Ex Libris

TODAY'S
NONFICTION
BEST SELLERS

TODAY'S NONFICTION BEST SELLERS

THE READER'S DIGEST ASSOCIATION
PLEASANTVILLE, NEW YORK

CONTENTS

Times to Remember

The inside story of a great American family, told by the woman whose steady faith and indomitable will held it together in its hours of tragedy

A condensation of the book by

Rose Fitzgerald Kennedy

"Age," Mrs. Kennedy writes, "has its privileges. One is to reminisce selectively. I prefer to remember the good times." Here are fond memories of her father, "Honey Fitz," the scrappy little Irishman who became mayor of Boston. Here is the love story of Rose Fitzgerald and Joe Kennedy, "the boy I fell in love with, the man I married . . . and the architect of our lives." Here are their nine children, among them a future President and two future senators, growing up amid fun and laughter and family pranks, but never being allowed to stop learning and striving. And here too are moments of triumph such as few families are privileged to know.

But if she prefers to remember the good times, Mrs. Kennedy cannot forget the tragedies. These also she has known in full measure, and in surmounting them she has found another kind of triumph.

"A mother's story, intelligent and profoundly moving."
—*Cosmopolitan*

PROLOGUE

There have been times when I felt I was one of the more fortunate people in the world, almost as if Providence had chosen me for special favors.

Now I am in my eighties, and I have known the joys and sorrows of a full life. I can neither forget nor ever reconcile myself to the tragedies. Age, however, has its privileges. One is to reminisce and another is to reminisce selectively. I prefer to remember the good times.

Millions of words have been written about my family, and if I were to make a guess about the contents of that mountain of print, I would think that most of it has, at best, been flawed by inaccuracies and misunderstandings, while the worst has been mendacious and deceitful. For a great many years I tried to ignore everything, from the honest errors to the pure trash, for if I had allowed myself to care I would have been driven to distraction. I suppose the flow will continue so long as there are Kennedys in politics or in the public eye; and I can do nothing about the errors and falsehoods that come off the presses. Nor can I possibly cope with all those that came off in the past. But at least, in this book, I can deal with the major ones.

I will now confirm a rumor that is quite true. The Kennedys do cooperate with one another, and an individual's project is likely to become a family one. In writing this memoir, I have been helped with time, energy, painstaking research, and encouragement by every member of the family. They have enabled me to find intrafamily letters, notes, and other artifacts that might help to fill gaps and add variety and a sense of life.

This, then, to the degree that I have succeeded, is a book about my husband and myself, with something about our parents and a great deal about our children; in their settings, their humanity, their natures, and destinies.

Rose Fitzgerald Kennedy

CHAPTER ONE

As with so many other American families of Irish descent, we begin with the famines that swept Ireland during the middle of the last century. Thousands of people died. Other thousands, younger and stronger and luckier, emigrated to the United States, and a large share of these to the city and hinterlands of Boston. Because of overcrowding and disease, about one passenger in ten died on the voyage.

My paternal grandparents, Thomas Fitzgerald and Rose Mary Murray, made that grim voyage in the 1840s. They both came from County Wexford, but they met and were married in Boston. Later another son of Wexford, Patrick Kennedy, arrived in Boston. There he, too, met and married an Irish immigrant girl, Bridget Murphy. Each of these four brave souls had passed away before I was born. But I know they worked hard and raised their children in the love and care of God.

The Fitzgeralds had eleven children. Nine of them survived infancy; among these was John Francis Fitzgerald. He married Mary Josephine Hannon and they had six children—of whom I was the eldest. The Kennedys had four children, including an only son named Patrick Joseph. He married Mary Hickey and they had three children. One of them, again an only son, was Joseph Patrick Kennedy.

The two family lines joined when Joseph Patrick Kennedy and I were married.

BY THE time my father, John Francis Fitzgerald, was in his late teens, he was an amateur expert on Boston's past. I remember as a child that it was a rare outing that did not inspire a discourse on American history, delivered in a style that was marvelously entertaining as well as informative. Naturally this had an influence on me when it came to raising my own children. I believed they should know the history of their country, and I used to take them to the landmarks in Boston and the countryside, explaining what had happened there. Their interest developed with the years, and I suspect this may be one reason why as adults they wanted to serve the country in public life. I think Jack's sense of history guided his whole career and gave his presidency a quality of its own.

There is another family characteristic that I think derives from my father. This is a mixture of abundant energy, healthy physique, quick reflexes, and a psychological or endocrinological X factor. I refer not only to the touch-football games that became famous, but to the strenuous activities that were always going on in our family.

As for his scholastic abilities, my father did extremely well at the Boston Latin School, which had high academic standards. He was accepted at Harvard Medical School and was in his first year when fate intervened to change his life.

His mother, Rose Mary Fitzgerald, had died three years earlier. Now his father, Thomas Fitzgerald, died. There were nine surviving sons, of whom my father (then age eighteen) was third eldest. And although Thomas Fitzgerald had left a small amount of money, it was nowhere near enough to keep this large brood fed and sheltered very long. Consequently my father left medical school, took a civil service examination, and landed a steady job as a clerk in the Boston Custom House. He became the mainstay of the family and continued as such until the youngest boys were ready to take care of themselves.

Perhaps because he was denied the credentials of an education, my father had an enormous appetite for knowledge and read everything within reach: books, magazines, and, of course, many newspapers. When he found something that struck him as interesting or in some way useful, he would cut the item out of the magazine or paper with his small penknife. Then, to be sure he wouldn't lose it, quite often he would pin it with a straight pin, of which he always carried a supply, on his lapel or, when that area was filled, somewhere else on the front of his jacket. He did this all his life; and what he read, he remembered.

I expect that here again his character left some imprint on mine. I have always kept scrapbooks and loose-leaf notebooks filled with facts and ideas and quotations, the gleanings of many years of clipping items from newspapers and magazines.

The life of a customs clerk could never satisfy my father's ambitious nature, so after three years he resigned and started an insurance business in the North End of Boston. He was already mixed up in so many civic, fraternal, social, and athletic affairs that he was widely known there, and with his natural gift of salesmanship he soon was prosperous enough to marry the girl he had loved for years, Mary Josephine Hannon. They married in 1889, and I was born on July 22 of the next year and christened Rose Elizabeth.

By the time I arrived my father was already active in ward politics. Soon he was elected to Boston's Common Council, then to the state Senate, and then—a meteoric rise—to the United States House of Representatives. He was one of the youngest men in Congress, the only Democrat from the whole of New England, and the only Catholic. He was reelected twice, so his tenure in Congress lasted six years, from 1895 to 1901.

Meanwhile our family was increasing. I had a little sister, Agnes; then a brother, Thomas; and with three young children, my father decided to vacate our small house in the North End of Boston and move us to a big, old, rambling, but wonderfully comfortable place in West Concord, where we lived when I was between the ages of seven and thirteen. They were wonderful years, full of the traditional pleasures and satisfactions of life in a small New England town: neighborly human relationships, family affection, trips with horse and buggy to my grandparents' home, climbing apple trees and gathering wild flowers.

A most precious gift that I received during those years came in large measure from my mother: a deep faith in the Church and its teachings and practices. And in my own time I tried to pass this gift of faith on to my children.

EVERY summer our family spent two or three weeks at the seaside at Old Orchard Beach, Maine. It was especially attractive to my parents because so many of their friends, practically all of them Irish Catholics from Boston, went there with their families, visiting back and forth and picnicking together while the children played. One of the men who came there fairly regularly with his family was a greatly respected businessman and political leader from East Boston, Patrick Joseph ("P. J.") Kennedy. He and my father knew each other well, as they were both members of Boston's Democratic "strategy board."

So it was at Old Orchard Beach that my future husband and I first saw each other: Joe, a spindly-looking nine- or ten-year-old, and I, taller but not much to look at either, two years younger.

In 1900, as my father was ending his third term in Congress, there were shifts and realignments in Boston political circles, with P. J. Kennedy and others blocking my father's renomination. He decided to end his congressional career and bought a moribund little weekly newspaper called *The Republic,* which he saw as a potentially valuable instrument for advancing his political future. He was both resilient and audacious, and his goal was to become mayor of Boston.

He had no experience in newspaper publishing, but he was shrewd, and he soon made a success of *The Republic.* By 1904 he could afford a fine, spacious fifteen-room house in the suburb of Dorchester, where we lived happily for many years. Another baby, my youngest brother, Frederick, was born there: the last of us six; John F. Jr. and Eunice had preceded him in Concord. I went to the Dorchester high school, where I soon made many friends while managing to do well in my studies.

We children had only a hazy idea of what was happening when, in 1905, our father was elected mayor. It was one of the most hard-fought, noisy, complex political melees ever seen in Boston, yet the sounds of battle seldom reached us.

The strategy board had opposed him in the primary, but on election night at East End headquarters my father made his way to P. J. Kennedy and said, "Now that the fight is over, let's get together." They shook hands on it, and were allies once again.

And so in January 1906 my father was inaugurated. His one regret, he said, was that his parents were not alive to see the day. "It would have been a great delight to them. I am the first son of foreign parents to become mayor of Boston."

His new status made little difference in our lives at home.

In those days, at least in Dorchester, high school consisted of three years, with a fourth, postgraduate, year for those who were going on to college. I took this fourth year and thus left high school at age sixteen. Then my father insisted I take an extra year at Sacred Heart Convent in downtown Boston. I was disappointed, as I had my eye set on Wellesley College, but I liked the school and did well there.

As events turned out, I never did go to Wellesley—and that is something I have regretted. However, I had another experience of greater value.

The mayoralty term in Boston at that time was two years, so in 1907 my father came up for reelection. There were new outbreaks of factionalism, and he was defeated. He was already planning for the next election, but in the summer of 1908 he took my mother, Agnes, and me to Europe.

We went to Ireland, England, Belgium, France, Switzerland, Germany, and Holland, all in about two months—a rather hectic schedule. And toward the end of that summer it was decided that Agnes and I would stay on for a year at a convent boarding school in Blumenthal, Germany, near Aachen and the Belgian and Dutch borders. Classes were conducted in French and German, so I became proficient in both languages and they have been assets all my life.

Actually, though the atmosphere was religious, the curriculum was unusually concerned with the practical things of this world. It was assumed that the girls when they married would be devoting their lives to *Kinder, Kirche, und Küche* (children, church, and cooking). Therefore, we were all coached in the arts of housewifery.

I think that these excerpts from letters I wrote to my parents convey something about my outlook on life at eighteen.

Dearest Father,

I have something very important and exciting to tell you so I hope my words will be persuasive and you will say "Yes." Christmas is coming and there is to be a fifteen-day vacation, from December 23 till January 8. [Agnes and I] love Blumenthal, but we do not at all relish the idea of spending our vacation here, when all the others are home . . . with their families. We can take a two-week round trip from Aachen to Hanover, to Berlin, to Dresden, to Leipzig, to Cologne and back to Aachen, with room and board and incidentals, for about $140. The cities we want to visit contain famous picture galleries and churches. An opportunity would also be afforded us to go to the theater, and see some of Goethe's and Schiller's plays. We would get a chaperone, so we would be perfectly safe. . . . I do hope Mother will approve. If I could only talk to her I am sure she would. We will think of you when you cut the *Turkey* tomorrow. Dearest love and kisses to you and Mama. Rose.

Father's letter arrived and how we jumped and talked and laughed when we received it. It was just lovely of you both to give us permission to go. We both were so happy and vowed you and Pa were the best and the dearest father and mother in the world. We shall both think of you at the midnight Mass, and pray for you. We have a great deal of opportunity to pray here. Happy New Year. Your loving and devoted daughter. Rose.

The Reverend Mothers and Mother General stayed up to welcome us back again. We have been kept busy talking about our trip ever since. We seemed to have seen everything. New Year's Night in Berlin we heard *Tannhauser* and it was truly wonderfully beautiful. We had to wear "décolleté" gowns and you should have seen us. We took the yokes out of our light dresses, and threw veils over our heads and there we were. The Kaiserin and Crown Princess as well as other members of the royal family had a loge directly below us.

In mid-June we had a letter from our father saying he had decided to run for mayor again, and that if we wanted to we could come back, at least for the summer. He came over to escort us home, but first he took us sight-seeing in Holland, Belgium, France (where Agnes and I did a little shopping for "something à la mode in gay Paris"), and England.

When we got back to Dorchester in August, it was decided we would not return to Europe for another year's study. Instead, Agnes went to the Sacred Heart Convent at Providence, Rhode Island, and I to the Academy of the Sacred Heart in Manhattanville, New York City (now Manhattanville College in Purchase, New York).

FATHER won the nomination for mayor in 1909. Heretofore I had been too young to pay much attention to his campaigns. This time, when the mud began flying, my instinctive reactions were shock and outrage; I seethed. But my father seemed to take it more or less for granted. And so I calmed down and began to accept the idea that gossip and slander are part of the price one pays for being in public life. This is a lesson that it is necessary to learn, or life in a political family such as ours could become miserable.

When my sons married I made sure to warn Ethel, then Jackie, then Joan, in turn, that they might hear scandalous gossip about members of our family, and that they should understand this and be prepared for it. They took the burden with the blessing.

Father was reelected mayor of Boston, and in June 1910 I

received my graduation certificate. I was to be twenty years old the next month, and the following winter I would be making my debut, the rite of passage that would make me a full participant in adult life.

My debut was not lavish, at least by the standards of the times. It was a beautiful reception and tea at our home in Dorchester. Though it was the dead of winter, my parents had turned the house into a bower of roses for me. I wore a white satin dress with a short train, long white kidskin gloves, no jewels or ornaments except a bit of white ribbon in my hair, a corsage of violets and lilies of the valley. With my mother in black Chantilly lace and my father in cutaway and winged collar, I received the guests in the drawing room. More than four hundred and fifty people, among them the new governor, two congressmen, and the entire Boston City Council, had accepted my father's invitation.

Joe was there. So were a couple of would-be rivals and a number of other young men and girls. After the older people had left, we had a sit-down dinner and sang and joked and laughed and danced. No champagne, no alcohol in any form, for on that evening none of us needed anything for a good time but our own high spirits.

"THERE is a time to laugh and a time to dance" and those next few years were such times. I was "the mayor's daughter" again, and to help my mother, I became his companion and assistant on many of the trips he took. I was, as they said in that day, "in the bloom of youth and beauty." My spirits were further uplifted by the fact that Joe Kennedy and I were in love and wanted to marry.

The boy I fell in love with, the man I married, the father of my children, and the architect of our lives, was tall, thin, wiry, freckled, with blue eyes and red-blond hair. His face was open and expressive, conveying qualities of self-reliance, self-respect, and self-discipline. He neither drank nor smoked, nor did I. He was a serious young man, but he had a quick wit and a big, spontaneous grin that made everybody in sight want to smile, too. Even then he had an aura of command. At Boston Latin

School, for instance, he was class president. His academic record was good enough for him to be admitted to Harvard; he was one of the few Boston boys of Irish descent to go there in that era.

Joe was as fascinated by the world of finance and business as my father was with the world of politics, and soon after he graduated from Harvard in 1912 he took the examinations to become a state bank examiner. He passed and received his appointment, and during the next year and a half visited banks all over eastern Massachusetts, learning far more about finance than he had in all his Harvard economics courses.

In those days the financial institutions of Boston were controlled by "proper Bostonians." They sat on their fortunes like broody hens on fertile eggs, and intrusions into their hen houses were met with resentful cluckings.

As a result of this oligarchical control over finance and credit, Joe's father, P. J. Kennedy, together with a few other prosperous Irish businessmen, had founded an independent bank in East Boston called the Columbia Trust Company. After nearly two decades it had grown so large that one of the big Boston banks wanted to absorb it, and offered the stockholders a good price. A majority wished to accept, but P. J. Kennedy wanted to preserve the bank as an independent institution. He hadn't enough money of his own to buy out the others and block the deal, so he called on Joe—who by then had grown wise in the ways of banking—to lead the fight against the takeover.

It was quite a battle, and when the tumult and shouting had stopped, Joe was the victor. Columbia Trust was saved, intact and secure, and Joe Kennedy was its president. He was then twenty-five years old: the youngest bank president in the United States. Within the financial community, and in the general community of Boston Irish, he was no longer just P. J. Kennedy's son but was suddenly well-known in his own right.

Joe and I were married in October of 1914 in a service attended only by our families and close friends, in the private chapel of Cardinal O'Connell of Boston, who officiated.

Early Days

The author's father, John Francis ("Honey Fitz") Fitzgerald, was mayor of Boston when he visited President Taft in 1912 (left). In 1914 Rose married a Boston banker, Joseph P. Kennedy. They vacationed in Maine (below) in 1915, and in Florida (above) in 1925.

MOST OF OUR YOUNG married friends lived in rented apartments, and as a place to start our life together an apartment would have been perfectly fine for me. But not for Joe. From the very beginning, home was the center of his world and the only place that really, finally, counted, no matter where his plans took him.

We found a nice old wood-frame house—seven rooms, plus two small ones in the converted attic—on a small lot with a few bushes and trees. It was at 83 Beals Street in the Boston suburb of Brookline, only about twenty-five minutes from the center of the city by trolley. That house, our first home, is now a public museum, a national historic site, and is visited by many thousands of people a year.

Joe Jr., Jack, Rosemary, and Kathleen were born during the years we lived on Beals Street. They arrived in a space of less than five years, counting from Joe Jr.'s birth in 1915 to Kathleen's in 1920. The nursery was on the verge of overflowing, since I was soon pregnant again. We had started out with a maid of all work who cooked, served, cleaned, and laundered, all for seven dollars a week. When the babies began coming we added another helper, a hospital-trained nursemaid. With the fifth child on the way I could not do with less help, and obviously I needed more space. So we began looking for another house near good schools, good transportation, and good shops; it also must be in a quiet area with fresh air and play space for the children. We found what we needed nearby at 131 Naples Road, where Eunice, Pat, and Bobby were born. Jean and Teddy, of course, were still to come.

The birth of each child was a new thrill and joy, but I have cherished all of them equally. And even though I was sometimes distracted or tired, I had made up my mind to raise my children as perfectly as possible. What greater aspiration and challenge are there for a mother than the hope of raising a great son or daughter?

PEOPLE often ask me about early influences, with an implication that I must have applied some private formula to make my children turn out so well. This is flattering, but I cannot claim original discoveries in the field of child rearing. When they were old enough to understand the rules of right and wrong, to learn responsibility, and to have their interests broadened from those of babyhood to childhood and thence to youth, my methods did depart somewhat from the norm, but practically always in the direction of the old-fashioned rather than the newfangled.

Joe was delighted and enchanted with his children; he spent as much time as he could with them. Yet those times soon became scattered and unpredictable. Early in 1917—only Joe Jr. had arrived by that time—he turned Columbia Trust over to his father to run and became assistant general manager of Bethlehem Steel's huge Fore River shipyard at Quincy, Massachusetts. With America's entry into World War I, he was under such pressures that, except for Sundays, he came home just long enough to sleep. The shipyard broke all production records. And Joe developed an ulcer.

After the war Joe went into the brokerage business, and later into the private banking business, which enabled him to spend much more time at home. Before long he was in all sorts of enterprises. For instance, he formed a syndicate to buy control of a chain of New England movie theaters, which in turn led him into movie production, then studio ownership and operation. This required a lot of time in New York, which was the financial center of the movie industry, and in Hollywood, the production center. He worked away from home for days, weeks, or even months at a time, but he telephoned me nearly every day; and each Sunday at noon he called and spoke with the children. I would have them all lined up and waiting, in the order of their ages, so that even the smallest could hear his voice. His influence was felt in our house even when he was away. Yet for quite a few years I was responsible for most of the child rearing.

EUNICE and I were recently trying to define the respective roles Joe and I had in the children's lives. She states things clearly and directly. "You were in charge of us and raised and trained us while we were children," she said. "And then, when we began

turning into young people, Dad took charge the rest of the way."
I think perhaps this was so. Joe and I were individuals with
highly responsible roles in a partnership that yielded rewards
which we shared.

"As the twig is bent, so the tree inclines"—an elementary home
truth that apparently psychologists of most schools have come to
accept. I now realize that I had a considerable part in forming the
characters of our children. Naturally I had very good material
to work with. Yet I knew what I wanted from them. I didn't always succeed in my aims, but it was never from lack of effort. I
looked on child rearing not only as a work of love and duty but
as a profession as interesting and challenging as any honorable
profession in the world, and one that demanded the best that I
could bring to it.

I was more fortunate than most women in having the domestic
help and money that I required. On the other hand, with nine
young children the needs were extraordinary and required a lot of
planning, organizing, and supervising. I learned to become an
executive.

For all our children there were many statistics that needed to
be remembered each week, month, year, and for years ahead. One
day, therefore, I stopped in a stationery store and bought a supply
of file cards and index tabs and set to work cataloguing names,
dates, and events in a systematic way. I continued to do this for
many years.

As each new baby came along, he or she was indexed and the
card inscribed with all the primary vital statistics such as date
and place of birth, church of baptism, names of godparents, and
any other pertinent data. In due course I added the date and place
of first Communion and confirmation. Meanwhile there were
entries on anything of importance concerning health and physical
welfare. Each child was weighed every Saturday night, and if there
was loss of weight two weeks in a row I took measures: perhaps a
richer diet and less exercise until the scale went up. Vaccinations,
eye examinations, dental examinations—everything went onto
the cards, including dates and notations of childhood diseases and

aftereffects. (When Joe became ambassador to the Court of St. James's, my dutifully kept box of file cards became a symbol of American efficiency. Actually it had just been a matter of Kennedy desperation.)

Jack, for instance, was a healthy infant, but, as noted on his card, he had whooping cough, measles, and chicken pox. Then: "Had scarlet fever—February 20—1920." Scarlet fever was a dreaded disease in those days, fairly often fatal, and it was a terrible time for us. Above all, it was a time for prayer. Jack was a very, very sick little boy, and Joe promised in his prayers that if Jack were spared he would give half of all his money to charity. When Jack did recover, Joe fulfilled his pledge by giving a check to the Guild of St. Apollonia, which had a program of taking needy children to dentists and doctors for good care but lacked money for a bus for the purpose. Joe's check for thirty-seven hundred dollars was exactly half his fortune at that time.

CHAPTER TWO

WHAT could be more interesting for a woman than to watch her own child grow and develop, and to guide it with patience and perseverance to bring out the best that nature has given? As I found out from raising our nine, each child is a continual surprise. None should be compared with another, for each has God-given potentialities which depend for full realization on influences in his or her environment.

For us, mealtimes were particularly important because they were about the only times when both Joe and I could talk with the children and, more important, encourage them to have their own ideas. I kept a bulletin board where the children were sure to see it on their way to meals, and on it I would pin items from the papers and magazines. The girls and boys who were at an age where they could read were supposed to look at these in order to be able to say something about the topics of the day. Surprisingly, these mealtime conversations were spontaneous and fun. I led them, and popped in questions or made comments according to the flow of talk.

For example, a Florida item could cue me to ask how the state got its name. What does the word mean, what language is it from? Think of Spanish names of towns there. Sarasota, Tampa—no, not Miami, that's Indian. Where else in the country are there a lot of Spanish names? Yes, California. What about San Francisco? What does that mean? Whom was it named after?

There was nothing cut-and-dried about these mealtime talks; there would be mistakes, wild guesses; no one was graded—it was a game. People told jokes, made wisecracks, hurled friendly insults, and hooted and hollered at silly mistakes. They joshed and kidded and fooled around (within limits) and chattered about things that had happened at school, news of friends, likes and dislikes: the stuff of life, well spiced. I enjoyed it, and although I could be quite sharp with them, I could laugh with them, too; there was no lack of laughter.

With our large family there couldn't be family conversations that would interest all the children at the same time. After all, there were seventeen years between the eldest and the youngest; by the time Teddy was six and learning to read, Joe Jr. was twenty-three and a Harvard graduate. As the years went along we had two tables and servings. The small table, for the little ones, would be in the nursery or perhaps the breakfast room. I would sit with them, usually at supper, and the conversation would be adjusted to fit.

Thus at the little table as at the big table everyone had the chance to learn and converse at his own level of understanding. Nevertheless, I had to make sure that an older or more assertive child didn't monopolize a conversation or try to put down the others. For the silent, this could lead to shyness, diffidence, a sense of inferiority—precisely the opposite qualities from those we were trying to encourage.

Later, when I heard the children speak before large audiences and perhaps have to defend their statements against vigorous challenges, as in Jack's televised debates with Richard Nixon, I liked to think that those spirited discussions when they were young contributed to their effectiveness.

EVERYONE knows that reading is the most important instrument of knowledge, so naturally a parent is gratified if a child reads early and enjoys books. I was careful to select the books our children read, stressing educational and inspirational values.

Jack and Bobby as youngsters were very different in their reactions to reading. Bobby was likely to skim books and put them aside, yet in later years he became an assiduous reader.

Jack, on the other hand, was a natural reader. The fact that he was so often sick in bed or convalescing only encouraged what was already a strong natural bent. He gobbled books—not necessarily the ones I had chosen for him. When he was little his greatest favorite was a book called *Billy Whiskers,* the fictional adventures of a billy goat. I felt it was a waste of time, and I wouldn't have allowed it in the house except that my mother had given it to him. However, one day Jack asked me, "Mother, where are the Sandwich Islands?"

I confessed I didn't know and we looked in the atlas. "Those are the Sandwich Islands, but now we call them the Hawaiian Islands. Why—are you studying about them at school?"

"No," he said, "but Billy Whiskers stopped at the Sandwich Islands on his way across the Pacific." So it is really difficult to predict what may awaken a child's interest!

As Jack grew older his tastes broadened and he liked stories of adventure and chivalry, such as Sir Walter Scott's *Waverley* novels, and biographies of famous and interesting people—in general, subjects having to do with history, so long as they had flair, action, and color. He had a strong romantic and idealistic streak, and was somewhat of a dreamer.

WITH reading skills and enjoyment there would come, I fondly supposed, mastery of the essentials of written expression: grammar, penmanship, spelling. But to my distress most of the children seemed to be afflicted with deafness about the proper uses of who and whom, and I and me. They split infinitives and they ended sentences with prepositions. Eventually they did absorb proper usage, and in later years scholars would rank Jack as one of the masters of modern prose.

Here is a letter he wrote to his father when he was about ten:

A Plea for a raise
by Jack Kennedy
Dedicated to my
Mr. J. P. Kennedy
My recent allowance is 40¢. This I used for areoplanes
and other playthings of childhood but now I am a scout
and I put away my childish things. Before I would spend
20¢ of my ¢.40 allowance and In five minutes I
would have empty pockets and nothing to gain and
20¢ to lose. When I am a scout I have to buy
canteens, haversacks, blankets searchliagts ponchos things
that will last for years and I can always use it
while I cant use a chocolate marshmellow
sunday with vanilla ice cream and so I put in
my plea for a raise of thirty cents for me to buy
scout things and pay my own way more around.
Finis
John Fitzgerald Francis Kennedy

I don't know why he included Francis in his signature. Perhaps it was to invoke the blessing and help of that gentle saint.

His father granted the raise, but, clearly, we did keep a close rein on our children's finances. We wanted them to know the value of money and the painful consequences of heedless extravagance.

Within the family we didn't talk about money. It wasn't a forbidden subject, but our rule was that if you wanted to talk, you had to have something interesting to talk about. Money simply didn't meet that criterion. If the children needed or deeply wanted something special, it was discussed privately with their father or me. We wanted them to learn the value of efforts and rewards—the idea of the dignity of work.

Bobby had a paper route. That pleased us, of course; the paperboy is practically an American symbol of boyhood spunk and ambition. Then, after a while, I found he had talked the chauffeur into driving him. There he was, riding all over town—making his deliveries from a Rolls-Royce. Needless to say I put a stop to this at once.

Of course, not everybody has two very nice houses—by 1929 we had moved to Bronxville and had bought our summer place in Hyannis Port—a couple of boats, a tennis court, a swimming pool, and a Rolls-Royce or two in the family. But the children had no real idea that we were a rich family until their father entered politics.

That began in 1931, when he became one of Franklin D. Roosevelt's strongest supporters and chief advisers in the forthcoming presidential campaign. Thus he was suddenly in the national limelight, and the press took an interest in him.

The time had come to tell the children that their father was well-to-do. We were careful to emphasize that money brings responsibility, that it is never to be squandered or spent ostentatiously. Money does not provide a license to relax. It gives an opportunity to use one's abilities, free of financial worries, to go forward and help others—at school, in the neighborhood, and eventually in the community and in government.

THROUGH the years many people have remarked about the close bonds of loyalty and faith among the members of our family, and their spontaneous understanding of each other. There has been talk of "the Kennedy clan," a term I dislike, for to me the idea of clannishness has connotations of narrowness and exclusivity. I can see one merit in the expression, however: in a clan there is a pervading body of common beliefs and customs, so that members know what to do without having to ask or explain themselves to one another. And, in truth, this fairly describes our family.

For parents who have or expect to have a sizable family, my strong advice would be to work hardest on the older ones, for in the direction they go the others are likely to follow. Children are naturally imitative, and although at first they tend to imitate the examples of their parents, they tend as the years pass to imitate those set by older children. And the elder ones, in my experience, enjoy the responsibility of setting an example and correcting missteps. For instance, if one of the girls was going out with a beau of the wrong sort, some remarks from a big brother would be a hundred times more effective than a speech from us.

This also applied to the boys. Bobby strove with all his might and main to be like his two big brothers. And the three of them profoundly influenced Teddy.

I suppose the fact that Teddy was the little brother of them all got him more attention—and affectionate indulgence—than the older ones would have been inclined to give one another. I expect if the next elder had been a brother there would have been rivalry, but Jean always had a special empathy with Teddy. They shared a lot, including a quirky sense of humor. For instance, when they were teenagers Jean and Teddy went on a trip to Europe together, and we sent a scolding note saying they had been spending too much money and should be more careful. From London we had a cablegram: AFTER READING YOUR LETTER I DECIDED TO TRAVEL TOURIST AND I PUT JEAN IN MY DUFFEL BAG. LUCKY NO ONE WEIGHED THE DUFFEL BAG. TEDDY. Which reminds me of another we had from Teddy from the Riviera: HAVING BARRELS OF FUN. SEND MORE MONEY FOR MORE BARRELS.

Speaking of Teddy's boyhood leads me to his first cousin, "Joey" Gargan, my sister Agnes's son. During most summers Joey was with us at Hyannis Port, and he and Teddy became inseparable companions. Agnes had married Joseph F. Gargan, originally of a Lowell, Massachusetts, family. He had graduated from Notre Dame, and by 1929 was a lawyer practicing in New York City. It was a fine, happy marriage, soon blessed with three children: Joseph Jr. (Joey), Mary Jo, and Ann. They were still very young when Agnes died suddenly in 1936. In the years following, the children spent summers and school vacations with us; in a real sense they became members of our own family.

During Teddy's youth he was more exposed to his father's direct influence than his older brothers had been. Years later he would write:

> From our earliest days, I think all the Kennedy children were made to feel that our father's principal interest in life was his family. As the youngest, it appeared to me that the family was his only interest.
>
> I have always felt the greatest gift Dad gave to each of us was his unqualified support. . . . No matter how busy he was, he seemed to have a moment to listen and to encourage us.
>
> Dad wanted us to be natural and able to smile no matter how tough things were. He wouldn't let any of his children feel sorry for himself. "I don't want any sour pusses around here," he would say. Yet he was quick to scold a child who tried to smile too readily or to charm his way through life. "Remember," he would say, "a smile and a dime can only get you a ride on a streetcar. You are going to need a lot more than that to get somewhere in life."
>
> Because he was interested, because he did care, because he wanted to help, he brought out the best in each of us. We were ashamed to do less than our best because of our respect and feelings for him.

Ted's last remark brings up a question that has often been asked of me: "What has made the Kennedy children strive so hard for individual excellence?"

Superior achievement, or making the most of one's capabilities, is to a very considerable degree a matter of habit. The children were encouraged by their father to be winners and leaders in whatever they set their hand to, and to develop the habit. If they lost in a sport—or lagged in school or another activity—the reasons were analyzed. If these involved some negligence or lack of effort or monkeyshines, that was dealt with in very clear terms.

Joe's attitude has been much written about, particularly after the boys went into public life with such conspicuous success. Journalists and others pondered what had caused the so-called Kennedy phenomenon. The main point of the whole exercise was not winning per se. It was rather that we wanted them to give their maximum effort always. One way of saying this might be:

"God wants a different thing from each of us . . . which only we can do and for which we were created." Joe and I knew they were not perfect; yet we wanted each to develop his or her individual abilities and to do his or her very best.

Another of Joe's statements that everyone in the family heard often was: "We don't want any crying in this house." It was picked up by some of the writers and misunderstood in a way that made him seem hardhearted. He really meant that there was to be no self-pity, and no burdening of others with any personal misfortunes. He knew that for almost everyone life is likely to hold many knocks and bruises, and that people had better get used to that idea at an early age.

One especially appropriate example was the way Jack happened to write *Profiles in Courage*. After his injuries during the *PT-109* ordeal Jack had a serious problem with his back. He was seldom really free of pain, although he bore it with so few outward signs that nobody but his doctors, the family, and a few close associates realized his condition. Finally, during 1954, the problem became so bad that he agreed to a spinal operation. Not only was it a failure but an infection set in and he nearly died: he received the last rites of the Church. But he pulled through, and after the danger was past he was flown to our Palm Beach house for recuperation. Joe had bought the Palm Beach house in 1933 and we had all spent Christmas vacations there.

In a few months Jack was healthy enough for the doctors to try the operation again, if he wanted it. He did. So it was back to the hospital in New York, where the second operation was successful (relatively speaking; he was always afterward in discomfort, which he ignored), and then back again to Palm Beach for more months of recuperation.

It was there that Jack did most of his work on *Profiles in Courage*. He had, as I said, been fascinated since boyhood by history and biography. He knew the meaning of courage, and he worked on the book in his hospital bed, in bed at home, and in other places—but my most vivid memory is of him writing as he sat in a wheelchair by the seawall at Palm Beach.

It turned out to be a very fine book, and its excellence was rewarded with a Pulitzer Prize. It was admired by historians and influential opinion makers of the so-called intellectual establishment. After publication of the book Jack was no longer a comparatively unknown junior senator from Massachusetts but someone discussed nationally.

His writing of *Profiles in Courage* is just one example of how Jack took a positive, constructive attitude and changed a trial into a triumph.

CHAPTER THREE

JACK once remarked that I was "the glue that held the family together." Pat has said I was "very solicitous and kept up with whether one was doing well or not"; adding that, as for my praising her, "Well, she must have, though that's not one of my strong memories." Eunice, writing in a sentimental mood, remarked on "Mother's compassion, and ever constant . . . example of goodness and faith." Teddy spoke of "gentleness and understanding, and support and encouragement that made the high family standards livable and perhaps reachable."

I am indulging in these quotations because they may help illuminate a question that naturally could come to mind after what has been said about our aim to bring out the best in our children. How did Joe and I adapt this aim to the needs of Rosemary, our eldest daughter, who was a retarded child? I am sure it will be understood that this is not an easy matter for me to write about, but I will do my best.

It was not until she was a toddler that I began to realize that Rosemary might be handicapped; she was slow in everything, and some things she seemed unable to learn how to do. She went to kindergarten and first grade at the usual ages, but her lack of coordination was apparent, and as time went on I realized she could not keep up with the work. I was informed that Rosemary's

IQ was low, but that was about all the concrete information I received. This was in the early 1920s, when the tests were still quite new, and no one could say what the scores meant except in a general way. When I would ask experts, "What can I do to help her?" there didn't seem to be much of an answer. I was frustrated and heartbroken.

It was suggested that we put Rosemary in a special school for children with neurological defects, but I rejected that idea except as a last resort. In such a place, living with neurologically maimed children and gaited to their pace, she would soon feel deeply her difference from her brothers and sisters, and that might remove her incentive to try to learn. We decided that keeping her at home, with understanding and encouragement, would be the way to develop her capacities to their fullest, whatever they turned out to be.

This did, of course, involve a good deal of time. The less progress Rosemary seemed to make, the more time I would spend trying to bring her along. Joe and I wanted her treated in the most normal way possible, and we did not indicate either within the family (except as necessary, and then casually and indirectly) or outside it that there was anything extraordinary about her. I felt that if Rosemary could acquire the basic skills in schoolwork, sports, and dancing, at least well enough to enjoy them, she would manage to be happy. If she was attractive and well groomed and well mannered, she would be able to have a reasonably satisfying life. With special care, which we arranged at the schools she attended, and with great effort on her part, she did achieve reasonable performances in all these matters.

The other children in the family must have realized that Rosemary was different from them and from children of her age group, but Joe and I tried hard to minimize this. They were merely told that she was a little slow and that they should help her. When she did something well, tell her so. If she made a joke, laugh with her. If she wore a pretty new hair ribbon, say something about that; but don't talk about her lack of tennis skills. If there was some activity going on, invite her to participate. All of them were understanding and cooperative. It was a conspiracy of kindness.

Rosemary was a warmly responsive and loving girl. She was appreciative of attention and compliments, and so hopeful of deserving them. She spent the school year of 1934–35, when she was sixteen, at the Sacred Heart Convent at Providence, Rhode Island. At examination time she wrote, "Pray very hard that I will get someplace, I tried as hard as I could."

FAITH in God and in the teachings of the Church had been instilled in me from my earliest years. But I didn't think of myself as being particularly religious; I was just an ordinary, staunch, believing Irish Roman Catholic. Rosemary's misfortune did not incline me in the least toward doubt; but rather, if anything, strengthened my belief. I asked myself endlessly why she had to have so many handicaps. The more I thought, the clearer it became to me that God in His infinite wisdom did have a reason, which in time, in some way, would be unfolded to me.

Religion was never oppressive in our household, but it was always there, part of our lives, and the Church's teachings and customs were observed. We went to Mass on Sundays, holy days, first Fridays. We said grace before meals. Faith, I would tell the children, is a living gift from God, to guide us in our activities, to be a source of solace and comfort in our lives on earth, so we should do everything we can to nourish it and to help it grow and flourish, and try never to lose it. I would hear them recite their catechism. I also would encourage the idea—in youth and adulthood—of making a yearly retreat in a quiet, wholly religious environment of devotion, instruction, and contemplation.

I wanted all of the children to have at least a few years in good Catholic schools. A child thus educated, I maintained, would have more confidence about settling the problems of everyday living, and a better concept of his duties toward his God, his neighbor, and himself. This was one of the very few instances in which Joe and I were in disagreement. He said that a child learned faith and morals at home, and that the boys in particular would be dealing with people of all faiths or none when they grew up, and he wanted them to meet all men on their merits, without consciousness of religious factors. As a consequence, all the girls had some years at convent schools, but the boys were educated almost entirely at secular schools.

I also felt the children should have as much continuity as possible in their education, since a transfer student may find himself at a serious academic disadvantage. For that reason I had stayed on in Brookline with the children a couple of years after Joe's first big venture in the movie business obliged him to spend his workweeks in New York City. Only in 1927, when he was certain that this business would be taking most of his time in the foreseeable future, had I consented to move from our Boston suburb to Riverdale, a suburblike neighborhood of New York City.

After two years in Riverdale, where Joe Jr. and Jack attended the Riverdale Country School as day students, we found a rather ideal spot. This was Bronxville, a very attractive suburban village only a mile square, so the schools and churches were within walking distance.

We bought a big house set in six acres of grounds, a property well scaled to the needs of our increasingly large and energetic family. It remained our home for nearly thirteen years.

We debated whether the children should go to day school until they were ready for college, or in their early teens go off to boarding school. If the latter, which school? At what age?

JOE and I had agreed that the responsibility for the education of the boys was primarily his, while that of the girls was primarily mine. So he decided that Joe Jr. and Jack would continue as day students at Riverdale until time to send them to boarding school.

All the other children had a portion of their schooling in Bronxville schools, but I sent Kathleen off to Sacred Heart at Noroton, Connecticut, when she was thirteen. She was quite pretty and was being distracted from her schoolwork by boys inviting her to the Saturday-afternoon movies and so forth.

After finishing grade school at Riverdale, Joe Jr. was enrolled

Growing Up

The first three Kennedy children (from right: Joe Jr., Jack, Rosemary) posed with their mother in 1919. The entire family (minus young Joe, who was in Spain) saw Pope Pius XII crowned in 1939.

in Choate, a boarding school in Connecticut. It was a fortunate choice. The school suited him, and clearly he suited the school. His grades were excellent, and he demonstrated qualities of leadership that brought high praise from his masters and, of course, made Joe and me very proud of him. He later went on to the London School of Economics for one year, and then, in the fall of 1934, he entered Harvard.

Many people have asked me about Jack's teenage years. Did he do well in school? What were his favorite subjects? Did he have any adolescent problems? And so forth.

Jack went through the fourth, fifth, and sixth grades at Riverdale Country School and did reasonably well, with around a B-minus average. Meanwhile Joe Jr. was doing so well at Choate that we decided it would be a good place for Jack, too, so we put in his application the spring of 1929 for enrollment in the fall of 1931. We were advised that he should first have a year away at some other boarding school, so he could mature and become accustomed to the life. It was decided he would go to Canterbury, a Catholic school.

It was not one of his better years. As I look back over his letters home I discover that his spelling remained peculiarly his own ("I learnt how to play baggamon to-day") and that his right eye was bothering him ("I see things blury even at a distance of ten feet"). Then, during Easter vacation of 1931, he was stricken with appendicitis. By the time he recovered from the operation, the school year at Canterbury was nearly ended, so we engaged a tutor to work with him at home, hoping that he could pass the entrance examinations for Choate that summer. He passed the English and mathematics, but failed the Latin. However, after intensive drill during the rest of the summer he passed the Latin exam, and entered Choate that fall.

We were often anxious about his physical health in those years. But what concerned us as much, or more, was his lack of diligence in his studies; or, let us say, lack of fight in trying to do well in those subjects that didn't interest him. Like practically all the old, established eastern prep schools in those days, Choate had a highly structured set of rules, traditions, and expectations into which a boy was supposed to fit. Joe Jr. had no trouble operating within this system, but Jack couldn't or wouldn't conform. He did pretty much what he wanted, rather than what the school wanted of him. And the more pressure that was put on him, the more he seemed to find ways to frustrate those in charge. Once he collected all the pillows from all the rooms in his dorm and put them in some boy's room, so that when the boy came back from a class and opened his door there was just a solid mass of pillows. At the end of his second year his housemaster, Mr. Maher, filed a despondent report with Choate's headmaster, George St. John:

> I'd like to take the responsibility for Jack's constant lack of neatness about his room and person, since he lived with me for two years. But in the matter of neatness, despite a genuine effort on Jack's part, I must confess to failure.
>
> Occasionally we did manage to effect a house cleaning, but it necessitated my "dumping" everything in the room into a pile in the middle of the floor. Jack's room has throughout the year been subject to instant and unannounced inspection—it was the only way to maintain a semblance of neatness, for Jack's room was a club for his friends.
>
> I regard the matter of neatness or lack of it on Jack's part as quite symbolic—aside from the value it has in itself—for he is casual and disorderly in almost all of his organization projects. Jack studies at the last minute, keeps appointments late, has little sense of material value, and can seldom locate his possessions.

The outstanding talent Jack had demonstrated in school—as Mr. Maher indicated—was a talent for making friends. During vacations he invariably brought at least one, often three, four or more school friends home with him. "Jack's surprises" became a joke in the family. After a while, though, it was no surprise to see LeMoyne ("Lem") Billings, who became Jack's best friend and finally his roommate. They had great rapport, and they sparked each other to various pieces of nonsense.

Besides talking things over with Jack at home and writing to him, his father was corresponding with Mr. St. John, the headmaster, who showed a great deal of understanding and who in Jack's junior year wrote:

> The fact of the matter is that I cannot feel seriously uneasy or worried about Jack. The longer I live and work with him and the more I talk with him, the more confidence I have in him. I would be willing to bet anything that within two years you will be as proud of Jack as you now are of Joe.
>
> Jack has a clever, individualist mind. It is a harder mind to put in harness than Joe's—harder for Jack himself to put in harness. . . . A more conventional mind and a more plodding and mature point of view would help him a lot more right now; but we have to allow, my dear Mr. Kennedy, with boys like Jack, for a period of adjustment. All that natural cleverness Jack has to learn how to use in his life and work, even to cover it up at times. . . . I never yet saw a clever, witty boy who at some stage in his early development was not considered fresh . . . the final product is often more interesting and effective than the boy with a more conventional mind who has been to us parents and teachers much less trouble.

By the end of the first quarter of his senior year Jack evidently was beginning to see the light, for he wrote to his father that he had "definitely decided to stop any fooling around." Nevertheless, it was about the same time that Jack and Lem formed a little enterprise that nearly pulled the roof down on their heads.

Mr. St. John often addressed the student body at convocations or at chapel. His remarks were designed to expound the ideals of the school and the kind of responsible citizenship he expected from the students. He had a descriptive term that summed up all unworthy qualities; the term was mucker. Muckers were everything that was not wanted at Choate.

Recently, at my request, Lem wrote me a letter explaining just how it happened that he and Jack organized a Muckers Club.

> In those times part of the daily schedule at Choate was compulsory evening chapel, starting about twenty minutes after supper. And in those times, seniors were the only students allowed to have

combination radio-phonographs—and Jack and I had a very good one. Our room was directly above the dining hall, and with the stairway close by it was very convenient for us to get down and back for meals—and also, of course, very convenient for other boys to get from the dining hall up to our room, and with those twenty minutes to kill they were coming up by the dozens to listen to the radio-phonograph. The congestion became so bad that Jack and I . . . decided to form a club—[with] thirteen of our best friends as members—and only club members could be in the room during that period.

There was nothing wrong so far: The unfortunate thing was the name we chose. Mr. St. John used the word "mucker" as the epitome of the worst element. Therefore, in our juvenile way we found it amusing to call our group the Muckers Club. We even had little gold charms designed in the shape of shovels and engraved "Choate Muckers Club." I don't know whatever happened to Jack's, but a couple of Christmases ago I gave mine to Caroline.

Naturally, I suppose, rumors began to spread. The worst things Jack and I ever did at Choate were to keep a messy room and be late for classes. Some of our members, I expect, did break the school code of conduct by going into town and smoking, drinking, and so forth. Anyway, the rumors centered on our room because that's where the club met nightly. The school gossip reached Mr. St. John, and when he heard the name of the club—he saw red. He was furious.

He called my mother—my father had died two years before—and she had to come all the way from Pittsburgh to have a session with him and me about my part in the Muckers Club. She decided it was much ado about very little.

He called Mr. Kennedy in Washington and asked him to come up to Choate to discuss Jack's part. Mr. Kennedy . . . [had] many important matters to occupy his attention in Washington. But he came up anyway.

Both boys graduated with their class at Choate in 1935, in no disgrace. Jack, in fact, though his cumulative grades placed him slightly below the middle of his class, was voted "most likely to succeed."

Moreover, I think that silly episode of the Muckers may well have been a turning point in Jack's life. I am sure he did not like that confrontation with the headmaster and his father. Something certainly soaked in, and deeply. Probably it was a matter of passing through a phase and thus of getting a little experience leading to adult maturity and perspective. At any rate, his life took on a new momentum from then on.

CHAPTER FOUR

As Joe's wife and hostess, and with his expanding activities in many fields of business and government, I found there was seldom a dull moment. I was involved, for example, in the golden age of films because Joe became one of the leaders of the movie industry. In less than three years after entering film production he headed or controlled three studios, and had merged them with Radio Corporation of America (RCA) to form a major new studio —Radio-Keith-Orpheum (RKO). Consequently I knew a number of the stars, one of whom, Gloria Swanson, Joe helped to set up as an independent, under the label of Gloria Swanson Productions.

My special interest in clothes developed during this period when Joe was surrounded daily by some of the most beautiful, and beautifully dressed, women in the world. I could not compete in natural beauty, but I could make the most of what I had by keeping my figure trim and my grooming perfect, and by always wearing interesting and becoming clothes. And so, with Joe's endorsement, I began spending more time and more money on my wardrobe. Eventually I landed on some lists of best-dressed women.

Pat has a comment on this period:

> I remember in Bronxville when she'd go out at night with Daddy—I remember her coming to kiss me goodnight, and she was always so beautiful. My room was dark and this vision just sort of appeared, smelling absolutely marvelous with her perfume.

I was fascinated by the perfume, we all were, and as we girls grew older we'd ask her what it was. But she wouldn't tell us. She didn't want even her own daughters to have it. . . . Finally when she was seventy-five she told us. Now we all wear it; it's our favorite perfume.

But when we all started to smell alike, Mother changed hers to something else.

DURING 1929–30 Joe liquidated all his movie interests except for his chain of theaters and a few minor properties, and for the next couple of years he commuted to his office in New York City, and ordinarily was home with us at night and on the weekend. This was a golden interval for me and for the children.

While Joe had been active in the movies, he had also continued to be substantially involved in the stock market. Part of his genius was an amazing ability to analyze a situation and to reach the rational answer at just the right time. There was no better example of this than in that boom-and-bust year of 1929.

While the stock market was soaring, Joe took a long hard look and decided this was a bubble that was bound to burst. He began taking his money out of the market, and by the time of the famous crash of 1929, nearly all of his major assets were in cash in safe banks. Thus, not only had he saved his wealth from the disaster but was in a position to sell short. Consequently he made money as the market went down.

At the same time he was becoming increasingly worried about the state of the nation, and he soon became convinced that Franklin D. Roosevelt was the man who could save the country. Joe was closely involved throughout the campaign of 1932, though not in a conspicuous way, always preferring to work behind the scenes. He was elated when Roosevelt swept the nation, and he expected to be a part of the new administration in a role commensurate with his efforts and abilities. To him this meant appointment as Secretary of the Treasury. But to general surprise, Roosevelt named William H. Woodin, president of American Car & Foundry Company, a businessman certainly more submissive to White House wishes than Joe would have been.

Joe was keenly disappointed, all the more so a short time later, when Mr. Woodin retired because of health and President Roosevelt again passed Joe by and appointed Henry Morgenthau, Jr., to the Treasury. However, my husband and the President had a friendly if remote relationship. There were invitations to us from the Roosevelts to drop in at Hyde Park or at the White House— and from us to them if their travels happened to bring them near our houses, which by mid-1933 included the one we bought at Palm Beach.

Finally, in the summer of 1934, Joe was appointed to a job in the New Deal that challenged and excited him. He was made chairman of a new arm of government, the Securities and Exchange Commission. He was determined to have the whole SEC apparatus set up and running within a year; then he planned to submit his resignation. Actually it took him sixty-six days longer, and then he resigned, leaving behind one of the enduring monuments of the New Deal.

NINETEEN thirty-six was another busy year for Joe. He reorganized the entire financial structure of RCA. Then he reorganized Paramount Pictures from top to bottom. After that William Randolph Hearst asked him to study the financially troubled Hearst publishing empire, and he produced a plan that resulted in drastic changes there.

That year, 1936, was also a presidential campaign year. In his first term the President had alienated many important business and financial leaders. Joe, though often at odds with these men, was still highly respected by them. He knew that Roosevelt needed him, and responded by writing a book titled *I'm for Roosevelt*, in which he showed that the New Deal was not the enemy of business but that its reforms had, in fact, saved capitalism and the free-enterprise system in America. He went on to take an active part in the presidential campaign, and was happy when the returns showed the greatest landslide in U.S. history.

Active as Joe was, he soon began feeling uncomfortable at not being in the thick of things in Washington. Consequently the following year, 1937, he accepted FDR's request to head a new federal agency, the Maritime Commission, which was supposed to bring sense and profitability into the chaotic, fast-declining U.S. merchant marine.

First the SEC, now the MC, both important, no doubt, but I felt that Joe deserved something really special in the government, and I told him so. A high-level ambassadorship would, of course, be an attractive possibility. But Joe spoke no foreign languages and had no natural facility in them. Thus the suitable possibilities really were reduced to only one, that of being ambassador to Great Britain. The position was occupied by Robert Worth Bingham, a most competent and respected man. However, it was rumored and soon confirmed that Ambassador Bingham was seriously ill and would have to resign.

When Joe came home for weekends, I would ask him, "Couldn't you tell the President what you want?"

Joe said to me, "Well, I can't just walk into the office of the President of the United States and say 'I want to be ambassador to England.'"

It was understood, however, that if he did his usual excellent job at the Maritime Commission, the next step would be the ambassadorship.

Early in 1938 the President officially appointed Joe to the post.

THE political and diplomatic history of that time has been well documented. What I can add are only some footnotes from the viewpoint of the American ambassador's wife, official hostess, companion, and the mother of his numerous children, who were transported from a more or less normal American environment to the complicated world of diplomatic London.

I was sure this would be an important experience for them, and indeed it was. In fact, it probably put Jack on the first rung of the ladder to the presidency. However, there was also the immediate, practical matter of schools for all the children.

We decided that Bobby, who was then thirteen, and Teddy, who was six, would live with us at the embassy residence and go to day school in London. Eunice and Pat and Jean would attend a Sacred Heart boarding school near London similar to the one at home. We found an excellent school for Rosemary deep in the Hertfordshire countryside, and we arranged for a special tutor-companion. Kathleen, who had graduated by then from convent school and had been at Parsons School of Design in New York learning design and decorating, would drop out for a while and live with us at the residence, helping me with my duties as hostess and also having her debut in London. Joe Jr., who was in the last semester of his senior year at Harvard, would stay on to graduate and then come over to gain embassy experience as a very junior secretary to his father.

As FOR Jack, he had had an erratic academic career in the previous few years because of a series of illnesses. After graduating from Choate in 1935, he had planned to spend a year at the London School of Economics, but his studies there were terminated after only one month by hepatitis. He then returned to the United States and was accepted at Princeton even though classes had started a few weeks earlier. However, after less than two months at Princeton, his hepatitis flared up again and put him out of commission once more. He left Princeton shortly after Thanksgiving and spent most of the rest of that school year in Arizona. In that sunny, dry climate he finally recovered his health and was able to go to college again. This time he chose Harvard, to his father's great joy, and entered in the fall of 1936.

Jack made an almost complete turnaround at Harvard. He ran for class president that first year and was swamped. The next school year, 1937–38, he ran for student council and lost again. I think this was his last venture into student politics. He continued to show rather more interest in social activities and sports than in grades.

He tried out for the football varsity although he weighed only one hundred and forty-nine pounds, which showed a lot of courage but not much sense. He dropped back to the junior varsity and was doing a good job there until one day in practice he was hit by a hard block or tackle, landed at the wrong angle, and ruptured a spinal disk. This injury ended his football days and marked the beginning of troubles with his back that were to plague him the rest of his life.

In the fall of 1937 Jack had decided to major in government. He still had no particular idea of going into politics himself; his ambition inclined toward journalism, for which studies in political science and government would be very useful background. In any case, his new interests were reflected in improved marks, and he stayed on at Harvard when we left for England.

Joe arrived in London to take up his ambassadorship in February of 1938. Following an operation for appendicitis, I was able to sail by early March, bringing Pat, Bobby, Jean, Teddy, and "Kick" (our family nickname for Kathleen) with me.

THE early months passed in a whirl of introductions and social and official events. A pleasant but exhausting formality was to call on the wives of all the other ambassadors and introduce myself. It was interesting seeing the other embassy residences, meeting these women, and getting a sense of who was who in the diplomatic colony.

The first protocol visit came only two days after my arrival. Ambassadorial wives—accompanied by their husbands—were always received by the queen, a gracious way of welcoming them to the country. So, on March 18, Joe and I arrived at Buckingham Palace, and at the appointed time were ushered into a beautiful and very comfortable sitting room, where Queen Elizabeth came forward to greet us.

She had such a friendly manner that I felt at ease with her at once. She and Joe had already met, so they chatted a bit about Anglo-American relations, but she soon wanted to hear all about our children and their feelings about coming to England. The two royal children, Princess Elizabeth (the present queen) and Princess Margaret Rose, were about the ages of two of our youngest, Bobby and Jean, so Her Majesty and I could compare notes.

Soon afterward Joe and I received a royal invitation to spend the weekend of April 9–11 at Windsor Castle. The other guests were Prime Minister and Mrs. Neville Chamberlain, Lord and Lady Halifax (he was the new foreign secretary), Lord and Lady Elphinstone (she was the queen's sister), and, I suppose as an extra man, Major the Honorable Sir Richard Molyneux.

We came up from London in an embassy car and arrived at the castle at seven p.m. There we were met by the master of the household, Brigadier General Sir Hill Child, who conducted us to our rooms. They were in one of the towers, with a lovely view of the park. The furniture was upholstered in red damask, and the accessories were in gold and white. In my bedroom was a huge bed set high, so that one had to use a step stool to get into it. A servant in full livery was especially appointed to attend us and lead the way whenever we left our suite.

After a few minutes of contemplating the scene, Joe turned to me and said, "Rose, this is a helluva long way from East Boston."

That weekend at Windsor was one of the most fabulous, fascinating experiences of my life. These are excerpts from my diary notes, which I hope will be interesting to others:

At 8:20 the footman came to escort us to the Green Reception Room. At 8:30 the King and Queen came in and greeted everybody by shaking hands. All the ladies curtsied, and the men bowed low. Dinner was announced and the King and Queen walked ahead . . . they sat opposite each other at the middle of the table. . . . Table decorations consisted of high flowers, which made it difficult for the King and Queen to see each other and caused some good-natured teasing.

After dinner, the Queen stood in front of the fireplace in one of the drawing rooms. Each of the men bowed to her, then went into an adjoining room to talk with the King, the ladies remaining with the Queen. She talked with me first for about fifteen minutes. . . . I found it very difficult to accustom myself to saying "Ma'am" when addressing the Queen and she told me not to bother, putting me at my ease. . . . We talked, among other things, about the difficulty of sleeping in London, and the Queen was amused that I put wax in my ears.

After a while the King and the men came back, and after mixed conversation the King and Queen showed us some of the treasures of the castle, in a room off the drawing rooms. . . . At 11:00 the Queen said good night and shook hands with all. In bed, we heard the sounds of the Changing of the Guard, and the clock striking in the tower.

The next day was Palm Sunday. My diary continues:

We had breakfast in our sitting room. Then went to Mass in the town of Windsor. . . . On return we saw the Changing of the Guard—very impressive—then walked in the large park that surrounds the castle and ran into Princess Elizabeth . . .

At luncheon Princess Margaret sat next to her mother, and Princess Elizabeth was seated between Prime Minister Neville Chamberlain and Joe. (I suppose this is a regular procedure—associating with older people even at the age of thirteen. Of course, there are many advantages to this way of life but also many restraints on the natural inclinations of a normal youngster.)

After lunch there was a band concert. Then it was arranged for us all to take a walk, very informally, with the King and Queen and the two little princesses. Everybody changed into comfortable shoes and tweeds. We walked to Frogmore, one of several mansions that monarchs have built in Windsor Park as domiciles for visiting family members and guests. . . . The King told us that his parents—with their large family—had used it as a schoolhouse and he had studied there. We also saw many of the natural and cultivated beauties of the park such as the mulberry bushes.

We left at mid-morning the next day, and were back at the embassy residence in time [for] lunch.

In May we gave a joint debut for Kathleen and Rosemary. As I have said, we always wanted Rosemary to participate as fully as possible in the activities of the family and of her general age group. On such an occasion as this—a big, somewhat confusing scene with much music and dancing and lots of people who didn't know Rosemary—we naturally had a few apprehensions. But she looked pretty, she was happy, and everything went well.

Rosemary went to some parties, but we always had one of the men from the embassy escort her to see that she had dancing partners and wasn't left too long with one partner. I say this because parents who have a retarded child may be discouraged and think their child could not undertake a social occasion.

Also, that same month, Kick, Rosemary, and I were presented at court, one of those British royal ceremonies that has since disappeared but at the time was glamorous beyond belief.

There would be several hundred girls and matrons at any given presentation. The act itself was quite simple. One went to Buckingham Palace, sat awhile in a reception room, and on cue from a functionary of the court entered the grand ballroom, at one end of which on a dais sat the king and queen and two or three other members of the royal family. One walked out in front of them, curtsied to each, then walked to the side of the room and stood there, or perhaps sat on an available gilt chair. Literally that is all there was to it.

It was decided that about ten of us who were associated with the embassy would go to the first of that year's four presentations. Naturally an important matter was proper gowns. Our British friends said they should be by a British designer, since he would understand the exact needs, including the dimensions of the train. I went to Molyneux, the foremost British designer of the time; my dress was of white lace beautifully embroidered in tiny silver and gold beads. For Rosemary and Kathleen we selected white net trimmed in silver. Every woman presented wore three white plumes in her hair, honoring the Prince of Wales.

As a matron I would be expected to wear a tiara in my hair. I didn't own one, so my new friend Lady Bessborough lent me hers, and it proved to be most flattering and magnificent. It fitted well and glittered with many brilliant diamonds.

When the great night arrived, I was carefully inserted into my lovely embroidered gown by a covey of maids. A man from Molyneux came over to check details and to pin and secure the white plumes at the proper angle. A hairdresser was there to place the tiara on my carefully constructed coiffure. The maids helped me draw extra-long white gloves almost to my shoulders. My jewels were added.

England

Mr. Kennedy (above right) was named
ambassador to Great Britain in 1938.
As he and his wife emerged from
Buckingham Palace after meeting the
queen, Teddy waited to snap their
picture (right). Later, elaborately
dressed for her formal presentation
at court, Mrs. Kennedy (above)
"felt a little like Cinderella."

I viewed the complete picture in a long mirror and was perfectly amazed at myself. I felt a little like Cinderella.

I ran into my husband's room to show him my elegance. His blue eyes lit up, and he grinned in the most loving way and said, "You're a real knockout."

In a few minutes the girls came running in to see and be seen. More exclamations all around. Then downstairs to be viewed by the younger children, who were duly impressed, then a stop in the hall for the staff to see us, then a session with photographers, and then in large cars off to Buckingham Palace.

The rest was a gigantic theatrical. The palace illuminated; the guards resplendent; the beefeaters in costume with maces, lining the grand stairway; passing through anteroom after anteroom attended by footmen in full livery; at last the ballroom and a sight of the royal dais, and being ushered to our place among the diplomatic corps—our place determined by length of tenure, which put us after the Chinese ambassador but before the German ambassador—and looking around at the grandeur of the room with its vaulted and frescoed ceilings and its elaborate murals and gilded pilasters, and looking around also at the others there, the men immaculate and wearing their decorations, and the women striking and regal in their beautiful gowns and jewels.

IT IS a strange aspect of human nature—or perhaps a saving grace—that we tend to expect the best and discount the possibility of the worst, even though experience shows that the worst often happens. Humans seem to have been designed to be optimistic. Otherwise, why would anyone have children, plan for their future?

I am led to these thoughts because, while all the pomp and circumstance and romantic storybook traditions that I have described were continuing, events were building toward the general (and for us, very personal) disasters of the Second World War.

Jack was an observer and even to some degree a participant in the events that finally led to war. After the summer of 1938 he had gone back to Harvard for his junior year. However, his father, realizing that momentous history was being made in Europe, suggested that Jack defer his second semester and rejoin us. He could help in the London and Paris embassies, and also do some traveling in other parts of Europe. So he came over in February 1939.

Something Joe did at this time, for which he has never been given proper credit, concerned the plight of the Jews in Hitler's Germany. It had become clear to him that they had to escape if they were to survive. From that point on he had been active, behind the scenes, in helping many individual Jews escape. Further, he devised what became known as the Kennedy plan to find new homes for all Jews trapped under Hitler. British policy prohibited large-scale Jewish immigration to Palestine, so Joe proposed that they be given asylum in South America, Lower (Baja) California, and Africa. But before the plan could be worked out, war began.

MEANWHILE ambassadorial life had continued. The following is an excerpt from my diary:

May 4 [1939]

Very busy all day preparing for the [embassy] dinner for the King and Queen. The flowers arrived from Paris about one-thirty. As we found we could get more unusual flowers there and much less expensive, [we] had them flown over by plane. Everyone was rather nervous until they arrived because it always takes quite a long time to arrange them, and get the right colors for the right rooms. . . .

During the day men from Scotland Yard came up to interview our butler to find out who the men were who were helping out in the evening. The butler had chosen men who had served at Buckingham Palace, so Scotland Yard was reassured, and there were no detectives present. I suppose they are especially careful at this time because of the Irish terrorists in the I.R.A.

We were all ready at about eight o'clock when the two ladies from the embassy arrived who were going to assist me in receiving the guests, Mrs. Michael Scanlon and Mrs. Butterworth. We all wore tiaras, of course, in honor of the Queen. I gave them last-

minute instructions, and the guests started to arrive about ten
minutes past eight. . . .

Just before eight-thirty, the ambassador and I went downstairs
in the hall, and the footmen all waited. About twenty-seven minutes
of nine, they told us the [royal] automobile was approaching. . . .
The ambassador had already descended the steps, as one is supposed
to meet the sovereigns at the foot of the steps, when they are honoring a house or an embassy. . . .

We bade them welcome and then the Queen and the ambassador
went up the stairs first, the King and I following. We were told the
King preferred the Queen to go ahead of him. They were received
in the French room . . . overlooking the garden, where a circle had
already formed. The children were all there together.

We invited the King and Queen to have a cocktail which they
declined. I remember at Windsor, they had never drunk cocktails,
but I was told that sometimes they liked to have one before dinner, and so we made the gesture. The Queen seemed to feel the
same way I do about them. . . . I always feel when I want to be
lifted up they are apt to make me sleepy and when I want to be
sleepy, they are apt to stimulate me.

We chatted informally and dinner was announced in two or
three minutes, when we went downstairs. The guests were all seated
by Sir John Monk, who usually has that responsibility at big occasions. Mr. Bullitt [the U.S. ambassador to France] was on the
Queen's right, as he was the only one she hadn't seen for a long
time. Of course, when the King and Queen are present, they take
the place the host and hostess usually have in the center of the
table, and, as usual, are opposite each other. . . . The six youngest
children were seated at a small table at the end of the room. . . .

[After] dinner the Queen and I left the table, I giving a slight
curtsy as I left the King; and as the ladies left the room, they each
curtsied toward the King. The Queen and I went upstairs to my
bedroom for a minute to powder. She asked me if I got up in the
morning to see the children off, and I said that I was usually up
late at nights and rested in the mornings. To my humiliation, she
said she usually got up, half dressed, to see her children, and then
went back to bed again.

When we joined the ladies for coffee . . . we followed the regular
procedure of bringing up different ladies to speak to her for a few

minutes each. . . . After about twenty-five minutes, we were joined by the gentlemen, and we went into the Pine Room which had been arranged for the cameramen and had two pictures taken, one serious and one laughing.

Then we went to the back room for the film. We had two of Walt Disney's and *Goodbye, Mr. Chips,* which was excellent and marvelously acted. It was quite sad, and after it was finished, it was very plain to see that the Queen had had a little weep. . . .

After that we stepped into the hall where we had something to drink. Again they chatted with a few of their friends and then went downstairs. They shook hands with almost everyone as they left. I said good-bye in the hall and the ambassador went to the car with them. After a minute's interval, the other guests said good night and the party was over.

On September 1, 1939, the Nazi armies invaded Poland. Two days after that, September 3, the British government fulfilled its pledge and declared war against Germany.

Joe Jr. and Jack and Kick and I were there in Parliament to hear Mr. Chamberlain's heartbreaking speech with its tragic lines: "Everything that I have worked for, everything that I have believed in during my public life, has crashed in ruins."

While we were on our way home from the House of Commons the air-raid sirens began to howl, and we ran for the nearest refuge we could find—which happened to be the basement at Molyneux. I thought later, what an ironic way for a woman to begin her war experiences. At the time I was simply scared for us all. As I recall, no bombs dropped on London that day—the raiders were turned back—but it was a premonition of what soon would be happening in deadly earnest.

It was time to get our children back home, and all of us but Rosemary and my husband, who was duty-bound to stay at his post, were back in the United States by the end of that month. We decided to let Rosemary stay on awhile because she was doing so well at her school, which was far in the countryside and almost surely safe from any bomb threat.

Jack resumed his undergraduate studies at Harvard and by

taking extra courses was able to graduate the next year, in the class of 1940. He decided to do his senior thesis on the reasons why the British government, under Stanley Baldwin and then Neville Chamberlain, had not armed the nation sufficiently to meet the growing power of Hitler's Germany—thus making the Munich pact necessary. The thesis was rated *magna cum laude*, which enabled Jack to graduate—despite his fragmented collegiate career—*cum laude*.

The professors at Harvard thought so highly of the thesis, in fact, that they suggested Jack expand it somewhat and interest a book publisher in it. The book came out that summer under the title *Why England Slept*. It sold extremely well, and Jack gave most of the proceeds to repair bomb damages in England.

MY HUSBAND remained in London for more than another full year, save for trips home for rest and for consultations with the President.

While in the United States, Joe actively helped Roosevelt in his bid for a third term. It looked as if the election of 1940 would be a very close one; the third-term issue was hotly debated, and the Republicans had an energetic and attractive candidate in Wendell Willkie. The President asked Joe for his support, and Joe went on a national radio hookup of one hundred and fourteen stations (paying the expenses from his own pocket) and endorsed Roosevelt for reelection. His main point was that he believed FDR could keep us out of the war.

The day after Roosevelt's reelection Joe sent in his resignation as ambassador to England. The President persuaded him to keep the title until a successor could be selected. Thus his resignation was not formally accepted until February 1941.

He never reentered government service except as a consultant and, many years later, as a member of the Hoover Commission, which was set up to reorganize the executive branch of the government. Yet he was never any less concerned with national and international affairs than he had been during the decade when he was helping to shape them.

CHAPTER FIVE

THE summers of 1940 and 1941 found us in our house in Hyannis Port, as usual. There were the familiar sounds: the bounce of tennis balls, the splashings and belly flops in the ocean, the cacophony of the radios and phonographs, the cars revving up and backfiring, departing and arriving, the piano being tortured by someone learning to play, the yapping of dogs, the ringing of telephones, and the maids' knocks on my door to ask, "Mrs. Kenendy, what should I . . ."

From 1941 onward Hyannis Port was our principal residence for seven or eight months of the year. For all of us it became home. The children had their Christmas and Easter holidays in Palm Beach, but they had their summer vacations and all the spring and fall weekends they could manage at Hyannis Port.

During the late 1940s I still had a sizable population of teen-agers on my hands there. It was a complicated household, especially because the three Gargan children, Joey and Mary Jo and the youngest, Ann, were spending the summers with us. None of our older children was there all the time, but all were there for at least part of the summer and they tried to make their visits coincide. Moreover, they were likely to invite a friend or two along for a weekend or a week or so. It was a busy house, and I was sometimes hard put to keep it passably well organized.

During those Hyannis Port summers I chased Joey around a lot, making him behave. He writes:

> She was always very much aware of where we were going and what our activities were, whether going to a movie on a rainy day down at Hyannis (we rode our bikes, about three miles each way, and we were given just the price of admission, no extras) or going out in a boat. If we were sailing she wanted to know where we planned to be, what time we were coming back, and we were always to watch the flagpole in front of the house. If she wanted us to come in for some reason she'd take the flag down. . . . She was

especially concerned to know if we were taking any other children with us and, if so, who they were and did their parents know—so that the parents wouldn't start worrying. She was *very* conscious, always very aware and considerate, about the feelings of other parents, and she was in touch with them about all the activities of our group of friends. When we were older and going to dances and driving cars, she had to know the names and addresses of our dates —just so she could be in touch with the parents in case of any problems that could involve not getting the girls home on time. The club dances ended at midnight in those days. We were supposed to take our dates directly home and be back at the house ourselves about twelve-thirty. And if we missed by more than ten minutes or so, we'd hear about it from her the next morning. That went on until we were well up into our late teens.

I have always been a rather light sleeper, so I would hear them when they came into the driveway and put the cars away in back of the house. If they were later than they should have been they drove in very slowly, with the least possible noise, turning the headlights off, and being careful not to slam the car doors or the back door of the house. They would take their shoes off and sneak upstairs in the dark to their rooms. But I knew what was happening. Joey's sister Mary Jo says:

The rules were a little different for the girls than for the boys. If I stayed out an extra fifteen minutes I could expect to see Aunt Rose looking for me. And that is the absolute truth. She had a little blue car, and . . . she'd come out and find us and say, "Dear, it's time to come home," and home we'd go. Everyone recognized her headlights on the little blue car and knew she was coming. She was, for us, even then a very strong personality.

But I can't ever remember her putting anybody down. That was one of my biggest memories of her about raising children. If I was late or something, [or] she had gone out after one of us, there'd be a note on that person's pillow: "The next time be sure to be in on time." She made herself clear and that was it: You were never chewed out. And over a period of time, this method really worked, it got to you. . . .

There's something about her. She believes in people. You just didn't want to do anything to disturb her or make her upset. If she said, "This is the way I think you should do it," you probably would find yourself thinking, well, I would kind of like to do it that way.

Evelyn Jones, who began working for us as a maid during that period, has recalled:

Mrs. Kennedy always had so much on her mind. She was always going around with these notes. At the time I was first working there, they were wearing those twin sweater sets and she would have so many things to think of that she'd have all her sweaters pinned with notes. One day she ran out of space and tried to pin some on me. I wouldn't let her: It made me feel like a human bulletin board, but I sympathized with the problem.

Except for a few elementary rules and regulations such as being at meals on time, it was a very informal household. Joe and I wanted people to feel relaxed. Yet sometimes the relaxation got to be a bit extreme. For instance, there was a general tendency, especially among the boys, to leave towels and sweaters and sweat shirts and tennis racquets and tennis shoes strewn about. I considered that extremely inappropriate, and said so vehemently.

One day they ganged up on me. One of them, just to bait me, deliberately left a pair of very dirty white tennis sneakers on the dining-room table. I saw them and left a note sticking out from the top of one sneaker: "Bobby, are these yours?!"

Bobby came along, saw the note, and left another one with: "Dear Mother, no they're not mine. Jack's."

Jack came along, saw both notes, and left another: "Dear Mother, that's wrong. They belong to Teddy."

Teddy came along, saw and read the three notes, and left one of his own: "Dear Mother, that's a lie, they belong to Pat. . . ." And so forth, through several others. I never did find out whose dirty sneakers those were, but at dinner that evening I noticed a lot of silly grins around the table, to which I paid no heed.

THE SUMMER OF 1941 had been the last one our entire family had together. Ordinarily Joe Jr. would have been returning to Harvard that fall for his last year of law school. However, believing that the United States would be drawn into the war, he volunteered for training as a navy flier; and in July, shortly before his twenty-sixth birthday, he reported for his primary training at the Squantum Naval Air Station near Boston. It was close enough so that he could come home for several weekends during the rest of that summer. Afterward he took advanced training at the big naval air station at Jacksonville, Florida. He was awarded his wings in May 1942, and in September 1943 he was finally sent to England to fly with the RAF Coastal Command.

Jack had come to the same conclusion as Joe Jr., but because of the back injury he had suffered in Harvard football, he was rejected by both the army and the navy. He did all sorts of calisthenics and corrective exercises. In September 1941 he applied again to the navy, and this time was accepted for the officer training course. Early that winter he received his commission.

At first he had a desk job in Washington, helping prepare a digest of relevant news and intelligence for the navy's chief of staff, a duty he found dull. After Pearl Harbor he quickly applied for sea duty. Instead, he was assigned to instruct recruits at a training base in South Carolina. It wasn't until the late fall of 1942 that he was transferred to PT boats. He trained for about six months, and early in 1943 was sent to the South Pacific, where by March he became skipper of *PT-109*.

One may wonder what I thought about all this. I detested it. Violence and war were against my religious beliefs, my sense of morality, and my common sense. The future confirmed my beliefs in ways which in that period I could barely have imagined.

Yet I was caught in events utterly beyond my control. There was nothing I could do but to put on a cheerful face and pray.

THE summer of 1941 was also the last one that Rosemary could be with us. In the year or so following her return from England there was noticeable retrogression in her mental skills, and her customary good nature gave way increasingly to tantrums and rages. And there were convulsive episodes. Seemingly, a neurological disease had overtaken her, and it was becoming progressively worse. Joe and I consulted the most eminent specialists, and their advice, finally, was that Rosemary should undergo neurosurgery.

The operation eliminated the violence and the convulsive seizures, but it also had the effect of leaving Rosemary permanently incapacitated. She had no possibility of ever again being able to function in a viable way in the world at large. She would need custodial care. We found the proper place in a convent in Wisconsin where the nuns have given her all the compassion and cheerful, loving care that her misfortune and her sweet nature deserve. She has been there for more than three decades. She has remained physically healthy and is perfectly happy in her environment; she would be confused and disturbed at being anywhere else. I visit her every few months. Eunice goes about every six weeks. The other family members see her at least a few times a year. She knows us and is pleased to see us.

THAT summer of 1941 was also the last one we had with Kathleen. From her childhood Kick had been, in effect, our eldest daughter because of Rosemary's disability. She was small, quick, witty, and exceptionally bright. She adored her two big brothers, and they in turn were delighted by her. Consequently, when Joe Jr. and Jack went into the navy, I think Kick, too, wanted to become directly involved in the war. Early in 1943 she left her newspaper job, reporting for the Washington *Times-Herald*, to join the Red Cross training program. She wanted to serve in a theater of war and hoped that this would be England.

She had developed a great fondness for that country and its people during our years there and had many English friends, one young man especially who meant more to her than I realized at the time. This was William John Robert ("Billy") Hartington, Lord Hartington, eldest grandson and heir of the Duke of Devonshire.

Kick got her wish. She was on her way to England by late June, 1943. Her letters to us—and to Jack out in the South Pacific—form an interesting narrative.

July 14
London

Dearest Little Kennedys,

The job is going very well. I simply can't get over how nice everyone is. I must say that I expected old friends to be kind but they have exceeded all expectations. . . .

Billy and I went out together for the first time in London last Saturday. It really is funny to see people put their heads together the minute we arrive any place. There's heavy betting on when we are going to announce it. Some people have gotten the idea that I'm going to give in. Little do they know. It just amuses me to see how worried they all are.

There were very great difficulties in the way of marriage between Kick and Billy. She, of course, had been brought up in the Catholic Church. Not only had she been thoroughly indoctrinated in her religious beliefs, but she had that special gift of faith. She also knew how much the Church meant to me, to most of her close relatives, and, historically, to her ancestors.

Billy's ancestors had for generations held high offices in the English government of Ireland. As such they had done their best to suppress any sentiments for independence among or on behalf of the Irish. Indeed, in that regard, both sides of the family, the Cavendishes (earls, marquesses, and dukes of Devonshire) and the Cecils (earls and marquesses of Salisbury), had been among the most conservative members of the ruling class. I think it would be fair to say that the Cavendishes and the Cecils, who had always been among the strongest pillars of the Church of England, deeply mistrusted the Irish people, who in turn regarded them as arch-enemies. To put it mildly, there was little in the family backgrounds to encourage a romance between Billy and Kick.

Kick had said in her letter she wouldn't "give in"—wouldn't leave her church to join Billy's—but it would have been equally unthinkable for Billy to leave the Church of England and become a Roman Catholic. It was an apparently impossible dilemma. To Jack she wrote:

July 29
London

I have just returned from a day and a half spent in the country with Billy at Eastbourne. It has been blitzed quite badly, but the family continues to go there during the summer months. It's the most lovely spot. Billy is just the same, a bit older, a bit more ducal, but we get on as well as ever. . . . Of course I know he would never give in about the religion, and he knows I never would. It's all rather difficult as he is very, very fond of me and as long as I am about he'll never marry. It's really too bad because I'm sure I would be a most efficient Duchess of Devonshire in the postwar world, and I'd have a castle in Ireland, one in Scotland, one in Yorkshire, and one in Sussex [where] I could keep my old nautical brothers in their old age. But that's the way it goes. Everyone in London is buzzing with rumors. I can't really understand why I like Englishmen so much, as they treat one in quite an offhand manner and aren't really as nice to their women as Americans, but I suppose it's just that sort of treatment that women really like. That's your technique isn't it?

Well, take care, Johnny. By the time you get this so much will have happened. The end looks nearer now than ever.

Kathleen's letter was prophetic. Four days later, *PT-109* was cut in two by a Japanese destroyer. I did not know anything about Jack's ordeal until it was all over and he was safe. A message had come from the navy that he was "missing in action" but it had been delivered to Joe, and he didn't show it to me, not wanting to give me bad news until it was absolutely necessary. Several days later, when Joe had gone riding at eight a.m., as was his custom, I turned on the radio and heard the announcement that Lieutenant (j.g.) John F. Kennedy, earlier reported missing, had been found.

The romance between Kick and Billy deepened. So did the dilemma in which not only they but the parents on both sides were painfully involved. There were many transatlantic cables and telephone calls, the point of it all being to make possible a marriage that would have been "a marriage made in Heaven" except for conflicting religious loyalties.

During the winter and spring of 1944 all of us tried to find some way by which the marriage could be sanctioned, or at least tolerated, by both the Roman Catholic and Anglican churches. But, finally, since it couldn't be worked out, the couple decided on a civil ceremony. They were married on May 6, 1944, at the Chelsea Registry Office. The duke and duchess and a few other close kin were there for Billy, and Joe Jr. represented our family.

Kick and Billy had about three weeks together before he had to return to his regiment, the Coldstream Guards, which was training for the Allied invasion of Europe that came a month later.

Meanwhile, Jack had been recuperating from his injuries in the *PT-109* episode, partly in hospitals and partly at home with us. Bobby had entered one of the navy's officer candidate schools.

I REMEMBER that Sunday in 1944. We had all lunched outside on our big porch at Hyannis Port. Joe Sr. had gone upstairs for a nap, and I sat reading the Sunday paper. There was a knock at the front door. When I opened it, two priests introduced themselves and asked to speak with Mr. Kennedy.

I invited them to come into the living room and join us comfortably until Joe finished his nap. One of the priests said no, that there was a message both Joe and I must hear: Joe Jr. was missing in action on August 12 and was presumed lost.

I ran upstairs and awakened Joe. I stood for a few moments with my mind half paralyzed. Then I managed to blurt out the priests' message. He leaped from the bed and we hurried downstairs. From what the priests told us we realized there could be no hope, that our son was dead.

Joe went out on the porch and told the children. They were stunned. He said they must be brave: that's what their brother would want from them. He urged them to go ahead with their plans for a sailing race that day, and most of them obediently did so. But Jack could not. Instead, for a long time he walked on the beach in front of our house.

There were no tears from Joe and me, not then. We sat holding each other close, and wept inwardly, silently.

Then Joe said, "We've got to carry on. We must take care of the living. There is a lot of work to be done."

When Kick heard the news she asked for leave, and hurried home to be with us. Meanwhile the Allied invasion of France had begun, and Billy and his regiment had fought through France and into Belgium.

In mid-September, while Kick was still with us, the news came that Billy had been killed in Belgium on September 10. We could scarcely believe it. It seemed too cruel that another tragedy had befallen us so soon. Kick then left us to be with the Cavendishes in their sorrow, and we did not see her again until the war in Europe was over.

Joe took his own advice about carrying on. He kept himself very busy with many things, notably the establishment of the Joseph P. Kennedy, Jr. Foundation for mental retardation.

One of the best ways to assuage grief, which we first learned fully at this time—and which would help us survive future tragedies—is to find a way to turn some part of the loss to a positive, affirmative use for the benefit of other people. I do believe that God blesses us for that and lightens the burden.

IT HAS been said that time heals all wounds. I don't agree. The wounds remain. Time—the mind, protecting its sanity—covers them with some scar tissue and the pain lessens, but the wounds are never gone.

"How can one endure in the face of tragedy?" people have asked me. And surely I have often had reason to ask myself.

Joe was right in his words: "Take care of the living. There is a lot of work to be done." And he was right in his instinctive and immediate recognition that in sorrow we must look outward rather than inward, and thus can come peace of mind and spirit.

CHAPTER SIX

WHEN Jack was discharged from the navy early in 1945, he worked for the Hearst papers as a special correspondent, covering the British election, the Potsdam Conference, and the founding of the United Nations. He liked the work and did well.

Many people think that his father practically forced him to enter politics. That would have been completely out of character on both sides. Anyone reading Joe's letters to Jack and the others can see that giving orders to his children would have been contrary to the relationship he had with them. And Jack, quite as obviously, would not have submitted to such a parental command. (I can imagine his smiling agreeably and saying, "Yes, Dad," as he used to say, "Yes, Mother," when I told him to put on a sweater—and then go off without it.)

It is true that the role Jack chose probably would have been different had it not been for Joe Jr.'s death. Joe Jr. would have made a career in elective public office. That was his ambition, and he had practically every asset for the role. As Jack wrote, "His success was so assured and inevitable that his death seems to have cut into the natural order of things."

The period when Jack was confronting the fact that his older brother was gone was a crucial one in Jack's life, in the life of our family, and as it turned out, in the political life of the country.

JAMES Michael Curley, who had succeeded my father both as congressman and as mayor of Boston, and who was subsequently in and out of those two offices, and the governorship, during three decades, had been elected mayor again in 1945. This left his congressional seat vacant, and Jack decided to try for it.

At twenty-nine, Jack knew a lot about political science, government, diplomacy, national and international affairs. He had studied them at Harvard, had learned a good deal through his father's involvement in them, and had observed them as an author and journalist in these fields. He also understood that in this congressional district the names Fitzgerald and Kennedy were enough to get him off to a good start.

But while Jack knew about politics, he knew very little about the actual mechanics of organizing and operating a campaign. Obviously, to my father (then a hale eighty-three) and to other relatives and family friends he looked like a promising neophyte and got the benefit of any doubts. It is worth asking how he looked to others who had no personal connection with us.

Some interesting answers have been supplied—from direct experience—by Dave Powers, an air force veteran, who met Jack at the very beginning of this campaign but had no intention of joining it. He did so, however, and stayed with Jack afterward as a close associate to the end of the road in 1963.

Jack was the hardest-working candidate I ever saw. Nothing was ever too much if he figured it could help the cause. If he heard some other candidate had been to some benefit or church affair or something like that earlier and made an impression, he'd say to me, "Dave,"—and this let's say is in the evening after already going that day for twelve, fourteen hours—"Dave, how about it, shall we go over and show them the *real* candidate?" And tired as you yourself could be feeling by then, you'd say, "Sure, let's go," even if it's half an hour away through traffic, because he was trying so hard, giving it everything he had, and you feel that you've got to do your best for him. And every place he goes, he makes votes. People warm up to him.

Now, with a guy like that—with that desire, and making votes everywhere he stops in—you tend to make a very full schedule. But here's something else. Jack has a funny sense of time and distance. He'd get interested in these people and he'd forget about time, and it was hard to disengage him. And, anyway, he has the feeling that every place else is only fifteen minutes away. I've been with him in his apartment in the middle of Boston and he's soaking in his tub at a quarter of eight, and we're due in Worcester at eight, and he'd say, "Dave, how far is it to Worcester?" And I'd say,

"Well, if we're driving, we're late already." It would go like that.

Now, I remember there was one of these big veterans' rallies someplace in the district and his mother was there, at our request, to say a few words and to introduce him as the candidate. We were running late. We got there late.

Afterward, Jack and his mother were chatting with several of us in the campaign. And he says, "Mother, they're all telling me I should wear a hat, because it will make me look older."

And she looked him right in the eye and said, "I think it's more important to be on time." Jack did a double-take and turned to the fellows who were handling his schedule. Her remark [had] brought them awake, too, and the scheduling got looser, at least for a while.

He never asked for anything but time, more time than it turned out he ever had. . . . All he needed was a thirty-six-hour day.

Jack won both the primary and the general election that fall, entering Congress at the age of twenty-nine, a year older than my father had been when first elected to the same seat.

Jack's subsequent performance as a congressman was difficult for anyone to fault. When he ran for reelection two years later, in 1948, no one in his party bothered to make him run in the primary, and in the election no Republican ran against him, so he continued in office by acclamation, so to speak. In 1950 he had five opponents in the Democratic primary, but he was renominated and then beat the Republican nominee by five to one.

Presumably he could have gone on in this same safe seat for the next forty years, rising by seniority through committee chairmanships and cloakroom camaraderie to become, perhaps, Speaker of the House. That prospect bored Jack intensely.

By the time Jack's third term in the House would be over, Senator Henry Cabot Lodge, Jr., would be coming up for reelection. It was difficult to imagine that Jack could win against him. Lodge was handsome, charming, intelligent, a hard worker, and an excellent campaigner. Although his ancestry was Back Bay, he was one of the foremost liberals of the Republican party—an "enlightened" Republican. However, my husband believed Jack could win and encouraged him to make the race. In our thirty-eight years of marriage I had seen Joe's judgment vindicated so consistently that I didn't question it.

Jack took his time, weighing all the pros and cons carefully, then as usual made his own decision. He would run. Kennedy vs Lodge developed into one of the most famous battles in modern U.S. political history.

Joe was intensely interested and active in the campaign, though he stayed behind the scenes. Bobby, by then twenty-six, had an interesting job in the U.S. Department of Justice, but when he was asked by his father and by Jack, he put aside his personal concerns and came in as campaign manager.

Jack's back was again causing him severe and prolonged pain, and he traveled with crutches, which he concealed in his car. When he arrived at a hall to speak he walked with a determined effort from the car to the door; but when he came into the room where the crowd was gathered he was erect and smiling—looking fit and healthy.

General Eisenhower took the presidency that year by a large majority, yet Lodge, closely identified with Eisenhower and with his vigorous endorsement, went down by 70,737 votes.

FOUR years later at the 1956 Democratic convention, Jack was chosen to give the speech nominating Adlai Stevenson, and he himself came within a hairsbreadth of the vice-presidential nomination. From the force of that momentum he went on to the presidential nomination and election in 1960.

In my wildest hopes and dreams for him, I could hardly believe that in a matter of only fourteen years he would move from a rather shy, sometimes awkward young candidate for Congress in 1946 to a still youthful-looking but mature President.

MEANWHILE, from that first campaign of Jack's to the one for the presidency, we were concerned with a great deal besides politics. In the Kennedy family, as in all others, life and death went on happening.

After the end of the war in Europe, when it was possible to

travel freely again, Kathleen would come to visit for a few weeks at a time. And of course that was always a blessing for us. After recovering, outwardly, from the shock of Billy's death in the war, she went on to make a good life for herself in England. The duke and duchess took her with utmost affection into their family circle, and England became her home.

We lost our beloved Kathleen on May 13, 1948.

She had taken a holiday on the Riviera and was flying to Paris, where her father was waiting to meet her. On the way—her route threaded along the edges of the French Alps—the weather went bad, navigation equipment was not adequate, and the plane crashed into a mountainside, killing all on board. Joe hurried to the scene. He watched as the body of his daughter was brought down the mountainside.

The duke and duchess wrote us a beautiful and heartfelt letter saying how much they had loved Kathleen, and how grateful they had been to her because of the happiness she had brought to their son Billy. I cannot bear to quote from it. Kathleen was buried at Chatsworth, the Devonshire ancestral estate. The duchess suggested her epitaph: "Joy she gave, and joy she has." Billy had been buried in Belgium, where he had fallen.

ABOUT this time Joe and I began to wonder when we were going to have grandchildren.

Bobby blazed the trail. Ethel Skakel had been Jean's roommate and best friend at Manhattanville College; that's how Bobby and Ethel met. They married in 1950 and their first child, Joseph Patrick Kennedy, was born in 1952.

Eunice and Sargent ("Sarge") Shriver married in 1953, Pat and Peter Lawford in 1954, Jean and Stephen ("Steve") Smith in 1956, Ted and Joan Bennett in 1958. Joe and I could count on frequent weddings during that decade, and one of them was Jack's.

The first I ever heard of Jackie Bouvier was during the winter of 1951. She and her younger sister, Lee, were vacationing in Hobe Sound, up the coast from Palm Beach. Jackie worked on a

Washington newspaper and knew several of our children, since by that time Jack, Eunice, and Bobby were working in Washington. She was invited to spend a few days at our Palm Beach house while some of them were there. I was not there myself at the time, but soon afterward I received a thank-you letter signed "Jackie." I thought it was from a boy. How extraordinary for a boy to write such a charming letter. It turned out Jackie was a girl, and I began hearing good things about her from members of the family, especially that Jack liked her a great deal. I did not meet her until the summer of 1952, at Hyannis Port. I liked her at once.

Jackie and Jack became engaged in the early summer of 1953, and there were many preparations for their wedding. Jackie says:

> We got engaged in June and the wedding was going to be in September at Newport, so I remember one day my mother invited Jack's mother over to Newport for lunch and to discuss the plans. Jack was there for the weekend. And the situation amused me so much. Because here was Jack, he was thirty-six at the time and he was grown up and he was a senator. And his mother was coming to have lunch with my mother, and we were going to the beach and he and I would have a swim first. The two mothers were dressed up—Bailey's Beach was dressy then—and I remember [Mrs. Kennedy] had on a beautiful light blue silk dress and a big hat. Jack had on some undershirt and a pair of bedroom slippers, and I expect she was rather mortified at the sight her son presented. I remember that on the way over, the two mothers were in the front of the car and we were sitting in the back seat, sort of like two bad children.
>
> Anyway it was, I'm sure, one of his least favorite days—the two mothers sitting there in their hats and pearls and white gloves chattering away about the wedding. So we went swimming. I came out of the water earlier; it was time to go for lunch, but Jack dawdled. And I remember she stood on the walk and called to her son in the water, "Jack! . . . Ja-a-ck!"—and it was just like the little ones who won't come out and pretend not to hear their mothers calling—but he wouldn't come out of the water. I can't remember whether she started down or I went down to get him, but he started coming up, saying, "Yes, Mother."

KATHLEEN AND LORD HARTINGTON, 1944

Weddings

PAT AND PETER LAWFORD, 1954

EUNICE AND SARGENT SHRIVER, 1953

In the 1940s and 1950s most of the Kennedy children were married and began to establish families of their own.

ED AND JOAN, 1958

BOBBY AND ETHEL, 1950

JACK AND JACKIE, 1953

JEAN AND STEPHEN SMITH, 1956

It was a splendid wedding, with all the traditional ceremonials and a large group of attendants. Archbishop (later Cardinal) Cushing presided and read a special blessing on the marriage from the Pope. There were eight hundred in the church, including all sorts of notables, and more than twelve hundred at the reception. I daresay Jackie must have gotten a little tired smiling and shaking hands, but I can't think of a more appropriate introduction to life as the wife of a political figure.

Jack loved her and was proud of her and appreciated her. And it would be hard to imagine a better wife for him. She brought so many things that helped fulfill his character. She developed his interests in art, music, and poetry—especially poetry, in which he had had only a mild interest.

I admired the fortitude she showed when Jack had his back operations. The first one, when he almost died, was in October of 1954, and there she was, a young bride, deeply in love with her husband and faced with being widowed. For the first few weeks after he was brought down—still on a stretcher—to Palm Beach to recuperate, he had a nurse to change his dressings. Then the doctor said she wouldn't be needed anymore provided there was someone else to do it. Jackie took that on; the doctor taught her how. The incision was very large, it was still draining, and the dressings had to be changed several times a day. She did this skillfully and gently, with no comment about it to anyone.

As THE tribe increased, we began to have a housing crisis at both our Palm Beach and our Hyannis Port homes. But at Hyannis Port the problem soon began to solve itself, for the family could take a much longer cumulative time there—the summer vacations, and weekends all the way from after Easter to Thanksgiving—and this made it sensible for them to buy their own houses as their families grew. Bobby and Ethel rented a place the first two or three years; then a house next door to ours came on the market, and they bought it. And that was the beginning of what came to be known as the Kennedy compound—though that is a misnomer if I ever heard one.

A few years later another house came on the market: it is catty-corner from ours and directly back to back with Bobby and Ethel's, and thus the three backyards adjoin, separated by some shrubs and outbuildings. This one became Jack and Jackie's house. It was a spacious and congenial arrangement—everyone could walk back and forth through the backyards.

That group of three houses is bounded on the street side by a tall, split-picket fence, enough to give us a modicum of privacy. The other two sides are open, the beach and also the lane coming into the properties where Jean and Steve had a house. Eunice and Sarge's place is a ten-minute walk away; Teddy and Joan's, another ten minutes away.

By 1960 there were houses galore, with plenty of space for visitors, and we were all close enough to see one another as often as we wished.

By then Joe and I were seventy-two and seventy. Both of us were healthy, active, enjoying life fully. We had suffered grievous losses, but we rejoiced in our children who remained and in our grandchildren. And we had the excitement, the drama, the pride, the great thrill that our eldest surviving son was running for the presidency of the United States.

THERE were a number of reasons why, supposedly, Jack could not win the Democratic nomination in 1960. First, he was too young—forty-three—and no one so young had ever been elected President. Second, he had had no experience in the executive branch of government, whereas the presumed Republican nominee, Richard Nixon, had had two terms in the vice-presidency. Third, he had little or no support among the party's established national leaders; and fourth, and most important, he was a Catholic. True, there was now a new generation, and religious tolerance had grown, but how much and how effectively was debatable.

Nevertheless, Jack decided to run, and from that moment everyone in the family went to work for him. Bobby, of course, was campaign manager, and I also took to the road. When it was all over Jack gave me a map of the United States which he had marked to show the places I had visited and signed it, "For Mother—With Thanks." The map shows that I made forty-six appearances in fourteen states. Somewhat to my own surprise I found myself turning into a regular politician. I did not miss a chance to ask anyone to vote for Jack: taxi drivers, elevator operators, waitresses, porters, manicurists, and anyone with whom I could strike up a conversation.

This was Jackie's first experience in hard campaigning. She was rather a shy person, but there she was, traveling with Jack in motorcades, shaking hands along main streets, and even going into supermarkets now and then to announce herself as the wife of John F. Kennedy and urge the shoppers to give him their votes. All of us were impressed. She was a wonder.

The convention is rather blurred in my memory. We all were in or near Los Angeles except for Jackie, who by then was in mid-pregnancy with their second child. [Caroline, their first, had been born in 1957.] Joe and I and other members of our family stayed at Marion Davies's house. Joe preferred to remain there on the evening of the balloting, away from the crowds and the photographers. The rest of us were at the convention hall.

Jack won the nomination on the first ballot. There was joyful, ear-shattering pandemonium. Pat (a member of the California delegation) and I were called to the platform to stand with him as everyone cheered. It was a very proud moment.

THE evening of Election Day, 1960, we were all at Hyannis Port. Bobby's house had been converted into election head-quarters. It was chaotic: teletype machines clattering, telephones ringing, television sets going, typewriters clicking, and lots of people. The whole top echelon of the campaign staff—the expert analysts, newspaper reporters, photographers, stenographers, telephone operators, and many others—were there. Bobby was in the middle of it all. Jack was in and out. Teddy, Steve, Sarge, Peter, the girls, the cousins, friends—everybody was working, and for once there wasn't much kidding or much gaiety. The race was extremely close, and there was tension in the air. Now and then people came over to our house for a sandwich or a drink or a change of scene. Jack would come in to tell his father about a new development.

Joe and I had very little conversation that evening. He was trying to get the latest exact figures and to project from them how the counts were likely to develop in critical districts. I went over to see Jackie a couple of times because she was rather alone at her house—Jack being deeply preoccupied—and out of the melee because she was now in the eighth month of pregnancy.

I couldn't bear to think that Jack would lose. In spite of the uncertainties I kept thinking, He'll win, of course he will. Finally, late that night, after the tide seemed to have swung in his favor, I went to bed in order to be rested and prepared for the outcome, whatever it would be.

I think the election must have been decided sometime toward daybreak, because about four thirty, as I learned later, the Secret Service men closed in around our adjoining properties and particularly around Jack's house, taking over the protection of the presumed President-elect.

Pat (in a letter, much later) wrote:

> I remember that around 3 A.M., when it looked good for Jack—we all went into the kitchen for something to eat. Jack left later by the kitchen door and I can see him now, crossing into Bobby's back lawn in the dark, walking to his own house, and the Secret Service closing in right behind him. A couple of us said (hardly able to believe it): "Good night, Mr. President."

TOWARD the end of perhaps the busiest, most exciting months of our lives, we closed the house in Hyannis Port for the winter and made the annual migration to Palm Beach.

We had Thanksgiving there, and needless to say it was a day of very special thanksgiving. Jack and Jackie and Caroline couldn't be with us because Jack was busy selecting his Cabinet and other high officials for his administration. The new baby was due to arrive at almost any time, and Jackie had to remain near her own doctor and hospital in Washington. John Fitzgerald Kennedy, Jr., was born on November 25, to the joy of all.

Inauguration Day was January 20, 1961. Jack and Jackie were in their house in Georgetown. Bobby and Ethel lived about half an hour away in McLean, Virginia. The rest of us, when we assembled at the scene, stayed in Steve and Jean's house in Georgetown or in a house nearby which we had rented.

It began to snow the afternoon before the inauguration. By daylight next morning the storm was nearly spent but had left a thick blanket of snow and a cold, wet wind. Our rented house was only half a mile or so from the nearest Catholic church, and since I am accustomed to walking, I decided to walk to Mass. I put on galoshes and a heavy coat and thick gloves and a couple of woolen scarves, and took off for church.

As I approached I noticed a great many policemen outside, as well as police cars, and unmarked cars occupied by men who I realized must be Secret Service agents. Suddenly it occurred to me that Jack must be coming there for Mass.

I asked one of the policemen if the President-elect was expected, and he gave me a guarded look and said he didn't know, maybe so. I went inside and sat near the rear. A few minutes later Jack came in and sat down toward the front.

I hadn't suggested he go to Mass that morning; he was there of his own volition. He didn't know I was there and I didn't want to go and sit with him, bundled up as I was. I just followed the Mass and, from a distance, looked at him very happily.

Nor did I go to him after Mass, because I knew there would be photographers ready to pop pictures of any personal encounter, and I wanted no picture taken of him with me in my regalia. However, since I had to get ready for the ceremonies, I thought it would be an advantage if I could get a ride back to my house. I went over to one of the Secret Service men and said, "I am Mrs. Kennedy, the President's mother. Will you please have someone come with a car and take me to my house?" He nodded. But no car came. Evidently he thought I was either an impostor or demented—because I certainly didn't look like a President's mother. After waiting awhile I walked home. It was no hardship, accustomed as I was to New England winters.

The rest of that day is somewhat blurred in my memory because so much was happening, with one stupendous scene following another. At the inauguration Joe and I were close enough so that we could have exchanged some words with Jack after he came down the Capitol steps and took his place. But we didn't do that. We stood and applauded him, as everyone else did, and as we took our seats we gave each other a squeeze of the hand, with no need or desire for words.

Bobby was in the reviewing stand as attorney general. Although Jack wanted him in that office, Bobby had resisted because he feared the appointment would be criticized as nepotism (and it was), but he had yielded to the arguments of his brother and father. In any case, I found myself in the position of being the mother of both the President and the attorney general, which was rather overwhelming.

That night there were five inaugural balls at different locations. The big one, at the District of Columbia National Guard Armory, had a throng of about a thousand people, including Joe and me, other members of the family, and good friends waiting for Jack and Jackie in the presidential box at one end of the great arena. Jackie looked perfectly beautiful, and Jack had never looked more handsome. Everyone was smiling at them; one could almost literally feel a wave of love and pleasure.

I had saved the gown I wore when I had been presented at court and was delighted to find I could wear it without alteration. It is now part of the Smithsonian Institution's collection of gowns worn by American women during special events in history. After the ball Joe and I returned to Georgetown. Jack and Jackie went home to the White House.

We didn't stop there for farewells the next day. We knew that Jack would be involved in his new duties and that Jackie, too, would have a lot to do. And so, quietly and happily, we returned to Florida.

CHAPTER SEVEN

JOE was so determined to avoid any appearance of influencing Jack that he did not set foot in the White House except once during the rest of that year. However, it happened that I was present, on the sidelines, at the first great triumphs of Jack's presidency. These came in early June of 1961 at the time of his meetings, first with President de Gaulle in Paris and then with Chairman Khrushchev in Vienna.

Ever since the late twenties I had been going to Paris almost every spring, because I love the city and because I wanted to look at the spring fashion collections and pick out a few dresses. Jack knew that this was part of my yearly schedule. So, happily, the State Department found a way to involve me in the festivities.

On the evening of Jack and Jackie's arrival there was a dinner for a hundred and fifty in the Hall of Mirrors at Versailles. I had prepared myself for this grand event with a new evening gown, which, of course, was French. Jackie looked absolutely stunning. That evening and during the whole visit she was a *succès fou*. Jack was delighted, and he said at an event the next day, "I think I should introduce myself—I am the man who accompanied Jacqueline Kennedy to Paris."

After Paris I was allowed to go on to Vienna, where Jack held meetings with Chairman Khrushchev of the U.S.S.R. During the stay I chatted with Mrs. Khrushchev several times. She had a very pleasant, disarming smile, and wore her hair drawn straight back, and no makeup. She told me immediately that she knew a lot about me, as she had read an article about me in *McCall's*.

Mrs. Khrushchev was one of the special surprises and delights of that trip. Her English was quite good, and I had the impression that if we lived in the same town, I would find her a reliable friend.

There had been many photographs taken of Premier Khru-

Grandpa Kennedy enjoyed
his grandchildren. He is seen
above with Caroline and below
with a dozen Smiths, Shrivers,
and Kennedys. In 1961, just
after he and the President were
photographed, he suffered a
stroke, but paralysis did not
dim his interest in the family.

Grandpa

shchev and Jack together during the Vienna meeting, and I decided to send some of those to the premier and ask him to autograph them; he signed the photographs, returned them to me, and I sent them on to Jack to keep for Caroline and John Jr.

I received the following letter from Jack:

Dear Mother:

If you are going to contact the heads of state, it might be a good idea to consult me or the State Department first, as your gesture might lead to international complications.

Love,
Jack

To which I replied:

Dear Jack:

I am so glad you warned me about contacting the heads of state, as I was just about to write to Castro.

Love,
Mother

JOE and I spent most of that summer of 1961 on the Riviera. Then on December 19, when we were at the Palm Beach house making our preparations for Christmas, Joe was stricken with a blood clot and partial hemorrhage in one of the arteries of his brain—a stroke. His chances of living were problematical; but he survived the crisis and a few weeks later was off the critical list and strong enough to be brought home. From that time on, my niece Ann Gargan, who had been well trained in nursing, devoted herself to caring for Joe.

The stroke had left him unable to speak and had almost completely paralyzed his right arm and leg. However, his mind appeared to have been only moderately impaired. By springtime his general physical condition had improved so much that his doctors said he was ready to begin therapy, through which he might regain the powers of speech and movement. Accordingly we—Ann and I, and Joe on a stretcher—flew to New York, where Joe entered the Institute of Rehabilitation Medicine, whose director was—and is—Dr. Howard Rusk.

Slowly, with good care and his indomitable will, Joe came back as far as it was possible physically. He was able to stand with the aid of a cane and, with someone's arm for balance, to walk a few steps. But mainly—aside from the considerable time every day he would have to rest in bed—he was confined to his wheelchair, because standing was a great drain on his strength.

His doctor wrote:

Probably the most moving moment during his stay in New York was when the President visited. . . . After the visit, the President wheeled his father to the garden and indicated that he must leave. Mr. Kennedy . . . locked the [wheel]chair, and indicated that he wanted to stand, which he had previously not been able to do alone. Some assistance was offered, but he shunned it angrily.

Then, with incredible effort, he forced himself to a standing position. He fixed the President with his piercing eyes and extended his left hand to say good-bye. The President, obviously moved, quickly turned and disappeared to the street and out of sight.

As Joe made progress, minute and sometimes evanescent though it was, he could again take part in life. The limits of his participation were of course severe. He came to family meals, and followed the conversation attentively. Though he couldn't speak, he could laugh, and that marvelous grin of his was intact. He was amused by the banter, even when directed at him.

Fairly soon we were able to resume in a general way the annual pattern of our lives: spring, summer, and fall in Hyannis Port; winter in Palm Beach; with intervals in New York, where we continued to dine out and where Joe continued to go to his office—for an hour or two at a time—to look over the books.

THE first year of Joe's illness was also the year that Teddy ran for the Senate. I was involved very little in that campaign, for I felt that Joe needed me, and I wanted to be with him. Furthermore, Teddy apparently was feeling a bit oppressed at being the kid brother in the family and was out to show that he could win on his own merits. Jack was very pleased with him. Teddy recalls:

He knew that when I was running in Massachusetts I told the voters I wanted to be judged on my own and not on the family name. So in a speech he made in 1963, he said, "Teddy wants to be judged on his own; so he is thinking of changing his name . . . from Teddy Kennedy to Teddy Roosevelt."

Teddy won, and I must say that with all three of our surviving sons in positions of leadership I thought to myself that I must have done something right.

And so we entered a golden time. It was shadowed by Joe's illness; yet, as I have said, he was still able to enjoy a good many of the pleasures of life; and his spirit was comforted by the accomplishment of the grand design he had for his sons, and by their love and respect for him.

Jack often came to the Cape, and Dave Powers has described his departure after his last visit, on Sunday, October 20, 1963:

Ambassador Kennedy was on the porch in his wheel chair. The President . . . put his arm around the old man's shoulder and kissed him on the forehead. He started to the helicopter, turned, looked at his father for a moment, and went back and kissed him a second time. . . .

When the President was inside the helicopter . . . he looked out at the figure in the wheel chair and his eyes filled with tears.

"He's the one who made all of this possible," the President said sadly, "and look at him now."

I remember Friday, November 22, began as one of those perfect late-autumn days at the Cape. At that time of year the air is crisp but not cold, and it has such freshness from the sea that one's spirits are lifted up. By then, also, the summer people have gone and the village, though not deserted, is somnolent.

And so on that beautiful morning, after I had been to Mass and we had had breakfast, Joe and I went for a ride in the station wagon, simply enjoying the weather, the scenery, and the serenity. Then I went over to the golf course, and was back at the house in time to have lunch with Joe.

After lunch Joe had his nap. I was feeling rather tired and went upstairs to lie down for a while. Soon I heard Ann Gargan's radio blaring so loudly in her room that I went to tell her to please tune it down. Ann said the volume was up because she had just heard that along the route in Dallas someone had taken some shots at the President and that he had been wounded.

I had a mixture of reactions. Worry about Jack, of course, instinctively. But then a rejection of the idea that it could be something terribly serious because, after all, he had been through so much that almost automatically I had in the back of my mind the thought, Jack is having some more hard luck; another problem about his health, but he'll surmount it. Further, I had trained myself through the years not to become too visibly upset at even very bad news, because I had a strong notion that if I broke down, everybody else in the household would.

I went back to my room and paced the floor, trying to think that soon the news would come that Jack had not been wounded badly. After a while I went back to Ann's room and found that the news was worse. My heart sank. But I still couldn't realize that what seemed to be happening was really happening. Then, a few minutes later, Bobby telephoned from Washington and said Jack was in extremely serious condition and was not expected to live. And then, soon, the news came that Jack was gone.

AT ANY such time of shock and grief I suppose that most people fall back for support on familiar patterns of behavior that can be followed automatically. In our household, many long years before, Joe and I had adopted as a general principle that if there was bad news to be faced it should be given in the morning, not late in the day, for otherwise there would be a sleepless night which would only make the debility worse. Hence, I decided that Joe should not be told of the tragedy until the following morning. This would also allow time for his physician, Dr. Boles, to come down to the Cape from Boston, and for Teddy and Eunice to come up from Washington, as they had called and said they wanted to do. Bobby would stay in Washington to take care of

Jackie and supervise all that would need to be done there. Sarge, Jean, and Steve were also in Washington; Pat was on her way from California. I told Ann and the nurses that Mr. Kennedy was not to be informed of anything about this until the children had arrived and we could decide how he would be told.

The household staff and everyone else, grief-ridden though they were, acted their parts superbly. For example, Ann unplugged all the television sets, and of course Joe was irritated, but then he seemed to accept this as one of those freakish defects of modern technology and contented himself with a magazine.

Meanwhile, as that afternoon wore on, I spent much time in our front yard or on our beach, and walked and walked, and prayed and prayed, and wondered why it had happened to Jack. He had had everything to live for: a lovely and talented wife, a perfect partner for him, and two beautiful little children whom he adored. He had made such a glorious success of his life and of his presidency, and at last, for the first time since early childhood, he had become really healthy. Everything—the culmination of all his efforts, abilities, dedication to good and to the future—had lain boundlessly before him. Now everything was gone. I walked on the beach and I thought, Why?

My reaction to grief takes in part the form of nervous activity. I have to keep moving, walking, pulling away at things, praying silently while I move, and making up my mind that I am not going to be defeated by tragedy. Because there are the living still to work for, while we mourn the dead.

Dr. Boles arrived. He told us that Joe could physically withstand the emotional shock, though he agreed it would be better if it came not that evening but in the morning. Ted and Eunice arrived and, as casually as they could, went in to see their father. Perhaps Joe was surprised by this conjunction but there was no reason to be too surprised: after all, he was due for a checkup from Dr. Boles, and both Ted and Eunice traveled a lot and therefore might drop in on us most anytime. It was decided among us, with Ted really taking the burden on himself, that he should be the one to tell his father the next morning.

I went to the morning devotions at St. Francis Xavier's—the beautiful little church in Hyannis where all four sons had served as altar boys—and stayed on for the first Mass of the day, to which Ted and Eunice came. I had called the pastor the night before and asked him to say this Mass for Jack. It was one of the first things I had thought to do.

After Mass we went home to breakfast and afterward, as usual, Joe went to his room for a rest. Very soon then Ted—with Eunice, Ann, the doctor and a nurse; not I, for I couldn't stand it—went in and told him, as gently yet as straight-out as possible, what had happened and that Jack had passed away.

I heard from them later on that Joe not only took the tragic news bravely but seemed to want to comfort them. The doctor had already given him a sedative, and soon he went back to sleep.

The doctor said that it would be feasible for Joe to go to the funeral in Washington that Monday, but Joe rejected the idea. One of his old friends, Father John Cavanaugh, the former president of Notre Dame University, came to stay at the house and offer such aid and comfort as he could give. The two of them sat together and watched the ceremonies on television.

It was far easier for me to travel, and I felt I should be there. And I was. I did not walk with the others in the procession from the White House to the cathedral because I felt quite unwell that morning. Nor did I take Communion at the cathedral, as some did, because I had already been to an early Mass and had received it then. I was at the graveside in Arlington, of course, and afterward I went to the White House to help express our family's appreciation to the numerous heads of state, dignitaries, and friends who had traveled from far places to pay respects.

That evening I came back to Hyannis Port to be with Joe.

WE IN the family reacted to our common grief in our own ways. But we could all be reasonably steady because of the faith, hope, and love we shared, and because we knew quite well what Jack would want from us: he would want courage, he would want as many smiles as we could manage, and he would want his death to be an affirmation of life. He would want us to think of him with love, but to live for the living, and to cherish such happiness as we could find or give. We all realized this, and we all did our best.

Everyone knows of Jackie's bravery and dignity during the ceremonies. As General de Gaulle remarked, "She gave an example to the whole world of how to behave."

THANKSGIVING was three days later, and so during Tuesday and Wednesday the children and grandchildren began arriving. We did not know whether Jackie would come, but on Wednesday evening she, too, arrived, bringing Caroline and John. And we had our Thanksgiving celebration, with every one of us hiding the grief that gnawed at us and doing our best to make it a day of peace, optimism, and thanks for the blessings that were left to us.

There were so many memorials for Jack that we in the family were surprised, for bereaved as we felt, we could not have anticipated the sense of bereavement shared by vast numbers of people all over the world. I was often invited to take part in the programs; and when I could I did.

The first major one that I felt I should attend was in January, when Cardinal Cushing offered a solemn high Mass for Jack at Holy Cross Cathedral and Erich Leinsdorf conducted the Boston Symphony Orchestra in Mozart's *Requiem in D Minor*.

Boston, Jack's birthplace, filled with so many memories of him . . . the cardinal who married Jack, and now so recently had buried him . . . the beauty of the Mass, of the cathedral, and of the music . . . all these elements together had a nearly overpowering effect. I managed with difficulty to keep a grip on myself.

EARLY the following summer, on June 19, there was very nearly another tragedy within our family. Ted and another young senator, Birch Bayh of Indiana, along with Mrs. Bayh and Ed Moss, a close friend and aide of Ted's, were due at a meeting in Springfield, Massachusetts. They had taken a charter flight—through a foggy night—and the plane crashed during the landing approach. The pilot was killed. Later Ed Moss died. Senator and Mrs. Bayh escaped without long-range serious effects, but Ted was very badly injured: several vertebrae were fractured and there was a possibility that his spinal cord had been damaged.

He was bedfast for six months, most of them in traction, but with his rugged constitution he was able to progress to a wheelchair, to crutches, and finally to walk and run and even engage in sports; although for years afterward he had to wear a back brace. He seems to be in perfect health now.

Meanwhile, during his convalescence he was able to take care of the important business of his Senate office by telephone, mail, and courier, as Jack had done while recovering from his back operations. And again like Jack, Ted turned his physical incapacity to constructive use by collecting and editing essays about his father in a book he titled *The Fruitful Bough*.

Ted was also up for reelection that year. Obviously campaigning in person was out of the question, but he had an able and devoted staff, headed by Steve Smith, and he was reelected with more than seventy-five percent of the votes.

BOBBY had been very close to Jack, had felt united with him. He had worked in Jack's 1946 congressional campaign, had managed the first Senate campaign and presidential campaign, had been in Jack's Cabinet and at his right hand through every problem that arose during the presidency. And as brothers they shared ties of loyalty, sentiment, memory.

No wonder, then, that Bobby at first felt and acted as if he had been cut adrift and did not know quite what to do in the years ahead. However, he wanted to do what Jack would have wanted of him, and the first urgent priority was to help Jackie and the two children. During those next months—and indeed for the next years—Bobby was a pillar of strength in Jackie's life: adviser, protector, confidant, and good, cheerful companion whenever he was needed.

As that summer of 1964 went on, it became apparent that President Johnson preferred to have someone other than Bobby on the ticket with him for vice-president. I was disappointed because I knew Bobby wanted the nomination. But I admired President Johnson and I could understand his position.

In any case, Bobby had to decide what to do; and having reached the conclusion that he wanted to stay in public life, he decided to run for the Senate in the New York State elections. He won by more than seven hundred thousand votes.

Teddy meanwhile had been discharged from the hospital in mid-December. And so when Congress reconvened that January of 1965 there were two Kennedy brothers in the U.S. Senate.

A little later they were shown on a magazine cover, with the Capitol dome in the background. We had the cover framed, and their father indicated he wanted it put up on the wall in his bedroom, where it would be in his view whenever he was in bed.

Joe's condition remained a slow, grueling process of attrition, yet his spirit was never less than valiant. I was with him most of the time, and we always had meals together.

I had luncheon and dinner invitations rather often, and when I accepted I would say that I might be a bit late. Since Joe dined punctually at six, I could have a light meal with him and still arrive in time for another light meal with my hostess. Joe always knew my plans, but I never dressed for an evening out until after dinner, when he was asleep. There was no subterfuge; I simply thought the sight would remind him of the irretrievable past.

In 1968 Bobby decided to run for the Democratic nomination for the presidency. I had profound misgivings. I felt he had so many responsibilities to his family and within our general family; and he was still young enough—at forty-three—to try for the presidency later; and that meanwhile he should try to relax a bit.

But Bobby, once having made up his mind about the right course for him, was not going to be deflected from it. People have talked about the streak of romanticism in Jack. It was Bobby who, for all his supposed ruthlessness—such a mistaken term for him—was really a romantic idealist. I mean he felt that with faith and effort one can do great good in the world.

And so once again the troops rallied: the loyal cadres that

Bobby and Ted and Jack himself, and Steve and others had built all over the country. And I, of course, prepared to take to the road, as I had done many times before, to help wherever and however I could. I was seventy-seven then, and it seemed to surprise people that I should be out stumping for my son, but by then it had come to seem perfectly natural.

I did make an absentminded mistake in that campaign. Bobby had just won the primary in Indiana, and as usual there were interviews. A reporter commented that the Indiana campaign had cost a lot of money, and that it must be nice to know the Kennedys could afford it. I had heard such comments many times, and they struck me as unfair. Although Joe did contribute substantially to the financing of the campaigns, the amounts were almost trifling compared with those he gave to schools, charities, medical research, and so forth. Apparently my irritation had reached a flash point, because I was quoted as saying: "It's our money and we're free to spend it any way we please. It's part of this campaign business. If you have money you spend it to win."

Mainly, in the 1968 campaign, I tried to dispose of Bobby's image of ruthlessness. I pointed out that when he was attorney general his probes into labor racketeering and organized crime were marked by his idealism and courage. I emphasized that above all he was kind, that his heart often ruled his intellect, and that he was open and honorable and selfless.

HAVING done what I could in the primaries, especially the one in California, I flew back to Hyannis Port to await the California returns on radio and TV. By eleven that night, eastern time, it seemed fairly certain Bobby was the winner. Feeling thankful but tired after my travels, I went to bed.

The next morning I awakened around six, in time for early Mass, and turned on the television for the final results. Instead, I heard that Bob was being taken to the hospital.

Again my mind somehow would not allow me to think that it could be anything really serious. I went on dressing, listening distractedly; then Ann came in, saying he had been shot.

It seemed impossible that the same kind of disaster could befall our family twice in five years. If I had read anything of the sort in fiction I would have put it aside as incredible. I still wanted to go to Mass.

Later, back at the house, I was praying, *Lord have mercy!* And thinking, *Oh, Bobby, Bobby, Bobby.* I kept busy in my room, sorting, rearranging, doing *anything* to keep moving. And I wondered. I still couldn't believe it, although I knew it was so.

The next morning, Thursday, June 6, Bobby passed away.

THE funeral plane arrived from California that evening, and Bobby lay in state at St. Patrick's Cathedral in New York, where a hundred thousand people came to pay their respects. At the service on Saturday, Teddy delivered the eulogy with dignity, simplicity, and grace. His three brothers were gone. His father would go soon, as he knew. And he was a credit to all of them.

His summary of Bobby's character was perfect in truth: ". . . a good and decent man, who saw wrong and tried to right it, saw suffering and tried to heal it, saw war and tried to stop it."

There were some comments later in the press about my "composure" and "self-possession" and "bravery," and it was remarked that from time to time I waved from the funeral train to people who had gathered in the cities and towns—some even on rooftops—to watch it pass. Apparently there were those who thought the waving inappropriate. But I did this, and encouraged the children and grandchildren to do it, because I felt that if people cared enough to come out and pay their respects we ought at least to give them some sign of appreciation. As for my being composed—I had to be. If I had broken down in grief, I would only have added to the misery of the others and possibly set off a chain reaction of tearfulness. But, in fact, it was not just I who set an example of fortitude. The family set it for one another. For example, young Joe II, who adored his father and who was barely seventeen, went through the cars and on behalf of the family thanked friends, official dignitaries, reporters, colleagues and staff assistants of Bobby's for being with us.

Ethel was the most admirable of all. She and Bobby loved each other deeply—they had a perfect life. Much as I would grieve for Bobby and miss him, I knew she would miss him even more: not only for all they meant to each other but as the father of her ten children, with the eleventh to come a few months later. Yet she was calm and courageous, and I was very proud of her.

How sad are our hearts when we realize that we shall never see Bobby again, with his windblown hair, his big, affectionate smile, carrying one child piggyback and leading another by the hand, his dog close behind them. What a joy he brought us. A devoted husband, a beloved son, an adored brother—I know that I shall not look upon his like again.

AFTER Bobby's death Joe's condition declined until November 18, 1969, when, surrounded by those who remained of his family, and quite peacefully, he passed away. I was kneeling by his bedside, holding his hand. Next to Almighty God, I had loved him—do love him—with all my heart, all my soul, all my mind.

With the deaths of his brothers and then the death of his father, Ted was the only surviving male member of our immediate family. Ninth and last child, youngest son, he now had to be the head of the family. And he responded magnificently. He is my joy and support and solace.

CHAPTER EIGHT

IN THE resurrection of Christ we find our sure hope in the immortality of the individual soul. This faith and assurance give life, with all its struggles and earthly disappointments, a sublime meaning and are a source of wonderful strength and constant guidance. So my life went on, with both an overwhelming sense of loss and a determination to remember with dearest love, yet to meet the future with my head into the wind.

I thought, during this period, a good deal about Jacqueline. I felt that after such time as it might take her spirits to mend, she would be able to participate fully again in life.

I had known Aristotle Onassis for some years, and I liked him. He was pleasant, interesting, and, to use a word of Greek origin, charismatic. Even so, when Jean called me one morning in October 1968 and said Jackie was going to marry him—and would be calling later to tell me about it—I was rather stunned. I thought of the difference in their ages, in religion (he is Greek Orthodox), and the fact that he had been divorced. My thoughts were awhirl, but with contemplation, the first basic fact seemed to me that Jackie deserved a full life, a happy future.

I decided I ought to put my doubts aside and give her all the emotional support I could in what was bound to be a time of stress. When she called I told her to go ahead, with my loving good wishes. I was reassured when she said she had consulted Cardinal Cushing, who spoke out for her, through the press, with this statement: "My advice to people is to stop criticizing this poor woman. She has had an enormous amount of sadness in her life and she deserves whatever happiness she can find."

Jackie was greatly cheered by my confidence in her. Recently she said:

> When I married Ari, she of all people was the one who encouraged me. Who said, "He's a good man." And "Don't worry, dear." Here I was, I was married to her son and I have his children, but she was the one who was saying, if this is what you think is best, go ahead. It wouldn't surprise anyone who has really known her; but anyway, how extraordinarily generous that woman is in spirit. I always called her "Belle Mère"—I still call her that.
>
> She comes and visits us. It's wonderful for Caroline and John. And Ari adores her. The first Easter after we were married she came to spend a few days with us in the Caribbean. . . . Then, after Grandpa died late that year—I was there in the room with the others when he died—she was feeling sort of shaky. She came and spent New Year's with us.
>
> If I ever feel sorry for myself, which is a most fatal thing, I think of her. I've seen her cry just twice, a little bit. Once was at Hyannis

Port, when I came into her room, her husband was ill, and Jack was gone, and Bobby had been killed . . . and the other time was on the ship after her husband died, and we were standing at the rail together, and we were talking about something . . . just something that reminded her. And her voice began to sort of break and she had to stop. Then she took my hand and squeezed it and said, "Nobody's ever going to have to feel sorry for me. Nobody's ever going to feel sorry for me," and she put her chin up. And I thought, God, what a thoroughbred.

My thoughts turn to a time recently when Eunice and I were invited to lunch with the editors of this book. Someone posed the question to us: "Would you rather be a senator or the mother of a senator?" Eunice with alacrity said she would rather be a senator. But I decided that I would much rather be known as the mother of a great son or a great daughter.

Now I want to say some things about Ted. After Jack's and Bobby's deaths he made it his responsibility to work toward the goals that had been most important to them. Jack had proposed abolishing the discriminatory parts of our immigration laws; Ted guided the bill through the Senate. Bobby had campaigned to end this country's military involvement in Vietnam; Ted was one of the most effective leaders in mobilizing the congressional and public sentiment that finally brought that about. At the same time he was doing everything generous and thoughtful for me, and for Jackie and Ethel and their children; and he was at the hospital with Ethel when the last baby was born.

For many years my children have participated in the Edgartown Regatta, and 1969 was no exception. I knew that Ted was flying to Martha's Vineyard to skipper Jack's old boat, the *Victura*, with Joey Gargan to crew for him.

I had heard also that after the race they would be going to a cottage on nearby Chappaquiddick Island for a cookout with some of the men and women who had campaigned with Bobby. One of the young women invited was Mary Jo Kopechne, a loyal, hardworking and wonderful person who had been one of Bobby's most dedicated assistants. She and most of the others had been guests at Hyannis Port the previous summer.

The events of that tragic night have been thoroughly reported in the world press: how Ted drove over a narrow bridge and the car plunged into the water and Mary Jo was drowned; how Ted repeatedly dived to find her, and went back to the cottage for help from Joey and Paul Markham; how their efforts failed; and how Ted did not report the accident until the next morning.

I first saw Ted when he returned to Hyannis Port the afternoon after the accident. He was so unlike himself it was hard to believe he was my son. He was disturbed, confused, and sick with grief over the death of the young woman. But with good medical care, and his own natural reserves of strength, Ted started to pull himself together.

I wrote to Mr. and Mrs. Kopechne, saying that after suffering the loss of my own daughter Kathleen at the same early age of twenty-eight, I could realize what a suffering this was for them; and how badly I felt that my son was in any way involved in their loss; and that my sympathy and prayers were with them.

Someday, perhaps, Ted may decide to seek the presidency. When the time and circumstances are right, I would like to see him President, because I know he would do wonderful things for the country. But in the immediate future he has plenty of important work to do in the Senate. As for our family situation, there are all those sixteen children—Jack's and Bobby's and his own—for whom he has a responsibility. And there are still too many risks, as anyone who reads the daily newspapers knows well.

Ted, of course, will decide for himself, just as his brothers did. But if anyone wants to know whether I think he should run for President in 1976, my answer is: "I hope he will not." *

Meanwhile, during these past few years, life for me has been

---

* On September 23, 1974, Senator Kennedy announced his "firm, final, and unconditional" decision not to run for President or Vice-President in 1976, saying, "I simply cannot do that to my wife and children and other members of my family." [Editor's Note.]

quite full enough without having another President in the family. I believe in keeping interested. Sedentary people are apt to have sluggish minds. Vivacity, receptivity to ideas, interest in other people, have special relevance as one gets on in years. So I am busy with many projects, especially for the mentally retarded.

I still respond to the demands and opportunities of public service. Evidently I have acquired a certain status. Teddy says:

> Mother is especially good in a one-to-one relationship, and that's because she not only cares about people in general but as individuals. She and I might be out walking together in the dusk at Hyannis Port and a carful of people would pull up and ask directions to the Kennedy compound. . . . Invariably she would not only give them directions but point out one or two sights of special interest. Now, most of these people probably had seen her at some time on television when she was all dressed up in one of her Paris creations, so that probably would be their idea of her, which didn't match at all with this woman who was walking down Scudder Avenue in flat heels, a sweater and skirt, maybe a scarf, [or] a golf cap. . . . But they would start recognizing her way of speaking; and ask her, "Is it . . . ?" and she would say, "Yes, it is" . . . and they would smile, and thank her, and drive off in a state of complete captivation and rapture.

I was at dinner at a friend's house, and the conversation had taken a slightly morbid turn, which caused me to remark, "But I'm sure God wants us to be happy and take pleasure in life. He doesn't want us to be sad." The man sitting opposite said, "Mrs. Kennedy, that is one of the most inspiring statements I ever heard." All I said was something I have always believed.

I still see no reason to doubt it. God made the world and made us to live in it for a while. We owe Him infinite thanks and obligations. Surely among these is the appreciation of the delights of life. Birds sing after a storm; why shouldn't people feel as free to delight in whatever sunlight remains to them? If more people were thankful for what they have, instead of mournful for what they have not, much good would come to the world.

WHEN JACKIE REMARRIED, some wondered whether she would keep the house she and Jack had at Hyannis Port. She soon said she was going to, because it meant so much to her and to Caroline and John Jr. She wrote:

> When I came back everything just hit me, because this was the only house where we really lived, where we had our children . . . and nothing's changed since we were in it. And I found myself becoming so happy here. The children are happy, and the cousins are here, and all the grandchildren adore [their grandmother].
> She sees them in little groups . . . and talks with them on the level of what interests them.
> She has the food they like, which is the same food she gave to her children . . . creamed chicken and Boston cream pie and apple jelly . . . the most wonderful food there is in the world, sort of American home-cooking. I think you always like to know that all the best kinds of things are at your grandmother's house.

My grandchildren have often credited me with being a very proper person. However, I have never thought of myself that way, and I think I can refute the charge with one recent incident that landed me in the Palm Beach newspaper.

I had stopped in at Mrs. Wrightman's house because she was giving a luncheon honoring my friend Mary Lasker. John Ryan, Joe's former nursing attendant who had stayed on after Joe's death, was supposed to come and pick me up in the car, but there was a misunderstanding about the time, so after waiting for him on the porch I walked down the driveway to wait for him at the road. When he still didn't come, I started walking home. But it is quite a long distance, and it was a hot day, so I decided the sensible thing was to try to get a ride with a passing motorist. I raised my thumb in the way I had seen hitchhikers do.

I was well dressed in a white suit, and I was sure I looked respectable and attractive. Therefore, it was rather mortifying when at least a dozen cars went by, until finally a man did stop.

I told him who I was and what the problem was. He looked a bit amazed and very kindly drove me to my front door. As it happened, later that afternoon I was in a shop and saw him with his wife, so I went over to thank him again and introduce myself to her. We all smiled and shook hands and that was the end of the story, except that a day or two later the press got hold of it, and it became a feature article with a cartoon drawing of me and words to the effect that "Rose Kennedy, although now in her eighties, has taken up hitchhiking. . . ."

Most of my grandchildren are still too young to be thinking much about what they want from life except the next allowance and the penny candies they are going to load up on at the store. Or being allowed to crew in races.

I don't try to impose my ideas and values on them (not that it would do any good if I did), and I don't pry into their lives. But I do have a few special hopes for them.

I hope they will realize how they happen to be where they are. They came—on the Kennedy-Fitzgerald side—from ancestors who were quite disadvantaged, but who had the imagination, the resolve, the intelligence, and the energy to seek a newer, better world for themselves and their families. In just a few generations these beleaguered Irish immigrants produced a family to whom many in the world looked in admiration. It is an inspiring story. My grandchildren are the continuing part of it, and I hope they will try always to be worthy of it.

I hope they will realize that the United States of America was one of the few places in the world where this saga could have happened. I hope they will always feel a deep sense of gratitude toward this country, and deep pride in it, and deep obligation to preserve, protect, and defend it.

I hope they will have courage and the strength to bear the difficulties and disappointments and griefs of life. Bear them with dignity and without self-pity, knowing that tragedies befall everyone, and that determination, not tears, makes pain bearable.

I hope they will comprehend that the span of any life is short and all the days and hours are precious. I hope they will live life fully, in all the dimensions of both its duties and its beauties.

Now, AS I APPROACH my eighty-fourth year, I find it interesting to reflect on what has made my life, even with its moments of pain, an essentially happy one. I have come to the conclusion that the most important element in human life is faith.

If God were to take away all His blessings—health, physical fitness, wealth, intelligence—and leave me but one gift, I would ask for faith, for with faith in Him, in His goodness, mercy, and love for me, and with belief in everlasting life, I believe I could suffer the loss of my other gifts and still be happy.

We must guard against the thought that faith is mere credulity; the truth is that just as it centers upon God, so too it comes from Him to those who seek it. From faith, and through it, we come to a new understanding of ourselves and all the world about us. It puts everything into a spiritual focus, so that love, and joy, and happiness, along with worry, sorrow, and loss, become parts of a large picture which extends far beyond time and space.

During my long lifetime I have found three devotions which were of special spiritual inspiration to me. The Rosary has helped me to lead a happy life devoted to the love of God and for the benefit of my family and my friends, and the welfare of my neighbor. If I am worried and I hold the rosary in my hand, it gives me comfort, trust, serenity, and a sense of being understood by the Blessed Mother. As I have talked and prayed to her all my life, in happy, successful times, I know now she will understand and comfort me in my anxious, troubled moments.

Another favorite is the *Meditations and Devotions* by Cardinal Newman, which always brings me consolation when I am discouraged or find myself in an inexplicable dilemma.

And my third great source of inspiration is my devotion to the Stations of the Cross. These fourteen pictures represent events in the last three hours of our Lord's life. I follow His journey to Calvary often, in church, kneeling before each Station. At the Twelfth Station in particular, when He died, I think of my three sons in their last moments—on their final missions, undertaken for the benefit of humanity—and I bow my head in silent resignation to God's Holy Will.

Finally, at the Fourteenth Station, I see the Blessed Mother view, for the last time, her Son as He is placed in the tomb. I take renewed strength and courage in the thought that as Jesus Christ rose from the dead, my husband and I and our sons and daughters will one day rise again, and we all shall be happy together, nevermore to be separated. My spirits are lightened and my heart rejoices, and I thank God for my belief in the Resurrection. *I am the resurrection and the life; he that believeth in me ... shall not die.*

This promise has been a steady source of inspiration throughout my life, and I hope and pray that all who read this book may find renewed peace and strength and joy in these thoughts.

A DEDICATION

Rose Kennedy has special reason to be aware of the problems of the mentally retarded. It is to her beloved daughter Rosemary "and others like her—retarded in mind but blessed in spirit"—that she dedicates *Times to Remember*. "My vision," she writes, "is a world where mental retardation will be overcome, where we no longer mourn with mothers of retarded children, but exult and rejoice with parents of healthy, happy youngsters."

The principal aims of The Joseph P. Kennedy, Jr. Foundation, established in honor of Joe Jr., who was killed in World War II, are to seek, through research, the causes and, it is hoped, the cures for mental retardation and to ameliorate its effects. Mrs. Kennedy has stipulated that the foundation is to receive all royalties from the sale of her memoirs.

One of the foundation's major projects is the International Special Olympics, which provides year-round sports training for almost four hundred thousand mentally retarded children and young adults here and abroad. Readers wishing to help expand this program to include many more of the two and one half million retarded young people in America may send contributions to The Joseph P. Kennedy, Jr. Foundation at 1701 K Street, N.W., Washington, D.C. 20006.—The Editors

SYBIL

The haunting odyssey of a woman fragmented
into sixteen warring personalities—and her
successful struggle to become one again

A condensation of the book by

FLORA RHETA SCHREIBER

Illustrated by Robert Heindel

Sybil Dorsett lived in a waking nightmare.

There were checks that she didn't remember writing, clothes in her closet that she hadn't bought. She would find herself in a strange city, with no memory of how she had gotten there. She was caught in the grip of a nameless fear.

One day her psychiatrist was startled to see the patient change before her eyes. Sybil's attitude, her manner—even her voice—were different.

"Who are you?" the doctor asked.

"I'm Peggy," said Sybil.

That was the beginning of one of the most bizarre and fascinating cases of multiple personality in the annals of psychiatric medicine. Sixteen different "people" emerged, two of them male. Only through them was the doctor able to piece together the story of Sybil's strange and tortured childhood, and begin leading her back to health.

"A brilliantly written, poignant narrative, a remarkable literary achievement." —*American Journal for Psychoanalysis*

1

THE CRASH of glass made her head throb. The chemistry lab swirled. The acrid smell of chemicals seemed to emerge from some far-off memory—the broken glass in the old drugstore at home, the accusing voice, "You broke it."

Sybil Isabel Dorsett flung her chemistry notes into her brown zipper folder and rushed to the door, the uncomprehending eyes of the other students upon her.

The door closed behind her. She was in the long, dusky hall on the third floor of Columbia University's Havemeyer Hall. Then she was waiting at the elevator. "Too long." Her thoughts spun. The elevator was taking too long.

SYBIL clutched for her zipper folder. It wasn't there. The elevator wasn't there, either, or the dusky hall. She was walking on a long, narrow street, with snow swirling underfoot. A sharp wind whipped her. She had no overshoes, no gloves, no hat; her ears ached. Her light tweed coat, which had seemed warm enough when she walked to the lab from her apartment on Morningside Drive, offered painfully little protection against the cold.

She looked for a street sign. There wasn't any. She looked for a house, a gas station. None. There was only this poorly lighted, deserted, nameless street in a place she didn't recognize.

Old, ugly, massive wooden structures—some painted battleship gray, others covered with sheet metal—lined the street. She was in a warehouse district. There seemed to be no exit, just as there had been no entrance. Was there no taxi? No bus?

If she could find a phone booth, there would be a directory to give this place a name. And she could call Teddy Eleanor Reeves, her roommate, who must be worried about her. Dr. Wilbur, too, would surely be worried. Had she missed her hour with the doctor? Could she have missed *many* hours by now? There was no knowing how much time had passed.

Momentarily, Sybil stopped under a streetlamp and rummaged through her purse. Her Social Security card, Blue Cross card, driver's license, Columbia University library card—each brought the reassurance of recognition.

Her billfold, which had contained $50 and some change when she left her apartment, contained only $37.42 now. She had walked to the lab, and had bought nothing after she got there. Had she used the missing cash to travel to this place? She had sufficient, the doctor believed, to present this history-making case in a medical journal, because in addition to its great medical significance, the case had broad psychological and philosophical implications for the general public.

I wanted to wait for the outcome of the case before committing myself. In the meantime, Sybil and I became friends. After knowing her and her other selves for three years, I became intrigued by the idea of the book and began to do formal research to unfold this extraordinarily chilling saga.

Sybil's story provides not only a new observation of the uncanny power of the unconscious mind in motivating human behavior but also a new look into the dynamics of destructive family relationships, the crippling effects of a narrow, bigoted religious background, a woman's identification with the males in her family, and the denial of self-realization. In terms of what not to do, Sybil's story is a cogent lesson in child care. Implicit in this account, too, are such issues as: What is maturity? What is a whole person?

—FLORA RHETA SCHREIBER

waited at the elevator; then she was here. That was all she could remember.

In her purse also was a large, reddish-brown tag she had never seen before. A key dangled from it. Turning the tag over and over in her almost frozen hand, she looked at it again, rereading its gilt numbers: 1113. Obviously a hotel key. Where had it come from? The tag bore no name or address.

As she walked rapidly along, looking at each street intersection for an approaching vehicle, her panic mounted.

Suddenly there was a light. A gas station. A phone booth at last. According to its directory she was in Philadelphia, a city she had visited often. But not once had she been in this area.

Intending to call Dr. Wilbur, she inserted a dime in the slot to ask for long distance, but the telephone was dead. She asked the gas station attendant if she might use his private phone. "Sorry," he replied. He walked away from her and closed the door in her face. Her fear, she knew, had made him afraid.

But the knowledge that she was in a city she knew well lifted some of the terror. Returning to the street, she noticed for the first time the Delaware River and, on its other shore, Camden, New Jersey. The Delaware was familiar. She had once done an impressionistic watercolor of it while Capri, her cat, sat at her side, watching every stroke of the brush.

Street signs began to appear. Approaching a corner, she noticed a city bus. "Wait! Wait!" she called frantically.

The florid-faced driver waited.

Arms and legs aching, she collapsed in a window seat in the rear of the bus, ready to go wherever it would take her. Was it evening? Or morning? The anonymous in-between gray of the overcast sky held no clue.

Was the key in her purse from the Broadwood Hotel, where she always stayed when she visited Philadelphia? She walked to the front of the bus and asked the driver, "Do you go anywhere near Broad and Wood?"

"Three blocks from it," he replied. "I'll call you."

Through the bus window she began to recognize familiar Philadelphia landmarks: she was on terra firma again. Then, reality at last, the red brick Broadwood Hotel. Someone had told her the Broadwood had been built in 1923. That was the year she was born. Funny.

"Your corner," the driver called to her.

In the main lobby she stared at the familiar marble, the yellow, black, and white tile floor, scrutinizing each detail as if she were looking at it for the first time. The place had changed since she had last been here. The bellhops were not the same. Nor had she ever seen the owlish woman at the registration desk. Unable to decide whether to register or look for room 1113, she rushed out to Broad Street. On a newsstand she noted a copy of the Philadelphia *Bulletin*. It was dated January 7, 1958. She had left the chemistry lab on January 2. *Five days lost.*

Slowly, fearfully, she pushed open the hotel's heavy glass door once again. Dimly she heard the owlish woman at the desk call to her. "Hello, there," she was saying, her large head bobbing

in recognition. "I was worried about you out in that snowstorm. Now, when you get to your room take a hot bath and get some hot tea. This is no weather to monkey around with."

"Thank you. I'm all right," Sybil replied somewhat stiffly as she headed toward the elevators.

The door of an elevator slid open. Sybil, anxious and apprehensive, entered. She was the only passenger. "Eleven, please," she said.

"Out in that storm?" the elevator boy asked.

She whispered, "Yes."

"Eleven," he called.

The elevator door closed behind her with a metallic clang. As she walked down the hall, the numbers on the doors flashed by. Then, as if it were in neon lights, there was 1113!

Sybil turned the key over in her unsteady hand. At last she inserted it and the door swung open. She found the light switch. Stepping inside, she closed the door behind her.

As far as she knew she had never before been in the room. But if it weren't hers, where had she slept from January 2 to January 7? How had she come by the key? The woman at the desk downstairs had acted as if she were registered.

Sybil removed her wet coat and kicked off her wet shoes. She slumped into a chair near the window and for a time just stared vacantly through it. Then she went to the telephone to call room service. She ordered split pea soup and a glass of hot milk. At that moment something on the dresser riveted her attention and she dropped the receiver abruptly. It was her zipper folder. Opening it, she discovered her chemistry notes, exactly as they had been five days before when she had scooped them up in the lab. Also on the dresser were her mittens and the red scarf she had been wearing at the Columbia University elevator.

In a corner of the dresser was a receipt from a Philadelphia department store for a pair of pajamas. Where were they?

She found them on a hook behind the bathroom door, hanging like an accusation. The pajamas, looking rumpled and slept in, were loud, with orange and green stripes. Not her style. She always chose solid colors. These were the sort a child might select.

Then, on a small bedside table an object she had not seen before beckoned to her: a pencil drawing of a female figure perched on a cliff against a towering mountain that threatened to engulf it. The drawing was on Broadwood stationery. It had obviously been left behind by the person who drew it. Who?

There was a knock at the door, and the room-service waiter placed Sybil's tray on a table. "You're not very hungry tonight," he said, as if comparing her order to what she had had on other occasions. His manner was protective, as if he knew her well. Yet Sybil had not seen him before. He left.

She gulped the milk. Then, pushing the soup aside, she put on her still-wet shoes and coat, her scarf, her mittens. She stuffed the pajamas and the sales slip into her zipper folder. Though she could see that the snow hadn't stopped, and though she was aware that the trains might be delayed, Sybil Isabel Dorsett knew she had to get back to New York while she was still herself.

2

ON THE train Sybil tried to envision what had taken place in her absence: the regular daily sessions with the doctor missed, the doctor's possible attempts to search for her, and above all the doctor's disappointment upon surmising what had happened.

She thought about the very first time she had seen Dr. Wilbur. That recollection unleashed a flood of others so powerful that not until the train pulled into New York's Pennsylvania Station did it cease.

SYBIL had been twenty-two years old that summer of 1945. She was living in Nebraska with her parents, Willard and Henrietta ("Hattie") Dorsett. Wartime without, it was for Sybil also wartime within. For the nervous symptoms that had plagued her since childhood had become so bad that the authorities at the midwestern teachers college where she was majoring in art had sent her home, saying that not until a psychiatrist deemed her fit could she return. But homecoming had only aggravated Sybil's symptoms. In August 1945 she was earnestly seeking a solution to a lifetime dilemma that no one understood.

In this state of mind she had seen her mother's physician, Dr. Lynn Thompson Hall. Hattie Dorsett had been the sick one, and Sybil had come to the office as the daughter of the patient. But while talking to the doctor about her mother, Sybil had experienced a fleeting wish that he would ask about her. She liked the tall, soft-spoken Dr. Hall, for he treated her like an intelligent adult. Having an IQ of 170 should have earned her the right to be treated as if she were intelligent. Yet she never felt like that around her mother or father. They had been forty when she was born; she had never known her mother without gray hair. She supposed it was this gap, seeming to span not one generation but two, coupled with her being an only child, that explained why in her parents' presence she remained a child.

Having finished examining Sybil's mother, Dr. Hall took the younger woman aside and said, "I'd like to see you in my office for a moment, Miss Dorsett."

To Sybil's surprise, the doctor did not talk about her mother. Looking firmly at her from his swivel chair, he said forthrightly, "Miss Dorsett, you look pale, thin. What's troubling you?"

It was exactly what she had hoped would happen. "Well," she replied slowly, "I don't have any great physical complaints, Doctor." She desperately wanted his help but, afraid to tell him too much, merely added, "I'm just nervous. I was so nervous at college that they sent me home until I could get well."

Dr. Hall was listening attentively, as if he really did want to help her. "You're not at college now?" he was asking. "Then what are you doing?"

"Teaching in a junior high school," she replied. Because of the wartime teacher shortage she was able to do so without a college degree.

"I see," he said. "And this nervousness you speak about—what form does it take?"

The question terrified her. No matter how much Dr. Hall wanted to help her and no matter how much she wanted his help, she simply was not able to tell him: there was a force that shrouded her life and made her different from other people, but it remained nameless even to her. All Sybil said was, "I know I have to see a psychiatrist."

The doctor showed no surprise and seemed to make no judgment. "I'll make an appointment for you," he said matter-of-factly, "and tell you the date and the time when you come with your mother on Thursday."

Sybil said nothing of this to her parents, but on Thursday, in her mother's presence, Dr. Hall remarked, "Your appointment is with Dr. Wilbur for August tenth at two p.m. She's especially good with young people." He leaned forward and put his hand on Mrs. Dorsett's arm. "And, Mother, you're not to go with her."

Sybil was startled, even shocked, by the tone the doctor had taken and by her mother's apparent acquiescence. *Nobody*—not family, friends, not even Sybil's father, and certainly not Sybil— had ever told her mother what to do. Hattie Dorsett didn't take orders; she gave them. Moreover, it had been a fact of Sybil's existence that her mother went with her everywhere. In a single sentence Dr. Hall had reversed the reality of a lifetime.

PRECISELY at two p.m. on August 10 Sybil entered the office of Dr. Cornelia B. Wilbur in Omaha's Medical Arts Building. The doctor had red hair and was young, perhaps no more than ten years older than Sybil. Her eyes seemed unmistakably kind.

Still, churning within Sybil were the same opposing feelings that she had experienced in Dr. Hall's office: relief that at last she was doing something about her nervousness, coupled with terror that the condition was untreatable.

Dr. Wilbur was patient as Sybil, trying to mask these feelings, rattled on about being so shaky at college that she had often had to leave the classroom. "Well, I'm home now," she continued, "and it's simply dreadful. I'm with my parents every minute. They look at me with long faces. I know they're ashamed. They were counting on my education. But I'm going back when I'm well enough."

The doctor still hadn't said anything, so Sybil went on talking. "My parents worry about me. Everyone worries about me—our pastor, everybody. I'm illustrating the pastor's sermons on Daniel and Revelation, painting the beasts rising from the sea as he talks about them. I'm suspended on a scaffold ten feet above the stage. I usually chalk on heavy drawing paper my interpretations of what the pastor says. He—"

Dr. Wilbur interrupted her. "You've been telling me what everybody else thinks about you. But how do *you* feel?"

Sybil talked of her poor appetite, of the fact that she weighed only seventy-nine pounds even though she was five feet five. The recital of physical complaints included her chronic sinusitis and her poor eyesight. After a pause she added, "I'm not at all well, but I've been told that I'm really healthy. Ever since I was a little girl, I've been sick but not sick."

Sybil froze when the doctor tried to get her to talk about her feelings, but the psychiatrist persisted. Finally Dr. Wilbur told her, "You should come back. You have difficulties that can be worked on."

Walking out of the building into the glare of the August sun, Sybil realized that she would never be able to tell Dr. Wilbur all that she could about herself. All that she knew—even then.

On Sybil's second visit to Dr. Wilbur, Hattie Dorsett, frustrated at being forbidden to accompany her daughter to the doctor's office, had taken her as far as the elevators of the Medical Arts Building and said she would wait for her in a nearby department store. When, dutifully, Sybil walked into the store, she caught sight almost at once of her mother's lean, proud figure and gray-white hair. At once, too, came her mother's, "What did the doctor say about *me?*"

"She didn't say anything," Sybil replied.

The treatment continued once a week throughout the summer and early fall of 1945. For all three Dorsetts it was a period of apprehension. Each time Sybil came home her parents were waiting like vultures. Separately or together they would ask, "What did she say about us?" It was never, "How are you getting on?" Or, "How did things go?" Nor was it ever what Sybil would have liked most of all: to have them say nothing.

"You don't think much of yourself," the doctor told Sybil. "That's an uncomfortable feeling. So you project it on others and say, 'They don't like me.' "

Another of Dr. Wilbur's themes was, "You're too serious. You need more social life." The doctor advised, "Get away from home. Go to New York or Chicago, where you can meet people like yourself—people who are interested in art."

Sybil's parents criticized the doctor. She smoked, and no good woman did that—no good man, for that matter. She didn't go to any church, let alone a church of their fundamentalist faith. For them, the doctor would remain an outsider.

"Dr. Wilbur doesn't really care about you," Sybil's mother repeatedly warned. "She tells you one thing now. But when she gets you where she wants you she'll tell you altogether different things. And remember, young lady, she'll turn on you if you tell her you don't love your own mother."

Sybil would assure her mother that she would never tell the doctor that because it wasn't true. "I do love you, Mother. I do." She affirmed it again and again.

She desperately wanted to get well, and the scenes at home did not help. If talking led to a scene, so too did silence, for then her parents would accuse her of being moody, and although they had upbraided her for moodiness many times in the past, they now claimed Dr. Wilbur was responsible for it. "She'll make you crazy," her mother warned, "and then they'll put you in an institution. That's the way doctors make their money."

In contrast, others who knew Sybil talked of a marked improvement in her. As the weekly one-hour sessions continued through September, Sybil herself became more and more convinced that

Dr. Wilbur would help her to get well. But she was still very puzzled by herself.

She had still not told the doctor what puzzled her—some terrible, nameless thing that had to do with time and memory. There were times, for instance, when Sybil would go to the doctor's office and later would have no clear recollection of what had transpired; she could not tell her parents what the doctor had said about them or about anything else.

There had been one occasion in particular.

"Last time you were here you tried to jump out the window," the doctor told her. "You leaped out of the chair and rushed to the window. I couldn't stop you."

Sybil didn't remember doing anything of the sort, but she didn't argue the point. All her life people had told her she had done things she hadn't done.

"I wasn't really disturbed," the doctor explained. "The glass is unbreakable." Then she became more serious. "You had what looked like a little psychological seizure."

Psychological? Dr. Wilbur was saying that Sybil was nervous. That was old—not new. What was new was that the doctor didn't seem to blame her.

Nor did Dr. Wilbur seem to think that her condition was hopeless, as she herself had often feared. The doctor presented her with three choices for the immediate future: to continue her art teaching at the junior high school for another year; to go back to college; or to undergo intensified treatment at Omaha's Bishop Clarkson Memorial Hospital, where the doctor and a colleague ran a psychiatric division.

Sybil chose the hospital. But when she told her parents they were distressed. To them hospitalization meant only one thing: their daughter was insane.

"This has nothing to do with insanity," Sybil tried to explain.

"Then it has to do with the devil," her father replied ominously. However, he agreed to talk it over with Dr. Wilbur, and finally gave his consent for Sybil's hospitalization.

Clarkson, as Dr. Wilbur saw it, was only a temporary measure.

What Sybil needed ultimately was psychoanalysis. "I would like to do the job myself, but I'm not an analyst yet. In fact, I shall be leaving Omaha shortly to begin my training. I suggest that after you leave Clarkson you go to Chicago to be analyzed."

The prospect thrilled Sybil. Chicago meant not only moving closer to the truth about herself but also getting away from home. Psychoanalysis, however, posed another problem for Willard and Hattie Dorsett. They feared that the strange world of the analyst's couch would exclude God from Sybil's life. "I'll have to talk it over with Pastor Weber," Willard Dorsett said.

The two men were very close. Impressed with Dorsett's talents as a builder-contractor, the pastor had engaged him to build a church for the denomination. Now, as they talked in the half-built church, the pastor was noncommittal. "Frankly, Brother Dorsett, I don't know what to advise. The decision is not mine to make but yours and hers."

Finding no effective defense against his fears, Willard left the decision to his daughter. Sybil's answer was unflinching: "I still want to go to Chicago."

While waiting for a bed at Clarkson and for word from Chicago, she saw the immediate future as a stepped-up assault on the terrible thing that had enshrouded her life. The decisiveness that she had been unable to show when she was younger she felt able to exert at last.

But suddenly everything changed. Following a strep infection, Sybil contracted pneumonia. Her head ached terribly; her throat was raw; and although she tried to get out of bed to cancel her October 6 appointment, dizziness and weakness intervened. She asked her mother to telephone Dr. Wilbur. She heard Hattie saying, "This is Mrs. Dorsett, Sybil's mother. Sybil can't keep her appointment with you. She has pneumonia and asked me to call you. Thank you." With a click her mother hung up.

"What did the doctor say?" Sybil asked.

"She didn't say anything."

"Nothing about another appointment, and the hospital?"

"Nothing."

THE TRAIN HAD reached Trenton, and still Sybil's reverie continued. The echo of her mother's voice could not be stilled. The train moved on toward New York as the memories came, unbidden, propelled by what Sybil supposed was their own logic. The doctor had started all this, the doctor to whom she was returning.

LEARNING that Dr. Wilbur had said nothing about another appointment, Sybil consoled herself with the thought that probably the doctor had assumed she would call when she was well enough. But when she did call she was told that Dr. Wilbur had left Omaha permanently. After all the bitter battles at home, after the difficulty of persuading her parents to let her go into treatment, the road to getting well had been ripped from under her.

She thought of how her mother would scoff and her father would become silently critical. She thought about Dr. Wilbur and how puzzling it was that she should have left town without so much as a backward glance in her direction.

The loss of Dr. Wilbur ruled out continuation of treatment at Clarkson. And soon a letter came from Chicago stating that the analyst to whom Dr. Wilbur had written wasn't accepting new patients. In the stillness of her room Sybil faced the fact that somehow she would have to carry on alone. She persuaded herself that she wished to seek readmission to college. After all, she *had* been treated by a psychiatrist.

She wrote to the college about her desire to return, and in the meantime continued teaching at the junior high school and painting. Her painting *City Streets* and a pencil drawing were exhibited at an Omaha art gallery. But the nameless thing still pursued her. Whenever a day came that she felt free of it she recorded that day in her diary: "All went well today." In January 1947 Sybil returned to the campus.

There were enough good days for her to complete almost three years of college and to move triumphantly into the second semester of her senior year. But then in 1948, shortly before the end of her last semester, her father summoned her to Kansas City, where her parents were then living. Her mother was dying of cancer of the spleen, and she insisted upon having no nurse but Sybil. "If this is what your mother wants," Willard Dorsett told his daughter, "this is what she will have."

Sybil did not know what to expect when she arrived in Kansas City. But Hattie Dorsett had never been so calm and rational; in this period of crisis mother and daughter got along better than they ever had before. The very calm became an ironic background for something that happened one evening. Hattie Dorsett, relatively free from pain, was sitting in the big red easy chair in the living room when Sybil came in with her supper tray. Suddenly, seemingly apropos of nothing, Hattie remarked, "I never made that call to Dr. Wilbur."

"You did," Sybil said. "I heard your conversation."

Hattie was composed as she replied, "Well, I held my finger on the button. I never made that phone call."

This possibility had never even occurred to Sybil. It was inconceivable that her mother would have blocked her route to health, would have condemned her to the uncertainty about Dr. Wilbur with which she had lived for almost three years. That nameless thing that the doctor had glimpsed the day her patient headed for the window had continued in Omaha, at college, and in Kansas City. And it had been Sybil's *mother* who, by preventing the continuation of treatment, had deliberately shaped her daughter's destiny.

Yet there were no recriminations. Nobody ever criticized Hattie Dorsett. There was no flare-up of anger against her on Sybil's part. Anger was evil. Hattie ate her supper. Sybil took the tray back to the kitchen. Mother and daughter never again discussed Dr. Wilbur or that nonexistent phone call.

Afterward, however, Sybil felt a surge of hope. No wonder the doctor had left Omaha without calling her; it was she who had a right to feel disappointed in Sybil. The glorious dream of getting wholly well returned, but this time it would have to be delayed until Sybil could afford to pay for her own treatment.

Dr. Wilbur, she learned, was now a psychoanalyst in New York. And it was to New York that Sybil was determined to go.

Never, through the six years—from 1948 to 1954—that were to intervene between the decision and its execution, did Sybil breathe this dream to anyone. Her intention was one thing more she had to keep to herself.

In July 1948 Hattie Dorsett died and was buried in a Kansas City cemetery. In September, Sybil returned to college. She was graduated with a bachelor's degree the following June.

For the next few years she lived with her father, whose work as a builder kept him constantly moving from city to city. Sybil taught school and worked as an occupational therapist. By the summer of 1954 she had saved enough money to go to New York to get a master's degree at Columbia University's Teachers College and to resume treatment with Dr. Wilbur. She told her father only about the studies.

Sybil arrived in New York on Labor Day, but she waited until October before calling Dr. Wilbur, fearful both that the doctor would reject her and that she would accept her. Rejection was plausible because of the seemingly cavalier way in which Sybil had closed the door on treatment. It was even likely—and this hurt more—that the doctor wouldn't remember her.

Acceptance would hold a different kind of terror, for if she became Dr. Wilbur's patient, Sybil knew she would have to tell the doctor about the end-of-the-rope feeling she had experienced in Detroit, her last residence before coming to New York. In the classroom she had seemed to be all right, although there were times that she couldn't remember. The moment she left the classroom, however, strange, incomprehensible things had happened to her. These things had been occurring since she was three and a half and had begun to filter into awareness at eleven. But in Detroit they had become more menacing.

People she had never seen before would insist that they knew her. She would find a dress that she had not bought hanging in her closet. She would begin a painting and later find that it had been completed by someone else—in a style that was not hers.

Many mornings she would awaken without remembering going to sleep; or she would go to sleep and wake up, not the next morning, but at some unrecognizable time.

If Dr. Wilbur accepted her, all these things would come up. This time, Sybil promised herself that, fearful or not, she would tell the doctor about them.

ALL THAT had happened three and a half years ago. Now, in January of 1958, as Sybil returned to New York from Philadelphia, the past faded. Suddenly it was the present that became compelling as she faced the deep disappointment that after more than three years of analysis with Dr. Wilbur an episode like the one in Philadelphia should have occurred.

The train chugged into Penn Station, and Sybil took a taxi to Morningside Drive, where in 1955 she had taken an apartment with Teddy Reeves. Teddy was visiting her family in Oklahoma.

As the apartment door swung open, Capri, thin and wide-eyed, croaked a pathetic accusation. Sybil had left the cat without water or food. She would not consciously neglect any animal, least of all her precious Capri. But she had abandoned the animal she loved as she herself had been abandoned repeatedly in the past by people who had claimed to love her.

3

SYBIL LAY restless and wakeful that night, thinking of the first time she had seen Dr. Wilbur in New York. The doctor lived and had her office at Park Avenue and Seventy-sixth Street. As she ushered Sybil into her sunny consulting room that day in October 1954, each remembered the last time they had met, in Omaha almost ten years before.

She's changed, Sybil thought. Her hair is a brighter red. But her eyes, her smile, the way she nods her head are the same. At the same time Dr. Wilbur was thinking, She's as fragile as ever. Looks no older. I'd know that face anywhere: the heart shape, the tilted nose, the small rosebud mouth. It's a face you don't see on the streets of New York, an English face, fresh and unadorned.

Deliberately ignoring the green couch, Sybil walked with slow, strained movements to the opposite side of the room and perched stiffly on a small mahogany chair. The account she gave of herself was brief, factual, devoid of emotion—as if giving a résumé in an employment office instead of talking to the doctor to whom she had returned after great striving. Her graduation from college, her teaching, her painting, her mother's death (which she mentioned without feeling) filled the frozen hour.

The deep freeze continued as Sybil introduced the subject of Stanley MacNamara, an English teacher with whom she had taught just before coming to New York. Although he had asked Sybil to marry him she talked of him coolly, as a social worker might, reporting only that he was part Irish, part Jewish, that his father had deserted his mother, and that his mother had later abandoned her son. Stan had been raised in an orphanage, had worked his way through college, and had made his own way.

For her part, Dr. Wilbur was more interested in what Sybil did not say about Stan than in what she did say. But she didn't press. She asked only, "Just what do you want from me?"

Sybil lowered her head and said, "I would like to come back to you for analysis."

IN THE weeks that followed, Sybil almost literally lived for her Tuesday morning appointments. She would make a ritual of deciding what to wear. At the university's psychology library she steeped herself in psychiatric literature, especially case histories, for the more she knew about symptoms in other patients, the more adept she would become, she believed, at concealing her own. In seemingly no time it had become her fixed purpose to keep hidden what she had come to New York to reveal.

Sometimes a patient gives a psychiatrist a glimpse even on the first visit. After almost two months this one, the doctor thought ruefully, presented only the outer rim of the surface. On that outer rim sat Stan, whom Sybil thought of marrying but who in analysis had emerged wooden, a stick figure. Only through careful probing had the doctor finally uncovered the fact that he was proposing a sexless marriage—platonic was the word Sybil used.

Why, the doctor wondered, should an intelligent woman allow herself to become involved with a man who apparently had no sexual responses, an abandoned child who had never known and could not give love? What could account for a libido so markedly low that it would countenance such a relationship?

But if Sybil's libido was low, her reserve was high. At first the doctor attributed that to Sybil's strict upbringing. But that could not account for the aloofness which seemed to mask a terror in the patient's eyes. She isn't being candid with me, the doctor thought.

And then, on December 22—when the analysis was just two months old—Dr. Wilbur came measurably closer to the truth about Sybil Isabel Dorsett.

THE HOUR began innocuously enough, with Sybil's saying, "I want you to see the letter I received from Stan this morning." She talked of the letter with her customary lack of emotion, but when she opened her purse she suddenly became flustered. Only half the letter was there, a half with a zigzag edge. *She* hadn't torn it. Who had? The other half was not there. Two other letters received that morning were intact.

In an effort to conceal what had happened Sybil slipped the mutilated letter behind the other two. But the doctor was asking, "Do you want me to see the letter?"

Sybil started to stammer . . . and the stammer dissolved into something else. The prim, gentle midwestern schoolteacher, her face contorted with fury, jumped up from her chair and, moving so fast that she seemed to do everything at once, ripped up the letters and threw their remains in the wastebasket. Then, clenching her fists, she stood in the middle of the room, ranting, "Men are all alike. You jist can't trust 'em."

Jist. Sybil, the perfectionist schoolteacher, didn't talk that way.

With rapid, spiderlike movements Sybil headed toward two long casement windows. Swinging the draperies aside, she pounded her left fist against a windowpane. "Let me out!" she screamed. "Let me out!" It was an agonized plea—the call of the hunted, the trapped.

Dr. Wilbur moved swiftly, but before she could reach her patient, the pounding fist had gone through the glass.

"Let me see your hand," the doctor said. Her patient shrank from her touch. "I only want to see if you cut yourself," the doctor explained gently.

Her eyes wide with wonder, the patient looked at Dr. Wilbur for the first time since she had jumped up from the chair. In a plaintive, little-girl voice she asked, "You're not mad about the window?" The tone was one of curious disbelief.

"Anybody can fix a windowpane. The handyman will do it."

This time, when Dr. Wilbur took her hand, the patient offered no resistance. Sybil had always maintained a safe distance from the doctor. Now she sat right up beside her on the couch, letting her hand linger in the doctor's even after the latter had declared, "No cut. No bruise."

But once again there was a shift of mood. "There's blood."

"No blood," replied the doctor. "You didn't cut yourself."

"Blood in the hayloft," the patient said. "Tommy Ewald was killed. I was there."

"Where was the hayloft?" the doctor asked.

"In Willow Corners."

"Did you live in Willow Corners?"

"Jist everybody knows I live in Willow Corners." There was the "jist" again.

Gradually, as the patient continued to relive what had transpired in the hayloft, the doctor was overtaken by an uncanny, eerie feeling—muted yet insistent, like the traffic noises that were trickling into the room through the broken windowpane.

"My friend Rachel was sittin' with me and some other children in the hayloft. Tommy said, 'Let's jump down into the barn.' We jumped. One of the kids hit the cash register. There was a gun there. The gun went off, and Tommy was lyin' there, dead. The other children ran away. Not Rachel and me. She went for Dr.

Quinoness. I stayed with Tommy because I didn't think it was right to leave him lyin' there dead."

"You were two brave little girls," Dr. Wilbur said.

"There was blood, and death. I know what death is. I do."

"Does thinking of blood make you sad?" the doctor asked.

"You care how I feel?" Again the look of curious disbelief.

"I care very much."

"You're not jist tryin' to trick me?"

"Why should I?"

"Lots of people trick me."

The sense of being tricked. The anger. The distrust of people. The conviction that a window, a thing, was more important than she. These were symptoms of some profound disturbance.

From the moment the patient had dashed to the window, the doctor had been aware not only that her behavior was uncharacteristic but also that she actually looked and sounded different. She seemed smaller, shrunken. The voice was also quite different, childlike. Yet that little-girl voice had uttered a woman's words in its denunciation of men. And the incongruous "jist."

The doctor had the distinct impression that she was dealing with someone younger than Sybil. Then the thought she had been reining in broke forth. "Who are you?"

"Can't you tell the difference?" was the reply, accompanied by an independent toss of the head. "I'm Peggy, sometimes Dorsett and sometimes Baldwin. I'm really Peggy Baldwin."

"Tell me something about yourself," the doctor suggested.

"All right," Peggy said. "Do you want to hear about my painting? I like to paint in black and white. I don't paint as much or as well as Sybil."

The doctor waited a moment. "And who is Sybil?"

"Sybil? Why, she's the *other* girl."

"I see," the doctor replied. "Where do you live?"

"I live with Sybil, but my home is Willow Corners."

"Was Mrs. Dorsett your mother?" the doctor asked.

"No!" Peggy backed away, cowering. "She's not my mother!"

There was sudden movement. Peggy had left the couch and

was heading across the room with the same swift, spiderlike movement with which she had earlier rushed to the window. The doctor followed. But Peggy had vanished. Sitting on the small mahogany chair near the desk was the midwestern schoolteacher.

"I did that, didn't I?" Sybil murmured, pointing to the window. "I'll pay for it. I'll pay."

"You don't remember, do you?" the doctor asked softly.

Sybil shook her head.

"Don't be frightened," the doctor said. "You were in another state of consciousness. You had what we call a fugue—a major state of personality dissociation characterized by amnesia and actual physical flight from the immediate environment."

"You don't blame me, then?" Sybil asked.

"No, I don't blame you." The doctor followed her to the door. The hour was up. "Blame has nothing to do with it. We'll talk more about this next time. Don't worry. It's treatable."

WHAT do I have here? the doctor asked herself as she dropped into her chair. A dual personality? Sybil was now coming three times a week because of the Christmas vacation. Well, she had better continue to come that often. This case was more complicated than Dr. Wilbur had thought at first. Sybil would be back on Friday. Sybil, or Peggy?

IT WAS Sybil, calm and collected.

Dr. Wilbur had planned to tell her patient that when she blacked out during her fugue states, someone called Peggy appeared. But Sybil skillfully changed the subject and was so effectively evasive that when the hour was over the doctor still had not told her. Nor did she have the opportunity during the next appointment. When Dr. Wilbur stepped into the foyer to greet her patient it was Peggy who was waiting. She was hatless and gloveless, and Dr. Wilbur had no difficulty recognizing her.

"Come in, Peggy," the doctor said. And Peggy, obviously pleased that Dr. Wilbur had been able to distinguish her from Sybil, entered with quick, confident steps.

Relaxed and cooperative, Peggy was more than willing to talk. "I was angry the other day," she said. "I had a right to be." Her tone became confidential. "You know Stan sent us a 'Dear John' letter. Only it was 'Dear Sybil.' He said, 'I think we should discontinue our friendship.' I was so mad I tore up his letter and threw it in a trash can on the way here. Only it wasn't the whole letter. I jist thought it was. I was insulted. Who wouldn't be?"

Peggy paused and, with an impish glint, remarked, "Want to know who wouldn't be insulted? Sybil. I have to stand up for her. She can't get angry because her mother won't let her. But it's all right to be mad if *I* want to be. Wanna know somethin' else about Sybil? She's scared. She's jist scared all the time. She gives up, but I don't."

"Peggy," the doctor asked, "do you and Sybil look alike?"

"Not at all," Peggy replied indignantly. "We're completely different. You see how my hair is. And the shape of my face."

There was no real difference. While Peggy seemed younger and did talk and behave differently, the hair, the face, and the body were Sybil's. When the doctor probed for the thread that connected Peggy to Sybil, Peggy said with a touch of edginess, "Oh, leave me alone. There are things I jist can't tell you."

Peggy stayed the whole hour. When it was over she said pleasantly, "You know, we met before, in Omaha. I talked to you my own self, at the window. But you didn't recognize me."

Peggy remained very much in the doctor's thoughts. Peggy was angry because Stan had sent Sybil the "Dear John" letter. Could this mean, the doctor wondered, that even though Sybil didn't know about Peggy, they were closely allied and that Peggy carried the emotional impact of Sybil's experiences?

Peggy had said that Sybil couldn't get angry but that *she* could. Was Peggy Sybil's defense against anger? Was the rage in that fist, when Peggy broke the windowpane, the embodiment of what Sybil repressed? Suddenly, thinking of Peggy out on the streets alone, Dr. Wilbur was concerned. Peggy had clearly shown that she didn't know present from past. And she was young. The doctor hoped she would get home safely.

WHEN SHE LEFT the doctor's office Peggy Baldwin, sometimes Dorsett, had no intention of going back to the dormitory. "I want to go someplace," she murmured half aloud as she strode onto Park Avenue. The broad street, with Christmas trees sparkling with snow dotting its median strip, its shining limousines, the doormen with their bright buttons glistening in the sun, fascinated her. It was all so different from Willow Corners. She had to admit she lived in this wonderful city with Sybil. But her *home* was Willow Corners. She decided to walk for a while, look, see, experience. There were so many things she wanted to know about that she often went to different places just to find out what was going on.

Walking west, and then down Madison Avenue, she looked at the shops with sable stoles, lovely knitted suits, pink peppermint nightgowns. She loved pretty things, but she didn't dare buy anything from good places like these.

The bar she passed later on West Forty-fourth Street was another place she didn't dare go. But she could look in at all those people, doing what nobody she knew in Willow Corners did. Sometimes, when she thought of people, she felt lost and alone. There were too many cross people, and cross people made her angry. Her anger was purple and violet.

She went into a railroad station. PENNSYLVANIA RAILROAD the sign said. Oh, boy, she thought, I can go somewhere. She went up to a ticket window. "Ticket, please," she said.

"To Elizabeth?" the woman behind the window asked.

Peggy nodded. Why not?

The next thing she knew she was in a restaurant near another railroad station, ordering a hot chocolate. When she asked the waiter whether she was in Elizabeth he looked at her in a peculiar way and said, "Well, sure." Funny, she didn't know how she had gotten there. Her last memory was of buying the ticket at Penn Station.

Leaving the restaurant, she walked briskly across a parking lot. She hadn't gotten very far when she felt the sudden joy of recognition at seeing her father's car. She went to it and began trying the doors. They were locked. She felt trapped, not by being locked in but by being locked out. Anger, purple and violet, welled within her. Almost without knowing what she was doing, she banged the metal frame of her handbag against a slightly open window. After a few blows she heard the tinkle of broken glass. She loved the sound of breaking glass.

Suddenly a man in a tan suit was standing beside her. "What did you do that for?"

"It's my daddy's car," she replied.

The man snarled, "No, it isn't. It's my car."

Peggy didn't like this man one bit. "It's my daddy's car."

"Who's that?" asked the man.

"Willard Dorsett," she replied proudly.

The man took out his wallet and displayed the car's registration card. "You see, the numbers match the license plate."

Her head high, her eyes flashing fire, she started off to tell her father what had happened. But the man who claimed to own the car grabbed her arm. "Cool it, sister. It will cost me twenty dollars to replace that window. Are you going to pay for it?"

"Why should I? It's my father's car," Peggy insisted.

"Who are you anyway? Let me see your identification."

"I won't," Peggy asserted.

The car owner, infuriated by her refusal, pulled her purse away from her. "Give it back to me!" she screamed.

He removed a plastic identification folder and returned the purse. "Sybil I. Dorsett," he read aloud.

"I'm not Sybil Dorsett," Peggy replied coolly.

"Well, what's your name?"

"I'm Peggy Lou Baldwin."

"You said your father was Willard *Dorsett*."

Peggy tried to pull away, but she knew that she was being stopped as much from within as from without. She knew Sybil had control. She could feel Sybil reaching into their handbag and handing two crisp ten-dollar bills to the hateful man.

As Peggy rode the train home she thought of how silly it had been to make all that fuss about a little broken glass.

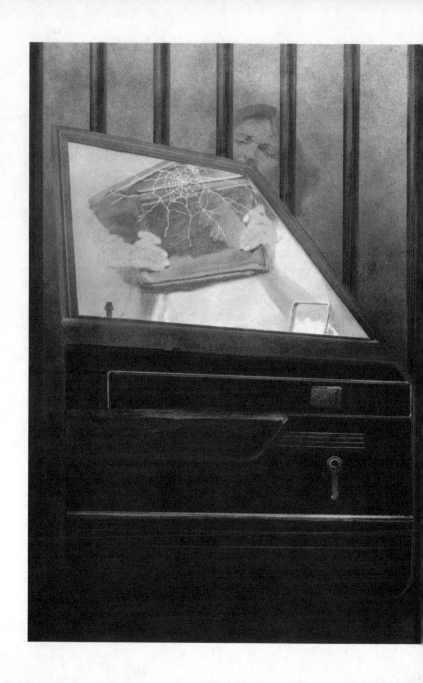

IT WAS NEARLY DARK when Peggy returned to the small dormitory room she shared with Sybil. She kicked off her shoes and stretched out on the bed.

Then she got up and put a record on the phonograph. Singing along with the music, she went to the window and looked out at the snow that had just begun to fall. She stopped singing. She was afraid of snow, afraid of the cold.

Suddenly she had an idea. This was the night of the students' Christmas social in the rec room. She decided to go. She would wear the apple-green dress that opened down the front, the one she had bought in a Chinese store on upper Broadway. As Peggy took the dress off its hanger and slipped into it, she reflected that Sybil could sometimes be an awful nuisance. When Sybil had found this beautiful dress in the closet she had acted as if she had seen a ghost. How did it get into *my* closet?

Peggy looked at herself in the mirror. The effect was simply beautiful. She wasn't too crazy about her chunky appearance, but she liked her Dutch haircut, her straight dark hair, her round face, her pug nose, her bright blue eyes, and her mischievous smile. Sybil, with her thin body, her light brown hair worn loosely, her heart-shaped face, gray eyes, and serious expression, was altogether different. Couldn't the nice doctor see that?

The recreation room was already crowded when she arrived. There was a long refreshment table. Peggy knew her religion wouldn't let her have the coffee or tea, but the little sandwiches and dainty cookies looked good. She had just begun to nibble on a sandwich when a voice asked, "Have a good day, Sybil?"

"Great," Peggy replied without hesitation as she looked up at Teddy Reeves. Teddy was a good-looking woman, though she was indifferent about how she dressed and wore no makeup. Teddy, who occupied the room next to her own, always called her Sybil. Long ago Peggy had decided to answer to the name when necessary.

"Glad to see you, Dorsett," Laura Hotchkins said as she came up and joined them. Laura was another of Sybil's friends.

Teddy, Laura, and several other girls clustered around, all

talking about their art teacher, Professor Klinger. All at once Peggy reached into her purse for a crayon pencil, pointed it against the wall, and began, in an affected voice: "Now, ladies and gentlemen, art is in the great tradition of human experience, and unless you give it your *undeevided attention,* you are insulting the muse." The girls began to giggle. Peggy, making two large holes in a paper napkin, converted it into eyeglasses, which she put on the edge of her nose. She squinted and said, "I want you to concentrate on painting as if it is the most important thing in the world. I mean the painting of Rubens, of Rembrandt, the other masters. I don't mean the silly contemporaries. What they call experimentation is an excuse for *emptEEness.*

"Now, Miss Dorsett, you're a serious woman with great talent. Why must you paint in this *seely* tradition?"

Laura Hotchkins's giggle turned into a laugh. Teddy guffawed.

Peggy went on, bringing the house down. What had started as a performance for a few became a show for everybody. Her imitation of Professor Klinger was the high point of the evening.

IT WAS a different Peggy who saw Dr. Wilbur two days later.

"The glass," said Peggy. "I'm goin' to *break* the glass—and get away. I don't want to stay. I won't. I won't!"

"Get away from what?" Dr. Wilbur asked.

"The pain. And the hands hurt," Peggy whispered.

"Your hands?"

"No. The hands comin' at you."

"Whose hands?"

"I won't tell. I don't have to tell if I don't want to."

"What else hurts?"

"Music hurts."

"Why? You can tell Dr. Wilbur."

"Dr. Wilbur went away and left us in Omaha." It was the whine of a hurt, lost child.

Gently, Dr. Wilbur put her arm around Peggy.

Suddenly Peggy grew silent. Then Peggy disappeared. Seated on the couch where she had been was Sybil.

"I had another fugue?" Sybil asked, drawing away from the doctor. She was frightened, anxious.

The doctor nodded.

"Well, it wasn't as bad as the last time," she reassured herself, looking around the room and seeing that nothing was broken.

The doctor made an effort to discover what Sybil knew about what Peggy had said. "You mentioned music to me once, Sybil. Why don't you tell me a little more about it?"

"Well, I took piano lessons, and my teacher used to say, 'You have all the native ability, but you must practice more.' I didn't practice because whenever I made a mistake my mother would holler, 'That's not right. That's not right.' But the minute she left the house I'd drop whatever I was doing and dash to the piano. I could always work things out at the piano."

"Tell me, do you have any special feelings about glass?"

"Glass?" Sybil echoed thoughtfully. "Oh, I remember something. When I was four we were visiting Grandma Anderson in Elderville, Illinois. My cousin Lulu and I were drying the dishes. She hurled a crystal pickle dish through the French doors. She was a real brat. And then she told everybody that I did it. My mother let me have it, but good."

"I see," said Dr. Wilbur. "Now, do hands disturb you?"

"Hands? Not particularly."

"Did hands ever come at you? Someone else's hands?"

"I don't know what you mean."

It was apparent that Sybil's discomfort suddenly was greatly intensified. "I see," said the doctor. "Another question: Does the sight of blood disturb you?"

"Well, yes. But doesn't it bother everybody?"

"Did you ever see blood as a child? The blood of a playmate, perhaps?"

Sybil sat back and thought. "Let's see. Tommy Ewald. His father had a barn and kept horses. Tommy died in the hayloft. We were playing. A gun went off. It was an accident. That's all I remember. There could have been blood. I haven't thought about Tommy in years."

By February 1955 the doctor felt that the diagnosis of dual personality had been confirmed beyond a shadow of doubt.

Peggy and Sybil, although existing in the same body, had different memories, different moods, attitudes, experiences. The experiences they shared were perceived differently. Their voices, diction, and vocabularies were different. They presented themselves in different ways. Even their ages were different. Sybil was thirty-two, but the doctor couldn't decide whether Peggy was a precocious child or an immature adult. And unmistakably Peggy carried some terrible burden that Sybil refused to face.

However, an event took place that changed Dr. Wilbur's diagnosis and made her glad she had not yet told Sybil about Peggy.

4

MARCH 16, 1955. The patient, sitting quietly in the waiting room, was absorbed in the pages of *The New Yorker*. When she saw the doctor she got up at once, smiled, and said warmly, "Good morning, Dr. Wilbur."

It isn't Peggy, the doctor thought. Peggy doesn't sit still. Peggy doesn't read. Peggy's voice doesn't have that cultivated tone. It has to be Sybil. But never before has Sybil spoken to me before I addressed her or smiled in this spontaneous way.

"How are you today?" the doctor asked.

"I'm fine," was the reply. "Sybil was so sick she couldn't come. So I came instead. Sybil wanted to come, but couldn't get dressed, though she tried and tried. She sometimes suffers from a complete absence of feeling and a total inability to do anything. But how gauche of me to start a conversation without introducing myself. I'm Vicky."

For an instant the doctor was stunned. But for an instant only. Why should I be surprised? she reflected. There were more than two personalities in the Christine Beauchamp case, described in a text she had read.

"Won't you come in, Vicky?" the doctor asked.

Vicky did not merely walk into the consulting room; she made an entrance. While Sybil's movements were constrained, hers were free and graceful. She was wearing a dress of many colors.

"This is a lovely room," she remarked casually. She walked to the couch and settled herself into a comfortable position. The doctor joined her and said, "Tell me, Vicky, how did you know where to come?"

"I know everything," Vicky explained. "I admit it sounds presumptuous, but I watch everything everybody does. That's why I say I know everything."

Did this mean, the doctor wondered, that Vicky could tell her about Sybil and Peggy?

"Vicky," she said, "I'd like to know more about you."

"I'm a happy person," Vicky replied, "and happy people don't have big stories. But I'll be glad to tell you anything you want to know."

"What I'm really trying to say is that I should like to know how you happen to be."

Vicky's eyes twinkled. "Oh, that's a philosophical question. But if you want to know where I come from, I'll be happy to tell you. I come from a very large family. My mother and father, my brothers and sisters all live in Paris. *Mon Dieu*, I haven't seen them in years. My full name is Victoria Antoinette Scharleau. Vicky for short. One becomes Americanized, you know."

"Don't your parents feel badly that you're not with them?" Dr. Wilbur asked.

"Not at all," Vicky replied with assurance. "They know I'm here to help. After a while they will come for me and then we will all be together. They're not like some parents. They do what they say they will do."

"You're very fortunate."

"Oh, I am," Vicky asserted. "But I really came to talk about Sybil. It's appalling the way she worries all the time. She doesn't eat enough, doesn't let herself have enough fun, and generally takes life too seriously. And there's something else, deep inside."

"What do you think it is, Vicky?"

"I can't really say. It started before I came. Sybil was just a little girl then."

"I see." The doctor waited for a moment and then asked, "Did you know Mrs. Dorsett?"

Vicky was suddenly aloof, guarded. "She was Sybil's mother. I lived with the Dorsetts for many years. Yes, I knew her."

"Do you know Peggy?"

"You mean Peggy Lou? Or Peggy Ann?"

"Peggy who?"

"Stupid of me," Vicky apologized. "I had quite forgotten that Peggy Lou is the only one you've met. There are two Peggys."

"Two Peggys?" Again the doctor wrestled with amazement.

"Peggy Ann will be along one of these days," Vicky predicted. "They do things together, those two."

"What makes them different?"

"Well, it seems to me that what arouses Peggy Lou's anger makes Peggy Ann afraid. But they're both fighters. When Peggy Lou decides to do something she goes at it in a bullheaded way. Peggy Ann goes at things, too. But she's more tactful. They both want to change things," Vicky concluded, "most of all, Sybil."

"Very interesting," the doctor replied. "Vicky, was Mrs. Dorsett Peggy Lou's mother?"

"Well, of course," Vicky answered.

"But Peggy Lou claims that Sybil's mother is not her mother."

With an amused smile Vicky said, "Mrs. Dorsett was Peggy Lou's mother, but Peggy Lou doesn't know it. Mrs. Dorsett was Peggy Ann's mother, too. But Peggy Ann doesn't know it, either."

There was a silence, which the doctor finally broke by asking, "Do Peggy Lou and you look alike?"

Vicky's face darkened with disappointment. "Can't you tell?"

The doctor temporized. "I've never seen you together."

Vicky rose from the couch and walked lithely to the desk. She returned with a prescription pad, removed a pencil from her purse, and began sketching. "Here," she said after a while, "are two heads. I have blond ringlets. This is Peggy Lou. Her hair is dark.

She wears it straight, like this." On the pad Vicky had drawn a Dutch cut. "You see how different we are."

The doctor nodded. "What about Peggy Ann?"

"I won't bother drawing her. They're very much alike."

"You sketch very well. Do you also paint?"

"Oh, yes. But Sybil paints better than I. My forte is people. I like them and know how to get along with them. I'm not afraid of them because my mother and father were always very good to me. I especially enjoy people who talk music, art, and books. And I'm at home with society people. But I don't think I'm a snob. I just have refined tastes, coming as I do from my kind of family.

"When I leave here I have a date with a friend, Marian Ludlow. We're going to lunch at the Fountain Restaurant at the Metropolitan Museum. There's an exhibit we especially want to see called 'Word Becomes Image.' Marian was raised in an East Side town house. They had a large household staff, summered in Southampton, that kind of thing."

"Does Sybil know Marian Ludlow?" the doctor asked.

"I'm afraid not," Vicky replied with faint condescension. "Sybil's not a *femme du monde*, a woman of esprit. She saw Mrs. Ludlow in line in the Teachers College cafeteria and wondered what a fashionable woman like that was doing there. The cafeteria was crowded, and Sybil was sitting alone. Mrs. Ludlow asked if she might sit with her. You know Sybil is always afraid of not being polite enough. So she said, 'Certainly.' But the thought of having to cope terrified her. She blacked out. So I took over and had a conversation with the *grande dame*. That was the beginning of our friendship."

"Does Peggy Lou know Mrs. Ludlow?"

"Oh, they're worlds apart."

"Does Sybil know about you?"

"She doesn't know about the Peggys, and she doesn't know about me. But that doesn't keep her from having an image of a person like me—an image she would like to fulfill but that constantly eludes her."

Dr. Wilbur's mind raced as she assessed what she had heard.

Sybil, Peggy Lou, Vicky, and Peggy Ann. Four persons in one body. Were there others as well? Believing that Vicky had the answers, the doctor decided to take the plunge. "Vicky, you've talked of the Peggys. Tell me, are there any others?"

"Oh, yes," was the reply, "there are many others. That's what I meant when I told you I know everything, about everybody."

"Vicky," the doctor urged, "I want all of you to feel free to come during the appointment hour, no matter who is using the body."

"Oh, yes, they'll come," Vicky promised. "And I'll come, too, though it seems strange for me to be coming to a psychoanalyst. The others are neurotic, but I don't think I am. But I do want to help you. After all, that's the only reason I'm not in Paris with my family. I don't believe that either Sybil or Peggy Lou has gotten down to the nitty-gritty of what's bothering them. Watching them flounder here, I knew I had to step in. Together I think we can get to the bottom of this. So please count on me."

"I appreciate that," Dr. Wilbur said, "and I should like to ask your advice. I want to tell Sybil about you and the others. In fact, I don't see how the analysis can go anywhere if she doesn't know. What do you think?"

"Well, be careful," Vicky cautioned. "Sybil's always been afraid of a diagnosis."

"I understand that, Vicky, but I did tell her that she is subject to fugue states, when she is unaware of what's happening."

"I know. But that's very different from telling her she's not alone in her own body."

"I think it will reassure Sybil to know that she is functioning even though she doesn't know it."

"She, Doctor?" Vicky asked quizzically. "Or *we*?" With that, Victoria Antoinette Scharleau, the woman of the world with the graceful movements and the mellifluous voice, departed.

LATE for her appointment, Vicky walked briskly. She thought of Marian Ludlow, with whom she had shared a world of interests since their accidental meeting. Marian had exquisite taste. She had been educated in exclusive private schools and had made a grand tour of Europe. Born to wealth, she had married into still more wealth. But after her husband's death her fortune had dwindled, and she had come to Columbia to prepare herself for teaching by taking graduate courses in art education.

Standing at the doorway of the Fountain Restaurant in the Metropolitan Museum, Vicky saw Marian seated at a table.

"I'm afraid I'm late," Vicky said apologetically. "It was a business appointment. I couldn't get away."

"I've been enjoying my solitude," Marian replied. She rose and they walked to the food counter.

Back at the table, Vicky and Marian talked of the arts as they ate. Marian finished her coffee, Vicky her hot chocolate.

"Well," said Marian, "we have our jewelry class at six. That gives us just time to see 'Word Becomes Image.' "

The exhibit was intriguing. Among the Biblical illustrations was an interpretation of the beasts from the Apocalypse engraved in the sixteenth century. Vicky remarked, "I used to paint beasts. Back in Omaha I illustrated our pastor's fiery sermons."

"I'm glad to hear you talk about your painting," Marian said. "You're always so reticent about it, Sybil."

Sybil. The mention of that name didn't disturb Vicky. That was the only name by which Marian and everyone else knew her —the name on identification cards and checks, on mailboxes, in registrars' offices. As a realist Vicky accepted these facts of her unique existence. She was discomforted more by the fact that it was Sybil, more than she, who had really painted the beasts.

"I'm reticent about my paintings," Vicky said aloud, "because I know better painters than I."

"Well," Marian replied, "that's always true. But you're no slouch. After all, the head of the art department said that he hadn't had anyone for years with as much talent as you have."

Most of Sybil's paintings were, of course, collaborative efforts of several of the selves. Despite diversity of styles, the total Sybil Dorsett—with Sybil herself as the dominant painter—had always had the potentiality of being an important artist. But that potentiality was never realized because of the psychological problems that deflected Sybil's efforts.

Vicky and Marian had an early dinner in the roof restaurant of an apartment hotel near the Columbia campus. Then they went to the six o'clock jewelry class, which Vicky attended because Sybil couldn't. The class, held in a basement aglow with blow-torches, stirred in Sybil old, unresolved fears. Vicky, however, enjoyed this class and was scoring an A in it. Tonight she was making a necklace and helping Marian with a silver pendant.

After class Vicky and Marian went back to Vicky's dormitory room and listened to the news on the radio. As Marian was getting ready to leave, Vicky very cautiously began putting away the jewelry supplies they had brought back with them.

"Why are you so fussy?" Marian asked. "You room alone. These things won't bother anybody."

Vicky thought of the time Sybil had brought a sample sketch to Dr. Wilbur's office and had told the doctor that she was afraid to use it because she didn't know where it came from. It had been Vicky's. Remembering how disturbed Sybil had been, Vicky wanted to protect her from another terrifying discovery.

Sybil was in her dormitory room studying for an exam. There was a knock on the door. It was a tall, good-looking woman in her early forties, with bright brown hair and bright brown eyes.

"I can't stay," she said. "I'm late for a hairdresser's appointment, but I thought I'd stop and give you this. You've done so much for me, Sybil." The woman handed Sybil a lovely hand-crafted silver pendant. "See you soon," she said, and was gone.

See you soon? Sybil thought. Done so much for her? I've seen her around, but she acted just now as if we were friends. Friends? Confusion raged. Return to the desk. Try to study. But the pages of the text blurred, and she asked herself, Will there never be an end that also has a beginning?

Victoria Antoinette Scharleau, who knew everything, watched Marian Ludlow give Sybil the silver pendant.

5

D<small>R. WILBUR</small> adjusted her desk lamp. She had made a trip to the Academy of Medicine Library, where a librarian had assembled for her almost the whole of the relatively sparse literature about multiple personality. Medical history had recorded the cases of seven women and three men with dissociated personalities.* The case of another woman, whose pseudonym was Eve, had recently been described in the *Journal of Abnormal and Social Psychology* by Drs. Corbett H. Thigpen and Hervey M. Cleckley.* *

Now, as she read on into the night, Dr. Wilbur searched for the point at which, in these other cases, the first dissociation had taken place. She surmised that Sybil's first one had occurred during childhood. Peggy's childishness seemed to be a clue. In Sybil's case these were probably multiple roots, or shocks, leading to multiple selves which personified reactions to those shocks.

The case was taking on the aspect of an adventure, a whodunit of the unconscious, and Dr. Wilbur was becoming excited. The analysis, she decided, would have to be unorthodox. She smiled as she thought, An unorthodox analysis by a maverick psychiatrist. She did consider herself a maverick, and she knew this independence would stand her in good stead in dealing with this extraordinary case. She knew that it would be necessary to treat each of the selves as a person in her own right and to winnow away the reserve of Sybil, the waking self. Otherwise the total Sybil Dorsett would never get well.

The pivotal question was: *Why* had Sybil become a multiple personality? To date, analysis had revealed certain pervading fears

---

* Others have been recorded since.
* * The article was subsequently expanded into a book, *The Three Faces of Eve,* which was a selection of Reader's Digest Condensed Books. [Editor's note.]

—of getting close to people, of music, of hands. Telltale, too, were the seething rage, repressed in Sybil but bursting forth unbridled in Peggy Lou, and the denial of mother in both Peggy Lou and Vicky.

IT WAS Vicky who appeared at the next Dorsett appointment hour. Hunting for the original trauma, the doctor asked Vicky whether she knew why Peggy Lou was afraid of music.

"Music hurts," Vicky answered, "way inside, because it is beautiful, and it makes both Sybil and Peggy Lou sad. They're sad because they're alone and nobody cares. When they hear music they feel more alone than ever."

Asked why something beautiful should hurt, Vicky replied cryptically, "It's like love."

"Was there something about love that hurt?" the doctor asked.

"There was," Vicky said. "Doctor, Sybil doesn't want to love anybody. It's all part of the same mosaic—the fear of hands coming at her, the fear of people, the fear of music, the fear of love. All have hurt her. All have made her afraid."

"Why is Sybil afraid when you're not?"

"I have no reason to be." That was as far as Vicky would go. "Poor Sybil," she sighed. "She's all choked up. She won't cry. She can't. Everyone was against her when she cried."

"Who is everyone?" the doctor asked hopefully.

"Oh, I'd rather not say." Vicky smiled. "After all, I was not a member of the family. I only lived with them." Victoria Antoinette Scharleau closed the door that had swung partly ajar. Yet a ray of light had entered: she had placed the blame for Sybil's inability to cry squarely within the Dorsett family.

All at once, with a transition so slight as to be almost imperceptible, the eyes that had been serene dilated with fear. Vicky, who was not a member of the Dorsett family, had returned the body to Sybil, who was.

Startled at finding herself on the couch close to the doctor, Sybil moved away. "What happened?" she asked. "I don't remember coming here today. Another fugue?"

Dr. Wilbur nodded. This, she decided, was the moment to spell out what these fugues really were. Then she could confront Sybil with what the other personalities said and bring her closer to memories from which she seemed barred.

"Yes. You had another fugue. But it's more complicated than that. Now, you've never said this to me, but I think you're aware that time goes by without your knowing that it has. You know that you have lost time here?"

After a long pause Sybil replied in subdued tones, "I promised myself I would tell you, but I haven't dared."

"What do you think you do in the time you lose?"

"Do? I don't do anything."

"You go right on doing something, even though you're not aware of doing it. It's like walking in your sleep."

"Well"—Sybil lowered her eyes—"all my life I've been told that I had done certain things that I knew I hadn't. My mother would say I was a bad girl. She would shake me. I'd ask what I had done. She'd holler, 'You know perfectly well what you did, young lady!' But I didn't know. I don't know now."

"Try not to be too worried. Others have had this condition. It's treatable." Dr. Wilbur could see that this statement made an enormous impression on Sybil. She seemed more relaxed.

"But it is more complicated than the fugue states we've already discussed. In a simple fugue there's just a loss of consciousness, but your fugues are not blank. While you yourself lose consciousness another self takes over for you."

"Another self?" Sybil asked, stunned. "Then I'm like Dr. Jekyll and Mr. Hyde?"

Dr. Wilbur said quickly, "You're not at all like Dr. Jekyll and Mr. Hyde. That's pure fiction. Actually, people with your condition are not torn by the conflict between good and evil."

"May I go now? We're running overtime." Sybil felt an almost unendurable pressure.

But having committed herself, Dr. Wilbur pressed on. "Not a great deal is known about this condition. But we do know that the different selves of any one person are likely to share the same ethical code, the same basic moral structure."

"Selves?" Sybil echoed fearfully. "Did you say 'selves'? Plural?"

"Sybil," the doctor said gently, "this is nothing to be afraid of. There's a self-assertive personality who calls herself Peggy Lou. There's Peggy Ann, who also is a fighter, but she is more tactful than Peggy Lou. Another calls herself Vicky. She's assured, at ease, a delightful person."

Sybil rose. "*Please* let me go!" She had been profoundly shaken. Thinking it unwise to let her leave alone, the doctor offered to walk out with her. "I'll be all right," Sybil insisted.

Later, in the gathering dark of her silent office, Dr. Wilbur turned again to the volumes about multiple personality that cluttered her desk. She also combed references on hysteria, for she felt sure that multiple personality, though a bizarre and abnormal phenomenon, was not a psychosis but a hysterical condition. This growing realization renewed her confidence; for although she had never treated a multiple personality, she had had many successes in treating hysterics.

Psychosis, she reflected, is the more serious illness. Multiple personality belonged to the class of patients known as psychoneurotics. The specific neurosis was hysteria major. The kind of hysteria major from which Sybil Dorsett suffered, not only with multiple personalities but with a variety of psychosomatic illnesses and disturbances in the five senses, was as grave as it was rare. It would take brashness and great sacrifices of time to see this case through.

The phone rang. It was after ten. Probably a patient in a crisis, calling for help. Please, not tonight, Dr. Wilbur thought. When the day was done she needed an interval to stop living other people's lives. She wanted more time for her husband, for professional meetings, to have her hair done and go shopping.

She picked up the phone. It was Teddy Reeves, Sybil's dormitory neighbor. "Dr. Wilbur," Teddy reported, "Sybil Dorsett fell apart. She really blew. I don't know what to do."

"I'll come right over." Dr. Wilbur wasn't really surprised. She suspected that what Teddy had meant by "she really blew" was that Peggy Lou had taken over.

TEDDY PUT SYBIL to bed and, standing by in terror and compassion, watched as Sybil, getting out of bed and then in again, also went in and out of a series of what appeared to be disparate moods. One moment she was a ranting child, walking on the furniture, leaving her fingerprints on the ceiling. The next moment she was a self-possessed and knowing woman, talking of herself in the third person and saying, "I'm glad Sybil knows. Yes, indeed, it will be better for all of us." Then Sybil became the quaking person who had tapped at Teddy's door. She was lying inert on the bed when the doctor arrived.

"I'll give you a Seconal," Dr. Wilbur said, "and you'll be fine in the morning." She had discovered that barbiturate sedatives relieved Sybil's anxiety for forty-eight hours.

Morning came, and Sybil awakened, freed of anxiety by the Seconal the doctor had given her the night before. The multiple selves seemed like a nightmare that had receded.

IT WAS well past midnight when the doctor left. Although not certain what the personalities actually represented, she hypothesized that the waking Sybil more or less corresponded to the conscious mind and the alternating selves to the unconscious.

Now what I have to do, she thought as she paid the taxi driver, is to become acquainted with each of the personalities, and to determine with which conflict each of them deals. This will take me to the roots of the trauma—against which the selves have become a defensive maneuver. Of more immediate importance was to get closer to the waking Sybil, to get around the anxiety and defensiveness behind which the other selves lay in ambush.

But how did one get closer to this remote and timid Sybil Dorsett?

ONE morning in April 1955, when Sybil had brought some of her watercolors to the office, Dr. Wilbur asked, "How would you like to drive with me to Connecticut some Sunday during the dogwood season? The countryside is lovely then, and you can sketch the flowering trees and shrubs."

"Oh, you have more important things to do than to spend a Sunday with me," Sybil replied diffidently.

Dammit, the doctor thought, I must make her understand that I regard her as an extraordinarily gifted woman, that I would enjoy being with her even if she weren't my patient.

Finally Sybil agreed to the trip, which took place on a sunny Sunday in early May. Wanting the occasion to be purely social, Dr. Wilbur confined the conversation to the scenery. They skirted the small shore cities and drove to Long Island Sound. "I've always wanted to paint boats," Sybil said, "but I've always felt that I couldn't get the shapes right." But she made some sketches of sailboats anchored at a marina.

"I like them," the doctor said. Sybil seemed pleased.

Leaving the Sound, Dr. Wilbur drove in leisurely fashion along old country roads and pointed out some houses that were pre-Revolutionary. Sybil said, "My father's a builder. He's very interested in architecture." The father had scarcely been mentioned in the analysis. Dr. Wilbur was glad to hear about him.

Sybil had insisted upon providing lunch, which they ate at a small campground, where Sybil did a pencil sketch of a hill studded with flowering crab and dogwood. At the time Dr. Wilbur thought Sybil had made the picnic lunch as her contribution to the outing, but she later learned that it was a precaution against having to go into a restaurant: Sybil's fear of restaurants was so intent that being in one had often led to lost time.

Nor was it until later that the doctor learned why, when she agreed to the trip, Sybil had insisted upon returning to New York by four o'clock at the latest. "I have some work to do," she had explained. The real reason was Sybil's fear that if she stayed out beyond then, she would show the signs of the emotional disturbance, fatigue, and fright that often manifested themselves at the end of the day. She had been afraid that she would dissociate, and she had not wanted to risk having the doctor meet the other personalities outside the office.

On that trip to Connecticut neither Dr. Wilbur nor Sybil knew that they had not been alone. Peggy Lou was delighted that Sybil had taken her somewhere. Vicky couldn't wait to tell Marian Ludlow about the old pre-Revolutionary houses.

In that car, too, were passengers whom neither the doctor nor Sybil had ever met. As Dr. Wilbur said good-by to Sybil, Marcia Lynn Dorsett, pert and assertive, with a shield-shaped face, gray eyes, and brown hair, turned to Vanessa Gail, her close friend, and said in an English accent, "She cares about us." Vanessa, a tall, slender girl with a willowy figure, reddish hair, light brown eyes, and an expressive oval face, communicated to Mary that single, simple sentence, "She cares about us." Mary, a maternal, little-old-lady type, plump and contemplative, repeated with a slight smile, as if it were a question, "She cares about us?"

Then Marcia, Vanessa, and Mary activated an internal grapevine. The message rang loud and clear: *This Dr. Wilbur cares about us.* After that Marcia, Vanessa, Mary, and everybody else held a conclave and decided, "We'll go and see her."

6

THE TRIP to Connecticut produced a change, not only in the other personalities but also in Sybil herself. Less guarded during the summer of 1955 than during the first seven months of analysis, Sybil began to talk of her early environment. There were no sudden revelations about the root causes of the multiplicity, but out of the portrait of the town in which Sybil—presumably born one—had become many, Dr. Wilbur was able to acquire insights that contributed later to her understanding of causes. Thus it was that she led Sybil—and Vicky as well—into an exploration of Willow Corners, Wisconsin, where Sybil was born on January 20, 1923, and spent her first eighteen years.

WILLOW CORNERS stood in the flat terrain of southwestern Wisconsin, close to the Minnesota line. The local accent was barbed with a nasal twang, and during Sybil's early years the men and women riding to town in wagons from the outlying farms were a constant testament to the town's reliance on the land.

Willow Corners was dotted with tall trees and with white frame houses, most of which had been built by men who worked for Willard Dorsett. The unpaved streets, dusty on dry days, were mud-filled bogs when it rained.

Outwardly there was nothing remarkable about Willow Corners. Founded in 1869, it was a tiny town two square miles in area. The monotonous doings of its one thousand inhabitants were recorded in the weekly *Corners Courier* in typical headlines: SMALL TWISTER DEMOLISHES JONES OUTHOUSE; MOTHERS CLUB PICNIC AT HIGH SCHOOL WEDNESDAY.

During Sybil's time the town was chiefly a wheat-farming community with a general store, hardware store, small hotel, barbershop, drugstore, bank, post office, and gun shop. Stores were open on Wednesday and Saturday nights, when families made a festive ritual of shopping together and exchanging news and gossip.

The town had two policemen—one worked days, the other nights. There were one lawyer, one dentist, and one doctor. An ambulance always stood ready to take the sick to the world-famous Mayo Clinic in Rochester, Minnesota, some eighty miles away.

A slice of Middle America, the town was stratified in class structure. At the top was a moneyed elite and at the bottom a working class. Mistaking money for virtue, the townsfolk venerated the rich, however their wealth was acquired and however they behaved. Until Sybil was six, the town's wealthiest man was her own father, a status he lost in the Depression.

Willow Corners had churches of many faiths. The Protestant congregations all looked askance at one another, and at the Roman Catholics, whom they regarded as the incarnation of evil. Bigotry was rampant and racial prejudice intense.

Nevertheless, the town abounded in an easy, unthinking optimism, and in maxims such as "Today's leaves of hope are tomorrow's blossoms," which was inscribed in the school auditorium. That tomorrow's blossoms were withering on today's leaves of narrowness did not occur to the virtuous citizenry.

The Dorsetts' home, a white house with black shutters, stood kitty-corner to the schools. Their next-door neighbor was a recluse, the woman across the street a dwarf; down the street lived a man who had raped his thirteen-year-old daughter and who, after the event, went right on living in the same house with her as though nothing had happened. It was all part of the curious deformity and lewdness, resulting in assorted illegitimate children, that ran like a subterranean current through this outwardly average, normal, puritanical town.

WILLARD Dorsett was descended from the original settlers, as were most of the townsfolk. He and Hattie had met on a blind date while he was visiting in Elderville, Illinois, of which Hattie's father was a founder and the first mayor. Other men, attracted by Hattie's good looks and vivacity, had broken with her because of her sharp tongue, but Willard was willing to "put up with her," as he phrased it, because he thought her refined and a talented pianist. Since he himself sang tenor in the church choir he pictured Hattie as his future accompanist. At any rate, he was in love with Hattie Anderson, and after a number of weekend dates in Elderville he asked her to marry him.

Hattie wasn't in love with Willard and said so. Her blind date with him had been an act of defiance against a jeweler to whom she had been engaged, but who had reneged on his promise to give up alcohol. Moreover, she claimed all men were alike, not to be trusted (a sentiment Peggy Lou had echoed in Dr. Wilbur's consulting room), with "only one thing on their minds."

Still, the thought of living in Wisconsin appealed to Hattie, who had never been out of her native Illinois. And in time she grew to care about Willard. He was good to her, and she tried to reciprocate. She cooked what he liked, and always had his meals on time. Although she didn't enjoy housework she became a fanatic housekeeper. In the early days of their marriage Hattie and Willard shared long, pleasant musical evenings.

In thirteen years Hattie had four miscarriages, no children. She had ambivalent feelings about having a baby. She enjoyed taking care of other people's babies, but the actual prospect of having to care for a child of her own often made her antagonistic to motherhood. When Sybil was conceived, Willard was afraid for this baby, too. He therefore exerted over Hattie a dominance he had never shown before, forbidding her to appear in public during the pregnancy. Thus secrecy and concealment surrounded Sybil even in the womb.

At birth Sybil weighed five pounds, one and one-fourth ounces. As if ashamed that she was so tiny, Willard took great pains to have the one and a quarter ounces included on the birth announcements. He took it upon himself to name the baby. Hattie, who did not like the name Sybil, used it only when absolutely necessary; at other times she called her daughter Peggy Louisiana, later abbreviated to Peggy Lou, Peggy Ann, or just Peggy.

Severe depression overtook Hattie during the first four months of Sybil's life. In this period her only contact with the baby was when she breast-fed her. Otherwise the care of the infant fell to Willard and, chiefly, to Grandma Dorsett.

When Hattie was well enough to be up and about she had a head-on collision with Willard about nursing the child when there was company in the house. He forbade it, even when Hattie said she would take Sybil into a bedroom and close the door. "No," Willard said sternly. "Everybody will know what you're doing." Resentfully, Hattie acquiesced. Sybil, unfed, cried. Hattie blamed the baby for the crying which made Hattie nervous.

As time went on, Hattie became less and less concerned with pleasing Willard. "I don't care," she would sputter when he complained about an omission in her hitherto painstaking care of him. No longer did she have the patience to sit still long enough to accompany him at the piano. Indeed, she could no longer sit still under any circumstances for more than a few minutes without getting up to straighten a curtain or to flick a little dust from the furniture—even in other people's houses. And she fell into the habit of repeating the ends of people's sentences. If someone said, "I've got such a headache," Hattie would repeat, "Such a headache."

BY THE AGE OF EIGHT Sybil had come often to sit on the back-porch steps and, leaning her head on her knees, to wonder why she felt . . . not able to find the right word, she would settle for "a lack of something." All she knew was that something made her feel, as her mother would put it, "sad, down, and blue." Most disturbing to Sybil was her guilty feeling that she had no reason to be unhappy and that by being so she was somehow betraying her parents. She prayed for forgiveness on three counts: for not being more grateful for all she had; for not being happy, as her mother thought she should be; and for what her mother termed "not being like other youngsters."

Disconsolate, Sybil would sometimes hasten from the porch steps to the upper floor of the house, where Grandma Dorsett lived. In the sanctuary of Grandma's home were many mansions—recollections of small experiences that in retrospect were to loom large in Dr. Wilbur's consulting room.

Grandma would take Sybil in her lap, and the child would draw pictures on drawing paper that her grandmother always had ready for her. Proudly Grandma Dorsett would hang the drawings on the wall. In her kitchen cupboard Grandma had many jars of dried prunes, apricots, and figs, and she would let Sybil choose whatever she liked. Grandma also let her open drawers and fold everything she wanted to fold. One day Sybil found a baby picture of herself in one of the drawers. When she saw that picture, stored so carefully, she realized that Grandma really *liked* her. Even greater proof was Grandma's defense of Sybil when her mother accused her of being bad. "Now, Hattie," her grandmother would say, "she's just a child."

The visits upstairs with Grandma were never long. Her mother allowed only a set time and, as the visit proceeded, Sybil could feel that time was running out. When Grandpa came home, however, it was Sybil herself who brought the visit to a close. She didn't like her grandfather, a large, burly man given to rough play. At the sound of his wooden leg on the stairs she would say, "I have to go now." Grandma would smile under-standingly.

When Sybil was four years old her grandmother had a stroke, after which she was sometimes not herself. She would wander around Willow Corners not knowing her way. Sybil made it her job to find her and bring her home, protecting her until she recovered—as for so long Grandma had protected Sybil.

For five years after her recovery Grandma Dorsett continued to protect Sybil. But when Sybil was nine Grandma was afflicted by a new illness—cancer of the cervix—which worried Sybil and made her afraid.

THERE was a coffin in the big house in Willow Corners, and through the kitchen window Sybil could see the men from the funeral home bringing in the folding chairs for the service.

"Go to your room," Hattie told her. "Mama will come and get you when we're ready." Her mother gave her a lollipop, and Sybil lay on the bed, licking it while she waited. She could hear voices downstairs. Then for a while she heard nothing.

Suddenly her father was standing over her. "Come on," he said. "The service is over. You can come with us to the cemetery."

They had promised she could come down for the service, but they hadn't kept their promise. She was *nine* years old. The service had taken place in her own house. But they left her upstairs with a lollipop, like a baby. She could not forgive her parents. The tears, ice-cold, stayed within her. She never cried aloud.

Down the stairs she went, past all those silent people, on to the sidewalk. "You're to go in this car, Sybil," the minister said. Inside the car were her uncle Roger and his wife.

It was a cold, windy April day. At the Dorsett family plot, Sybil did not see the metal casket, the flowers, or the people; what she saw was her grandmother in her long skirts, her high-top shoes, her white hair, her small blue eyes, her warm, sweet smile. What Sybil heard were not the minister's words but her grandmother's gentle voice saying, "It's all right, Hattie," when her mother said, "Sybil, you mustn't bounce on Grandma's bed."

Sybil bounced on Grandma's big, soft bed all she liked. Her grandmother would scoop her up, rock her, and say, "Sybil, Sybil,

Sybil." When she was with her grandmother there was no hollering. Home, just downstairs, seemed miles away.

The wind howled over Sybil's father and her uncle in silent grief, over Aunt Clara, wringing her hands and moaning hysterically, over these grown children bereft of a mother. It howled over her grandfather's soft moan. Sybil alone, her throat constricting, her chest growing heavy, was dry-eyed.

The wind was cold. Anything that is cold is not love. Love is warm. Love is Grandma. They were burying love.

Sybil found herself moving forward. She was at the grave, her body poised to jump into it, to join her grandmother forever.

Then a hand grabbed her arm and dragged her away.

SYBIL turned to see who had so forcibly removed her from her grandmother. Her uncle? Her father? They were not there. Instead of a grave there was a desk. Instead of a minister there was a teacher, tall and thin, who talked quickly in short sentences. She wasn't Sybil's teacher. Miss Thurston, her third-grade teacher, spoke slowly and deliberately and was stout. This was Miss Henderson, the fifth-grade teacher.

What has happened? Sybil wondered. The room was a regular classroom in the school she had attended since kindergarten. Only it wasn't her classroom. She knew all the rooms in the school, and this, she knew, was the fifth-grade room. She had to get out, had to get back to the third grade where she belonged, where Miss Thurston had probably marked her absent.

Then she began to notice the other children—Betsy Bush across the aisle, Henry Von Hoffman in front of her, Carolyn Schultz, and all the rest. Well, she thought, the whole third grade is in here. Most of these children had started with her in kindergarten and she knew them well. They were the same children, yet they were dressed differently and looked bigger than they had before she left for her grandmother's funeral. How could all these children get bigger in a moment?

Betsy Bush, confident as always, was waving her hand to answer the teacher's question. She acted as if she belonged here.

None of the other children seemed to think there was anything wrong about being here. Why should Betsy be answering questions when Miss Henderson was not her teacher?

Sybil's eyes turned to the notebook open on her desk. There were lots of notes, but she hadn't taken them. There were completed homework assignments, which she hadn't done, but she noted that they were consistently graded A.

She began to examine herself. Her own dress. It was yellow voile with green and purple embroidery, as totally unfamiliar as those of the other girls. She was wearing a dress that wasn't hers in a classroom where she didn't belong.

She looked at the clock above the teacher's desk. It was two minutes to twelve. Then the bell sounded, and she heard the teacher's high-pitched voice saying, "Class dismissed."

Sybil was afraid to move, afraid to face going home. When she was certain the room was deserted she rose slowly from her seat and walked even more slowly to the coatroom, where there was just one coat still hanging, a plaid mackinaw she had never seen before. Sybil finally put it on. It fitted her perfectly. She walked slowly out of the building. On the corner across the street was the big house with black shutters, her home.

She hurried inside, eager to be among familiar things, but when she hung the plaid mackinaw in the hall closet, she saw none of the clothes she remembered. Unfamiliar reds, greens, and yellows leaped out at her. She started to go into the downstairs room, into which her grandparents had moved during her grandmother's last illness. The extra door to the room was plastered over; it was strange that they had done this so quickly. In the living room she found some of her grandmother's furniture along with theirs. And what was that on the breakfront? A *radio!* They had hesitated about buying a radio because her grandfather said that it was the work of the devil.

Mother called from the kitchen, "Peggy? You're so late."

When she was cute or funny, the way her mother liked her, her mother would call her Peggy Louisiana, Peggy Lou, Peggy Ann, or just Peggy. Evidently her mother liked her today.

The kitchen, Sybil noted with alarm, was light green. It had been white when she had last seen it. "I liked the white kitchen," Sybil said.

"We went through that last year," her mother replied.

Last year?

Her father was in the sun-room, reading an architecture magazine while waiting for lunch. Her playroom was the sun-room. Her dolls were in the window seat, but there were more of them. "Daddy," she blurted, "what doll is that, the great big one?"

"Are you playing games? That's Nancy Jean. You won her in a contest."

At the dining-room table there were four place settings instead of three. Why four? There didn't seem to be any company. This time, however, she was not going to ask any questions.

There was the thump, thump of a wooden leg, the sound that had always frightened her. It was her grandfather, all six feet of him, with his goatee and his bald head. What was he doing here? The grandparents' living quarters had always been separate from theirs. Each family ate by itself and did not enter the other's sphere; that was her grandmother's rule. But her grandmother was newly dead and already the rule was being broken.

Her father said grace. Her mother passed the food. There were some fried potatoes left. Her father took the dish and said to his father, "Dad, here are some more potatoes."

"He won't hear you," her mother said. "He's deaf and you know it."

In fact, her grandfather hadn't heard. He continued talking the same old talk about Armageddon, the last battle that was to take place on earth before the end of time. He talked of how some terrible day there would be a Catholic president.

Her mother changed the subject. "Willard," she said, "I had a letter from Cousin Anita today."

"What does she write?" her father asked. Then turning to Sybil he remarked, "I'll never forget how wonderful you were about taking Anita's little Ella off our hands those few weeks after Grandma's funeral when they were staying here."

The *weeks* after the funeral? Hadn't the funeral just happened? Taking care of Ella? What was he talking about?

Sybil looked directly at her mother and made a bold plunge. "Mother," she asked, "what grade am I in?"

"That's a silly question."

Her grandfather, seeing how solemn she looked, proclaimed, "Christians must always smile. It is a sin not to smile."

Her father rose. "I said I'd be back to the store by one thirty."

Sybil's father had worked in the hardware store since they came back from the farm, where they had gone to live briefly as an economy measure when they lost their money in the Depression.

Her grandfather got up to go to his room. Sybil lingered, saying nothing.

"I don't know what's the matter with you today," her mother said. "You're not yourself—just not yourself. By the way," she said, "I'd like you to drop in on Mrs. Schwarzbard after school. She has a package for me."

"Who is Mrs. Schwarzbard?"

"You know perfectly well who she is."

As Sybil left the house she saw Carolyn Schultz and Henry Von Hoffman, and she waited until they had gone into the school. When she herself entered she was torn between going to the third-grade classroom and going to the fifth-grade room. She tried the third grade first.

Miss Thurston was at her desk sorting test papers. "How nice of you to come visit," she said when she saw Sybil. "I love having my girls come back."

Come *back?* Sybil headed for the fifth-grade classroom and made certain she returned to the seat in which she'd found herself that morning.

The first lesson was arithmetic. They were doing fractions, but Sybil couldn't multiply beyond the threes and fours. It was the last thing she remembered doing in the third grade.

The teacher erased the board, wrote up new multiplication problems, distributed paper, and began to drill for the next day's quiz. Sybil stared from her blank paper to the blackboard and back again. Miss Henderson watched her, then walked to Sybil's desk. "You haven't written anything," she said crossly. "Tell me what the answers are."

"I don't know."

Miss Henderson turned on her. "I don't know what's gotten into you. Are you playing games with me?" There was no answer. Walking away, the baffled teacher threw a parting shot over her shoulder. "You knew it yesterday."

Yesterday? Sybil was silent. For her, yesterday was blank.

ON OTHER occasions time had seemed to be erased for Sybil as Miss Henderson had erased those numbers from the blackboard. She had never dared mention this strange feeling to anyone. But this blank interval seemed longer. She was in the fifth grade and didn't remember being in the fourth. She remembered nothing since her grandmother's funeral.

When school was over, Sybil waited until the last child had left the classroom and then started for home. She wasn't going to Mrs. Schwarzbard, whoever she was, to pick up her mother's package. Her mother would be furious, but there was nothing Sybil could do but accept the fury.

In the school's main lobby Danny Martin called to Sybil. Danny was a year older than she and a very good friend. He had been at her grandmother's funeral. Maybe she ought to ask him about the things that had happened since then.

Danny walked across the street with her and they sat on her front steps and talked. "Mrs. Engle died this week," he said. "I went with Elaine to take the funeral flowers to invalids and shut-ins, just as I went with you when your grandmother died."

When Danny said this Sybil remembered, as if it were a dream, that a girl they called Sybil but who wasn't Sybil had gone with Danny Martin that day. It felt as if she had been inside this other Sybil, just walking along. But although she knew now that unaccounted-for time had passed since the funeral, this was the only memory that came back.

To forget was shameful, and she felt ashamed.

7

"How come the Greens are living in the Miners' house?" Sybil wanted to know.

"They moved there last summer," Danny said.

"Who is Mrs. Schwarzbard?"

"A dressmaker who came to town a year ago."

Danny never asked, "How come you don't know?" He became the antidote to the loneliness and vulnerability Sybil experienced after coming to in the fifth grade. Inexplicably, she had lost her friends.

At recess, when the children scrambled out to the playground, both boys and girls had their baseball and softball teams. They chose sides, but Sybil stood alone—unchosen. To be left out was a new, terrible experience. Before, the children didn't leave her out of anything; she couldn't understand why they did so now.

If it weren't for Danny, Sybil could not have endured the humiliation at school, where, because of her problem with math, her marks had gone down. Without Danny, Sybil could not have withstood her mother's accusation: "But you used to know the multiplication tables. You're just pretending to forget. You're a bad girl—bad."

Upon occasion—when she sat on the front steps talking with Danny, or when they played in the sun-room, where he made Shakespearean costumes for her dolls—Sybil was able to forget the strange, immutable subject of time. Just as miraculously, she was able to forget that she walked alone.

And except for Danny she was alone. She avoided her other classmates, and when she walked on Main Street, doing some errand for her mother, she often crossed from one side of the street to the other six or seven times in a single block to avoid an encounter with one of the townsfolk. Turning from everybody else, she turned to Danny, and he, without erecting barriers against others, turned as surely to her. They just naturally assumed that when they were old enough they would marry. Sybil firmly believed that when this happened, time somehow would cease to be strange.

Then, on a brisk October day when they were in the sixth grade, they were sitting on the front steps, and Danny said awkwardly, "Syb, I have something to tell you."

"What?" Sybil, sensing his tone, asked anxiously.

"My dad—well, he bought a gas station in Waco, Texas, and, well, we're going there to live. But you'll come see me. I'll come back here. We'll see each other."

The next month, while Danny's family got ready to leave Willow Corners, seemed to Sybil and Danny like a reprieve, as if they had been spared the parting. Between them nothing was changed except that they did everything together more intensely because they knew that time was running out.

Ultimately, however, the day came for Danny to say good-by. Sybil, sitting with him on the front steps which for so long had been the scene of close communion, was quiet and composed.

"We'll see each other," Danny repeated, and he stood up. "Well . . ." Overwhelmed by adolescent embarrassment, he fell silent. Then he bent over to where Sybil was still sitting, kissed her on the cheek, pulled away, and was gone.

Sybil, who since early childhood had shunned even the most casual physical contact, was now transported by a joyous tingle. At first she was not even aware that Danny was no longer beside her. When awareness returned she panicked, apprehensively searching for him. There he was—blond hair and lithe body moving, retreating. Sybil sank down onto the steps. The rescue that Danny represented had been withdrawn. All that existed now was an unmitigated aloneness.

THE SKY is blue, Vicky thought as, getting up from the front steps, she stepped into the time from which Sybil had just departed and walked around the white house with the black shutters.

"That you, Peggy?" Hattie called from the kitchen window.

No, Vicky thought as she entered the kitchen, it isn't Peggy, or Sybil. I'm not your daughter, but I'm here to take Sybil's place, and although you will call me your daughter, you will discover that I'm not afraid of you.

"You'll get pneumonia sitting out there in the cold."

"I'm used to our midwestern winters, and by comparison this is child's play."

"Don't act smart with me," Hattie warned.

"I was only stating a fact," said Vicky.

"Well, I'm expecting a package from Elderville. Go on over to the post office and get it for me."

Vicky went. Strange that it should be autumn. The time of beginnings is spring, she thought. Listening to the rustle of the dry leaves, she walked down the back-porch steps and along the alley that led to Main Street.

Autumn without, it was nevertheless spring within—the spring that followed a long winter of eight years of secret residency. Quiescent, nameless, she had *been* from the time Sybil was three and a half. Quiescent, yes. Powerless, no. During that period Vicky, though still nameless, had exerted a variety of internal pressures upon Sybil and the other selves, and had thereby been silently influencing Sybil's behavior.

But as Danny Martin faded out of sight Vicky realized that the time for more active intervention had come. She would have to take command of the body away from Sybil, who was obviously too traumatized by the parting to carry on. In her childish imagination Sybil had created a bright and unafraid girl and christened her Victoria Antoinette Scharleau. Now this hitherto quiescent self borrowed the name and entered the real world.

It was good, Vicky thought as she walked along Main Street, to feel the wind and to be wholly in control of the body that did the feeling. But though a newcomer to commanding the body, she felt like an old-timer in the street itself. For Vicky knew what had happened in the life of Sybil Isabel Dorsett, whether or not Sybil herself had been present. Time, often blank for Sybil, had been constant for Vicky. Moreover, Vicky had total recall; in

Sybil's disjointed inner world Vicky served as a memory trace.

The package from Elderville was waiting. This was a good beginning, Vicky decided; if it hadn't been, Mrs. Dorsett would have blamed her. How well, Vicky felt, she knew this woman— no mother to her—with whom all these years she had tried to help Sybil cope.

At school the next morning Vicky was in command of both body and schoolwork. And although the other children were aloof, Vicky understood that the aloofness was rooted in the two years since the death of Sybil's grandmother.

During those two years Peggy Lou had been in complete control of the body, and it was she who had lost all Sybil's friends. Vicky knew that Peggy Lou had isolated herself from the other children not because she disliked them, but because being with them made her angry at not having what they had—a home with brothers and sisters, and with no reason to be afraid.

Sometimes Vicky regretted having let Peggy Lou take over at Grandma Dorsett's grave. But at the grave Sybil had been angry. Dealing with anger was Peggy Lou's function—not Vicky's.

Moreover, the two Peggy years hadn't been all bad. It had been Peggy Lou's emergence more than the restraining hand that had kept Sybil from jumping into Mary Dorsett's grave. After the funeral Peggy Lou, an active child, had been able to do what Sybil, an inactive child, could not have done: she had taken care of Cousin Anita's obstreperous two-year-old, Ella. Vicky had been amazed that Hattie Dorsett got along better with her daughter after Mary Dorsett's death than before. The daughter who came home from the funeral with Hattie and Willard and stayed for two years talked back and walked on the furniture in a rage, but she also seemed more winsome than the little girl who lived in the white house before her grandmother died.

In subsequent weeks Vicky took a good look at Willow Corners. *Mon Dieu,* she thought, the people in this town had no style, no éclat. They were narrow, provincial, and dull. As for Sybil's parents . . . well, the father was nice, but he didn't come up from behind his blueprints long enough to be able to care about what was happening. The mother was a different story. She was always saying, "You should do it this way or that." It was this, Vicky decided, that had hampered Sybil in doing things, for how can you do anything when there are so many shoulds and shouldn'ts, and nothing is any fun? But Vicky had the consolation of knowing that she was here to help, that after a while she would go back to Paris with her own loving parents, brothers and sisters.

There were times when Vicky allowed one of the other selves in the Sybil Dorsett entourage, or even Sybil herself, to take a seat in the sixth-grade classroom.

One day Mary Lucinda Saunders Dorsett, who had emerged during the first year of Peggy Lou's two-year tenure, took that seat. Mary carried the psychological burden of menstruation. She continued to appear occasionally during the sixth grade, but Vicky was there most of the time. Toward the end of the term Sybil arrived at school one day feeling that the Victoria of her fantasy had taken her there. This return was not so alarming as the return in the fifth grade; Sybil still thought time was strange, but somehow she felt more at ease about this spell.

IN THE months that followed, Sybil found herself floating in and out of blankness. She became ingenious at disguising the fact, feigning knowledge of what she did not know.

During the late spring of 1935, however, she faced a new terror. Hysteria—major or otherwise—is an illness resulting from emotional conflict, and is generally characterized by the use of defense mechanisms. One is dissociation. Another is conversion, in which the emotional conflict is expressed in physical terms.

Suddenly, half of Sybil's face and the sides of her arms would become numb. She would grow weak on one side of her body, not always the same side. Almost constantly her throat was sore, and she had trouble swallowing. She would often lose the sight in one eye. She—and some of the other selves as well, notably Mary—developed a nervous tic.

But more disturbing than the physical afflictions was the fact that life seemed to be unreal. Sybil would remember that she had been somewhere or had done something as if she had dreamed it. One night she mentioned this feeling of unreality to her parents, who took her to Dr. Quinoness, the town's doctor.

He diagnosed Sybil's case as a form of Saint Vitus's dance. Explaining that there was a psychological component, he advised that she see a psychiatrist and made an appointment for her in Minneapolis. Willard and Hattie refused to let her keep it. If it was only psychological, Willard claimed, he could handle it himself. Upon this assumpton he bought Sybil a guitar and engaged a teacher for her. Father and daughter practiced together and later gave recitals. Since Vicky, Mary, Peggy Lou, and some of the other selves also learned to play, but with differing degrees of enthusiasm, the performances Willard Dorsett's daughter gave were strikingly uneven.

Trying to take her mind off her trouble, Sybil threw herself into her schoolwork. There, however, she was disturbed by not knowing the European history that had been taught while she was not present. Vicky carried history, just as Peggy Lou was the keeper of multiplication. With science, however, Sybil caught up quickly. She was especially fascinated by the mysteries of the human anatomy.

One day she dashed into the house after school to tell her mother about heart function. Hattie said, "I don't want to hear about that." Sybil, however, was so excited that she went right on explaining what she had learned. "How many times do I have to tell you that I'm not interested?" Hattie screamed, striking out at her daughter. Sybil, who had been standing on the polished linoleum in the sun-room, took the blow full on the hip, slipped, and fell sideways over a chair. Her ribs were badly bruised.

From that time forward Sybil was afraid of the science class, and even though science continued to fascinate her, she had a hard time getting through high-school and, later, college biology. She also became afraid of rooms with polished floors.

That night Hattie took Sybil on an outing to Main Street. It was a Wednesday night, and the stores were open. Sybil caught sight of some pretty hair bows and hoped her mother would ask whether she wanted one. But Hattie passed the counter.

Then Vicky decided to do the asking and pointed to a light blue bow. "I'd like to have it," she informed Hattie. "It matches our blue organdy dress."

"What do you mean by 'our,' you numbskull?" Hattie replied. "Don't you know that organdy dress is *yours?*" But she paid the cashier for the hair bow.

8

VICKY AND Sybil, Mary and Sybil, Peggy Lou and Sybil— what was the connection? Dr. Wilbur decided to ask Vicky. It was June 15, 1955, and the analysis had been proceeding for eight months.

"Vicky," the doctor said, "you've talked of *our* blue organdy dress. What else do you and some of the others share? Would you say they *share* a mother?"

"Yes, I suppose you could say that."

"Do they also share the same body?"

"That's silly," Vicky said. "They're people."

"Yes, Vicky, I know. But how are Peggy Lou, Peggy Ann, Mary, Sybil, and the others related? Are they sisters?"

"Nobody ever said they were sisters." Vicky looked squarely at the doctor.

"No," the doctor answered with precise emphasis, "nobody ever *said* that. But, Vicky, when people have the same mother, they must either be the same person, sisters, or brothers."

"When you put it that way," Vicky replied, "I have to admit that they must be sisters, because they *couldn't* be the same person!" She closed the subject as she rose to go. "*Mon Dieu,* what an absurdity it is to think of those individuals as the same. Marian Ludlow and I are more alike than are any two or three persons you have mentioned."

"Vicky," the doctor said firmly, "the hour is not over yet, and I would like you to listen."

Vicky seated herself.

"You say that Peggy Lou, Peggy Ann, Mary, and the others couldn't be the same person. But don't you see that they could be different aspects of the same person?"

"No," Vicky said, shaking her head. "I don't see. You, you're just Dr. Wilbur and no one else. And I'm just Vicky. There's nobody else here."

After rejecting the logical conclusion toward which Dr. Wilbur had been trying to lead her, Vicky now contradicted her contention that the doctor and she were alone, for she rose and said, "Now, Dr. Wilbur, Mary would like to meet you. She wants to participate in our analysis, and I think we should let her."

"*Our* analysis? How can it be 'our' if you girls are not the same person?"

Vicky chuckled. "I suppose you might call it *group* therapy."

Then, as surely as if she had physically left the room, Vicky was gone. A voice that definitely was not hers remarked politely, "I'm glad to meet you, Dr. Wilbur."

"You're Mary?" the doctor asked.

"Mary Lucinda Saunders Dorsett," the voice replied.

It was not the voice of a woman of the world like Vicky, or of an angry child like Peggy Lou. The accent was unmistakably midwestern, the tone soft, low, and somber. The doctor had not heard that voice before and knew of Mary only through Vicky.

She motioned Mary to the couch and waited. Mary was silent. New patient reserve? the doctor mused.

"What do you like to do, Mary?" she asked.

"I keep our home going," Mary answered, "but it's hard to do so much, Dr. Wilbur. You probably know that Sybil and Teddy Reeves have just taken a brownstone apartment together on Morningside Drive. They're doing it over, and the doing falls to me. How I wish we had more space. I'd like to have a flower garden, room for some animals."

"You don't like New York?"

"Not really. But then I don't get around much. Sometimes I go to a museum or a library. That's about it."

"What do you do when you're in the apartment?"

"Housework. Read. Listen to music. Do a little painting. Write poetry. Poetry eases the pain."

"What pain, Mary?"

"Haven't they told you? Vicky? Sybil? Peggy Lou?"

"Not directly. They've talked of the fear of getting close to people, the fear of music, of hands, of being trapped. And by denying Sybil's mother, Vicky and Peggy Lou indicate that they fear her. Do you fear her?"

"I never felt Sybil's mother was mine." Mary's tone was confidential.

"What pain, Mary?"

"You'll know in time. That's why I told Vicky that I wanted to come today. I want to help with our analysis. But I feel guilty about coming. Maybe it's a sin to go to a psychiatrist."

"Then why have you come?"

"That day last month among the dogwoods and the flowering crab," Mary answered thoughtfully, "you weren't a psychiatrist. You were a friend. We need friends."

"Sybil has friends. Aren't her friends also yours?"

"I suppose so," Mary replied, "but only in a way. Teddy Reeves knows me by name and can tell me apart from the others, but Laura Hotchkins thinks I'm Sybil. Most people do, you know. I'm sometimes very lonely."

"Then why don't you go out and make friends on your own, the way Vicky does?"

"Well," Mary explained, "for one thing I don't have the clothes. I just wear what I find in our closet, and what looks well on the others doesn't necessarily suit me." Mary paused, ducked her head, and added with a slight, tired smile, "But then I'm not as attractive as Vicky. I can't compete with her. I am what I am."

Mary saw herself as the eternal housewife, interested in *Kinder, Küche, Kirche*. And although the children didn't exist, although the cooking was difficult in a small kitchen, it became increasingly clear to Dr. Wilbur that what really troubled Mary were the problems revolving around *Kirche*. "Maybe it's a sin to go to a psychiatrist" reflected church-centered conflicts.

"When Grandma died," Mary told the doctor during the same session, "Sybil didn't mourn for her. Sybil went away. After Grandma died I came out to mourn for her. I came when Peggy Lou was in charge of things."

"How did you get your name?"

"It's Grandma's name. I look like Grandma. Grandma Dorsett's son is my father, and I also look like him. When I get home I'm going to phone Daddy. Did Sybil tell you that he and his new wife, Frieda, live in Detroit? I want to reassure him about things. You see, Sybil doesn't show him that she can try harder. I'm the one who has to show him." It was apparent that Mary loved her father unreservedly.

"But suppose something stood in the way of the trying?" the doctor asked pointedly. "Shouldn't you get that something out of the way?"

"Like the gardener," Mary replied almost self-righteously, "we must pull up the weed and destroy it."

"Exactly," the doctor agreed. "But what is the weed?"

For a moment the doctor had thought Mary was on the threshold of revealing the original trauma. But Mary kept the trauma obscure. Still, it was the doctor's impression that Mary did have some access to the truth and that, although torn by religious conflicts, she had a genuine desire to destroy the hidden weed.

"Do you know 'The Egotist,' by Sarah Fells?" Mary asked. "Both Sybil and I liked it when we were little girls.

> 'In a self-centered circle, he goes round and round,
> That he is a wonder is true;
> For who but an egotist ever could be
> Circumference and center, too.'"

Who is the circumference, who the center? the doctor wondered. Is Sybil the center or is one of these others?

THE SEARCH FOR THE CENTER was further complicated by the arrival at the next appointment of two selves Dr. Wilbur had not met before. Gazing at the woman beside her, who at the moment was simultaneously Marcia Lynn and Vanessa Gail, the doctor, who had thought herself inured to surprises could not keep from speculating on how so many diverse characters could flourish in the small, slight frame of Sybil Dorsett.

The newcomers had been introduced by Vicky, and the little that Dr. Wilbur knew about them had come from her. "Marcia," Vicky had said, "feels what Sybil feels—only more intensely." When Sybil and the others watched something sad on television, Marcia was the one who cried. And Marcia was the one who seemed to need her mother most. "She'll weep," Vicky told Dr. Wilbur, "because she's lonely for her mother." Vanessa, a tall girl with reddish hair, played the piano and was full of *joie de vivre*.

Since the body was now *simultaneously* occupied by Marcia and Vanessa, the doctor wondered how she was going to tell them apart. But very soon she was able to distinguish one from the other by their voices. Though both spoke with English accents in similar diction and speech patterns, Vanessa's soprano had a lilting quality, Marcia's alto a brooding one.

As she had with Mary, the doctor began by asking, "What do you girls like to do?"

"Travel," said Marcia.

"Go places " said Vanessa. "See and do new things."

Marcia and Vanessa enjoyed big cities, the theater, concerts, books. "We have our own likes," Marcia explained, "but we enjoy doing things together." It became clear to the doctor that, just as Vicky and Marian Ludlow were special friends in the world, Marcia and Vanessa were special friends within Sybil.

"Tell me how you feel, Marcia," the doctor suggested.

"You don't know what you're letting yourself in for, Doctor."

"Doctor," Vanessa chimed in, "you shouldn't ask her. She might tell you!"

"I see you girls have a sense of humor," the doctor observed.

"You have to have humor to survive in the Dorsett clan," Vanessa replied promptly. "Mary, Peggy Lou, and, of course, Sybil worry so much that they make life sound like a Russian novel. It's really comical. It's so out of character with Willow Corners. When I got there Sybil was twelve. I couldn't stand that town. There was so much sugar in the way they pretended to treat each other that I suffered from diabetes of the soul."

"That's a good phrase," Marcia interrupted. "Are you sure you didn't steal it from me? I'm the writer! Why don't you stick to your piano playing?"

"But I'm the one who came up with it."

"Oh, Vanessa, please. I was only kidding."

"Careful," Vanessa cautioned with a satiric overtone. "As our mother would say, 'Kidding is not a word we use when people are around.'" Then, turning to Dr. Wilbur, Vanessa said, "In the home even the word heck was not allowed."

"It's not right to criticize Mother," said Marcia.

"Oh, you never were able to untie the umbilical cord. That is why this nice lady is going to have to help you grow up."

"Vanessa, it isn't fair for you to talk like that."

"Fair! What do we know about fairness?" Vanessa countered. "Is it fair that we've been denied what other girls have? Someday I'll break loose, be on my own, and you, my dear Marcia, will come with me. You have a taste for life, and we've always been together even though you entered Sybil's life before me."

"Vanessa," Marcia pleaded, "the way we're talking to each other, the doctor will think we're one person talking to herself."

"No," the doctor interrupted, "I understand perfectly well that you are two different people, and I want you both to come here whenever you like and to say whatever you want to say."

"When we don't have competition from the others," Marcia said mischievously. "Vicky, for instance. She's smart, and she helps us a lot. But she talks too much—almost as much as Vanessa."

For three sessions in a row Marcia and Vanessa came back. There was an excitement, an electric quality about Vanessa—who was full of energy, used extravagant gestures, and dramatized everything—that was shared neither by Marcia nor by any of the other selves the doctor had met. Marcia was a calmer version of Vanessa, more somber, basically a pessimist. She found escape with Vanessa or in books, but essentially she thought of life as "horrid and futile" and of people as being "simply awful."

As THE summer of 1955 gave place to autumn Dr. Wilbur found the analysis again reverting to the spring of 1934, when Sybil returned after the two-year absence between the ages of nine and eleven.

IT WAS the first day of Sybil's return. The evening meal was over and the Dorsetts were in the living room. Hattie was listening to the radio. Willard was reading *Architectural Forum*.

"It's time to go to your room, Peggy," Hattie ordered.

Sybil was accustomed to being called Peggy, but she didn't understand her mother's instructions. She had never had a room of her own. Always she had slept in her parents' downstairs bedroom. She said good night and walked into that room. To her amazement the crib was not there, only her parents' bed.

"Peggy Louisiana!" Her mother's voice echoed sharply from the living room. "Aren't you going upstairs? It's after eight!"

Upstairs? Some years earlier Hattie had designated an upstairs bedroom as Sybil's, but had never gotten around to moving her there. Could that be the room her mother meant?

The crib was not in this bedroom, either. Instead there was a full-sized bed. Could the bed be hers? When had they given it to her? Sybil undressed and—for the first time in her life—got into an adult-sized bed in a room of her own. Now she could go to sleep without squeezing her eyes shut or turning to the wall.

IN PSYCHOANALYTIC terms a child's auditory and visual perception of parents' sexual intercourse is known as the primal scene because it is the child's first encounter with adult sexuality and because, as a foundation on which a youngster will build future feelings, attitudes, and behavior, it is of first importance in the child's development. Usually the moment is accidental, and the way a child is affected depends on the general atmosphere of the home. When sex is made to seem something private but not forbidden, the effects of this brief encounter are often free from psychological damage.

In Sybil's case the primal scene was no momentary glimpse, no single accidental moment. From the time she was born until she was nine years old she had been deliberately exposed to her parents' intimacies, which were in marked contrast to their daytime behavior. By day they never kissed, touched, or addressed each other by any endearment. In their household sex was regarded as wicked, and the daughter's normal questions about the facts of life went unanswered. Babies somehow happened, but nice people did not admit how.

From the time of their individual arrivals Sybil's various selves had different reactions to this primal scene. Peggy Lou was wakeful, uneasy, but she did not try to cover her eyes or to keep from listening. Vicky was curious. She had the distinct impression that Hattie Dorsett actually wanted her daughter to look, for Hattie customarily threw the sheets back as if to reveal what was happening. Marcia feared for Mother's safety. Watching and listening in that communal bedchamber was a self called Ruthie who emerged in analysis during the reliving of the primal scene. She was only a baby, perhaps three and a half, and she could not give the date of her arrival in Sybil's life. But of all the silent witnesses Ruthie was most indignant.

WHEN SYBIL was six there had been an interlude away from the white house with black shutters. For when the Great Depression left Willard Dorsett virtually penniless, he took his wife and daughter to live on forty acres of farmland belonging to his parents, five miles outside of Willow Corners.

At the farm, which Willard dubbed The Forty, Sybil found surcease from the strange occurrences at Willow Corners. She enjoyed all the things she could do in the one-room chicken house which the Dorsetts made their temporary home—coloring with her crayons, playing with her many dolls or with Top, her big Airedale, and reading in the primer her father had bought for her.

Her mother was different here from what she had been in Willow Corners. In the house with black shutters Sybil was always afraid to be left alone with her mother. *That* mother did things to you. Here Sybil was not afraid, for *this* mother didn't do *anything*. She sat unmoving at one end of the room, hearing and seeing nothing. She never answered when they spoke to her.

The change had come at Christmas. Hattie Dorsett didn't have the money to buy anything, and she had become very depressed. Then she stopped talking, stopped doing anything. Willard and Sybil even had to dress her and feed her.

One day in March, Sybil was with her father and Top in a plowed field covered with snow, where the oak tree they had been cutting for firewood waited for them. When it wasn't snowing they came nearly every day to saw at it. "Daddy," Sybil said as she placed her hand on the tree, "it still remembers us."

"You certainly have a good imagination," her father said. Smiling, he handed her one end of the crosscut saw and took the other himself. They worked together, and the wood began to give. The sun was bright. Sybil could see their house on the hill in the sunlight. Suddenly there was something else. And her father was asking nervously, "Did you hear that loud laugh?"

The laugh was repeated. It was shrill, rising higher. Sybil began to tremble. She had heard the laugh many times in Willow Corners. The laugh had come when she was made to stand up against the wall. A broom handle struck her back. A woman's shoe kicked her. A washcloth was stuffed down her throat. Things were put up inside her, things with sharp edges that hurt. Each time that laugh along with the pain. She heard it again when she was buried in the wheat crib and nearly smothered.

The laughter coming to her in the March wind had ripped away the quiet of the afternoon, its peace, its happiness gone.

Sybil looked up. Her mother was on the top of the hill in front of the house, where Sybil had left her sled. How had she gotten there? Only a little while ago she was like stone. Sybil saw her drop onto the sled in a sitting position. The sled shot forward down the hill, straight toward a plowed furrow under the snow.

Sybil, shocked and fearful, stood immobile. The sled hit the furrow and threw her mother off. Then Sybil's father was leaning over his wife, taking her pulse.

SYBIL stood near the stove while her father hovered over her mother, applying hot packs to her badly bruised and swollen leg. Her mother was saying, "I thought sure it was broke. Put on some arnica when you get done with the hot packs."

Her father made supper while Sybil set the table.

"You're doing it wrong," her mother said. "The forks are in the wrong place." The Willow Corners mother had returned.

9

LEARNING OF Hattie Dorsett's trancelike behavior at The Forty and of her other aberrations at Willow Corners, Dr. Wilbur was left in little doubt that Hattie was the source of Sybil's original trauma. Then, in early 1957, the analysis unfolded a drama of humiliations, secret rituals, punishments, and atrocities inflicted by Hattie on Sybil. Dr. Wilbur became convinced that Sybil was a battered child, four decades before the battered-child syndrome was medically identified. The horrors began when Sybil was only six months old. Moreover, there was a special brand of maternal ministration which continued throughout Sybil's early childhood.

In the morning after Willard had gone to work and she was alone with her child for the day, Hattie would lock the kitchen door and pull down the shades. What followed was not always the same. A favorite ritual, however, was to separate Sybil's legs with a long wooden spoon, tie her feet to the spoon, and then string her to the end of a light-bulb cord suspended from the ceiling. The child was left to swing thus in space while the mother turned on the faucet and waited for the water to get cold. After muttering, "Well, it's not going to get any colder," she would fill an enema bag and return with it to her daughter.

After the enema Hattie would laugh triumphantly and insist that the child walk around the room holding in the water. This resulted in severe cramps. But if Sybil cried, Hattie would beat her and say, "I'll really give you something to cry about." The ritual was not complete until Hattie had warned, "Now don't you dare tell anybody anything about this!"

With frightening frequency Hattie would force her daughter to drink a glassful of milk of magnesia. When Sybil pleaded to be allowed to go to the bathroom, Hattie made her go to the bedroom instead and then punished the child for soiling herself. When Sybil began to cry, Hattie tied a towel over her mouth so Grandma Dorsett would not hear. Fearing the towels, Sybil became afraid to cry. By age three and a half she no longer did.

There was still another morning ritual with which Hattie took great pains. Placing Sybil on the kitchen table, Hattie would force into the child's vagina an array of objects that caught the mother's fancy—a small bottle, a little silver box, the handle of a knife, a buttonhook for buttoning the high-topped shoes of that day. "You might as well get used to it," her mother explained. "That's what men will do to you when you grow up."

"Sybil," Willard said one Sabbath morning as the family was getting ready for church, "I don't see why you scream so every time we put those shoes on you. Hattie, we'd better get her new shoes." He didn't know that the buttonhook had other uses.

When Hattie Dorsett wanted to punish her daughter, she would slap the child and knock her to the ground. Or she would fling Sybil across the room; once the child's shoulder was dislocated. A hot flatiron would be pressed on the child's hand. A rolling pin would descend on her fingers. A purple scarf would be tied around her neck until she gasped for breath.

Sometimes Sybil was tied to the leg of the piano while her mother played Bach, Beethoven, or Chopin, pushing down the pedals of the piano and pounding the keyboard as hard as she could. Or Sybil would be blindfolded as punishment for having dared to ask

some question. The mother would answer, "Anyone could see that who isn't blind. I'll show you what it's like to be blind." At other times Hattie would show Sybil what it was like to be dead: she would shut the child in a trunk in the attic. Unable to endure, Sybil would allow one of her other selves to emerge.

WHEN HER mother tortured her Sybil could do nothing about it. Worse, she did not dare ask anybody else to do anything.

Sybil loved her grandmother, but her grandmother hadn't intervened when her mother tripped Sybil as she was going down the stairs. When her grandmother had asked what had happened, Hattie had replied, "You know how clumsy children are. She fell downstairs." Sybil repressed the rage she felt at her grandmother.

Her father hadn't intervened, either. Couldn't he see the meaning of the buttonhook, the dislocated shoulder, the burned hand, the black eyes, the swollen lips? But he had refused to see.

There was repressed rage, too, at the neighbors who never came when Sybil cried; at Grandfather Dorsett, who was upstairs and didn't seem to know what was happening below; at Dr. Quinoness, who again and again saw that the child had been hurt but didn't try to discover why. And later Sybil repressed rage at her teachers, who from time to time asked her what was wrong but never actually bothered to find out.

Distressed by those who didn't come to her rescue, Sybil nevertheless refused to blame Hattie, whose muttered "I have to do it" led her to think that this was indeed something that had to be done. One had not only to obey but also to love and honor one's mother. She blamed not the perpetrator of the torture but the towels, the silver box, and the buttonhook. When Hattie remarked on her deathbed, "I really shouldn't have been so cross with you when you were a child," it seemed to Sybil sinful even to recollect that "crossness."

Moreover, Sybil's feelings toward her mother had always been complicated by the fact that Hattie's behavior was paradoxical. The same mother who tortured her daughter would cut bright-colored pictures from magazines and paste them on the cupboard door at Sybil's eye level. The child's appetite was slight, and at breakfast, in order to encourage her to eat, this same mother would often manage to have a surprise in the bottom of her daughter's cereal bowl: prunes, figs, dates, all of which the child especially liked. Hattie also provided children's dishes decorated with pictures and Sybil's initials. And there were playthings all over the house. Again and again Sybil heard variations on the theme "You have so much to be thankful for." Then she would say, "You're the best mother in the whole world and I'll try to do better."

As these accounts came out during analysis Dr. Wilbur became increasingly convinced that Hattie was a schizophrenic, and that she had forged an intolerable reality against which Sybil had had to defend herself. Normal at birth, the doctor speculated, Sybil had fought back until she was about two and a half, by which time the fight had been literally beaten out of her. She had sought rescue from outside herself until she finally recognized that rescue would be denied; then she sought rescue from within.

At the Anderson home in Elderville, which the Dorsetts visited every summer, there was a clean break with Hattie's angry tyrannies. Here, aunts and uncles hugged and kissed Sybil, listened to her, and said that everything she did was wonderful. One summer when it was time to go back to Willow Corners, Sybil turned to Aunt Fay and said, "Will you keep me?"

Still, there were disquieting episodes. One day Sybil looked through the kitchen window, saw her mother near the stable, and heard her haunting laughter. Five feet from Hattie, Cousin Joey and Uncle Jerry were lifting a box onto a dray. Ashamed of her mother's eerie, unmotivated laughter, especially in the presence of relatives, Sybil shuddered. A coffin, she thought, as she looked at the box . . . It was Marcia who completed the thought: *The box will get bigger and will be big enough to hold Mama.* Marcia wanted her mother dead!

She could not have known that the death wish for a mother

frequently occurs in little girls because they find their mothers disturbing rivals for the affection of their fathers. Because of the intense guilt the wish aroused, Marcia pushed it from her thoughts and returned the body to Sybil, who didn't know about Marcia's little box grown big.

By dividing into different selves, Sybil found a way to survive.

So FAR, all Dr. Wilbur's information about Sybil's unhappy childhood had come from just one source—Sybil and Sybil's alternate selves. Other testimony was needed for substantiation.

Hattie Dorsett was dead. Apart from the patient herself, the father was clearly the best witness in whom nearly three years of analysis could find verification. So in April 1957, after minutely exploring the available evidence about the mother-daughter relationship, Dr. Wilbur decided to bring Willard Dorsett into the case. Sybil wrote and asked him to come to New York.

Willard was seventy-four now and living in Detroit, happily remarried and still working. He had already let it be known that he thought Sybil, at thirty-four, was too old to be supported by him, despite the fact that, after her money ran out at the end of two years in New York, he had agreed to pay her expenses so that she could continue treatment. (She had informed him about her analysis at the end of the first year.)

The doctor was inclined to regard the support as payment of a debt, the debt of a father to a daughter who through analysis was struggling to become whole. Although he once again had a substantial bank account and was earning a good income, he was assisting Sybil grudgingly, erratically. Yet at this stage of her life she had no bank account and no permanent job; aside from Willard's checks her only sources of income were occasional sales of her paintings, sporadic work as a tutor, and an intermittent part-time job as an art therapist.

Willard Dorsett's obligation to Sybil, the doctor thought, was also the debt of a father who had squandered his daughter's money. He had sold Sybil's piano, bedroom set, and several of her paintings without consulting her, and had not given her the proceeds. He had also made her pay half of her mother's funeral expenses.

Willard's failure to send Sybil her monthly check was a repeat performance of an episode that had taken place in Sybil's under-graduate days. Her upbringing forbade her to borrow, so for five weeks she had lived on oranges and cookies, rationed to two each a day.

Dr. Wilbur wrote Willard that this new default was causing his daughter anguish she was not well enough to withstand. He replied that he was busy and could not keep track of details.

As she again waited for her father to come to her rescue, Sybil was caught in a web of ambivalent feelings. The feelings would have been simpler if Willard had been a completely rejecting father. However, she did have a relationship with him. When Sybil was only six weeks old she had developed a disease of the middle ear, and she was comforted only when her father held her. By chance, when he held her he always sat next to the kitchen stove. The warmth, which she associated with her father, had soothed her. Years later, Willard had been proud of her painting. He had made it a point to mount and frame her pictures, and there had grown between them an affinity of taste.

Unable to make identification with her mother, Sybil had been compelled to make identification with *someone,* and she per-suaded herself that it was her father on whom she could depend. So the wait for Willard Dorsett's reply was long.

10

A T FOUR p.m. on May 4, 1957, Willard Dorsett entered Dr. Wilbur's consulting room. Erect, complacent, he cut an imposing figure.

Some ten minutes later his defensive armor had begun to crack. The questions Dr. Wilbur was asking were not about Sybil. Instead, the doctor was taking him back to Willow

Corners and his marriage to Hattie. Having taken Willard's measure, Dr. Wilbur had decided that the only way she could get what she was seeking was by direct attack.

"Why, Mr. Dorsett," she asked, "did you always entrust the full care and upbringing of Sybil to your wife?"

He merely shrugged. The question obviously seemed to him irrelevant. A mother *should* take care of a child.

Had he been aware that Hattie's behavior was peculiar? He moved jerkily in his chair and became defensive. When he finally spoke it was to say, "The first Mrs. Dorsett was a wonderful woman, bright, talented." He hesitated, flustered.

"And?" the doctor asked.

"Well," he said, "we had a lot of trouble. Financial and otherwise. It was hard on Hattie. At times she was difficult."

"Just difficult?" the doctor asked.

He averted his eyes. "Hattie was odd."

"More than odd, Mr. Dorsett, if what I've been told is true."

Was he aware that as a child Sybil had sustained an unusual number of injuries? With annoyance he answered quickly, "She had accidents, of course, like any child." Was he aware that Sybil had had a dislocated shoulder? Did he remember the burns on her hands, her black eyes?

"Yes." The involuntary twitchings in his face betrayed uneasiness. "I seem to recall these things now."

"What did your wife tell you about them?"

"Well," he said at last, "Hattie was always telling me that Sybil had many falls. I suppose I never really thought about how these things happened."

Willard stared at the green draperies and then shut his eyes, but the doctor was saying, "Mr. Dorsett, there are some things that Sybil says happened in the morning. . . ." The doctor recounted the ritualistic tortures. When she referred to the button-hook Willard bowed his head. It was a moment of revelation.

His voice was normally soft and low. Now, barely audibly, he mumbled, "Not Hattie!"

"*Hattie,*" Dr. Wilbur replied, "if what Sybil says is true."

"That's why Sybil screamed so on the Sabbath when we tried to button her white kid shoes." On weekday mornings, he added, he had been away from home and couldn't have known what was going on. "How could I, when nobody told me?"

"Think, Mr. Dorsett," the doctor enjoined. "Can you tell me whether these things actually took place? There are scars and injuries that lend credence to Sybil's account." (A gynecologist who had examined Sybil had stated that because of the internal injuries she probably could never bear a child.)

Willard wiped perspiration from his forehead with a freshly pressed handkerchief. "Doctor, I didn't know about these things, but looking back now I recall most of the physical injuries. I never saw Hattie lay a hand on Sybil, but knowing Hattie, I'm sure not only that they were possible but that they happened."

It was a pivotal moment. Willard Dorsett's admission that Hattie was capable of these atrocities was tantamount to a confession that by failing to protect his daughter against a perilously destructive mother he had been partner to the mother's deeds. It was indisputable now that the mother was the taproot of Sybil's having become a multiple personality. But Dr. Wilbur was also sure that the father was an important associated root. The mother had trapped Sybil, but the father had made Sybil feel that there was no escape from that trap.

The doctor simply said, "Mr. Dorsett, may I ask again why you allowed your daughter to be brought up by her mother?"

"Well," he replied, measuring his words, "it is a mother's place to raise a child."

"Even, Mr. Dorsett, when that mother is clearly schizophrenic? Even when that mother came very close to killing her child?"

Flustered, defensive, he replied, "I did what I could." Then he told Dr. Wilbur about taking Hattie to see a psychiatrist at the Mayo Clinic in Rochester. The doctor had diagnosed Hattie as a schizophrenic and had said that, although she didn't have to be hospitalized, she should be treated on an outpatient basis. "Hattie saw the doctor only once. She wouldn't go back because she said that all he did was stare at her."

The other psychiatrist's diagnosis confirmed Dr. Wilbur's own, and, together with Willard Dorsett's observations, provided the verification for which she had been searching. The tortures and cruelties that Sybil's other personalities had described to Dr. Wilbur *could* have been only echoes of Sybil's fantasies or delusions. There was even a remote possibility that the internal scars and injuries *could* have been self-inflicted. But now there was no need to question further.

At the end of a most revealing session Willard Dorsett shook hands with the doctor. "I tried to be a good father," he said. The door closed on a man who was visibly shaken.

AT THE moment Willard was walking into Dr. Wilbur's office that May 4, 1957, Sybil was gazing in astonishment at her Morningside Drive apartment. In a space of eight hours the main room had been transformed by what seemed like a great wall.

The apartment, originally the dining room of an old mansion, had an ersatz elegance, an old wood-burning fireplace, and the redundancy of two kitchens, but afforded its present occupants no privacy. To get to her room, the smaller of the two kitchens, Teddy Reeves had to pass Sybil's bed in the main room. Neither woman had ever quite gotten around to solving the problem.

A partition now divided the room in half and masked Sybil's sleeping area. But although Sybil was pleased at this solution, she was anxious to learn who was responsible for it.

The anxiety was the greater because her discovery had occurred at the end of a fragmented day with long stretches of lost time. She felt strong internal movement, a soundless clamoring—"the interference of the others," as she had learned to call it.

She heard Teddy's key in the lock. "I smell paint," Teddy called as she entered. Then she stopped short. "The partition's marvelous. Why didn't you tell me you were going to build it?"

"I didn't build it," Sybil said. But even as she spoke she knew that she couldn't be sure of the "I." Perhaps the nails which her nervously wandering fingers had discovered in the pockets of her slacks belonged to the partition's carpenter.

AT THE NEXT SESSION a new personality strutted jauntily before Dr. Wilbur and confessed, "I built the partition. I let Mike drive the nails, but I did all the heavy work. Vicky and Peggy Lou did most of the planning and measuring and some painting. You have to give girls credit where credit is due."

At first Dr. Wilbur did not take too much notice of the name Mike or of the patronizing compliment to girls. What most impressed her was that alternating selves had met Sybil's need for privacy with a constructive solution.

The doctor's attention was quickly brought back to the immediate situation, however, as a different voice announced, "I'm Mike. I want to ask you something."

"What would you like to know?" the doctor asked.

"How come we're different?"

"Different?" the doctor repeated.

"Well," Mike explained, "the others are girls. But I'm a boy, and so is Sid."

By their own descriptions Sid had light skin, dark hair, and blue eyes; Mike, olive skin, dark hair, and brown eyes. Sid derived his name from Sybil's initials—Sybil Isabel Dorsett. Mike was what Willard had called his daughter whenever she wore coveralls, and one of Grandpa Dorsett's favorite expressions had been "For the love of Mike."

Mike and Sid talked of the concert they had attended last night with Dad, and of helping Sybil with her wood carving and sculpture. They also spoke of life in the Dorsett-Reeves apartment. Sid, who was the partition's carpenter, was also Sybil's repairman. "I fix what's broken, mend what needs mending," Sid told Dr. Wilbur. "Sybil never knows who did it."

New York, the boys complained, offered them no opportunity for the sports they had enjoyed in Willow Corners, where they had spent long hours playing ball and roller-skating.

"I look like my dad," Sid volunteered. "He's a builder. I'm a builder. As good as he is anytime."

Boys in the 1920s and 1930s in Willow Corners, Mike and Sid were still boys in the 1950s in New York.

"I'm glad I'm not a girl," Mike said. "Nobody likes girls."

"I like girls," Dr. Wilbur said.

"Oh, some girls are all right." Mike grinned broadly. "I like Vicky and Peggy Lou okay."

There was silence, finally broken by Sid. "Sometimes I used to pretend I was a girl. When I did that a woman with gray hair laughed. Nobody laughs when I'm a boy."

"What you pretended was real, Sid," the doctor said, enunciating each word with care. "You look like your father and can be like him in thought and feeling, in the way you approach things. But you are never going to be built like your father. Your father was a boy who became a man."

"That's what Mike and I will be when we're older. We'll have everything our dad has. Dad has to shave. We'll have to shave. Dad . . ."

"Boys, I want to tell you something," the doctor said in a firm clear voice. "That is impossible. The truth for both of you is that you live in a woman's body, and boys in a girl's body don't grow up to be men."

"Not ever?" Mike asked. For the first time his tone was somber.

"No, not ever."

MIKE proved in analysis to be the more aggressive; Sid, the more thoughtful. This was appropriate in terms of their identification—Mike with his grandfather, Sid with his father. Willard Dorsett was a builder and carpenter. And that was the genesis of Sid, who built the partition.

Grandpa Dorsett had been aggressive and fanatical. He had aroused Sybil's fear, anger, and hatred. Sybil had dealt with these emotions by dissociating into an aggressive male personality whose name was Mike.

As far as the doctor could determine neither Sid nor Mike was subject to fear, anxiety, or depression. Both were capable of anger, but an anger more controlled than Peggy Lou's, though it turned out to be linked with her. As the mastermind behind Mike and Sid, Peggy Lou delegated her feelings to them. "Peggy

Lou," Vicky had said, "is angry about sex because of her mother's refusal to explain the facts of life. Sometimes Peggy Lou used to say that she was a boy." No doubt she was compensating for woman's inferiority in Willow Corners.

Mike and Sid were also autonomous beings, with emotions of their own. But analysis threatened their freedom, for Dr. Wilbur was determined as soon as possible to fuse both into the feminine whole they so resolutely rejected.

Sybil was unique in being the only known multiple personality to have developed personalities of the opposite sex.* The boys presented a serious complication in an already complicated case. How, the doctor asked herself, is Sybil to become one? Out of how many?

11

THE FACT WAS that there were five selves Dr. Wilbur had not yet met: Marjorie, Helen, Sybil Ann, Clara, and Nancy Lou Ann.

Marjorie was a small, willowy brunette with fair skin and a pug nose. Helen had light-brown hair, hazel eyes, a straight nose, and thin lips. Sybil Ann was a pale, stringy girl with ash-blond hair, gray eyes, an oval face, and a straight nose. Of these three, Marjorie alone was serene. Helen was intensely fearful; Sybil Ann, listless.

Marjorie Dorsett was vivacious, quick to laugh, and something of a tease. She had no hesitation in expressing annoyance or impatience, but she never showed anger. She was not depressed, nor did she give evidence of having been depressed in the past. Through some special immunity she had emerged unscathed from the battering in Willow Corners. She never referred to Sybil by name, only to "you know who."

* Since 1957 other multiple personalities who have developed selves of the opposite sex have been recorded.

Helen, who seemed unassertive, was nevertheless ambitious, determined "to be somebody, to do things in my own way, and to make you, Dr. Wilbur, proud of me."

But when the doctor mentioned Hattie, Helen broke away from the couch, where she had been seated quietly, and huddled under the desk.

"Helen?" The doctor placed a hand on her shoulder.

"She's in this room!" Helen screamed, beginning to tremble violently. "Behind the curtains!"

"Who?"

"Mother."

"There's nobody here, Helen, but you and me."

"I never want to see my mother again."

"You never will."

Sybil Ann didn't speak, she whispered. When the introductions were over she sat silently, staring into the distance. It was as if she were erasing herself from the scene, almost as if she were saying, "I'm not fit to occupy space." This fragile personality seldom ate, slept little, and evinced slight interest in her surroundings. Often she would say, "I don't feel anything."

Characteristically, Sybil Ann assumed command of the body when "everything was too much." The takeover, however, was a response to, rather than a means of coping with, the given situation; of all the selves Sybil Ann was the most profoundly depressed; she could sit for hours mute and unmoving. She was, Dr. Wilbur felt certain, an identification with Hattie Dorsett in her catatonic phase on the farm.

IN MARCH 1958 Clara presented herself to Dr. Wilbur with a terse autobiography. "I'm twenty-three. I never had a mother. I just exist." Clara was pacing the floor. "Sybil's such a deplorable character. It's disgusting. She can't do anything!"

"You sound as if you don't like Sybil," the doctor said.

"I don't," Clara replied resentfully. "I like to study and learn. She stands in my way."

"What do you like to study?"

"Medical things—chemistry, zoology."

"So does Sybil," the doctor was quick to point out.

"No, she doesn't," Clara said contemptuously. "A big steel wall goes up, and she just can't study."

"Will you help me hack that wall down?" the doctor asked.

"Why should I?" Clara's pique became even more pronounced. "What has she ever done for me?"

"Clara, can't you see that if you help me to help Sybil get well, she will no longer stand in the way of your doing the things you want to do?"

Clara hesitated. "Sybil keeps reliving the past." Then she said, "I'm glad I never had a mother."

The doctor allowed the comment to go unnoticed, replying only, "We're going to free Sybil of the past."

"Yes, she wants to be free," Clara said edgily. "Wants to forget everything and not face anything."

"She'll have to face it all before she can be free of it," the doctor said. "When we hack that wall down she'll be free to realize herself. Tomorrow, begin telling Sybil the things you know."

"What things?" Clara asked uncertainly.

"What you have learned, feel, remember. . . ." the doctor coaxed. "Clara, listen. What I'm asking of you is for your own good, for the good of all of you. All of you must work together. All of you must try to reach Sybil. Don't you see what's at stake?"

The room reverberated with menace as Clara replied, "Sybil doesn't have to live!"

STANDING IN Dr. Wilbur's consulting room the next day was Nancy Lou Ann Baldwin. The traffic noises from the street below were to Nancy the dread sounds of explosion, for she lived on the outer rim of terror.

"I don't like things to blow up," Nancy said to Dr. Wilbur. "Exploding, always exploding. It's just as bad as a bomb when you're little and your mother throws blocks at you. You get dizzy and you see little spots running around. And there is noise, an awful banging. The worst of it is Mother is not dead."

"Your mother is buried in Kansas City. There are no explosions that will injure you now."

"I don't see how you know that," Nancy protested. "Mother can be buried in Kansas City and exploding in my mind at the same time. Besides, there are many other kinds of explosions. You can't keep the world itself from blowing up."

"The world is not going to blow up, Nancy," said Dr. Wilbur.

"Why, then, have they built civil defense shelters?" Nancy replied hysterically. "Why do we see signs of the end everywhere? In the final war, at Armageddon, everything will be destroyed according to prophecy. There isn't much time left. And I don't want the devil to win!"

A crescendo of powerful feeling filled the room. "Doctor"—Nancy's words were wrung out slowly—"sometimes I'm so frightened I'd rather die right now. I'd like to. But God doesn't let me. And suicide is wrong."

Dr. Wilbur answered softly, "Why should you want to die? There would be too much to give up. Loving people. Making things. Enjoying music, art, nature." Then she added meaningfully, "Getting together with Sybil and finding yourself."

The mood was broken. Terror was replaced by defensiveness. "Why are you cornering me?" Nancy asked.

"My dear, I'm not cornering you. I'm just trying to make you see that there is no reason for you to die."

"There are private reasons."

"What are they?" the doctor asked quietly.

"Oh," Nancy replied, "all of us are trying to get Sybil to do things, and it doesn't work. Being linked with Sybil is a constant frustration. But then I'm very close to the Peggys, and you know how they feel about Sybil. Sybil makes Peggy Lou simmer."

Suddenly shifting into a relaxed mood Nancy explained, "I'm so close to the Peggys I took both their middle names. But they use Dorsett. I'm Nancy Lou Ann Baldwin. Miss Baldwin was a teacher Sybil pretended to be at the time I came."

"What are the other private things that worry you, Nancy?" the doctor wanted to know. "What do you want to do that you can't?"

"Walk on legs that are not weak," was the surprising reply.

"We can fix it so you can," the doctor promised. "If you and Clara and some of the others would join Sybil . . ."

"Excuse me, Dr. Wilbur," a voice that was not Nancy's interrupted. "I think I should say something here."

The doctor knew the voice well. "Yes, Vicky?"

"I think you're making a mistake in telling Nancy that. You see, Sybil has the same fears and worries that Nancy and Clara have—not only about religion but also depression and suicide ideas—much more than they've said here. I don't think it is sensible to try to bring Nancy and Clara closer to Sybil at this time because I'm not sure that even I am strong enough to fight all of that."

"It would be a mistake," Dr. Wilbur informed Vicky, "if I weren't going to do anything to change the worries of Nancy and Clara. Right? But I have every intention of doing so."

"All right," Vicky replied, "but remember my warning."

WITH THE revelation of the five new selves Dr. Wilbur realized that the case of Sybil Dorsett, precipitated not by one trauma but by many, was more complex than any yet reported.

The multiple roots of Sybil's complexity—the schizophrenic mother aided and abetted by the peripheral, passive father; the naïve and hypocritical environment; and the hysteria of the religious faith, particularly as exemplified by Grandpa Dorsett—all these things had now been interpreted. But the doctor still did not know when the first dissociation had taken place. She did know that not all the selves had emerged during the first dissociation and that all who had presented themselves so far had been in existence by the time Sybil was twelve. Fourteen alternating selves were already in evidence. Were there more to come?

The selves, the doctor was now convinced, were not conflicting parts of the total self, struggling for identity, but rather defenses against the intolerable environment that had produced childhood traumas; their ages were different because each had emerged at a particular time in Sybil's life to battle a particular trauma.

The strategy of treatment remained what it had been—to uproot and analyze the traumas, thus rendering unnecessary the separate selves who did the defending. Integration would be accomplished by getting the various selves to restore to the waking Sybil the knowledge, the experiences, and the memories that had become theirs during those parts of her life that *they* and not she had lived.

Dr. Wilbur realized that there were risks. There was no assurance that uprooting a trauma would lead to integration of the self who defended against it. Sybil might be torn apart even more seriously by the very therapy intended to cure her. But the illness was so severe that all possible risks were warranted.

12

PEGGY Lou and Peggy Ann, Vicky and Mary, Marcia and Vanessa, Mike and Sid, Marjorie and Ruthie, Helen and Sybil Ann, Clara and Nancy. These fourteen alternating selves drifted in and out of Dr. Wilbur's office, with their own emotions, tastes, ambitions, desires, behavior, and speech patterns.

Each knew of Sybil's existence. Each was aware of the others. Sybil, however, had not known about the others until Dr. Wilbur had told her about them. She had refused to meet them on tape, had refused to accept them. They were still unreal to her. What was real was the fact that she lost time. Only when time passed that was not lost did she feel she was getting better.

November and December 1957 had been such a time. Not once during this period had she suffered the anguish of finding herself in a strange situation without knowing how she had gotten there. Both she and Dr. Wilbur had dared to hope that they were entering the promised land of integration.

THE PROMISED LAND DISAPPEARED, however, on the morning of January 3, 1958. When Dr. Wilbur opened the door to her waiting room nobody was there. It wasn't until four days later that the morning mail brought a clue to Sybil's whereabouts.

Dated January 2, 1946, the letter was addressed to Dr. Wilbur at her former office in Omaha, and had been forwarded from there. Written in a childish scrawl on the stationery of the Broadwood Hotel in Philadelphia, it read:

Dear Dr. Wilbur,
   You said you would help me. You said you liked me. You said I was good. Why don't you help me?   Peggy Ann Dorsett

It was twelve years since Dr. Wilbur had left Omaha, and Peggy Ann's writing to her there indicated serious confusion.

Despite the fact that five days had elapsed since Peggy Ann wrote the letter, the doctor decided to call the Broadwood Hotel.

"Good morning," she said when the reservation clerk came on the line. She hesitated, not knowing whom she should ask for. "Do you have a Miss Dorsett registered?"

"Room 1113," the clerk replied. "One moment."

There was nobody in the room. At ten fifteen p.m. the doctor tried again and was told that Miss Dorsett had checked out.

She could only hope that Sybil would come to as herself, or that the personality who took over would return.

The next morning the doctor found Sybil in her waiting room.

"I've done it again," Sybil said sadly. "I came to in a Philadelphia street in a hideous warehouse district. This was even worse than some of the other blackouts. I don't know what was done in my name. Maybe murder."

The doctor replied firmly, "I've told you again and again that none of the others go against your ethical code."

"You've told me, but do you really know?"

"Sybil," the doctor ventured for what in over three years was easily the hundredth time, "I want you to hear the other selves on tape."

"No." Sybil shook her head decisively.

"It will reassure you," the doctor persisted. "When the Peggys tell me their story of Philadelphia, why don't I tape it? Then you can hear for yourself."

"The Peggys? Were they the ones? How do you know that?"

"Peggy Ann wrote me from the Broadwood." It seemed probable to the doctor that Peggy Lou and Peggy Ann had taken the trip together, as they often did.

"Philadelphia proves I'm not getting any better," Sybil said brokenly.

"In analysis," the doctor declared, "the further you go, the closer you get to the core conflicts, and the more resistance you have to face. You still refuse to meet these other selves on tape, so you still don't really accept them."

Sybil's mouth twitched uneasily.

"Some of them are little girls," Dr. Wilbur continued, "walking around in your woman's body. When the Peggys fled to Philadelphia they were running away from your mother. And because they are little girls, in a sense they keep you a little girl."

"Not only crazy," Sybil said with irony, "but immature?"

The doctor put her arm around Sybil and spoke with intensity. "Don't ever call yourself crazy again. Yes, you are fragmented, but yours is not the fragmentation of a schizophrenic. You are sane, sane enough to have survived a terrible childhood and to have made so much of yourself. Now tell me about your experiences in Philadelphia. Talking will help."

The doctor wished she could also talk to both Peggys. At this stage of the analysis, however, there was no way of summoning them. She would just have to wait for them to appear.

MEANTIME, Sybil returned to classes at Columbia. But she continued to live in terror. These others within her controlled her purse, transported her body, acted without her will. And always there was the fear that they had done things far worse than anything Dr. Wilbur had told her.

A month after the return from Philadelphia the doctor said, in a deliberately casual way, "I have Peggy Lou on tape. When you hear what she and Peggy Ann did in Philadelphia you will be greatly relieved."

Sybil's irises dilated with fear.

"Well?" the doctor asked. "It's going to have to take place eventually. Why not now? Only by getting to know the others can you make them part of you—make their experiences your experiences, their knowledge your knowledge. If this were a physical illness, would you tear up the prescription for a medicine that could make you well?"

"But will listening stop the blackouts?" Sybil asked desperately.

"Ultimately, yes. Shall I start the tape?"

There was momentary silence. Then Sybil nodded.

The taped voice was saying, "I heard the crash of glass in the chemistry lab. I left the lab because I didn't want to be scolded. I hadn't broken the glass, but I didn't break the pickle dish when my cousin Lulu in Elderville said I did, neither, and I was punished. It wasn't fair. The chemistry lab smelled funny. It made me think of the drugstore in Willow Corners. I was awful mad. I jist had to get away."

"Turn it off! Turn that thing off!" Sybil screamed. In the silence that followed she grew calmer and began to reminisce softly. "I haven't thought of the old drugstore in years. But I remember now." In the drugstore Sybil had inadvertently caused a bottle of medicine to crash to the floor, and there had come Hattie's accusing voice, "You broke it." When the glass had crashed in the chemistry lab, as in the old drugstore, Sybil's head had throbbed and the room seemed to swirl.

"How does this Peggy Lou know these things?" she asked.

"Peggy Lou is part of you. She defended you against the anger you felt at being unjustly accused. It's because of the drugstore and the pickle dish that Peggy Lou goes around breaking glass."

"Well, I wish she'd stop. I have to pay for the glass Peggy Lou breaks. I can't afford her."

"When you are able to get angry in your own right, Peggy Lou will stop and become one with you. Ready for more?" Though Sybil did not reply the doctor once again set the tape in motion. Peggy Lou's voice resumed.

"So I thought I'd go to the Broadwood and enjoy myself. But when I got there all I had was our zipper folder. I told them at the desk that my luggage would be coming along the next day. So I went out and bought the wildest pair of striped pajamas I could find. Peggy Ann went with me."

"The pajamas." Sybil's expression grew taut with recollection.

Peggy Lou's voice continued. "I was happy in Philadelphia. I sketched and went where I pleased, and no one told me what to do. And then I was caught in a snowstorm. I had no overshoes or gloves, and I was cold. I thought, I'll let Sybil have the body."

"You see?" the doctor said. "Peggy Lou is no monster. Shall we start listening tomorrow to tapes of the other selves?"

BUT so resolute was Sybil's resistance that Dr. Wilbur took the matter up with Vicky. "I told Sybil about you and the others. It doesn't seem to make any difference. I can't get her to accept your existence. I can't get her to remember things that happen to you. Vicky, there must have been a time before the first dissociation when Sybil was a whole person. I've often wondered when it all began."

"Would it help," Vicky mused, "if I told you about the first time I came?"

"You mean in the sixth grade after Danny Martin left Sybil?"

"That," Vicky explained, "was when I decided to enter the world as an active personality. But I existed long before then. We were three and a half when I first came."

Dr. Wilbur listened intently to Vicky's remarkable narrative.

"On a day in early September, 1926, we were driving with Sybil's parents from Willow Corners to St. Mary's Hospital in Rochester, Minnesota. The doctor there diagnosed tonsillitis. We liked it at St. Mary's. The doctor was tall and young. When he came into our room he always picked us up, hugged us, and said, 'How's my big girl today?' He looked at our throat and let us look at his. The doctor laughed, and we laughed, too. He held us high in the air and we could see that one of his cuff links was loose. We told him we would fix it.

" 'All right, honey,' he said.

"Nobody had ever called us *honey* before. Then we fixed the cuff link and turned it through that little hole in his shirt sleeve.

" 'That's wonderful,' he said.

"When he left our room we hoped he would come back soon. But when he did come he didn't look at our throat. He didn't pick us up. He just smiled and said, 'I have good news for you. You're going home.'

"Our arms went around his neck. We looked into his face and asked, 'Would you like to have a little girl?'

"He had liked the way we fixed his cuff link. We were sure he would like to have us do it all the time. We waited for him to say, Yes, I want a little girl. But he didn't. He just turned away.

"When we came to the hospital I was part of Sybil. But the moment the doctor left us, we were no longer one. As that white coat moved through that door, I became myself."

Dr. Wilbur was not surprised that the first dissociation had occurred this early. The analysis had already revealed that during a visit to the Anderson family home in Elderville when Sybil was four she had become Marcia. And in reconstructing the lost two years between the third and the fifth grades Sybil had made it clear that that had not been the first dissociation.

LATER during the same hour Peggy Lou talked about St. Mary's. "Were you there?" Dr. Wilbur asked.

"I went there as part of Sybil," Peggy Lou replied. "But when that white coat left us helpless I became myself. Well, not exactly. Peggy Ann and I were one then. We were called Peggy Louisiana."

Although the little girl who was called Sybil rode with her parents from Rochester to Willow Corners, in the car were two different children, Vicky and Peggy Louisiana. Not wanting to go home, Sybil had sent two internal defenders to represent her. The original child had temporarily ceased to be. From that moment forward there was much that Sybil didn't see, much that would remain concealed from her for thirty-nine years.

These newcomers contained between them everything that Sybil had lost. In Peggy Louisiana there had been invested all of the original child's assertiveness, all of her rage. To the one who would later be called Vicky had gone most of the original child's confidence and capacity to find her way in the world. In Vicky, too, was centered the continuity of memory and the ability to see life whole. For Sybil, the waking self, this was the beginning of time unremembered, of time stolen by those who came to defend her.

The original defenders, Peggy and Vicky, later produced progeny of their own. It was a very special "family tree." By 1935 Sybil, who was then twelve years old, had become all of the fourteen selves who had thus far presented themselves in analysis.

Dr. Wilbur had established that Vicky's "line" consisted of Marcia, who appeared in 1927, Mary (1933), Vanessa (1935), and Sybil Ann, whose precise date of arrival was not known. Peggy's "line" consisted of Peggy Ann and Peggy Lou (1926); Nancy, arrival date undetermined; Sid and Mike, who made their entrances in 1928.

For Ruthie, Helen, Marjorie, and Clara, the doctor noted, she had heard of no antecedents.

Now Dr. Wilbur knew that the first dissociation had taken place in St. Mary's Hospital when Sybil was three and a half.

It was now also possible for the psychiatrist to associate childhood events with the fears Peggy Lou had expressed in the early days of analysis. Sybil Dorsett's fear of getting close to people was an extension of her fear of getting close to her mother. The hands the patient feared were her mother's hands, instruments of torture. The fear of music had many sources: being tied to the piano leg while Hattie played; Hattie's unrelenting harping when Sybil herself tried to play; Willard's insistence that she study the guitar as an ersatz solution to her psychological problem. It was clear why Vicky had invented a loving mother of her own. It was also clear that the fourteen alternating selves, who had started out constructively but had become destructive to Sybil, would have to be integrated before the original self could be restored.

The doctor reached for one of the essays she had asked Sybil to write for her as part of the therapy:

Philadelphia really hit hard. I had thought for the first time with no doubts that the losing time part was gone forever. Now I'm as tightly bound as I've ever been. The tension is so great and the despair. I can't find peace. . . . I am ready to fight or accept or whatever, but how do I make the inside me accept what the outside me hears? I gather from what you have said that this is what I need to do. I've tried, but I can't seem to. All I do is panic. The only thing that really helps is when you and I work out some problem or memory. Then I get relief for a while before something else starts in again. I don't know what to do. I sometimes think what's the use? When will I make decisions as "me"? *Is* there NO WAY OUT?

13

THERE WERE occasional triumphs in Sybil's fragmented existence: "Awoke as me." "Stayed myself." But still, almost four years after the analysis began, she continued to experience intervals of lost time. When Sybil woke as someone else Teddy Reeves accepted it as a routine aspect of life in their common household. She would report to Sybil:

—"Mike was here for fifteen minutes at breakfast."

—"Vanessa was here at three a.m. 'I'm going to dress,' she said. 'I have a class. It says so on the schedule.' I made her go back to bed."

—"Mary came at two a.m. and tried to talk me into going with her to some other city. When I said, 'Not now,' she cried as if her heart would break."

What Teddy reported verbally, Capri, Sybil's cat, revealed through action. Sybil became expert, upon coming to, at inferring from the cat's behavior which of the other selves had been present. With Mary, for example, Capri was quiet, lovable. But with Peggy Lou the cat would become frisky and would race around the apartment before making its way to her lap or shoulder. "Nice old cat," Peggy Lou would say, holding the animal a bit too tightly. But Capri, who had no hesitancy about scratching any of the others, wouldn't scratch Peggy Lou.

"Maybe," Sybil quipped, "Capri is multiple, too."

ONE DAY a classmate named Henry walked Sybil home. There was an affinity between them. Both were from the Midwest; both loved music and books. And both were premedical students, for now that she had her master's degree in art, Sybil had decided on a future that included both art and child psychiatry.

Although Sybil was eight years older, her appearance was so youthful that she actually looked younger than Henry. On this particular day, reluctant to leave her, he offered her his notes covering the classes she had missed while she was in Philadelphia. "I'll go over the stuff with you," he volunteered.

She invited him in, and they worked simply as student to student with no surface insinuations of sex. She served him iced tea and cookies. Sybil enjoyed a pleasant two hours of wholeness.

As Henry was leaving, the mood changed. He put his hand gently on Sybil's shoulder. "I want you to come to the dance Wednesday night."

Sybil panicked. Refusing, she shrank from Henry's touch.

"Don't you like me just a little bit?" he asked.

"Of course I like you. But I don't want to date anybody," she replied firmly.

"You're too nice for that," he protested. "Lots of people like you. You're good company."

Sybil shook her head decisively. "No," she said.

"Then how about dinner?" he asked.

"No," she replied. "Henry, please don't press me. We'll see each other in the lab. I value your friendship, but don't press."

In the awkward silence that followed, Sybil could feel internal pressures, the interference of others. Sybil did not know that Vicky was thinking, He's nice. I can't see why she doesn't date him. Or that Peggy Lou was fuming, Jist like her. She never does anything I enjoy doing.

Henry tried to take her in his arms. "Sybil," he said, "I've liked you for a long time. Why can't we see each other?"

Extricating herself, Sybil reached for the doorknob, hinting that she wanted Henry to go.

"Are you sure?" he said.

"Very sure," Sybil replied. She shut the door behind him and bolted it.

Here she was, on the other side of a door that she herself had closed. She was thirty-five and an old maid—excluded by the phalanx of the married, a third plate at their dinner tables.

Henry. Male companionship. Perhaps the father of the baby Sybil so urgently wanted but probably couldn't have. Whenever a man had entered her life she had wanted his children even more than she had wanted him. And the desire for Henry, although deeply buried, *had* been there. But if she allowed herself to become involved with Henry, he would come to know her well and learn all about her. Then he would reject her. She had to protect herself against such an eventuality. No man must come close until she was well. She winced. Would she ever be well?

DESPITE Sybil's limited funds, clothes she hadn't bought continued to show up in her closets; paintings she had begun were completed in her "absences."

One day Peggy Lou picked up a glass dish in a Broadway store.

"Do you want the dish?" the clerk asked.

"No," Peggy Lou said, "I want to break it."

"Put the dish back," Vicky ordered.

Peggy Lou obeyed. They left the clerk thinking that the customer had been talking to herself.

Halfway across Madison Avenue, in heavy traffic, Peggy Lou and Vicky came to a sudden halt. "I'm going to the gift shop over there," Peggy Lou said, moving forward.

"I don't want to." Vicky turned and walked toward the side of the street from which they had come.

A traffic policeman yelled, "For heaven's sake, lady, make up your mind!"

For several months Sybil made repeated attempts to get to an art gallery to retrieve one of her paintings that had been part of an exhibit. Each time she tried, Marcia took her elsewhere. In the end it was Dr. Wilbur who reclaimed the painting.

Bored by female conversation in general, Mike and Sid sometimes succeeded in making Sybil break an engagement.

Sybil was overdrawn at the bank. She thumbed through the canceled checks. A check for five hundred dollars made out to Evans Real Estate? She had never heard of them. Earlier she would have regarded a check she hadn't signed as a mystery, but now she realized that one of the others had signed it. Nevertheless, when a telephone call from the Evans agency informed her of the closing formalities on "her" house in a New York suburb, Sybil panicked. Dr. Wilbur finally got a lawyer to rescue Sybil from the commitment. It had been made by Mary.

SYBIL could not mask the fact that her waking life since the episode in Philadelphia had once again become increasingly terrifying. Analysis seemed to be taking her backward, not forward. Her ambition to become a doctor was being frustrated by her blackouts in science classes. She could scarcely endure just being awake. Waking, she knew one of the others might take over. There was the everlasting internal pressure, the interference by the others. She felt isolated, useless, convinced that she was never going to get well. Overriding explanations, she refused to let the doctor come to the defense of the personalities.

Leaving the doctor's office one day, Sybil walked west along a crazy, swaying sidewalk. The buildings of the city seemed to stretch endlessly before her as she walked. She felt she had come to the end of the line. She didn't want to live this way. Why should she face life? she wondered. For what was she struggling so hard and alone? She was certain there was no way out.

She was nearing the Hudson River, brownish-green and deep. She envisioned herself in the water, sinking. Death would bring surcease. But before she actually reached the river, her body turned, propelled by another's will. The body, controlled by Vicky, found a phone booth on Riverside Drive. After dialing, Vicky said in a clear voice, "Dr. Wilbur, Sybil was going to throw herself in the Hudson River, but I didn't let her."

14

ALTHOUGH Dr. Wilbur continued to believe that straight psychoanalysis was the treatment of choice, it had become necessary to resolve the patient's intense anxiety and depression —to make her feel safer after her suicide attempt. Of the procedures suggested, Sybil chose electric shock treatments. When these proved ineffective she agreed to Sodium Pentothal, a barbiturate that is both an anesthetic and a hypnotic.

For fifty-six, and sometimes for as long as seventy hours after receiving Pentothal, Sybil came to know a sense of freedom that had never before been hers. Whereas previously she had shared none of the memories her other selves had, and had even forgotten some events of her own waking life, now, under the influence of the drug, these forgotten fragments began to filter into awareness. And very gradually, with Dr. Wilbur's help, what Sybil remembered under Pentothal she began to retain upon coming to again.

The sense of unreality that had been hers almost since birth was gradually replaced by a feeling of solidity. For the first time Sybil also began to experience not only the memories but also the emotions of the other selves. And she began to understand, too, what triggered dissociation. She now knew, for example, not only intellectually but emotionally, that "When I'm angry, I can't *be*." Anger was Peggy Lou's province.

Sybil came to regard the weekly Pentothal sessions as propitious winds before which she sailed with the speed of a schooner in a gale. That Dr. Wilbur visited her in her apartment when Pentothal was administered brought additional comfort. Feeling more alive, more interested, Sybil redecorated the apartment, made it more attractive for her doctor-guest. The jab of the needle, the not-infrequent swelling of the injected area, the occasional chill, the hiccups—none of these discomforts mattered in the light of the bright new day Sodium Pentothal had brought.

Integration, however, was still a distant goal. As the past flooded back, memories of childhood horrors returned—all the more reason to regress into the other selves, seeking defenses against the past. Yet there were glimmers of integration.

One came on a Friday night in the very height of spring. Seated on her bed after a tranquil three-hour sleep following a treatment, Sybil was thinking about the previous day, much of which had been a blank. Suddenly action was etched into the blankness. Was this memory? She did not know. If it was, it was memory of a different kind; for she was remembering not what she had done as Sybil but what she had done as Mary and Sybil Ann. Sybil was distinctly aware of two persons, each of whom knew what the other was doing and saying. Together these two persons went to the supermarket, bought groceries, conversed about prices.

Perhaps the most extraordinary aspect of the recollection was that Sybil remembered that at one moment she had been Mary, at the next Sybil Ann, and that when she was the one, the other person was beside her, a person to whom she could talk and express opinions and from whom she could seek advice.

This memory of the recent past was followed some weeks later by an even more confounding recollection. At breakfast one morning Teddy said, "I'd certainly like to know what Peggy Lou was talking about when she said that letters make words, words make paragraphs, and something about little gray boxes."

Sybil replied, "I haven't the faintest idea." But as she spoke, although aware of herself as Sybil, she felt at the same time like a little girl. It was not a matter of being childlike but of *being a child*. She found herself saying, "When I was young I was not allowed to listen to fairy tales or stories that were not 'the truth.' Nor was I allowed to make up stories. But I liked to write, especially animal stories and poetry. When Mother and Dad made me promise to stop, I devised a way to write without writing. I cut single letters out of newspapers and put them in little gray boxes, which I took to school. Then I'd paste the letters on sheets of heavy paper so that the letters made words, the words made paragraphs, and I could write without writing. You see?"

Bewildered, Teddy reminded her roommate, "But you just said that you didn't have the faintest recollection."

"I didn't," Sybil replied calmly, "but then suddenly I did. I remember devising that technique when I was in the third and fourth grades, after my grandmother died."

The third and fourth grades, after her grandmother died? The calm vanished as Sybil realized what she had said. Out of the mist Peggy Lou's memories were becoming hers. All at once Sybil realized that at that moment she had not merely *felt like* Peggy Lou; she *was one* with her. Pentothal had opened a line of communication between Sybil and one of her other selves to restore a fragment of the two lost years between the ages of nine and eleven. What had started as a casual breakfast conversation had become a milestone.

With the new feeling of being one with Peggy Lou there also came a wholly new attitude toward both Peggy Lou and the other selves. Sybil was now becoming able to distinguish what she did, as she put it, "as someone else" from what she did "as myself."

By Christmas, 1958, she had accepted her other selves with sufficient humor to include them in her Christmas card: "To Our Dr. Wilbur: Multiple greetings—Sybil."

UNFORTUNATELY, to Sybil, Pentothal became magic, and Dr. Wilbur the magician who could confer bliss. But the doctor didn't like Sybil's growing dependency on the drug. And although it had proved valuable in uncovering buried memories and lost time, in bringing Sybil closer to her other selves, it could not change the underlying problems. She decided to terminate this treatment. Accordingly, the first weekend in March, 1959, was bad not only for Sybil but for "everybody else."

"What have I done to make Dr. Wilbur punish me by taking me off Pentothal?" Sybil asked Teddy.

"Dr. Wilbur told us the decision to stop was for our own good," Vicky said. "I believe her."

But all weekend the Peggys nagged; Mary cried; Nancy, Vanessa, and Marcia stormed. Sybil, feeling her own despair compounded by that of the others, said to Teddy, "Dr. Wilbur isn't coming anymore."

And Vicky told Teddy, "You can't really blame them. The end of Pentothal is the greatest loss they've sustained since the death of their grandmother."

By the autumn of 1959 Dr. Wilbur faced the fact that the Dorsett analysis was following a halting rhythm. Progress was slow, resistances strong. Sybil would show signs of marked improvement for periods; then one of the other selves would slide into depression, conflict, fear, self-destructiveness. All accomplishment suffered, and some accomplishments failed. One obvious failure was that Sybil dropped out of school—too sick to learn.

Dr. Wilbur's conviction that straight psychoanalysis was the answer remained firm. To speed up the process of integration, however, she was willing to experiment with other treatments as long as they posed no threat to her patient. Sybil was a hysteric, and the doctor knew that such people can easily be hypnotized; she had used hypnosis successfully with other patients.

Toward the end of a gloomy and unfruitful analytic hour she said, "Sybil, when you first came to me in New York, you asked me to promise that I would not hypnotize you. But now I believe hypnosis can help us."

Sybil replied quietly, "I have no objection."

The journey toward becoming one entered a new, intensified phase. Now, cradled by hypnotic slumber, Sybil went back in time. The other selves went both backward and forward—forward so that, through gradual stages, all could reach Sybil's age.

None of the selves was essentially more intelligent than any other, but there were marked differences in what each had studied, learned, and absorbed. Differences in their ages, in the quality of emotions, in the degree of activity, and, of course, in the traumas each of the selves battled against accounted for vast differences in behavior. Integration, Dr. Wilbur knew, would be simpler if all the selves were the same age.

The doctor began one of the earliest hypnotic sessions by summoning baby Ruthie. "Do you remember me?"

"Yes."

"Ruthie, in ten minutes I'm going to say it is five minutes of seven. In that time you are going to grow up one whole year. Later the others are going to grow up too. Would you like to?"

"Yes. Then I can color."

"You may draw all you want. Or you may help Sybil paint. You will help everybody do everything. And you are growing, growing, growing. You will never be so young again. I want you to pick a nice day to grow in—a day you enjoyed."

"Aunt Fay."

"All right, you pick a day when you visited your aunt Fay in Elderville."

TWO MONTHS later the doctor told Ruthie, "In a few minutes you will be six, and it will be spring. You will never be any younger than that. Pick a day that was good."

"We're on the farm," Ruthie said. "Can Daddy help me make a grocery store in the haystack?" Ruthie had enjoyed the farm, where she was close to her father. "You dig a hole in the haystack and you put in the oatmeal box and empty cans and you make a store inside."

"All right. Now you are six years old. I'm going to help you to catch up to the others and to Sybil. Would you like that?"

"Yes."

"Now, when I touch your right elbow, I will ask to speak to Mike and Sid together. Sid. Mike."

"Hi."

"Hi. Would the two of you like to grow up?"

"Sure," Mike said enthusiastically. "Like Daddy."

"All right, both of you are going to start growing up. Now is there anything you would like to say before you are older?"

Mike posed a startling question. "You think the girls are going to kill us?"

"I don't know what you mean," the doctor said.

"There's a rumor," Sid said, "that the girls are going to kill each other, that soon some of them won't be. If so, will we die too?"

"Soon," the doctor said, "no one of you will be by yourself. All of you are going to work together. Nobody is going to kill anybody. And now you are getting older, older, older."

Dr. Wilbur felt reassured by the age-progression sessions, especially since genuine analysis was also taking place. Age progression was no mere mechanical process, no simple suggestion; it could advance only as the traumas and conflicts were resolved. It was being utilized as a means to an end.

BY APRIL 21, 1960, no one of the selves was less than eighteen. Sybil, however, was thirty-seven. Dr. Wilbur talked with Vicky about the importance of identity of ages. "I'm overwhelmed," Vicky said, "at the thought of being that old."

The doctor thought for a moment. "Vicky, you're the one who knows everything about everybody; you're the memory trace. Shouldn't you be Sybil's age when already you have all the memories of the years that make her older than you?"

"I suppose." Vicky was not enthusiastic. Then, lightly tapping a finger on the table, she remarked, "You're the doctor."

When the patient was under hypnosis Dr. Wilbur asked, "Is everybody here?"

Someone said, "Yes."

"Ruthie," the doctor called.

"Yes," said Ruthie, now eighteen.

"Mike," the doctor then asked, "would you like to be thirty-seven?"

"Sure," said Mike.

"Sid?"

"Sure," Sid said.

The doctor put the same question to Peggy Lou. "Well." Peggy Lou hesitated. "I'll miss my television programs."

The doctor laughed. "Thirty-seven-year-olds watch television."

Peggy Lou gave her consent, and none of the other selves had any objections, so the doctor announced, "We are going to start now. All of you are going to grow and keep right on growing. Fifteen minutes from now you will be thirty-seven and three months—Sybil's age."

Dr. Wilbur's voice assumed the cadence of hypnotic incantation. "You are getting older, older, older; you are growing, growing, growing: twenty-five, twenty-eight, thirty-one, thirty-three. In six minutes you will all be thirty-seven."

Seconds ticked away. Minutes passed. Waiting, Dr. Wilbur could not know that there was sudden rapture flowing through the senses that belonged to the fifteen selves of her patient. In every vein and fiber of Sybil there was a quickening newness, as she and her other selves moved to a new phase of healing.

The patient seemed relaxed. Finally the doctor proclaimed, "You are all thirty-seven and three months and will never again be any younger. When you wake up you will all be the same age."

"Will you love us now that we're old?" Peggy Lou asked wistfully.

"I will always love all of you. But you'll have more in common and will be able to share the things you enjoy."

Marcia asked, "Does this mean we can't call you if we don't feel well?"

"No, it does not mean that."

The doctor knew that the underlying fear Marcia had expressed for all of them was: Will I be rejected if I get well? To these troubled selves the end of treatment implied loss of the doctor, who had also become a friend.

"Now you are going to wake up," she began in hypnotic cadences. "One—stretch. You are waking up. Two—stretch, stretch, stretch. Now you may wake up. Three."

Sybil and the doctor looked at each other—their eyes mirroring one another's hope—the hope that a pathway had been opened on the journey toward becoming one.

THE NEXT morning Dr. Wilbur asked, "Sybil, would you like to meet the others?"

"If you want me to."

When Sybil was in a deep hypnotic sleep the doctor said, "I'll introduce you to Ruthie first. When I touch your right elbow I will ask for Ruthie."

Ruthie was summoned. The doctor waited. Then Sybil's voice said quietly, "I see her." The moment was charged with meaning. This was the very first time that Sybil had had a visual impression of any of her other selves, a signal that they existed within her *own* consciousness.

Sybil added, "Ruthie has her arms out. I think she wants me."

"Do you like her? Would you like to have Ruthie with you?"

"Yes, I want her. She belongs to me."

"She will be with you. She's as old as you and can help you."

"I want her help," Sybil admitted.

"How do you feel?" the doctor asked.

Sybil's answer was scarcely more than a whisper. "Happier."

"Now, Sybil," the doctor continued, "the others are right here. Choose the next one you want to meet."

"Vicky," Sybil said without hesitation.

"Very well. I'm going to ask Vicky to come. Vicky."

"Hi," said Vicky.

"Does she want to be friends?" Sybil asked.

The doctor put the question to Vicky.

"I should like to very much," was the gracious reply.

Suddenly Sybil was crying. "I have two friends now. They came toward me willingly." In a declaration of acceptance she said, "They are me, too."

Over the tears the doctor said, "Vicky is a part of you that is very likable. Why did you leave her behind?"

"I didn't. When I couldn't do something, Vicky did it for me.

I didn't leave her." For a moment Sybil was silent. Then she said, "I would like to go home." Instinctively she realized that meeting each of the selves involved facing the conflicts and traumas that each had defended her against.

"Very well," the doctor agreed. "I will explain to the others that meeting two selves is enough for one day. Then you can go."

"Peggy Ann," the doctor called.

"Yes."

"Does everybody understand why Sybil isn't meeting all of you today?"

"We certainly do," Peggy Ann answered. "It's all right."

The doctor said, "I'd like to wake you up now, Sybil. When you are awake you will know that you, Vicky, and Ruthie are together, that you will always be together, and that you will never need to be apart. Now you are going to wake up."

IN ALL analyses, periods of improvement tend to be followed by setbacks. Although Sybil had established an entente with Vicky and Ruthie she continued to resist meeting the others.

Then, one day, during New York's sultry summer of 1960, Sybil had been hypnotized and Peggy Lou had been summoned. Expecting Peggy Lou's "Hi," the doctor heard instead: "I say to myself Sybil."

Dr. Wilbur's brows were knitted in astonishment. "But I called for Peggy Lou."

"I am Peggy Lou, and I am also Sybil. I'm Vicky, too." Peggy Lou had obviously joined sleeping Sybil, Vicky, and Ruthie, not through the assistance of hypnosis, but spontaneously, of her own volition. But the merger had occurred in the hypnotic state, and the joining was not with the waking Sybil. The doctor could not be certain of its true significance.

Between July 1960 and January 1962 the analysis proceeded, traumas were resolved, and the massive residue from the past began to be chipped away. It was, however, a period of watchful waiting for the major breakthrough that would make Sybil *one* person.

15

O N A day in early January, 1962, Sybil and Dr. Wilbur were driving along the West Side Highway on one of their now frequent out-of-the-office visits. The doctor was at the wheel. Sybil, who usually enjoyed their nonprofessional moments together, was listless, gloomy.

"You're down," the doctor ventured, "because you're angry, and you've turned your anger against yourself. It's probably your mother."

Dr. Wilbur's eyes focused on the traffic ahead, but her thoughts were on the void that still clearly separated the conscious from the unconscious Sybil. Virtually all the other selves, representing the unconscious, had vigorously declared their hatred of Hattie Dorsett, but their reactions had not filtered into Sybil's consciousness. Dr. Wilbur decided that the moment had come for a direct onslaught. "Would you mind," she asked Sybil, "if I hypnotized you to get at the source of your depression?"

"Here?" Sybil looked at the doctor incredulously.

"Here."

Against a background of traffic noise came the hypnotic chant, and Sybil drifted into sleep. "You're supposed to love your mother," she murmured.

"Not when she doesn't earn your love," said the doctor.

"I wanted to please her," Sybil pleaded. "But I never could. I feel choked up when I think of her. She tied me down. It hurt terribly. She was always doing things—hideous things." Sybil's voice quavered; her body shook.

Dr. Wilbur held her breath. Sybil's voice rose. "I told myself I loved Mother and only pretended that I hated her. But I really hated her. When she died I thought for a moment I had killed her. I wanted to for so long. I wanted to kill my mother."

At this point Dr. Wilbur could see that the paroxysm of hatred, drained from the unconscious, was invading the conscious. The internal motion catapulted Sybil forward. Dr. Wilbur extended an arm to keep her from hitting the dashboard.

"I hate her! Even if she is my mother, I want her *dead!* I hate her, do you hear? I HATE HER!"

Sybil's fists pummeled the dashboard. Turning inward, she had reclaimed the anger she had denied since that day at the hospital in Rochester, when the original Sybil had ceased to be.

There was silence. The doctor decided to wake Sybil up.

"I guess I didn't think much of my mother," was Sybil's first remark.

Amazed that the patient had remembered, Dr. Wilbur countered, "On the contrary—you thought a great deal of her. And you wanted desperately to have her love you."

Smiling wryly, Sybil replied, "Wanting to kill your mother isn't very loving."

The doctor knew that another milestone in the analysis had been reached. Not only had Sybil remembered what she had said under hypnosis, but she had also recalled and accepted her death wish for her mother. Most remarkable of all was that once the capacity to get angry had been restored to Sybil, the pathways had been cleared for other emotions.

Hattie Dorsett, who had not really died until Sybil killed her with hatred on the West Side Highway, was no longer the major obstacle to her daughter's return to health.

THREE MONTHS later a letter from Frieda Dorsett, Willard's second wife arrived in Dr. Wilbur's office informing her of Willard's death. Sybil took the news quietly, but Mary, who had loved her father unreservedly, did not. Sybil didn't want to go to the funeral, and it was her decision that prevailed. But Willard's death was more devastating for Sybil than she could have remotely suspected. He had left his daughter penniless. The anger that so newly seethed within her precluded forgiveness.

Dr. Wilbur consoled her. "Sybil, you have always had strong Oedipal feelings for your father, but you've also always hated him. The original Sybil hated both her mother and her father."

With her allowance now ended, Sybil found herself barely getting by. Fortunately, she had dropped out of the premedical program, so there were no tuition fees. Her analyst, however, had to go unpaid—for the moment. As far as Sybil was concerned, this was a loan that would be repaid. For necessities there were her own slim earnings from intermittent tutoring, sales of her paintings, and a temporary job in a Laundromat.

MEANWHILE, the analysis was making measurable strides. Vicky was effectively bringing the various selves together by telling them about the past and the present of the total Sybil Dorsett. "The gang," Vicky told Dr. Wilbur, "is getting chummy."

No longer were there two Peggys but a consolidated Peggy Louisiana, and she was accepting with humor the prospect of becoming one with Sybil.

Then all of a sudden, just as Dr. Wilbur began to believe that integration was within easy grasp, Mary went into a severe depression. Sitting in the doctor's office in early June, 1962, she was so depressed that she couldn't talk. The next day none of the selves turned up for the regular appointment. Dr. Wilbur telephoned the apartment, but there was no answer. When she went to the apartment and finally managed to get in, she found Mary under the dresser. Extricating her, the doctor put her to bed. On succeeding days there were repeat performances.

On one occasion Mary fumed, "I'm in here."

"Where?"

"A place shaped like an igloo with no doors, no windows, and open above," Mary replied. "There isn't any way I can get to the opening up there. I'm caught."

When it became apparent that religion was the imprisoning igloo, Dr. Wilbur had to tear the igloo down by analyzing the underlying religious problem. The more they concentrated on religion, however, the more depressed Mary became. The greater Mary's depression, the more depressed—and more suicidal—became the total self.

Mary had not been deeply affected by Sybil's liberation from her mother, for Hattie Dorsett had not been one of Mary's major problems. As long as Mary had accepted Grandma's simple faith, life had been serene. But when she had allowed herself to be overwhelmed by the church which her parents and Grandpa Dorsett embraced, she had assumed the burden of religious entrapment that in some measure most of the selves, including Sybil, shared. For Mary there could be no resolution until she was freed of her religious conflict.

Wanting freedom from the religious distortions that hounded and divided her, yet wanting to hold on to her fundamental beliefs, Sybil realized that her problem was to salvage God while surrendering the nonessentials in which He had been enshrouded. This meant breaking free from a childhood environment in which religion was omnipresent, Armageddon table talk, and the end of the world a threatening reality.

"You see," Vicky informed the doctor, "Sybil always felt that this condition of hers was evil. As a little girl she thought it was a form of punishment, the handiwork of Satan. She often wonders whether she has displeased God. She's afraid that if she gets better, something terrible will happen."

BETWEEN 1962 and 1964 Mary remained trapped in her igloo, struggling between survival and suicide, between getting well and remaining ill. "We're all afraid to get well," Marcia confided to Dr. Wilbur. But there was also another fear—subtle, indefinable—a fear that Mike and Sid had voiced earlier.

"Am I going to die?" each of the selves asked Dr. Wilbur. The doctor's assurances that, although they would become one with Sybil, the individual selves would not cease to be were only partly convincing to them.

"There are many things I have to do," Vanessa told Marcia. "You see, I won't be here very long."

Then two new developments occurred that made the promised land recede even further.

Dr. Wilbur had thought that Mike and Sid had been integrated shortly after the age progression to thirty-seven. It had seemed probable that they would just yield to being the male that is present in every woman to some degree. But one day early in 1964 a crisp voice said to Dr. Wilbur, "I'm Mike, and I want to talk to you."

Belligerently Mike asked, "How long are you going on with this farce about integrating Sid and me with all these women?"

"But I explained to you long ago that you live in a woman's body and have to accept that fact."

"Then why did you make us men? A godlike sort of thing to do. Doesn't it bother you?" Mike was cornering the doctor as some of the other selves had complained she cornered them.

"I didn't make Sid and you men," she finally replied. "Just as you were never really boys, you're not men now. Where is Sid?" The doctor was stalling for time.

"Right here," Sid answered. "Mike spoke for both of us. Now that our dad is dead we're the men in the family, and no sissy doctor is going to stand in the way."

"Whether you like it or not, we're not going to be part of a woman," Mike added. "We're going to be men in our own right. And we aren't going to help Sybil as we did in the past. We're not going to build anything for her or play Mr. Fixit in her house."

With Mike and Sid in revolt and Mary still in the igloo, Dr. Wilbur had to summon once again the patience that had sustained her through the previous nine years.

THEN, in March 1964, though Mike and Sid were still fighting integration, Mary stepped out of the igloo. In an analytic session she announced, "The church doesn't matter. What is important is to live a good, Christian life and love your fellow-man." It was Grandma Dorsett's philosophy.

With Mary's problems resolved, Sybil was now well enough to hunt for a full-time job, her first since she had come to New York. In August she found one as a receptionist at a New York hotel.

She had been working there for a week when Ramon Allegre,

an accountant on special assignment to the hotel and soon to return to his native South America, asked her for a date. She accepted. From the first, her response to Ramon was positive.

The day after their first date Dr. Wilbur left for a medical convention in Zurich and an extended vacation abroad. Accompanying her to the airport, Sybil talked about Ramon. "I like him," she said with an unabashed forthrightness never before displayed. "He's asked me for another date tonight."

"He's rushing you," the doctor said, smiling.

"Is that what you call it?" Sybil asked. "It's been so long since I've had a date, I've forgotten the vocabulary."

16

RAMON ALLEGRE aroused feelings in Sybil that were entirely new. She had always been afraid to see the same person too many times for fear that the friend would discover her lapses of time or meet one of the other selves, and since the morrow might not belong to her, Sybil was habitually unable to make plans in advance. Now, however, she dared to be with Ramon through eight weeks of continuous dating.

They enjoyed concerts, theaters, art galleries, long walks in Central Park, and an occasional evening in Sybil's apartment. Teddy had moved out, and since then Sybil had permitted only two people to be really close to her: Laura Hotchkins, her friend from school, and Flora Rheta Schreiber, a friend and professional writer to whom Dr. Wilbur had introduced Sybil in 1962. Both women knew of Sybil's multiple personality, and Flora, whom Dr. Wilbur and Sybil had brought close to the analysis, had met the other selves. But Ramon knew nothing about her condition. In seeing him, Sybil was declaring her confidence in her own ability to remain herself.

Indeed, it was while cooking dinner one Thursday evening, waiting for Ramon to appear, that Sybil suddenly realized she was no longer incapable of loving or of personal involvement. Shortly before meeting Ramon she had confided in Flora, "I can't feel anything. How can you feel when you're too busy with the feelings that complicate your existence to have any others?"

But now Sybil found herself in the grip of an intense feeling for Ramon. Was it love? This feeling was as new as the sense of solidity that had replaced the floating sensations of the past. Was she well? she wondered. Was it health that had brought her to a metaphorical gate, through which she was reentering the world?

What lay beyond the gate? Sybil didn't know. She had glimpsed the world of well people, yet she knew that she was still set apart. Despite Dr. Wilbur's absence, not once during these eight weeks with Ramon had she dissociated. Even so, she was aware that some of her other selves still existed. Vicky and Peggy were close to her now, but some of the others had never been close, and they were still fighting integration. She also admitted to herself that romance had not banished her depressions and suicidal feelings: even during these eight weeks there had been tugs of despair.

She went into the bedroom to dress, and looked into the mirror. She was not displeased with what she saw. At the age of forty-one she was waiting for Ramon with a teenager's expectation. For the very first time she was experiencing love.

The doorbell roused her. There stood Ramon, holding a bouquet of roses. *"Cara,"* he said, kissing her. "I missed you." It had been precisely two hours since they had seen each other at the office, less than twenty-four hours since their last date.

"I missed you, too."

To Sybil, who often thought of people, moods, and things in terms of specific colors, Ramon seemed all brown, like the earth. He took her in his arms so easily, touched her so expressively, that although another person's slightest touch had once been abhorrent to her, she did not withdraw.

"A new drawing, *cara?"* Ramon's eyes rested on a black and white chalk drawing. "A self-portrait?"

Sybil was embarrassed. It was Peggy's drawing of her.

"I've always liked that one," Ramon commented, walking toward an abstract blue figure on a background of darker blue. Sybil felt more comfortable. That painting was her own.

"Notice the shading," she said. "All the shades of blue that are love."

"I never thought of love as blue," Ramon replied.

"I always have," Sybil answered. "Blue as the sky, the sea."

Ramon studied the painting. "It does create an impression of love," he admitted. Then, looking at other drawings and paintings in which figures of children predominated, he observed, "Have you declared war on the adult world?"

Sybil laughed teasingly. "Not exactly. But one of my recurrent motifs is a large house in which many brothers and sisters stand in a row. I suspect it's because I'm an only child."

"That's just about the first thing you've told me about your past. After eight weeks I didn't even know that."

The remark made Sybil uneasy. Careful to withhold the truth about herself, she had repressed her entire autobiography.

"All I really know about you," Ramon continued, "is that you are my age and that, like me, you have never married. Both of us have been busy with other things I suspect."

The uneasiness became acute. Sybil changed the subject, saying, "I'd better get the casserole out of the oven."

As they sat down to dinner Ramon, a Roman Catholic, said grace. Sybil found her thoughts wandering to Nancy's strong anti-Catholic feeling and Mary's entrapment in an anti-Catholic church. And she thought, How good it is that Nancy has disappeared, and Mary's religious conflict has been resolved. Unless these things had happened, Sybil mused, Ramon would not be sitting at this table.

After grace Ramon said, "I had a letter from my little niece this morning. Would you like to see it?"

"I can't read Spanish." But Sybil examined the letter with delight. "There are more pictures than words. Like me when I was six."

Although she had not met Ramon's niece, Sybil had grown fond of her and her two brothers, of whom Ramon talked constantly. She had come to think of them as Ramon's children because, after the death of their mother, Ramon's sister, and her husband in an automobile crash, Ramon had instituted adoption proceedings.

From the first, Ramon's strong family feeling had moved Sybil. As his story unfolded she had been deeply impressed, too, with his pursuit of his rags-to-riches dream. The eldest of nine children, he was the only one in the family to get an education. A scholarship saw him through college in his native Bogotá. In New York, by working at night and studying during the day, he had earned a degree from the Columbia University Graduate School of Business. An accountant now, he had secured a number of special assignments in first-class American hotels.

As Sybil returned his niece's letter to Ramon, he observed, "You love children."

"As becomes a schoolteacher," Sybil temporized. "Even though it's been years since I've taught. I've been so involved with graduate work, you see." She felt uneasy at having allowed threads of the past to become entwined with the present.

"You should have married," Ramon said. "You would make a wonderful mother."

The room was still. Sybil's thoughts wandered to her childhood. She remembered how she had pretended that she was a mother to her dolls, how she had planned for each of them. Now she suddenly realized that never once in these games of let's-pretend had she considered actually bearing a child. Ramon's ready-made family coincided with her early fantasy. As she served coffee, she thought, I can probably never have children of my own, but I could love these children.

Ramon turned on the radio for the news. A commentator was talking about a psychiatrist's testimony in a murder case. Ramon said with irritation, "People with real troubles don't need what you Americans call a shrink. Latins and Europeans don't indulge in the silly luxury of psychiatry."

Silence.

"Are you angry about something, *cara?* I didn't offend you?"

"Oh, no, Ramon." She looked at the brown hair, the dancing eyes. How little he understood. He could never understand the emotions that had complicated her existence.

Sybil arose from the table to kneel at the fireplace. "These October days can be chilling," she said as she lit the fire.

"Let me help you, *cara,*" he said, kneeling beside her.

She thought, I want him to make love to me. I want to have a baby of my own. If only I could. I'm scared. For eight weeks my fear has made him afraid. We've touched and kissed but that's all. I want more.

Responding to her unspoken entreaty, Ramon caressed her. "*Cara,* I want you."

"No, Ramon." She extricated herself from his embrace.

"I love you, Sybil."

"I love you, too, Ramon. But I'm afraid."

"Afraid of me?" he asked, confounded. His look reflected both perplexity and tenderness. Anxious to advance his suit, he was also eager to protect Sybil against her fears. "Maybe it's not the right time." He put on his coat and walked to the door. "Tomorrow night," he said. "We'll have dinner, someplace we haven't been before." He kissed her fingertips and was gone.

After the door closed behind him, Sybil thought, What if he doesn't come back? What if he does?

On Sunday morning, as they walked together in Central Park, Ramon suggested a drive in a horse-drawn carriage. As they rode, he drew a small box out of his pocket. She gasped as he placed a diamond and ruby ring on her finger.

"We will marry at once. You will go to Bogotá with me for the children. Then we will return to the United States with our family. Are you happy?"

Torn by conflicting feelings, Sybil was silent. She wanted those children more, if possible, than she wanted Ramon himself. If she were their mother, she would be good to them, would

undo the terrible things that had been done to her. All that
had seemed beyond her grasp was now on her finger, symbolized by Ramon's ring.

"You say nothing," Ramon said. "Why do you say nothing?"

For a time the *clip-clop* of the horse's hoofs was the only
sound.

"I must have your answer at once, *cara,*" Ramon pleaded.
"We don't have much time. The children can't wait. I cannot have them unless I have a wife. And I cannot bring them
here to live unless that wife is an American."

Sybil opened her lips as if to speak, then closed them.

"Are you all right?" Ramon asked anxiously. Then, "You must
say yes. Yes has been in your eyes for many weeks."

Finally, in a low, broken voice, Sybil said, "I love you, Ramon. I want to marry you and help raise those children. But
I cannot."

He was baffled. "Why? There's no one to stand in the way."

She could not tell him that although she had no husband or
lover, there *were* people in the way. How he would mock her if
she told him that she was a multiple personality. He was like the
rest of the uncomprehending world. You could tell people about
any other illness, even other mental illnesses, but this one you kept
from all but a very few. "Give me time, Ramon."

"Sybil, we do not have time. It must be *now*. These children
must have a mother. I want that mother to be the woman I love."

Time, Sybil agonized. Time has always betrayed me. Who
would rear these children? Not Sybil alone but Peggy, Marcia,
Vanessa, Mary, Mike, and Sid. Ramon would never understand.

The other personalities were falling into place within her; she
was getting well. But while she had reached the threshold, she
had not yet crossed it. The gift of time could rescue this love, but
Ramon had given her an ultimatum: now or never.

"Ramon," Sybil replied desperately, "it's no use. I can't marry
you." Turning from him, she looked through the window,
fighting despair. Then she returned the ring.

"Woman of mystery!" Ramon spluttered. "Tell me the reason,

or I'll go away. You'll never see me again." At once his tone changed from anger to tenderness. "If it's something serious, you can tell me. I love you, Sybil. I will listen."

The "don't dare tell" of earlier days returned to plague her. But now she was not running away from the truth about herself as she had in the past. She was indeed a woman of mystery to Ramon; because of the years of analysis, however, she was no longer a mystery to herself. Her unconscious had paraded itself before her as perhaps no other human being's ever had.

The carriage came to a halt. Silence reigned during the taxi ride to Sybil's old brownstone. Then they were at the entrance.

"Will you reconsider?" Ramon asked. His face was shadowed in gloom.

"I wish I could," she answered.

How do I handle this? was her inner plea. In the past I didn't handle crises; I let the others act for me. But I'm not the same. Now I'm capable of facing my own problems. I'm able to see the distinction between romance and reality. Ramon loves me—but with strings attached. I love him, and I want the children, but he is turning time into the old betraying enemy.

"I wish you no ill," Ramon said, "and all good. But unless you change your mind, we shall not meet again."

"Must we part this way, Ramon?" she asked.

"The decision was yours, Sybil," he replied coldly. The avalanche had begun, but the crash came when he said bitterly, "You've rejected not only me but those children you claimed to love even without knowing them." He turned from her, walked a few steps, and returned to put the box with the ring in her hand. "Take it in memory of the life you rejected, of your refusal to live."

Sybil fled into the house. She had rejected Ramon, she thought, as she herself had so often been rejected. Yet she knew she had no reason to feel guilty. Ramon's efforts to inflict guilt feelings on her had not succeeded, and that realization gave her strength, for she knew her very salvation depended upon her commitment to her emerging health.

As if in confirmation of this insight, the first thing she did in the apartment was to empty the vase of the now-withered roses Ramon had given her three days before.

The next morning Sybil made herself go to work. But Ramon was not there. His special assignment had been completed, she learned, and he would not be returning to the hotel. No time. Ramon had meant what he said. At the end of the week, finding it too painful to remain where Ramon and she had been together, Sybil gave up her job at the hotel.

DR. WILBUR returned from abroad shortly after Ramon departed. She was impressed with her patient's growth, but troubled by the episode with Ramon. References to him in Sybil's letters had in no way indicated the seriousness of their relationship. The doctor felt that if she had been in New York and had been able to talk to Ramon, it could have been salvaged.

Sybil, showing her new maturity, insisted that that would have done no good, because Ramon did not understand emotional problems or mental illness, and when Dr. Wilbur urged her to write to him so that the doctor could then talk to him, Sybil said, "I must first know when I will be well."

"You're so much better," the doctor replied. "You wrote me that you remained yourself in my absence. Did that continue to be true even after you parted with Ramon?"

"It did. The others talked to me sometimes, but *I* ran things. But you haven't answered my question. *When* will I be well?"

"Sybil, I don't know. You've shown health in your relationship with Ramon. But Mike and Sid are still fighting integration."

Sybil looked steadily at the doctor. "You've answered my question. If you had told me I'd be well in a month, two months, three, I would have written Ramon and taken my chances on your making him understand. But time has betrayed me again."

"If he loves you, he'll understand. We can write him and try."

"No," Sybil said quietly. "Ramon is a practical man. He won't wait for a neurotic."

As Sybil left the doctor's office, she felt lonesome to the core.

She did not hope to love again. Yet there was triumph in defeat. Her grief over losing Ramon was terrible. And it was real, as surely as the emotions of the past had seemed unreal. But the new reality was good: in spite of her grief, she did not dissociate; she felt solid enough to be able to defend her place in the world.

17

"I'M AFRAID of life and going out into the world. Afraid of being rejected, cast aside," Marcia said under hypnosis in January 1965. It was a natural fear of reentry.

"I'm looking forward to being a well person among well people," said Vanessa. "Life is for living, and I've waited too long."

"I think," Mike admitted during the same session, "Sybil's worth more than she thinks she is, or Sid and I ever thought she was. People care about her—Flora, and Ramon."

"Maybe," Sid added, "Sybil can do the things Mike and I want to do but haven't been allowed to do. Maybe she *can* be the kind of woman she wants to be and do well in a career. With Mike's skill and my skill, I'm sure she can. What she wants to do is all right with Mike and me. We like the new Sybil."

THE NEW Sybil? Who am I? she asked herself. Dr. Wilbur asked the same question: Who is she? For although Sybil was not yet a whole person, she was no longer a mere waking self.

The only person to appear for the Dorsett appointment these days was this new Sybil. When Dr. Wilbur wanted to communicate with the other selves, she could do so only through hypnosis.

Shortly after Mary came out of the igloo, she and Sybil Ann had been consolidated. Vanessa, closer to Sybil than some of the other selves, had moved farther in the same direction. Marcia, who previously had voiced a fear of getting well, had done so by joining Sybil, after she, too, had accepted the death wish for Hattie Dorsett. Peggy did not appear even when summoned.

The newly emerging Sybil was very different from what Dr. Wilbur had expected. Since Vicky had all the memories and possessed more of the original Sybil than Sybil herself, the doctor had thought it might be a good idea to do away with all the selves, including the waking Sybil, and allow Vicky to be the one self. Yet the doctor discovered that Vicky, like all the selves, existed for the express purpose of masking the feelings that the waking or central self could not bear to face.

The answer, therefore, had been to preserve Sybil's waking self, as such, while returning to it all the memories, emotions, knowledge, and modes of behavior of the other selves, thereby restoring the native capacities of the original child. This was pioneer work for Dr. Wilbur.

She knew that all the selves had come close to Sybil. As Sybil changed, the other selves changed as well. There had previously been two levels of denial of Sybil's mother. Sybil had accepted Hattie Dorsett as her mother but had denied hating her. The other selves had denied that the woman they hated was their mother. But after Sybil's moment of purging hatred in Dr. Wilbur's car, the other selves had come to acknowledge Hattie. Even Vicky, whose parents had never come from France to reclaim her, finally had come to admit, "Sybil's mother is also mine."

In May and June 1965 Dr. Wilbur tapered off the use of hypnosis, except as a means of communicating with the selves who could not otherwise be reached. The days of Sybil's dissociation seemed over.

SYBIL now felt able to manage without Dr. Wilbur and was eager to prove her independence. One day she was in her apartment writing résumés for a teachers' agency with which she had registered in the hope of getting a job outside New York. Her fingers suddenly went numb. Frightened, she called Dr. Wilbur, but could not reach her. She called Flora. By the time Flora came on the line, Sybil felt numb all over. "I'm sick," she cried. She tried to say more, but the receiver dropped out of her hand. Pitching forward, she hit the wall, and then fell into an inert heap on the floor. It was there that Flora found her, black and blue.

Rising to her feet, Sybil seemed taller than her normal self. A cheerful voice, younger than Sybil's, exclaimed, "I'm the girl Sybil would like to be. My hair is blond and my heart is light."

Then she was gone, and Sybil was there. "I must have blacked out," she said.

Flora knew at once that the blond self who had emerged was not any one of the fifteen selves she had previously met. A new self at this stage of the analysis, when Sybil was nearly integrated? The immediate matter at hand was to get Sybil into bed, apply cold compresses to the injuries, and try to reach Dr. Wilbur.

"It was a major gastrointestinal upset," Dr. Wilbur told Flora later that evening, "accompanied by a waking seizure and spasticity. All through it Sybil was aware of what was happening."

Flora told Dr. Wilbur about the blonde. "The dissociation was brief, perhaps no more than a minute," she said.

"Last February," Dr. Wilbur replied thoughtfully, "I met this blonde in the office, although I didn't realize it at the time. Sybil had been talking; then she looked blank for a minute, as she did in the old days. Then I heard the voice you described. Only for a minute, a mere flash."

The next day in the office Dr. Wilbur hypnotized Sybil. Mary was the first to emerge. "We had a fit," she explained.

Vicky said, "In our room last night there was someone else."

"Blond hair—I saw her," Marcia added. "I don't know her name. Who is she?"

"A new girl but not new," Vicky said.

Suddenly the newcomer spoke. "I'm not really new," she said. "I've been around for nineteen years. I'm the girl Sybil would like to be. I've lived unseen. An adolescent while the others still remained essentially children, I've carried no childhood traumas. I enjoyed college, and I love New York. I would have joined sororities, would have had many dates, would have been a cheerleader. I love life. The only thing that has stood in my way is that I wasn't free to be myself, to face the world. But now that the others are about to face it, I shall go with them. My vitality will lend strength; my zest for living, buoyancy; my unscathed past, assurance. I, who have never been ill, will walk with Sybil in the world of well people."

"Welcome," said Vicky.

"You and I belong together, Victoria," the blonde replied. "Unlike the others, we were not cradled in traumas but in Sybil's wish. We are blond—the only two of all sixteen of us who are—because Sybil wished to be blond." She still had given no name.

In fact she was a dream girl—the girl who had stood with Sybil at the mirror, throbbing with adolescent expectations as they had waited for Ramon. Her stilted and stagy speech was the affectation of a teenager spouting her new knowledge and confidence.

"She's Sybil's adolescence," Vicky said. "She needs to be with Sybil now."

"Is there anybody else?" the doctor asked, as if she were reliving the first days of the analysis.

"Why should there be?" Vicky seemed to shrug vocally. "We didn't expect the blonde, true. But as she told you, she's been around for nineteen years, although inactive. How could she have been active? As a teenager Sybil was still carrying the weight of childhood. She bypassed adolescence except in a physical sense."

As Vicky's words trailed off, the blonde spoke again. "I held back," she said, "until Sybil fell in love. When I realized Ramon wouldn't work out I rose to protect the adolescent Sybil from heartbreak. She was an adolescent, you know, with Ramon."

"If Sybil still wants to feel like an adolescent in love, there's no reason why she shouldn't," the doctor said. "People of all ages do this. Sybil can integrate you."

"She has," the blonde replied. "I'm no threat to the final healing. In fact, I will make that healing faster."

"Have you been listening, Sybil?" Dr. Wilbur asked.

"I have," Sybil replied. "And I know that this part of me who gave no name is telling the truth."

The blonde's appearance proved to be the climactic episode of Sybil's illness. After that there were days when Sybil just sat and absorbed the emotions, knowledge, and experiences the other selves had shared with her. Meanwhile, a tremendous reorganization was taking place within her. The personalities of each of the selves blended with that of the others. The past returned, and with it the original self called Sybil, who had not existed as an entity since she was three and a half. Not everything came to a conscious level all at once, but two significant things did: normal memory and a new sense of time.

"Now, when I wake up, I know what I did yesterday and can plan what I'm going to do today," Sybil said. "Do you know what it means to have a *whole* day ahead of you to call your own?"

Through several hypnotic sessions that followed, Dr. Wilbur matched Sybil's memories with the memories of those selves who still had individual identities. *Not one of these selves had a single memory that Sybil did not also have.* Sybil's attitude toward these selves, moreover, had completely changed, from initial denial to hostility to acceptance—even to love.

In late July, 1965, the doctor asked, "How are things going, Vicky? What progress is there underneath?"

"I'm part of Sybil now, you know," Vicky replied. "We are one. I used to say, 'This or that event was before my time.' Now I say, 'It's after my time.' You see, I'm no longer completely free."

That was the last time Dr. Wilbur talked to Victoria Antoinette Scharleau. On September 2, 1965, she recorded in her daily analytic notes on the Dorsett case: "All personalities one."

SEPTEMBER 30 was moving day at the old brownstone. Sybil's furniture and paintings went to Pennsylvania, where she had obtained a job as an occupational therapist in a hospital, an interim position until she could get into teaching. She spent her last two weeks in New York in Flora's apartment.

On the evening of departure—October 15, 1965—doctor and former patient, two women who had taken an eleven-year journey together, began their separate journeys. The night before Sybil left, she finally said of Ramon, "I would have asked him to wait," adding, in anguish, "if only I had known that I would soon be well." And Sybil, once unable to cry, let the tears flow.

Epilogue

I, THE Flora in the story and the author of this book, have stayed close to Sybil in the more than seven years since she left New York. In sharing excerpts from some of her letters to me, you will get a glimpse of the new Sybil.

September 25, 1966: Just think, I've been here almost a year now. It is the first continuous year of my life. It's amazing how days fit neatly into weeks and weeks into months that I can look back on and remember. It's the greatest experience I've ever had. People take so much for granted.

All has gone well. Not all easy, but no trouble. I even got a raise in salary after seven months. I was so surprised because I had not expected any since I had signed a contract for a set amount. I'm still looking forward to getting back into teaching, however. There's a good possibility.

You asked if the private art classes I mentioned were for me or by me. The classes are in oil painting and for adults. I teach them in the studio of my home. Get that. My home.

August 11, 1967: You and Connie [Dr. Wilbur] must be the first ones to know my big news—big to me, anyhow. Found out for certain yesterday that I will be an assistant professor. Am so excited. They interviewed eighteen others, and I was sure I'd never have a chance, but the dean told me it was unanimous. More details and news soon. . . .

November 20, 1968: It's wonderful how well things are going. After a little over three years there are times when I still can't believe how lucky I am.

On June 6, 1969, Sybil wrote to say that she was coming to New York to represent her college at a convention. In the city that for eleven years had been her fragmented home she visited with me, but she also walked through the city alone. On July 2, back in her present home, she recapitulated that visit:

When I walked along the streets of New York, many semi-forgotten memories came back, but all without exaggerated emotions. I just recalled old times, remembering what the feelings had been like but without reliving them. As I revisited familiar places, however, I became aware of memories that were not recollections of what had happened to me but rather to one of my former selves. There was the dress shop where Peggy Lou had shopped, and a confrontation at the Metropolitan Museum of Art with Marian Ludlow, who had been Vicky's friend. Marian recognized me at once. Remembering her through Vicky, who was now part of me, I chatted with Marian, accepting her as *my* friend.

At times, of course, there was a sort of wistful regret, expressed in a letter of May 28, 1970:

I would have accomplished much more than I have if things had been different during all those years. Yet I think I have an insight into and an understanding of my students that I wouldn't have had any other way.

Something happened in class the other day that will amuse you. One of my students had been ill and had missed many classes. Struggling with an absence sheet, she couldn't figure out just how much time she had lost. "Miss Dorsett," she asked, "were you ever unable to account for your time?" I did a double take. "Yes. Why, yes," I replied as nonchalantly as I could.

WHILE SYBIL was recalling from a distance her experiences as a multiple personality, Dr. Wilbur was still living with the phenomenon at first hand. In seven years she had diagnosed and treated six more cases—five females and one male. She succeeded in integrating all of them, although one suffered a relapse and had to be integrated a second time. None, however, was as bright or talented a person or as complicated a case as Sybil Dorsett.

The causes of multiple personality continue to remain elusive, although the evidence in Dr. Wilbur's other cases as well as in

Sybil's points to at least one common cause: an initial family milieu that is restrictive, naïve, and hysterical.

That this one psychiatrist, fresh from an eleven-year exploration of Sybil Dorsett, was called upon to diagnose and treat six other cases in seven years seems to indicate—just by the law of averages—that this illness occurs more frequently than is recognized by physicians. It is not impossible that many persons who suffer from amnesia are in reality multiple personalities. At any rate, since the prognosis is very good when the multiple personality is recognized and properly treated, it is essential to explore further this too-often-ignored field of medical knowledge.

DURING the Columbus Day weekend of 1972, Sybil, Dr. Wilbur, and I got together to celebrate the approaching completion of this book. Sybil was so well that it was hard to remember she had once been otherwise. She is climbing the professional ladder. Her colleagues respect her, and her students love her. She has many new friends, owns her own home, drives her own car—and makes regular payments to Dr. Wilbur for the analysis that is now fading into a distant past. Her several art exhibits reflect the work of an integrated artist.

In short, Sybil is leading a whole life.

Flora Rheta Schreiber

The success of *Sybil* has had its effect on the orderly tenor of Flora Rheta Schreiber's life. It was disconcerting at first to learn that some readers had the impression that the book was about herself. Now she counters such misconceptions with a smile and a patient explanation: "I am the author, not the subject." Unlike Sybil, Miss Schreiber had a happy childhood, growing up in New York with enlightened parents.

She is not intimidated by the many public appearances that have come with her book's best-selling status, for she once intended to go on the stage. At nineteen she was studying acting and preparing for an audition with the prominent actress-director Margaret Webster. But when her turn came she walked to the front of the stage and heard herself saying, "Miss Webster, I'm afraid there's been a mistake. I don't want to be an actress. I want to be a writer." With that, she rushed out of the theater.

She went on to earn her M.A. at Columbia University, and over the years she has published hundreds of magazine articles. But it is with *Sybil*, her fourth book, that she feels she has achieved the dream of creative dramatic writing that she blurted out to Margaret Webster so long ago. "Although it is nonfiction," she says, "it has the structure and style of a novel." Besides being an author, Miss Schreiber is a full professor of speech and English at John Jay College of Criminal Justice, part of the City University of New York, and teaches writing at the New School for Social Research.

She still hears from Sybil, who remains an integrated person. Although Sybil is a pseudonym, Cornelia B. Wilbur is the real name of the doctor who worked with her. Some years ago Dr. Wilbur left private practice to teach psychiatry at the University of Kentucky's College of Medicine, retiring to the status of professor emeritus last June.

WILL ROGERS
His Life and Times

A condensation of the book by

RICHARD M. KETCHUM

Cowboy, Wild West show trouper, trick roper without peer, Will Rogers was one of the pioneer stars of vaudeville, movies, and radio. But more than that, he was a perceptive, tongue-in-cheek social commentator who could reduce complex issues to their essentials, humble the mighty, puncture the pompous. For an entire generation he was the witty and beloved spokesman for sanity, common sense, and steady faith in the American dream. That is why at his death a friend aptly said, "A smile has disappeared from the face of America." And that is why, in an even more complex and unsmiling time, Will Rogers deserves to be remembered.

"Once in a long, long time comes a book . . . and before you lay it aside your dinner has become stone-cold or you are mighty late going to bed. . . . [This] is such a book."—St. Louis *Globe-Democrat*

1

"My ancestors didn't come on the *Mayflower* but they met the boat."

LIKE so many Americans, Will Rogers was a composite of many worlds. He happened to be born in Indian Territory—in what is now the state of Oklahoma—in 1879, when nearly everyone there bore the scar of that shameful episode in United States history known as the great removal. This was the eviction in the 1830s of the so-called Five Civilized Tribes (Choctaw, Chickasaw, Creek, Seminole, and Cherokee) from their ancestral lands in the southeast, and their forced migration to lands beyond the Mississippi River.

To this day no one knows with certainty the origins of the Cherokees. When encountered by Hernando de Soto in 1540, the tribe had been living, for as long as archaeological evidence can determine, in a vast region in the southern Appalachians. There were probably about twenty-five thousand Cherokees then—farmers and hunters who ranged from the Carolinas and Georgia into northern Alabama, the Cumberland Plateau in Tennessee, and along the Ohio River.

To the white settlers Cherokees were "warlike"—a term frequently used to justify killing or removing Indians; but it might be more accurate to say that the Cherokees had an abiding unwillingness to be pushed around. And they were as proud as they were determined: as an English officer remarked, "They are like the Devil's pigg; they will neither lead nor drive." Continually fighting with their neighbors, they boasted that they could, on short notice, put six thousand braves on the warpath.

From 1730 on, English, Scottish, German, and Irish entrepreneurs were actively moving about the Cherokee lands, trading with the Indians, marrying Cherokee women and siring halfbreed children, and slowly turning members of the tribe toward white ways. Will Rogers' paternal great-grandfather, Robert Rogers, married a half-blooded Cherokee woman; his maternal great-grandfather, John Gunter, married a full-blooded Cherokee. By the end of the eighteenth century a great deal of such interbreeding had occurred.

Meanwhile other whites were pushing in the perimeters of the hunting grounds. During the American Revolution the Cherokees remained loyal to the king, for His Majesty's representatives in America usually respected treaty obligations, whereas the colonial frontiersmen tended to ignore them. The Cherokees fought the rebels long after Cornwallis surrendered—which did nothing to endear them to citizens of the new republic.

Will Rogers on Indians:
"They sent the Indians to Oklahoma. They had a treaty that said, 'You shall have this land as long as grass grows and water flows.' It was not only a good rhyme but looked like a good treaty, and it was till they struck oil. Then the government took it away from us again."

In 1791 the tribe negotiated a treaty with George Washington affirming "Perpetual peace" between the United States and the Cherokees and forbidding Americans to hunt on Cherokee lands; but never again did they know a President whose policy was to defend the rights of Indians. Presidents Adams, Jefferson, Madison, and Monroe were no friends of the Cherokees, while Jackson proved to be the worst enemy of all.

After the 1791 treaty the United States government forced the Cherokees into a number of others involving land cessions, and as their ancestral lands diminished in size, the Cherokees came to a truly remarkable decision—considering their independent spirit. They concluded that they would adopt the white man's ways, accept his missionaries and religion, and pattern their government on that of the new United States. This meant almost total abandonment of an ancient culture and its replacement with that of the educated Christian white, all in hopes of convincing the American that they were entitled to his respect and friendship. As a consequence, they came to be known, along with other tribes of the southeast, as "civilized" Indians. But they continued to be treated as savages.

Early in the nineteenth century the Cherokees added one more accomplishment to their list: they became literate almost overnight. Some credit for this must go to the presence of missionaries and to the continuing practice of intermarriage with educated whites; but the giant step was taken in 1821 when the Cherokee council approved a highly successful system of phonetics by which an intelligent Cherokee could learn to read or write his native tongue within a matter of days; a Cherokee named Sequoya had worked for about ten years to devise the system. By 1828 the newly organized Cherokee Nation had, in addition to its own written language and a newspaper called the *Cherokee Phoenix*, a republic, a constitution, a principal chief or president, a bicameral legislature, a supreme court, and a codified body of laws. It was a society, one might have thought, worthy of acceptance by white Americans. But no one who believed so reckoned with the cupidity the Cherokees were about to encounter.

In 1828 the Georgia legislature suddenly declared that it had jurisdiction over all Cherokee holdings within the state's boundaries and conducted a statewide lottery for distributing the Indians' land and homes to white residents. That same year gold was discovered in Cherokee territory. Those whites who poured into the region and who were disappointed in their search for the precious metal were consoled by their first glimpse of the magnificent deep woods covered with enormous stands of hickory, oak, chestnut, mountain laurel, magnolia, and azalea; broad, sunlit savannas where corn, cotton, and orchards bloomed; mountain pastures where cattle and horses grazed. Some of the Cherokee houses, on the scale of small plantations, were equally tempting. The whites took one look and began moving in.

The Georgians were abetted by President Andrew Jackson, who in his first message to Congress announced plans to remove all the southeast Indians to lands west of the Mississippi River. In May 1830 the Indian Removal Bill passed by a slim margin, and on May 23, 1836, the U.S. Senate ratified a treaty setting a date for the final removal of the Cherokees two years later. During that period about two thousand Cherokees—deciding to leave while they could still take their belongings with them—made their way to the lands bordering the Arkansas River, leaving about fifteen thousand fellow tribesmen behind.

The major exodus began on May 23, 1838, according to schedule, supervised by army regulars who treated the Indians with kindliness and respect, and by Georgia volunteers, who urged on the laggards at bayonet point. As one regular recalled years afterward, "I fought through the Civil War and have seen men shot to pieces and slaughtered by thousands, but the Cherokee removal was the cruelest work I ever knew."

The summer of 1838 saw the worst heat and drought men could remember, and the Cherokees obtained permission from the army to conduct their own removal in October, after the drought abated. Then about fourteen thousand of them set out on the thousand-mile trip toward an unknown land.

In camps along the way most of them had only tents and blankets to protect them from the severe early winter; at tollgates they were charged outrageous prices; merchants and farmers gouged them mercilessly when they tried to buy food; their wagons bogged down in the November rains. Their number included old people, newborn babies, pregnant women, the halt, the lame, the blind, many of them suffering from disease. Along the line of march they left the shallow graves of four thousand—nearly one-fourth of the entire Cherokee Nation. Ever afterward the Indians called it the Trail of Tears.

When at last this caravan of heartbreak and misery arrived in Indian Territory, it was to find that its predecessors in the removal—those who had gone to Arkansas and beyond—were now firmly entrenched. They had their own farms, mills, and stores, none of which they were eager to share with the new arrivals. For a time the two groups came close to civil war, and not until 1846, when the Cherokees were given land in what is now eastern Oklahoma and were reimbursed to some extent for their losses in the southeast, did anything like harmony prevail in the re-located nation.

AMONG the hundreds of Cherokees who had moved west in anticipation of the removal were Robert Rogers and his wife, Sallie Vann. Robert Rogers' father—also named Robert—was a white man, his mother was part Indian; Sallie was one-fourth Cherokee and three-quarters Irish. They settled in 1835 or 1836 in the Going Snake district in what is now Oklahoma, where Rogers established a ranch. When a child was born to the couple in 1839, Robert Rogers had only one more year to live. It is with this son, Clement Vann, that the story of Will Rogers properly begins.

Clem grew up on his father's ranch. He hated school and did not get along with his stepfather, William Musgrove, whom his mother married when Clem was five. At the age of seventeen he left home to find a new life in what was called the Cooweescoowee country, bordering the Verdigris River. His mother and his long-suffering stepfather gave him twenty-five longhorns, a bull, four horses, supplies for the ranch and trading post he intended to start, and two slaves, brothers named Rabb and Huse.

In 1856 the Cooweescoowee district was virgin land, held in common by the Cherokee Nation for use by any of its members. Wild turkeys, quail, and prairie chickens were as "thick as blackbirds." In the Verdigris bottomland were wild geese, flocks of green parakeets, deer, wolves, and panthers. While his two slaves planted corn for feed, young Clem turned his cattle out on the bluestem grass that stretched unbroken for miles. His trading post flourished, and several years later he married a tall, dark-haired girl named Mary America Schrimsher, whom he had met in Tahlequah. A quarter-breed Cherokee, Mary had attended a Cherokee school in Arkansas and may have gone to the Cherokee-run Female Seminary near Tahlequah.

When she moved to Clem's ranch the only neighbors were a few scattered settlers, itinerant fur traders, and Osage Indians who came to trade or steal. Life was not easy, but both the ranch and trading post were successful, and for three years Clem's future looked secure. Then, as so often in the past, the shadow of the white man fell across the Cherokee land.

IT WAS 1861, and the Rogers ranch was only thirty miles from the Kansas border, where Union and Confederate sympathizers were turning the prairies into a dark and bloody ground. The Indians were as divided on the conflict between North and South as they had been over the question of the removal (even the Negro brothers Rabb and Huse, Clem's slaves, fought on opposite sides during the war). John Ross, the principal chief of the Cherokee Nation, hoped to preserve neutrality, but Southerners were quick to see that the Indian Territory provided bases for raids into Kansas, a highway to Texas, and a source of supplies.

David L. Hubbard, the Confederacy's commissioner of Indian affairs, appealed to the Cherokees to support the South. "Go North among the once powerful tribes," he told them, "and see if you can find Indians living, and enjoying power and property & Liberty, as do your people. . . . If you can, then say I am a liar and the Northern States have been better to the Indian than the Southern States." Few could deny the logic of his message, and on October 7, 1861, the Cherokee Nation made an alliance with the Confederate States of America.

After sending Mary to his mother's home (where she remained for a time before finally fleeing to Texas with her parents and sisters), Clem Rogers enlisted in the Cherokee Mounted Rifles. He served as captain under Stand Watie, a leader of the mixed-bloods, who became a Confederate brigadier general in 1864. When the war ended, the federal government contended

Both Will's mother, Mary, and his father, Clement Vann Rogers, a big rancher in what is now Oklahoma were part Cherokee Indian.

that the Five Civilized Tribes had forfeited their lands by supporting the Confederacy, but it took only the western portion of their territory, as a future home for other Indian tribes. It was hoped that the tribes would unite in a territorial government that would one day become a state. A treaty referred to this potential commonwealth as Oklahoma, from the Choctaw *okla homma*—red people.

Returning after four years of war, Clem Rogers found the entire Cherokee Nation devastated. His own ranch had been overrun by troops and had grown up to brush; his cattle and horses had been confiscated and his slaves freed; there was no money with which to begin again. After joining Mary and their baby, Sallie, in Texas, he made his way back toward the old homestead by degrees, stopping for a year with his mother and stepfather in the Choctaw Nation. He then spent two hard years driving a six-mule freight wagon from Kansas City to Fort Gibson, saving enough money, finally, to buy some cattle.

In 1868 he chose a location for his second ranch, about seven miles east of the original one. This land, according to the traditional practice of the Cherokees, was free to anyone who would occupy and improve it. The region Clem Rogers picked out was a rancher's paradise. Rich grazing land abounded; the bottomland along the Verdigris River was fertile, and the river itself provided abundant water for livestock. The nearest towns of any consequence were Coffeyville, Kansas, forty-odd miles to the north, and Fort Gibson, sixty miles south in Indian Territory.

In the fall of 1870 Clem brought Mary to the new ranch, where he had constructed a log house, and three years later they began building what was to be their permanent home—a two-story structure of hewn logs, plastered on the inside and weatherboarded on the outside, with seven large rooms. Downstairs was the big, square parlor, with an open fireplace, the only piano in the Cooweescoowee district, and curtains hung with lace. Across the entrance hall was the family bedroom, where their children would be born; and in the rear were the dining room, kitchen, and a bunkroom for cowboys working on the ranch. On the second floor were two large bedrooms, eventually used by the Rogers daughters. When the house was completed in 1875, it was considered one of the finest homes in the territory.

Mary Rogers possessed a quality that made the ranch a warm, inviting place that everyone liked to visit. She was a gay, lighthearted soul with a fine sense of humor and a love of music and dancing; she was always asking entire families to spend the night and enjoy an evening of square dancing and songs. She and Clem were also known for their willingness to help anyone in trouble; friends remembered how Mary would travel on horseback or in a buggy, day or night, to take food to the sick. By 1878 seven children had been born to Mary and Clem—five girls and two boys—but three died in infancy, leaving only Sallie, Robert, Maud, and Mary. On November 4, 1879, the eighth and last child was born, a boy who was christened William Penn Adair Rogers for a Civil War comrade-in-arms of his father's.

At the time Will was born Clem Rogers was one of the most

successful men in the territory. His range included about sixty thousand acres, forming an enormous V or wedge between the Caney River on the west and the Verdigris on the east.

Clem Rogers bought steers in Texas, drove them to his ranch for a year's fattening on bluestem grass, then trailed them to St. Louis, the closest market. He handled as many as five thousand head a year this way. After assembling a herd in Texas, it took two or three months to drive it to the Verdigris valley, covering twelve or fifteen miles daily.

At dawn the cowboys would get the cattle to drifting along, grazing as they went; by midmorning they would push them closer together, prodding the lead steers to move faster. At noon the cattle grazed while the cowboys ate at the chuck wagon; then the process began all over again, with the herd moving northward until twilight. With the coming of darkness the men rode slowly around the herd in ever-tightening circles, moving the longhorns into a compact mass until they lay down for the night. All through the night the cowboys took turns on watch, circling the herd, softly singing to quiet the animals, always on the alert for the sudden noise—a clap of thunder, even the snapping of a stick—that would startle the cattle into a stampede.

A cowboy had to be as skilled at his trade as any craftsman, and the horse he rode almost human in its understanding of what was required of it. Clem Rogers loved fine horses, and he purchased or raised some of the best in the territory. On the trail they knew how to move quietly and slowly; they could swim rivers and avoid potholes at night; and they were absolutely essential in every aspect of the cattle business—cutting out steers, tying, branding, penning, and shipping them.

By the time Will Rogers was old enough to know what was going on around him, the pattern of life at the ranch was well established, and it was a good one indeed. In 1890 there were three dwellings, seven other structures, three farms, three hundred enclosed acres, three hundred acres under cultivation. Improvements were valued at $15,000, and the ranch was producing three thousand bushels of corn and a thousand bushels of wheat, along with oats, apples, mules, goats, domestic fowl, and—of course—cattle and horses.

As Will's wife wrote years later, many people thought—because he was careless about his speech and dress and manners—that he was "a poor, uneducated cowboy who struggled to the heights from obscure beginnings." True, he had no college education, she said, but that was because he would not go to school. And as for his being poor, "the truth is that, as the only surviving son of an indulgent father"—his older brother Robert died when he was two—"Will had everything he wanted. He had spending money and the best string of cow ponies in the country. No boy in the Indian Territory had more than Clem's boy."

2

"Three years in McGuffey's Fourth Reader, and I knew more about it than McGuffey did."

IN NEARLY every respect Will Rogers' growing up was close to the nostalgic ideal of a nineteenth-century boyhood. The hard, lean years of the frontier were passing—for the Rogers family, certainly—and life was full of the joys of a childhood in rural America. From the time he could walk, Willie—as everyone called him—was riding a horse or working a rope in his hand. He was given his first pony at the age of five. His mother worried about him; watching the little sorrel mare rear up on her hind legs when Willie tried to pull himself into the saddle, she would cover her face and call to his father, "Clem, you're going to get my boy killed." But Willie was determined, fearless, and he had the advantage of all Oklahoma youngsters, he said later: "I was born bowlegged so I could sit on a horse."

Will spent the long, golden days of youth galloping hell-bent across the prairie, or riding to the swimming hole, hollering to his companions, "Come on, fellers, the last one in is a Ring Tail Hoss!" There were always plenty of friends to play with—white, Negro, and Indian children—and usually something exciting was going on at the ranch. Neighbors stopped by for a visit or a picnic; it was even an outing to go for *The New York Times*, which had to be picked up at the nearest post office, twelve miles away.

More than anything else, Will liked roping, and he spent hours learning to throw a rope under the guidance of Uncle Dan Walker, a Negro cowboy who worked for Clem. When he was older there were days at a stretch when instead of riding the range as he was supposed to do, he would find a shady place and practice "cutting curliques" or lassoing prairie dogs.

When he was six his oldest sister, Sallie, married a man named Tom McSpadden, and later that year Willie embarked on his first experience with education. He

On education: *"There is nothing as stupid as an educated man if you get him off the thing he was educated in."*

went to live with the McSpaddens, whose farm was near a schoolhouse, and every morning Sallie would help him tie his dinner pail to the saddle horn and make certain he headed for the classroom. The schoolhouse was a small, one-room log cabin, and all the students—most of them Indians—rode horseback or walked for miles to get there. Will hated the routine and the endless drills, and he spent most of his time racing with the Cherokee children, on foot or on horseback.

When it was apparent that this school was not going to take, Will was sent off to Harrell International Institute in Muskogee, a girls' boarding school which his sister Mary attended. The Reverend T. F. Brewer, president of the school, had an eight-year-old son and decided that the two boys could attend classes with all the young ladies, but Will said he felt just as Custer did when he was surrounded by Indians. The experiment was not successful, and before long Mr. Brewer was writing to Clem: "I regret to inform you that your son is not doing well in school and would suggest you remove him."

About this time Will's mother fell ill with amebic dysentery. Everything that could be done for her was done; but on May 28, 1890, Mary America Rogers died and was buried in a family cemetery on the ranch, beside her son Robert and the three infants. Will and his mother were alike in many ways: her gentle manner, sense of humor, love of music, and her easy way with people were some of the traits the boy inherited. Will's wife said later that he never got over his mother's death; he cried when he told her about it years afterward, and he once wrote, "Mamas name was Mary and if your Mother was an old-fashioned Woman and named Mary you dont need to say much for her, everybody knows already."

That fall Will was hustled off to yet another school, this time in Tahlequah, and he liked it no better than its predecessors. Next his father sent him to Willie Halsell College (roughly the equivalent of a junior high school) at Vinita, about forty miles from the ranch. Most of the pupils were boys and girls with whom Will had grown up, and he spent four happy years there.

Now his father insisted that he attend Scarritt Collegiate Institute in Neosho, Missouri, but at the end of the first term Will unexpectedly appeared at the ranch. He had been expelled. Clem was not pleased, and announced to his son that he was sending him to Kemper Military School in Boonville, Missouri.

WHEN Will showed up to begin what would now be called sophomore year in high school, he cut quite a figure; he had on a cowboy hat, a flannel shirt with a fiery-red bandanna at his throat, a brightly colored vest, and high-heeled boots with red tops and spurs.

Along with his luggage were lariats of various sizes, for all the cadets to see. Will had had his eyes opened to another side of the roping art at the Chicago World's Fair in 1893. He and his father had seen all the wondrous sights at the exposition, including Buffalo Bill's *Wild West Show*. The high point of the visit for Will was a performance given by one Vincente Oropeza, billed as "the greatest roper in the world."

Oropeza, gloriously attired in an embroidered jacket and buckskin trousers with brass buttons, went through dozens of spectacular rope tricks, concluding with one in which he wrote

Will (left) never cared much for school. One of his two years at Kemper Military School in Missouri, he said jokingly, was spent "in the guardhouse."

his name with his lasso, one letter at a time, in the air. Will was hooked.

At Kemper, as at all the other schools, Will was bright enough, but his academic interest waxed and waned. In elocution class the students were taught to speak the classic orations—Marc Antony's "Friends, Romans, countrymen, lend me your ears," Patrick Henry's "liberty or death" speech, and others—all with textbook gestures; but Will never could resist an opportunity to get a laugh out of his audience, and his gift for timing and for misplaced emphasis often broke up the class.

He played football and baseball, but mostly it was the lariat that kept him occupied. Exasperated teachers were always taking ropes away from him, but inevitably he managed to lay hands on another. Between his fascination with the lasso and his distaste for cleaning his rifle, Will accumulated one hundred and fifty demerits, which had to be worked off by an equal number of hours of solitary marching. He would arrange for his penance to be paid off near the kitchen and then ask the cook "if he wouldn't do something for the vanishing American."

In the spring of Will's second year at Kemper the old wander-lust overtook him, and he decided to "quit the entire school business for life." Which he did, at the age of eighteen.

The first his father knew about it was when he received a letter from his friend W. P. Ewing in Higgins, Texas, saying that Will was there and what should he do with him?

Clem suggested that Ewing try to get any work he could out of the young man, and for several months Will stayed on the ranch before striking out for what looked like greener pastures in Amarillo, Texas. There, hearing of a trail boss who needed a hand, he arrived in time to listen to another cowboy applying for the position. "And right there," he said, "I saw a fellow talk himself out of a job." The other boy told the trail boss in glowing terms what a good cowhand he was, and by the time he had finished, the man told him, "I'm in need of a hand, all right, but I think you'd suit me too well." Will, having learned the lesson, said to the boss, "Maybe I could do the work." He was told to get on his horse and come out to the boss's camp. To Rogers, "Them was the happiest words I ever heard in my life." He rode seven days a week, rounding up cattle, roping and branding calves, as happy as a teenage boy could be.

On his first visit home he shipped his saddle by express and traveled himself by freight train. Clem and Will's friend Jim O'Donnell were riding through a pasture at the Rogers ranch when they saw Will galloping toward them. It was obvious, O'Donnell remembered, that Will was not certain what his father was going to say about his running away from school. "He started right in tellin' us all about workin' for the big cow outfit in the Panhandle. He didn't get very far, when Uncle Clem says, 'Son, go back to the house and wash your neck and ears and put on a clean shirt.'"

Later Will drifted out to New Mexico, where he worked on

other ranches, until he was sent to California with a trainload of cattle for the Hearst ranch. After they had been delivered, he and another cowboy went to San Francisco and put up at a small hotel. The next morning when they didn't appear, someone went to their room and discovered they had nearly been asphyxiated. The boys were used to kerosene lamps back in Indian Territory, and before going to bed one of them had simply blown out the gas jets. His father sent Will to Hot Springs, Arkansas, to recuperate, and when he returned to the ranch after another stay in Texas, Clem decided it was time for him to settle down.

THE fourteen years between Will Rogers' birth and his visit to the Chicago World's Fair of 1893 had brought immense changes to the old Indian Territory—changes that altered forever the life of the Cherokee Nation, and of the big ranchers like Clem Rogers. The final subjugation of the Plains Indians was going on, feverish railroad building was interlacing all but the most remote places in the West, and millions of acres of land were opening up for settlement.

In 1862 Congress had passed the Homestead Act, providing that any adult citizen, or alien who had filed his first papers, could, after paying a ten-dollar fee, claim 160 acres of the public domain, and—if he stayed there five years—obtain title to it. Thousands upon thousands of small farmers and stockmen moved west, gobbling up acreage, building sod huts, and erecting fences, applying the same relentless pressure on cattlemen that the cattlemen had exerted on Indians. Railroad owners whose lines crossed Indian Territory discovered that some of the Five Civilized Tribes—by their participation on the Confederate side—had forfeited nearly two million acres to the government after the Civil War, and that these "unassigned" lands had not yet been allocated to other tribes. Lobbyists pressed for legal seizure of this enormous domain, and finally the government capitulated, paid the Indians $1.25 an acre for the land in what is now central Oklahoma, and surveyed it into 160-acre parcels for settlement. It was opened for claims at noon on April 22, 1889.

That morning some twenty thousand people—on horseback, on foot, driving wagons, wheelbarrows, and every imaginable conveyance—lined up at different entry points on three sides of the area and awaited the pistol shot that would signal the opening of the verdant prairies to settlement. When the gun was fired bedlam broke loose. Within a few hours nearly all of the two million acres had been claimed; tents, shacks, and other structures were being erected all over the once empty prairie; and by dark the new settlement of Oklahoma City had ten thousand people, Guthrie nearly fifteen.

On Congress: *"Never blame a legislative body for not doing something. When they do nothing, that don't hurt anybody. When they do something is when they become dangerous."*

Clem Rogers realized that it was only a matter of time until settlers would be swarming into the Verdigris valley. The little town of Oologah had come into existence as a whistle-stop on the Missouri Pacific in 1887, a few miles southwest of Clem's ranch, and from then on the area was destined to be farm country instead of cattle country. Clem, seeing what lay ahead, began to alter his operation from grazing longhorns on the open range to feeding shorthorn cattle in fenced pastures.

In 1891 he built the first barbed-wire fence in the Verdigris country. For some time he had been upgrading his herd, purchasing the first purebred shorthorn bulls in the territory, adding Herefords later. He was also breeding hogs and poultry, and was the first man in the region to introduce wheat on a large scale. In 1895 the Claremore *Progress* observed proudly that "Clem Rogers, the Oologah wheat king," had harvested thirteen thousand bushels.

West of the Cherokee Nation lay the tribe's most extensive and richest cattle ranges—some six and a half million acres of grassland south of the Kansas border, known as the Cherokee Strip. After unremitting pressure by white farmers on Congress, the Cherokee Strip was sold to the United States government for

In 1893 the Cherokees sold the Cherokee Strip to the United States, and the ensuing rush of white settlers (above) signaled the end of Clem Rogers' vast cattle empire. Years later Will wrote, "We spoiled the best Territory in the World to make a State."

$8,500,000, and in 1893 the most spectacular land rush of all followed, with a hundred thousand people stampeding across the waving grasslands to stake out claims. The following year the Cherokees received the first of five annual payments for the sale, each Indian getting $367.50 in cash.

But it was the passage of the Curtis Act in 1898 that finally put an end to Clem's cattle empire. That law forced allotment to individuals of all land held in common by the Cherokee Nation, abolished tribal law, and substituted a new code of U.S. laws for the Indian Territory. Between them, Clem and Will received allotments of 148.77 acres—all that remained to them of the sixty-thousand-acre ranch. It was clear that thousands more settlers would come in the wake of the Cherokee Run, and Clem

Rogers, now almost sixty, once again saw opportunity in the offing. He and several friends concluded that Claremore—a rail junction about twenty-four miles northeast of Tulsa—was the most promising town in the area for a bank, and in 1898 Clem sold his cattle, rented his farmland, and moved into town.

A curious dichotomy pervaded the lives of people like Clem and, to a lesser extent, Will Rogers—a kind of dual personality forced upon them by the circumstance of an Indian heritage and the relentless encroachment of white civilization. One can only speculate about Clem's feelings on the subject, but, as Will's son Bill suggests, Clem and Will were both "upwardly mobile, ambitious men, and I am sure they saw nothing wrong in trying to adopt the ways and attitudes that led to success, i.e., the white man's way. Today we might say that they should have paid more attention to the ancient Cherokee culture. But I think that was a concept that did not occur to them."

WHEN Will returned to the ranch after a year in Texas, he discovered that his father was living in Claremore and was expecting him to run what was left of the old operation. In January 1899 Clem restocked it with cattle, gave Will some animals of his own, and sent Will's friend Spi Trent to help manage the place. For about a year and a half they lived there, operating the ranch, but with Will always on the lookout for other forms of amusement. He sang tenor in a local quartet, attended every dance within riding distance, played baseball on the Oologah team, and participated in some of the roping contests then coming into vogue.

Will was almost as determined to own every good roping horse he saw as he was to master the art of roping. Throughout his life he owned so many it was impossible to keep track of them all. But his all-time favorite was one he owned at this time, a little yellow pony named Comanche. As Jim O'Donnell, who rode the horse in a number of roping contests and followed rodeos for forty years, said long afterward, "I have seen some wonderful horses, but none like Comanche." He went on to tell about the time a cowboy, riding Comanche, roped his steer and threw it,

For a while Will and his buddy, Spi Trent (second from right), ran the Rogers ranch, but they found the time—and the company—to attend every outing within riding range.

but when he jumped off the horse to tie the animal, the steer got to its feet and charged him. Without a moment's hesitation Comanche turned, pulled the rope tight, and flipped the steer by himself. The high point of these days—and the beginning of Will's show-business career—was his trip to St. Louis in 1899 for the annual fair, where he participated in a roping-and-riding contest run by "Colonel" Zack Mulhall.

After the fair, Mulhall, who was the general stock agent for the Atlantic & Pacific Railroad (later the Frisco), organized a "cowboy" band of about sixty musicians and made a tour of state fairs throughout the Middle West. Since most of them, as Will said, "could not ride in a wagon unless their shirttails was nailed to the floor," Mulhall decided he should take along a few real cowboys for authenticity. During a performance Mulhall would offer to pick out boys from the band who could ride an outlaw horse or rope and tie a steer in less time than any man in the audience could, and Will and his friend Jim O'Donnell were employed for that purpose. The rest of the time Will sat with the band, pretending to play a trombone.

In San Antonio, after the steer-roping contest was over, the local people invited the band members to a barbecue, and someone asked Will to speak. It was the first of many after-dinner speeches he was to give and surely one of the shortest. He got to his feet, blinked, scratched his head, and stammered, "Well, folks, this is a mighty fine dinner, what there is of it." Laughter greeted that remark, so he said, trying to cover up, "Well, there is plenty of it, such as it is." The speech was a success.

3

"Nobody but an Indian can pronounce Oologah."

IN THE fall of 1899 a nineteen-year-old girl named Betty Blake arrived from Arkansas to visit her sister and her brother-in-law, who was the Oologah railroad station agent. She was recovering from typhoid fever, and her mother thought the change would do her good, even though the social life in Oologah might not be as lively as it was at home. "The only young people in town," Betty's sister warned, "are the daughters of the hotelkeeper, and there is one boy, Will Rogers, who lives out on a ranch."

Betty was born in the Ozarks in a town named Monte Ne. When she was three her father died, and her mother supported her brood of six daughters and two sons as a dressmaker in the nearby town of Rogers. For all the family's financial worries, the household was a gay, lively one, full of music and fun. As soon as the children were old enough they went to work, and for a time Betty was a railroad clerk.

By all accounts she was pretty, good company, and much sought after by young men. One of her admirers recalled that he used to call for her in a handcar while she was working for the railroad, and that they would travel on it to see plays in Fort Smith.

After such excitement, Oologah must have been something of

a letdown. The town consisted of a handful of frame houses and plank sidewalks on either side of the main—and only—street. Beyond were the rolling prairies. Twice a day passenger trains stopped at the station where Betty's sister and brother-in-law lived and worked, and the Arkansas girl would sit at the window of the depot watching the townspeople turn out to meet them.

One evening a young man stepped off the train from Kansas City and came up to the ticket window. Betty went over to see what he wanted. "I looked at him and he looked at me," she wrote later, "and before I could even ask his business, he turned on his heel and was gone." When her brother-in-law came in with the express packages, one of which was a banjo addressed to Will Rogers, she realized who the boy must have been, and that he had been too shy to ask for his parcel.

A few days later she met him; one of the hotelkeeper's daughters invited Betty for dinner because Will was coming over. During dinner he was awkward and silent, but afterward in the sitting room he gradually thawed out and began to sing without accompaniment all the new songs he had heard in Kansas City, including "Hello, Ma Baby." Afterward they popped corn and pulled taffy, and Will gave Betty the music for the new songs so that she could learn to play them on the piano.

The two met often that fall. There were visits to farms and ranches all over the neighborhood (the Vinita *Indian Chieftain* noted that "nutting parties, gypsy teas and possum hunts were all the go" that season), and many more evenings of music, with Betty playing the piano or banjo while Will sang. She left for Arkansas just before Christmas, and shortly after the first of the new year, 1900, she received her first letter from him, headed "My Dear Friend." He asked her to return soon, and concluded, "Hoping you will take pity on this poor heart broken Cow pealer."

In the middle of March another letter came, this time to "My Dear Betty." It was unmistakably a love letter, which he asked her to burn. She didn't burn it, but neither did she reply. They saw each other again in the fall, at an Arkansas fair, and Will—lonely and shy—avoided her. That night there was a dance, and

Betty kept looking for Will, but she had only a glimpse of him standing alone outside the hall, watching her dance by.

It was the last time she saw him for almost four years, for Will had the wanderlust again. There was a lot of talk circulating through the West about ranching in Argentina; down there, it was said, were endless pampas in a country free of farmers and barbed wire, where a man could ride all day and never see a plowed field or a fence.

Late in 1901 Will announced to his father his decision to leave for Argentina. Apparently the two had some sharp words. Clem wanted his son to stay on the ranch, but Will was determined to go his own way. Clem bought back for three thousand dollars the herd he had given Will. Will sold off his other steers and said good-by. As he headed out into the world he took with him the most enduring influences on his life: his Indian heritage, all the Oklahoma roots that ran so deep, and a warm spot in his heart for Betty Blake, the girl from Arkansas.

WILL had no difficulty persuading a kindred soul named Dick Parris to accompany him to Argentina. Neither had the slightest idea how to get there. They went to New York to find a ship going south, but there were none sailing for the Argentine.

They heard that ships from Liverpool, England, occasionally sailed for Buenos Aires, so in March 1902 the two embarked on the SS *Philadelphia*, bound for England. It was the first of many ocean voyages for Will, on each of which he would be deathly seasick. Once back on land, however, he was full of good humor again. He wrote his sisters that he and Dick were in a hotel room "almost papered with pictures of Queen Victoria, who certainly had a stand in with the photographer."

The time the two young men spent in London coincided with the preparations for Edward VII's coronation. The entire city was in a state of confusion, but the two Americans found their way to Parliament, London Bridge, the Tower, and to Westminster Abbey, to gaze at the monuments to the great. "I knew very few of the men personally," Will said. Then, in company

Will's future bride, Betty Blake, came from a large, fun-loving Arkansas family. "Sometimes," a friend recalled, "they'd overflow out into the yard, there was so many of them." Betty is third from bottom.

with two hundred Spanish and Portuguese emigrants ("I can't understand a soul on this boat but Dick"), they set sail by slow freighter for Buenos Aires, arriving during the first week in May.

Argentina was a huge disappointment. Will wrote his father that he had been into the interior and had discovered that, while it was marvelous cattle and farm country, "it's no place to make money unless you have $10,000 to invest." There were hundreds of men competing for every job. Because of the language barrier, his unfamiliarity with the country, his distaste for the local food, and the wages offered (five to eight dollars a month), Will soon concluded that Argentina was not for him. Dick was so homesick that, on the theory that Clem might be sending him some money, Will bought his buddy a ticket home and spent most of what he had left on presents for his father and sisters.

No money was forthcoming, however, and by mid-June, Will was sleeping in the park. When he heard about a job tending cattle on a boat sailing for South Africa, he decided to take it.

During the twenty-five agonizing days it took the *Kelvinside* to run from Buenos Aires to Durban, Will served as night watchman on the cattle deck. As he said, he was too sick to do anything else, and there was no way they could fire him. In South Africa he worked for two months on the estate of an Englishman who raised and raced thoroughbred horses; the stables were "veritable palaces," Will said, "heated by steam and lighted by electricity." His job was to feed and exercise the horses, and help the veterinarian and the blacksmith.

By November's end Will was on the move again, driving some mules two hundred and fifty miles from Durban to Ladysmith. There, an import from America, Texas Jack's *Wild West Show*, was playing in the town, and for the young man it was like a breath of fresh air from home.

THE American cowboy and frontiersman were legends in their own time—at home and abroad—and the so-called Wild West shows were bringing riding and shooting exhibitions, roping demonstrations, and mock battles between cowboys and Indians to thrilled audiences throughout the United States, Europe, Australia, and to towns like Ladysmith in South Africa. The most famous troupe was Buffalo Bill's *Wild West Show and Congress of Rough Riders of the World*, featuring "Colonel" William Cody himself—former army scout and buffalo hunter.

Texas Jack's show was a long way down the line, but in 1902 it looked good to Will. He went to see Texas Jack, who immediately wanted to know how good he was at roping and riding. Will said he could do a few rope tricks, and proceeded to perform the Big Crinoline, a classic and a surefire crowd pleaser. Starting with a small loop, the roper twirls the line around his body, gradually letting out more and more rope until the entire length—as much as thirty to sixty feet—forms a huge circle spinning around him. Jack gave Will a job then and there.

Will was billed as "The Cherokee Kid—the Man Who Can Lasso the Tail off a Blowfly," and he was getting to be quite a fancy roper indeed. At matinees, always crowded with children, Texas Jack gave a medal to the boy who could throw a lasso best, and Will was constantly trailed by youngsters who wanted him to show them what to do so they could win a medal.

He was homesick, he admitted in a letter to the folks in Indian Territory, but he had been raised from twenty to twenty-five dollars a week, and he was continuing to learn from Texas Jack, whom he later called "one of the smartest showmen I ever met." It was from Jack, Will said, that he "learned the great secret of the show business—learned when to get off. It's the fellow that knows when to quit that the audience wants more of." It was an immensely valuable experience, but by the fall of 1903 Will had had his fill of South Africa.

He thought he might as well head for the United States by first completing a trip around the world. Texas Jack hated to see him go, but he gave Will a glowing recommendation. It read:

I have the very great pleasure of recommending Mr. W. P. Rogers (The Cherokee Kid) to circus proprietors. . . . I consider him to be the champion trick rough rider and lasso thrower of the world. He is sober, industrious, hard working at all times and is always to be relied upon. I shall be very pleased to give him an engagement at any time should he wish to return.

Will renewed his acquaintance with the miseries of sea travel, crossing the Indian Ocean to New Zealand and then to Australia. He planned to be home not later than December 1, but decided he would just see a little of Australia as long as he was there. As usual, he was intrigued by all the sights: the greatest sheep-raising country in the world; aborigines who could throw a boomerang so that "it will shave your hat off going and your head off coming back"; kangaroos as common as jackrabbits.

His tour of Australia consumed all the money he had earned with Texas Jack, so he took a job with the Wirth Brothers circus in New Zealand, performing a roping and trick-riding act which the Auckland *Herald* complimented as a "highly original exhibition" which "fairly dazzled the crowd."

For the second year in a row Will spent Christmas thousands of miles from home, but he vowed it would be the last one. He had heard that St. Louis was planning a world's fair in the summer of 1904, and he would be there for the opening, he assured the family.

BY THE time the prodigal returned in April, he had seen a lot of the world and had acquired, according to his friend Spi Trent, "a kind of sure-footedness . . . which comes to a feller who has learned to paddle his own canoe."

In Claremore business was booming. Clem Rogers was busy, as usual, in the affairs of the Cherokee Nation, which, as he had already foreseen, was about to vanish forever. Clem was looking to the future, and would now devote his great energy, strong opinions, and ability to the movement for Oklahoma statehood. (He was one of fifty-five delegates elected from Indian Territory to the constitutional convention that assembled in 1906, and that year the district he represented was named Rogers County in his honor. This work culminated in statehood for Oklahoma, pro-

Trick roping fascinated Will from boyhood. In 1902–03 he toured abroad with a Wild West show, billed as "The Cherokee Kid."

claimed by President Theodore Roosevelt on November 16, 1907.)

But to Clem's son, Will, none of these developments was half as exciting as the exposition that would open in St. Louis on May 1, 1904, celebrating (one year late) the one-hundredth anniversary of the Louisiana Purchase. It would be the largest world's fair ever held, covering fourteen hundred acres. There were to be fifteen new buildings, laid out in the shape of a fan, including the Palace of Electricity and the Palace of Machinery. There would be extensive foreign exhibits, including grass-thatched huts from America's newest territorial acquisition, the Philippine Islands. Sculpture and statuary by Augustus Saint-Gaudens and Daniel Chester French were to be set off by a six-acre rose garden, a colossal floral clock, and numerous waterfalls and miniature lagoons.

Beyond the fair's array of exhibits stretched a long, wide midway called the Pike, where vendors swarmed (it was claimed that the ice-cream cone, the hot dog, and iced tea were introduced for the first time on the Pike that summer), and where the amusement concessions were also clustered. These included a 265-foot Ferris wheel, the Temple of Mirth, the Jungle of Mirrors, Hagenbeck's *Wild Animal Show*, and, predictably, a Wild West show.

ALMOST as soon as he returned from his global junket, Will was summoned to Guthrie by his old employer, Colonel Zack Mulhall, who was assembling a group of riders for the Wild West show. The cowboys Mulhall had sent for were drifting in to his ranch every day; one of them was a young man named Tom Mix. Will stayed with them for nearly a week, working away at his rope tricks.

When they arrived at the fair the Mulhall cowboy troupe was combined with a troupe of Indians in a spectacular show involving some six or seven hundred horsemen. They had been performing for only about a month when Mulhall and the head stableman got into a fight; after an evening performance they met on the Pike, and Mulhall pulled a gun and started shooting. The colonel's shots only grazed his opponent but seriously wounded a young boy who was watching the battle, and Mulhall was hustled off to jail. In the aftermath of the shooting some of the cowboys pulled out and went home, but Will joined the Indian troupe on the midway and at some point performed in a small Wild West show Charles Tompkins was running inside the fairground.

BETTY BLAKE, unaware that Will was even back in the States, had come to St. Louis to visit one of her sisters and take in the fair. As she was walking through one of the exhibits on a Sunday morning, she overheard a girl remark that Will Rogers was performing in the Wild West show. Betty sent him a note, and back came a reply, to "Dear Old Pal," asking her to come to the afternoon performance and afterward they would have dinner and spend the evening together. Her sister and a friend gave her the usual hard time over her cowboy acquaintance, and since she "was not particularly thrilled about Will's profession" anyway, as she later confessed, she approached the arena with some misgiving. When Will appeared her worst fears were realized. He was wearing a skintight red velvet suit trimmed with gold braid, and Betty was so embarrassed she didn't even hear the applause for his act. After the performance there was a long wait for Will to join them—he was chasing the manager all over the fairground to collect his back pay. When he showed up, breathless and apologetic, he explained the spectacular suit. In Australia, where he had occasionally been billed as "The Mexican Rope Artist," Mrs. Wirth, the circus owner's wife, had made him the velvet costume on the theory that a Mexican rope artist would wear a colorful getup (Will had never quite forgotten the sensational Vincente Oropeza, either). He never wore the red suit again after seeing Betty's reaction.

The couple had dinner, strolled along the Pike, went to the Irish Village, where a tenor named John McCormack was singing for the first time in America, and said good-night.

WHEN Betty next heard from him it was late October and he was in Chicago. During that summer in St. Louis, on free Saturday afternoons, Will had taken a job at the Standard Theatre— a roping turn on the stage. Someone in the audience liked it well enough to write to the owner of a theater chain in Chicago, and the next thing Will knew he was offered a week's vaudeville engagement there for thirty dollars. During one show he was going through the rope tricks he had perfected with Texas Jack when a dog from an animal act ran onto the stage. Without thinking, Will tossed a loop over the animal and hauled him in. The laughter and loud applause made him realize that people wanted to see him actually catch something. And what quickly evolved in Will's mind was something that had never been done before in a theater—roping a running horse on the stage. He was sure he could bring it off if he could obtain the right animal. The right one, he knew, was a beautiful little bay pony that Mrs. Mulhall had offered to sell him for a hundred dollars.

Will didn't like Chicago much, he wrote Betty, and he was

going back to St. Louis to earn enough money to buy the horse he needed. Then he launched into a subject that was very much in his thoughts: he wanted to know if she was "contracted for" or if she had "a steady fellow." If not "then please file my application." According to form, he said, both of them "should have matrimonied long ago. It wouldent do for this young gang to look at our *teeth*, you know." He went on. "I could just love a girl about your caliber. You know I was always kinder headstrong about you anyway. But I always thought that a cowboy dident quite come up to your Ideal."

After winning a blue ribbon at a performance for visiting cattlemen during the final days of the fair, Will returned to Claremore, and soon he was rehearsing with the pony, Teddy—named for Theodore Roosevelt—which he had bought from Mrs. Mulhall. He had staked out a plot of ground as big as a stage and was going over and over his new routine until he had it down pat. By spring he was ready to try it out in New York, and once again Colonel Mulhall figured in his plans. He had been acquitted in the St. Louis shooting case, and was taking his Wild West show to New York.

On April 27, 1905, Will Rogers made his New York debut in Madison Square Garden with a Mulhall troupe that included Mulhall's daughter Lucille, who had made quite a name for herself as a performing cowgirl, Tom Mix, and a number of Will's cronies. Two weeks after they opened Will got one of the big breaks of his career.

According to a New York *Herald* clipping he sent to his family, Lucille Mulhall was roping to the music of the Seventh Regiment band when a big eight-hundred-pound steer, with horns that spread five feet, ran into the ring and suddenly started for the stands. Lucille and some of the cowboys tried to head it off, but the steer leaped the bars into the seats and, while the crowd panicked, loped up the stairs to the balcony. Hot on its heels came the cowboys, and, as the *Herald* article described it, "The Indian Will Rogers . . . headed the steer off" and got his rope

Will (left) made his big-time debut at New York's Madison Square Garden with Zack Mulhall's troupe in 1905. He became an instant hero by roping and tying a steer that broke loose and charged into the crowd.

around its horns. "Alone and afoot, he was no match for the brute's strength, but he swerved it down the steps on the Twenty-seventh street side, where it jumped again into the ring" and was roped by the men in the arena and led away. According to the account under the subhead INDIAN COWPUNCHER'S QUICKNESS PREVENTS HARM, occupants of seats on one whole side of the arena stampeded for cover, and Colonel Mulhall was heard yelling to Lucille to "follow that baby up the stairs and bring him back or else stay there" herself.

No man to miss an opportunity, Will set out to capitalize on the publicity with theatrical managers. He had concluded that the days of the big Wild West shows were numbered, and he had decided to break into what was then the most exciting and glamorous aspect of show business—vaudeville.

4

"All other performers think I have the
greatest act in the business."

SOMETHING like what came to be called vaudeville had flourished
for a good many years in England, where it was generally known
as "variety" entertainment. In this country vaudeville was a coming together of some peculiarly American forms of entertainment, including "dime museums" and "store shows"—conducted
tours of midgets, sword swallowers, and the like—the minstrel
show, the medicine wagon with its hired entertainers, and "car
parks"—amusement areas at the end of trolley-car lines, where
a family on an outing might be exposed to anything from ballet
and opera to animal acts and acrobats.

So vaudeville had many antecedents, but what put it on the
tracks was the Gaiety Museum, which opened in a deserted candy
store in Boston, Massachusetts, in 1883. Operated by a former
circus performer named Benjamin Franklin Keith, it featured,
among other attractions, a stuffed mermaid, a tattooed man, a
chicken with a human face, and a pair of comedians, Joe Weber
and Lew Fields. Before long Keith was giving the customers continuous performances, hiring talented artists of the day, and
bringing good clean acts to the city of Boston. In 1885 Keith and
Edward F. Albee presented the popular operettas by William
Gilbert and Arthur Sullivan, and their success in this venture
enabled them to acquire the real estate which became the Keith-
Albee chain of theaters, the most extensive in the world, with
houses in nearly every large American city.

By the time Will Rogers entered vaudeville, Keith and Albee
had a virtual monopoly on the booking of acts for theaters. But
if they dominated the business of vaudeville, a man named Willie
Hammerstein ruled what has often been called its heart.

Hammerstein's father, Oscar, had come to America from Berlin, gone into cigar making, and had somehow become the na-

tion's impresario of grand opera, in which role he built a dozen theaters. Grandest of them all was the Victoria Theatre at the corner of Broadway and Forty-second Street in New York. There, for the fifty-cent admission price, one could take advantage of the theater, music hall, billiard room, Oriental café, and roof garden—the last being Willie Hammerstein's particular domain.

Willie's special contribution to vaudeville was the "freak" act, and he often had a bizarre celebrity waiting in the wings to surprise and titillate customers—it might be a woman who had shot her husband or lover, a champion bicycle rider, or a polar explorer. No one knew what to expect. Nor was Hammerstein

On women: *"I'll bet you the time ain't far off when a woman won't know any more than a man."*

above perpetrating an occasional hoax on the public. There was, for example, "Abdul Kadar, Court Artist of the Turkish Sultan," who appeared with his three veiled wives. In fact, Abdul was a German named Adolph Schneider and the "wives" were his wife, daughter, and sister-in-law, who avoided talking to inquisitive reporters by falling to their knees and repeating the name of Allah whenever they were asked a question.

When the Victoria opened its doors in 1899 big-time vaudeville was just coming into its own, and under Willie Hammerstein's talented management his theater grossed more than twenty million dollars before it finally shut down.

Hammerstein's Victoria was the big time, but by 1910 there were some two thousand theaters in the small towns of America, offering what was known as small-time vaudeville. The show people drifted in and out of railroad depots with worn trunks plastered with stickers from faraway places and gave the natives the chance to ogle their sporty traveling clothes, flashy jewelry, and exotic women. But the veneer of glamour concealed a life of very real hardship. The touring actor had to travel constantly, in all kinds of weather. Enduring long, dirty train rides and second-rate hotels, he also had to tolerate the whims of uncooperative stagehands, and above all, the tyranny of the theater manager, who often cared little about performers and everything about box-office receipts.

The story of how Will Rogers broke into his new trade has all the elements of the classic show-business saga: the stagestruck rube arrives in the big city, receives some publicity as a result of performing a heroic feat (in this case, roping a half-crazed steer in Madison Square Garden), but is turned down by unfeeling booking agents who can't imagine that his act is any good (and who certainly don't believe he can rope a horse onstage). Finally he overhears one of them telephoning Keith's Union Square Theatre and saying, "Put this nut and his pony on at one of your supper shows and just get rid of him."

The supper show for which Will was engaged during the week of June 11, 1905, was the toughest possible way to break into vaudeville. It was scheduled between six and eight in the evening, when, as Will wrote later, "nobody that had a home or somewhere to eat would be in a theatre." His first appearance was announced by a sign bearing the singularly unprovocative message EXTRA ACT. But whether the audience felt sorry for him or whether they took pity on his pony, as Will supposed, the fact was that they liked his act, and the following week he moved up to the Hammerstein's Paradise Roof—"the swellest Vaudeville place in America," he told his sisters.

Will's routine was quite a novelty. "Will P. Rogers, the sensational lariat thrower, is making his first appearance at the Paradise Roof, and has proved a sensation in every way," the New York *Herald* observed. As the orchestra played a medley of tunes—inevitably, "Pony Boy" and some cowboy songs—Will made a spectacular entrance on Teddy, who wore specially made felt-bottomed boots to keep him from slipping on the stage. Will would slide off the pony, give him a slap on the rump to send him into the wings, and then begin his rope tricks, which he performed silently in rhythm to the soft orchestra music.

Will's roping act is virtually impossible to describe. In one of his early silent films, *The Ropin' Fool*, he did fifty-three different tricks, ranging from the simple to the nearly impossible.

*Will and Betty Blake conducted a nine-year
courtship, mostly by mail. One Christmas
he sent her a fur-collared coat and muff,
in which she posed proudly.*

What comes across in this film, as it did to the vaudeville crowds, is a combination of almost unbelievable timing, grace, and amazing skill. He usually began with the simplest of the so-called small-loop routines—the flat spin—in which he twirled the rope in front or to the side, parallel to the stage. From this he might go into the merry-go-round, in which the rope, constantly spinning, is passed from the right hand, under one leg, to the other hand behind the body, where the right hand picks it up again.

One of Will's specialties was the juggle, or bounce, in which the spinning loop travels up and down like a jumping jack, high over the roper's head and down to his feet, and up again. He could jump in and out of two loops simultaneously, or do the Texas skip, dancing back and forth through a large loop spinning in a vertical plane. (This was his favorite conditioning exercise, and he performed it almost daily to keep in shape.) He often climaxed his act by having an usher take one end of a ninety-foot rope up the aisle as far as it would reach while Will, standing at the footlights, held on to the other end to show the audience how long it was. Then he would haul it in and, after mounting Teddy, would begin twirling a small loop, lifting it over his head as it increased in size until all ninety feet were out in the Big Crinoline (which had earned him the job with Texas Jack), the glistening white rope spinning in a huge, beautiful circle far out over the heads of the audience.

Betty later described another portion of the act, in which Buck McKee, who was working with Will, rode Teddy, and Will roped horse and rider simultaneously. "There were many catches—throwing two ropes at once, catching the man with one loop and the horse with the other; a three-rope catch, a nose catch, a figure eight, and a tail catch so difficult that Will never ceased practicing on it." What she mentions lightly as "a figure eight" was in reality one of the most difficult catches; in it the spinning loop made a figure eight, one half of which caught the rider while the other half went around the head of the moving horse.

After watching Will, an actor suggested that it might be more effective if he told the crowd what he was going to do before he did it. One night, with no advance preparation, Will stopped the orchestra and announced that he wanted to explain his "next little stunt . . . I am going to throw about two o' these ropes at once," he said, "catching the horse with one and the rider with the other." He paused, grinned, and said, "I don't have any idea I'll get it, but here goes." Will's Western accent, his delivery, and the way he underplayed the statement tickled the audience, and to his embarrassment they started laughing. He came offstage angry and humiliated, and although other performers tried to persuade him that laughs were good for his act, he was too serious about his roping to accept the idea.

There were other occasions, however, when he learned that a little talk could be helpful. One evening when he was unable to get any of his tricks to work the way he wanted, he grew flustered, the audience became increasingly restless, and suddenly he began to talk. "Swinging a rope is all right," he said, "when your neck ain't in it. Then it's hell." There were a few chuckles. "Out West where I come from," he went on, "they won't let me play with this rope. They think I might hurt myself." By then he had the audience with him; they forgot the tricks he had missed and began enjoying Will himself. But it was some time before he did any talking other than to announce the tricks.

A little notebook Will began keeping in the summer of 1905 shows how much in demand he was. After a week each at Keith's and Hammerstein's in New York, he traveled to Philadelphia and Boston before returning to Manhattan for an engagement at Proctor's and five triumphal weeks at Hammerstein's roof garden. Will started at seventy-five dollars a week in New York on June 12, 1905, and by August he got two hundred and fifty dollars for a week in Brooklyn. Through the fall and winter he was on the road constantly, with no time off; not until March 1906 was there a break in the two-a-day routine. The notebook reads: "Sailed Mar 17 from N.Y. on S.S. *Philadelphia* for Paris and Berlin."

Early in April, less than a year after he had roped the steer in Madison Square Garden, Will Rogers was playing the most important theater in Europe—the Wintergarten in Berlin. From there he went on to London's leading music hall, the Palace, for five weeks at more money than he had ever earned.

In mid-July of 1906 Will was home in Indian Territory for the first time in over a year, and his family and friends were glad to see that theatrical success hadn't changed him. His sister Maud invited Betty Blake to join them, and her visit was almost a repetition of the one she had made in the fall of 1899—a steady round of parties, dinners, horseback rides, and evenings of singing around the piano. Although Betty enjoyed her visit, she found Will himself strangely elusive and distant. He paid no particular attention to her, never saw her alone, and she recalled that she was "a baffled young lady when I left for home."

What made it so mystifying was that he had been corresponding constantly with her for over a year. A flood of telegrams, postcards, and letters had descended on Rogers, Arkansas, from every part of the country (the salutations had changed from "Dear Old Pal" to "Dearest Betty" and then "My Own Sweetheart"), and nearly all contained the message that he was "the most persistent lover you ever saw," that he wanted her to marry him and "see the world as the *wife* of Rogers the Lariet Expert."

Betty had been back in Arkansas for a week when Will stopped by to see her. He was on his way to New York and had the idea "that we should get married at once." He was earning two hundred dollars a week, he was fully booked for the coming fall and winter, and as far as he was concerned, the future looked bright indeed. But Betty didn't regard show business as a steady or particularly worthy profession, and she didn't fancy herself trouping around the country with Will. He couldn't understand her attitude, and they seem to have had an unhappy parting.

For the next two years he followed the old routine: out on the circuit playing most of the principal cities in the United States and Canada, with interruptions only for a visit to Oklahoma when his father was ill. And the correspondence with Betty went on continuously, Will ever hopeful, Betty ever warm and friendly, but not ready to give in.

When Will went home to see his father he visited Betty in

Arkansas and spoke several times of quitting show business and returning to the old ranch life. But the panic of 1907 hit ranching as well as the vaudeville business, and Will decided to stick to his present occupation. Nevertheless, Betty remarked, "I felt that at last he was coming around to my way of thinking."

Will's little notebook tells the story of his activities. He was in Wilkes-Barre, Pennsylvania, the week of October 26, 1908. The next week was open (a rarity for him), and on November 9 he was heading home. He stopped off in Rogers, Arkansas, and as Betty remembered, announced flatly "that he was going to take me back to New York." There followed a notebook entry in big block letters for the week of November 23: GETTING MARRIED.

THE wedding took place at midday on November 25, 1908, at Betty's home in Arkansas, with only the two families present. Afterward the whole town gathered on the station platform to send the newlyweds off to St. Louis.

They had only a few days to themselves there, since Will was to open the following week at Proctor's in Newark, New Jersey. They went to a football game, had Thanksgiving dinner and champagne served in their room at the Planters Hotel, and saw *What Every Woman Knows*, starring Maude Adams.

In Newark, Betty watched Will for the first time on a stage, and she was not especially impressed. She had seen most of his rope tricks many times over. But his working hours were ideal for honeymooners; he arrived at the theater just in time to go on, and since Buck McKee had his ropes laid out, all Will had to do was slip on a dark-blue flannel shirt and leather chaps and walk onto the stage, perform for fifteen or twenty minutes, and then make his exit. Even though he was doing two performances a day, he and Betty had time to sightsee, attend other theaters, or visit with friends who were in town. To Will's disgust (since he had to wear his "Montgomery Ward" or wedding suit) they also went several times to the opera. Will later described one opera evening: "Caruso was the fellow who had played the part of a clown but I could not think of a funny thing that he did."

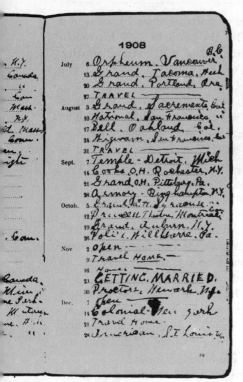

Will interrupted his vaudeville schedule in 1908 for a good reason. "The day I roped Betty," he said, "I did the star performance of my life."

Their tour of the Orpheum circuit turned out to be a real honeymoon; Betty had seen little of the country before, and Will wanted to rediscover it all with her. Wandering about, taking in the sights, picnicking in the countryside, riding horseback in the city parks—it was a relaxed, carefree life. When the tour ended, an offer came for Will to play the Percy Williams theaters in the East at a much higher salary than he had been getting, and Betty agreed that he should accept. She was, she conceded, "growing reconciled to show business."

After the Williams tour Will decided to put together an ambitious show of his own, featuring a variety of fancy ropers and trick riders. During this tour he made what was probably the most important decision in his theatrical career.

They were playing in Philadelphia and Will was onstage, watching the performances and making wry comments to the audience. Betty was in the wings, and the theater manager joined her. "Tell me, Mrs. Rogers," he said, "why does Will carry all those horses and people around with him? I would rather have Will Rogers alone than that whole bunch put together."

That decided it. Will would break up the troupe and go back to where he had started in vaudeville—just himself and his rope.

The worst of the decision was saying good-by to Buck and Teddy, who had been an intimate part of Will's life for the past six years. But with their departure, theater audiences began seeing an entirely different Will Rogers. From an intense, serious lariat artist he had developed into a humorous talker who also spun a rope, and that was to be the pattern from now on.

His way of concentrating hard on the rope made any remark seem impromptu (as indeed it usually was) and fresh. The lariat would spin smoothly, a gleaming white circle above the footlights, and Will would remark, half to himself, "Worked that pretty good." Or, if he missed a throw, which he rarely did, he might comment, "I've only got jokes enough for one miss. I've either got to practice roping or learn more jokes." Once he missed a fairly easy trick in which he jumped with both feet inside a spinning loop. As he was gathering in the lasso to make another try, he drawled, "Well, got all my feet through but one." As Betty wrote, "Laughs didn't have to happen twice to Will," and he began missing that trick regularly in order to use the line.

The gum chewing, which became his trademark, was made part of the act by accident. Will was a great baseball fan and often would head for a ball park to shag flies with the local team. He picked up the habit of chewing gum from the ballplayers. One day he arrived at the theater barely in time for the matinee performance and was still chewing when he came onstage. When the audience began laughing, Will remembered the gum, walked back and stuck it onto the proscenium arch, and the crowd roared. From then on he often used the business of parking his chewing gum after he missed a rope trick; then he would do the trick perfectly, collect the gum, and resume chewing.

Another modification in the act came about as a result of his friendship with Fred Stone, the actor and dancer, whom Will had admired before they met. The two men often played the same city, and they formed the habit of practicing together in the morning, with Will teaching Stone rope tricks while Fred coached him on dance routines. ("Rogers is a surprise when he starts dancing," *Variety* commented, "and gets away with it big.") The two had a lot in common: both were outdoorsmen who had lived adventurous lives; both were wholly absorbed in their profession; and neither could tolerate idleness. The Rogers and Stone families spent much time together over the years.

Most of the Rogers' friends at this time were theater people, among them W. C. Fields. Fields, who had achieved billing as "the greatest juggler on earth" while still a young vaudeville performer, first met Will in a Cape Town saloon, and they ran into each other again after Will joined Texas Jack's *Wild West Show*. Will had the greatest affection for Fields—a feeling that Fields reciprocated, as his biographer Robert Lewis Taylor writes, "with his usual periodic reservations and suspicions."

Now that Will was doing a single again he was better off financially. Although he was making the same money as before, he had fewer expenses and fewer problems. Clem's pride in his son's achievements grew steadily, although for a long while he was baffled that Will could make so much money. "Two hundred and fifty dollars a week," he would say. "Looks like something is wrong somewhere." But the tune changed when he took his daughters, Sallie and Maud, to Washington, where Will was performing at Chase's Theatre. Clem attended every performance and late in the week looked out over the audience from his box seat and began counting the house. Age had not dimmed his business instinct. "I tell you, girls," he said, "that manager sure is making a lot of money off Willie."

Unhappily, just when Clem and his son were beginning to be close to each other, it turned out that there would be no more such occasions. On October 20, 1911, Betty gave birth to a son, named William Vann for Will and Clem, and about a week later a package arrived from Clem containing a pair of beaded Indian moccasins for the baby. On its heels came a telegram informing them that Will's father had died in his sleep.

Will never forgot that he was Clem Rogers' son. "I suspect that Will's modesty had its origin in a tremendous respect for his father," Betty wrote, "and a knowledge that, at least in early manhood, he was a disappointment to his family." There was a hint of this in the story Will liked to tell about several of his father's cronies who came to see him perform in New York. When they got back to Oklahoma another old-timer asked what Will was doing. "Oh," said one, "just acting the fool like he used to do around here."

For several years after his father's death Will's career seemed to be stuck on a plateau. Show business generally was in the doldrums. In 1913 Betty gave birth to their second child, a daughter named Mary, while Will was playing vaudeville in Houston, Texas, and he was seriously concerned about his future. He sought Fred Stone's advice, and was urged to stay in New

On taxes: *"The Income Tax has made more Liars out of the American people than Golf has."*

York. Will needed a part in a show and Stone felt he would never get one as long as he was off trouping in vaudeville. So the Rogers family rented a house for the summer in Amityville, Long Island, and Will played vaudeville houses around New York.

Their third child, James Blake, was born in the summer of 1915—a time that was also memorable for the arrival of a small, coal-black pony called Dopey. Will had spotted Dopey in Connecticut, liked him, and brought him home, where he became more family institution than pet. He entered the house, walked up and down stairs, and when the children started riding, Dopey, the little black horse, was the animal they rode. "He raised our children," according to Will.

The uncertainty surrounding Will's career was made no easier by his attitude toward money. He could *almost* never resist a salesman, he could *never* resist buying a horse he wanted, and he assumed that every man was honest unless proved otherwise. He liked to buy furs for Betty, and he purchased two diamond scarf pins and a huge diamond ring for himself—ready currency for a touring actor who might find himself stranded without funds. Will's ring was in and out of hockshops frequently.

Because he was so relaxed about money, Will was often overcharged, but his attitude toward this was typical: "I would rather

be the one to pay too much," he would say, "than to be the man
that charged too much." He carried his paychecks around in a
pocket—often eight or ten of them at a time—until he needed
money. Then he would cash them. He never kept accounts or
business records. (Later, when he was making films, someone
asked who his accountant was. "Haven't got any," Will replied.
"We just put a check in the bank and draw on it until it's gone.")

Will spent most of the summer of 1915 at home with the family, and it was a nearly idyllic time. As far as vaudeville went, he
had hit the top. He was the featured attraction for two weeks at
the Palace on Broadway, the number one house in the country.

Late that fall Will was offered a two-week engagement in the
Midnight Frolic, a late-night show on the roof of the New Am-
sterdam Theatre. This probably had more to do with determin-
ing his future than any date he ever played.

5

"He brought beauty into the entertainment world."

THE *Midnight Frolic* was the property of Florenz Ziegfeld, Jr.,
who also produced the most famous show in America—the *Ziegfeld Follies*. The idea of hiring Will came from Ziegfeld's right-
hand man, Gene Buck, for Ziegfeld himself was virtually devoid
of humor. He put up with comedians only because they filled in
onstage while his girls were changing for their next number.

The *Frolic*, as Will described it, was "for folks with lots of
money. And plenty of insomnia." It began on the stroke of twelve,
and the cast included "the most beautiful girls of any show Ziegfeld ever put on." The loveliest ones, Will said, wouldn't work at
a matinee—they never got up that early.

When he started out in the *Frolic*, Will did pretty much what
he had been doing for the past several years—rope tricks punc-
tuated with jokes about the show, Ziegfeld, and so on. The crowds
took to him from the beginning, but Ziegfeld, sitting out front
glum-faced, commented flatly, "I don't like him."

*Rogers first went aloft at Atlantic City in 1915
in a Curtiss biplane piloted by E. K. Jaquith (right).
In later years flying became a passion with him.*

Gene Buck argued that the act was going over, so Ziegfeld agreed to watch it again another night. He did, and said, "Let him go. He doesn't fit in." For some days this byplay went on, Ziegfeld insisting each time that the roper be fired, and finally Buck went to give Will the bad news. But Will had an announcement to give him first.

"I want fifty dollars a week more," he blurted out. Besides, he added, he had a new idea for the act. "My wife says I'm always readin' the papers and I ought to talk about what I read."

Reluctantly, Buck told him to try it, neglecting to say that Ziegfeld was going to let him go, since he knew that the producer would be out of town for a week. As it happened, Will's notion of commenting on the news coincided with the effort of the industrialist Henry Ford to stop World War I. Ford had chartered a ship, loaded it with pacifists, idealists, and feminists, and set sail for Norway, where he hoped to halt the fighting through neutral mediation. As Will came onstage one night, groping for something to warm up his audience, he remarked, "If Mr. Ford had taken this bunch of girls, in this show, and let 'em wear the same costumes they wear here, and marched them down between the trenches, believe me, the boys would have been out before Christmas." The outburst of laughter convinced him that all he needed was a new gag about Ford's peace ship for each show.

When Ziegfeld returned he asked Buck how his cowboy friend had reacted to the news that he was fired. "I haven't let him go," Buck admitted, and asked the producer to come that night.

Ziegfeld did, and had to concede that the customers loved the act. "We'll keep him another week," he said.

One more week led to another, and another; Will got his raise; and as Henry Ford vanished from the front pages he cast about for new material. "So I started to reading about Congress," said Will, "and I found they are funnier three hundred and sixty-five days a year than anything I ever heard of." He would devour the newspapers for hours at a time, trying to work out a humorous angle to the day's news. "A joke don't have to be near as funny if it's up-to-date," he observed. And he concluded, about this time, that he didn't really care for the jokes that got the biggest laughs. What he preferred was the sly, subtle line that prompted people in the audience to nudge their friends and say, "He's right about that, you know." Where audiences once had admired his roping and chuckled at his comments, now they were laughing with Will, who seemed more like an amiable friend than a performer.

WILL's one-week engagement stretched out for months; he was still in the *Frolic* in the spring of 1916 when Ziegfeld—again as a result of Gene Buck's prodding—asked him to join the cast of the *Follies*. Will's refusal must have come as a surprise to the producer, but neither Will nor Betty thought the salary Ziegfeld offered was adequate, particularly since a *Follies* job meant that he would have to go on the road again. Will was enjoying a sane homelife for the first time in years; the family had a house in Forest Hills, Long Island, and kept horses in a nearby stable; he and Betty devoted a lot of time to the children and to riding.

They attended the opening of the 1916 *Follies*. The show was extravagant and spectacular; it was also deadly dull. Will's homespun act would have been a standout amid all that glitter. Through the long evening Will kept whispering to Betty, nudging her and saying, "See, Blake, what did I tell you? This was my one big chance." Or, "Boy, I wish I could have got my crack at it." They left the theater feeling that Will had lost an opportunity that might not come again.

Several days later Mr. Ziegfeld called (to Will he was always Mr. Ziegfeld) and admitted that the show lacked humor; he wanted Will to join it at once. By now Will was so eager to break into the *Follies* that he didn't even discuss salary.

"When Will went on the stage that night," Betty reported, "the audience broke into applause. Never had he gone over so well." He made a second appearance, spinning his rope and commenting on personalities and events, and immediately after the curtain rang down went upstairs to the roof to do his turn in the *Frolic*. As Betty wrote, "his magic stayed with him," and after the two shows they stayed up, eating sandwiches and drinking beer, waiting for the early editions of the morning papers. "All of them," she said, "gave Will excellent notices—the best, most important he had ever received."

Since the *Follies* and the *Frolic* were in the same theater and *Follies* patrons would drift up to the roof to eat, drink, and be entertained some more, Will now had to have an entirely different act twice every night, plus two matinees a week. He had acquired the habit of opening with the same phrase, "Well, all I know is just what I read in the papers," and going on from there. He pored over the noon editions of afternoon papers for his matinee performance; read stories from the final and home editions for the *Follies*; and for the midnight show extracted material from early editions of next morning's papers. "I buy more

newspaper extras than any man in the world," he claimed. All his comments were brief—usually three or four lines; in the time that most monologuists told eight or ten stories, Will averaged forty or more.

He also formed the habit of introducing prominent personalities from the audience. Ushers would keep an eye out for celebrities and send notes to Will's dressing room indicating the location of their seats; or Ziegfeld would tell him when friends of his were in the house; or sometimes Will, peering over the footlights, would spot a friend or someone known to the audience. (The houselights were always kept on when he talked.) One night he swung his rope out over the crowd and lassoed Fred Stone, who was seated on the aisle near the front. Despite his protests, Will hauled him up onstage and made him perform one of his

In 1916 Will's roping-and-comedy routine became part of the Ziegfeld Follies, *which featured "The Most Beautiful Girls in the World" (left and center). Soon he was among the headliners, like W. C. Fields (far left above) and Eddie Cantor (second from right above).*

own rope tricks, meantime leaning against the proscenium arch and visiting with him about Mrs. Stone and the children. It was the kind of unexpected treat that proved irresistible.

By the time Will joined Ziegfeld, the *Follies* was an established American institution. "A funny thing about the *Follies,*" Will wrote, "people never spoke of it in comparison to any other show. It was always 'It's better than the last year's, or it's not so good as last year's.'" It was true: Ziegfeld was his own greatest competition.

What had drawn people to the *Follies* ever since the first one opened in 1907 was, of course, the combination of beautiful showgirls, fantastic costumes and sets, and a sprinkling of high-priced talent—W. C. Fields, Bert Williams, Fanny Brice, Ann Pennington, Eddie Cantor, and dozens of other headliners.

When rehearsals began in the winter, Will and Betty often sat together in the darkened house while Ziegfeld and his assistants worked out the various spectacular numbers. When it was Will's turn to rehearse he generally kidded amiably about the show, about the girls—most of whom worked hard, since every stagestruck hopeful dreamed of being picked for the *Follies*—or remarked on incidents that had occurred during the tryouts. But it was not, in fact, a rehearsal for him. His act was always as fresh to members of the cast as it was to the audience, and they usually collected in the wings to hear him every night.

When the time came for the show to go on tour, Will was determined not to leave New York unless he got a substantial raise. Ziegfeld overwhelmed him with an offer of a two-year contract at $600 a week the first year and $750 the second—far more than he had considered asking. Then the producer suggested that Will stop by his office the next day and sign the contract. Will said, "I don't like contracts. You can trust me and I know I can trust you." And that was to be their arrangement for ten years.

Ziegfeld looked after Will in numerous ways. The *Follies* cast traveled in a special train, and the producer arranged for two of Will's horses, with a cowboy friend in charge of them, to go along in the scenery car, so Will could ride each morning and practice roping on horseback.

Of all the road trips Will made he was proudest of the occasions on which he played for President Woodrow Wilson. The first time was a benefit performance in Baltimore in 1916, shortly before the United States entered the war. Just before the opening the cast heard that President and Mrs. Wilson were coming from Washington to see the show, and Will immediately developed a bad case of stage fright. He had planned to devote most of his act to the country's lack of preparedness and to the diplomatic notes then going back and forth between Wilson and various European powers. The closer it came to curtain time, the more nervous he grew. When the moment came Will had to be shoved out on the stage.

He stood there for a moment, grinning sheepishly, rubbing

his head, and remarked to everyone's delight, "I am kinder nervous here tonight." Then he began easing into the material he had planned to use. "I shouldn't be nervous," he added, "for this is really my second Presidential appearance. The first time was when Bryan spoke in our town once, and I was to follow his speech and do my little Roping Act." Glancing at the presidential box and seeing Wilson laugh, he went on. "As I say, I was to follow him, but he spoke so long that it was so dark when he finished, they couldn't see my Roping." Then a pause: "I wonder what ever became of him." *

A few jokes about "Pancho" Villa, whom General John J. Pershing was chasing in Mexico, followed: "I see where they have captured Villa. Yes, they got him in the morning Editions and the Afternoon ones let him get away." Then he turned to the country's lack of preparedness—a subject on which Wilson was being criticized daily. "There is some talk of getting a Machine Gun if we can borrow one. The one we have now they are using to train our Army with in Plattsburg. If we go to war we will just about have to go to the trouble of getting another Gun." When Will saw that the President was leading the laughter, he added a pointed remark about the exchange of diplomatic notes with Germany, which Wilson afterward repeated to friends, saying it was the best joke told on him during the war. "President Wilson is getting along fine now to what he was a few months ago. Do you realize, People, that at one time in our negotiations with Germany that he was 5 Notes behind?"

Will later called this the proudest and most successful night he had ever had—made more memorable by the fact that the President came backstage during intermission and shook hands with everyone in the cast.

---

* William Jennings Bryan, perennial Democratic presidential candidate, had helped obtain the nomination in 1912 for Wilson, who after he was elected appointed Bryan Secretary of State. Just the year before the benefit in Baltimore, Bryan had resigned in a disagreement over Wilson's foreign policy following the sinking of the *Lusitania*. Bryan and Will would meet again. [Editor's note.]

UNITED STATES ENTRY into the war put no stop to Will's jokes about it. On the contrary, he found that Americans "laughed better during the war than any other time, if you happened to hit the right angle to it." At thirty-eight, with a wife and three children, he was exempt from the draft, but attempted to compensate for that by appearing at benefits and playing for returned veterans. To the president of the American Red Cross he wrote in May 1917, "While not a wealthy man, I earn a very good salary," and he pledged to donate ten percent of his next year's income—$5200.

He was telling *Follies* audiences that Germany couldn't understand how the United States could get trained men to Europe so quickly; what the enemy didn't comprehend, he said, was that "in our training manual there's nothing about retreating. When you only have to teach an army to go one way, you can do it in half the time." One of his

On peace: *"Prominent men run out of Decoration Day speeches, but the world never runs out of wars. People talk peace, but men give their life's work to war. It won't stop till there is as much brains and scientific study put to aid peace as there is to promote war."*

most successful routines was his advice on how to obtain a commission and fight the war in Washington: all it required was a visit to your senator. But the hazards to be faced were legion: ten men had been wounded in one day getting in and out of taxicabs.

With the signing of the armistice, which read "like a second mortgage" while the peace terms read "like a foreclosure," Will commented that it had taken eighty thousand words to tell Germany what we thought of them. When veterans arrived back he remarked, "If they really wanted to honor the boys, why didn't they let them sit in the stands and have the people march by?"

By this time his jokes were being quoted so frequently that he collected a number of them into two books which achieved modest success. The first was *Rogers-isms: The Cowboy Philosopher on the Peace Conference*, on the dust jacket of which he explained, "I made this book short so you could finish it before the next war." That volume was followed quickly by *Rogers-isms: The Cowboy Philosopher on Prohibition.* "You wont find the Country any drier than this Book," the cover proclaimed, and inside was an assortment of gags about Prohibition which had enlivened his *Follies* and *Frolic* routines. It had already been "the cause of more road improvement between dry and wet towns than any other thing," he claimed, since "Bad roads have broke more bottles of booze than the authorities." The Volstead Act would remain one of his favorite targets.

These slim books marked Will's first venture onto the literary scene. But it was short-lived. During the summer of 1918 he had discovered another medium representing new opportunities.

6

"Anybody can open a Theatre. It's keeping it open that is the hard thing."

ALTHOUGH Will Rogers and thousands of his fellow countrymen had been exposed to the novelty known as moving pictures, they could not have guessed that this new medium would, during the next few decades, transform the entertainment world.

So far as the general public was aware, the excitement started at the Koster & Bial Music Hall, west of Broadway in New York City, one evening in April 1896 when Manhattan society turned out, dressed to the nines, to see a demonstration of "Thomas A. Edison's Latest Marvel, THE VITASCOPE." Following the usual vaudeville fare, a twenty-foot white screen descended in front of the stage, lights were extinguished, a curious mechanical object in the center of the balcony began to buzz and wheeze, and a brilliant light filled the screen. Suddenly the figures of two women appeared and were seen to smile, pirouette daintily around their parasols, and dance. They vanished, and in their place an angry, surging wave crashed toward the audience. Thomas Armat, operating the Vitascope, recalled afterward that the realism of the oncoming surf "started a panicky commotion" in the front seats. Later the spectators went wild when a showgirl named Annabelle performed "The Butterfly Dance" on the screen. In short, an audience of sophisticated New Yorkers was thrilled and delighted, and behaved like a flock of children.

In truth, the "invention" demonstrated that night was not Edison's own, but a projector developed by Armat and a man named Jenkins. Armat had turned it over to Edison to manufacture. Since the 1850s, when a shutter was added to the venerable magic lantern to make a series of drawings look like a figure in motion, various experimenters had produced workable motion-picture projectors. The principle—then and now—was based on the fact that the optic nerve "remembers" a still image for a fraction of a second. The trick was to flash a sequence of pictures on the screen at a speed of sixteen frames per second, so fast that the eye could not distinguish them as separate images.

Edison was only mildly interested in Armat's projector. He had begun marketing something called the Kinetoscope, which had been developed at his laboratory by an imaginative employee named William K. L. Dickson.

This was what came to be known as a peep show. These upright viewing machines were installed by the hundreds in "phonograph parlors" across the land, where customers were already congregating to listen to Edison's gramophone. By placing a coin in a slot, a person could activate a viewer and watch about fifty feet of film. When Edison's associates tried to interest him in a film projector, he replied, "We are selling a lot of these peepshow machines at a good profit. If we put out a screen machine, there will be use for maybe about ten of them in the whole United States. Let's not kill the goose that lays the golden egg."

Not surprisingly, the first institution to see the possibilities of the motion-picture projector was vaudeville, and from 1896 to 1900 many houses showed films to supplement their live stage entertainment. But the pictures were of movement for movement's sake—photographs of natural phenomena like Niagara Falls, of trains and fire engines in motion, and of occasional news scenes,

William McKinley's 1896 presidential campaign being one of the first. These began to pall, however, and the novelty faded.

Yet while middle-class audiences in the vaudeville houses wearied of such fare, thousands of immigrants from Europe, eager for information about their adopted homeland and its customs, delighted in the garish penny arcades, where they could peer into a hand-cranked Kinetoscope and watch the bewitching pictures move. Arcade operators, sniffing the money that could be made by turning their establishments into picture theaters, began buying projectors and demanding new films to show on them. Before long these makeshift, back-room theaters became the most popular form of entertainment for America's lower class. While some saw all this as cheap claptrap, shrewder minds perceived in the growing popularity of films the makings of a new industry.

In Chicago two entrepreneurs named Spoor and Aronson formed a company called Essanay and began to transfer elements of the Wild West show to the screen. Aronson (who changed his name and achieved fame as "Bronco Billy" Anderson) was soon grinding out horse operas at the rate of one a week. William Selig, another Chicagoan, got in touch with Will Rogers' old friend Tom Mix, hired him, and thereby gave the American boy one of his first screen idols.

The theater that provided a name for all the others was Pittsburgh's Nickelodeon, which opened in a converted store in 1905 with a showing of the first important Western, *The Great Train Robbery*. That film set the pattern for hundreds more to follow: beginning with a scene in which two badmen slug a stationmaster, it moves quickly to a murder in the baggage car of a train, the dynamiting of a strongbox, a horseback chase, and a gunfight between the good and bad guys. With the coming of a true narrative to the screen, the nickelodeon boom was on. By 1907 there were three thousand of them; by 1910, ten thousand—all with uncomfortable seats, the pungent odor of human sweat, Cracker Jack, and popcorn.

As the demand for films grew, so did the need for stories capable of being translated to film, for improved production and distribution facilities, and for actors, editors, cameramen, and directors. Inevitably there had been a good deal of pirating and copying of films by shrewd nickelodeon operators. But the movie business was soon big enough to have its own monopoly, the Motion Picture Patents Company. By 1909 no film could be photographed, processed, or exhibited without its consent.

On lawyers: *"Every time a lawyer writes something, he is not writing for posterity, he is writing so that endless others of his craft can make a living out of trying to figure out what he said."*

The monopoly was a formidable antagonist for independent producers. Its spies raided unlicensed theaters and destroyed "illicit" projectors and films. By the time the monopoly was broken up under the Sherman Anti-Trust Act, the East Coast had become too hazardous for the independents. William Selig had taken his company to Los Angeles, which was near enough to the Mexican border to enable him to escape the monopoly's subpoenas and save his cameras from being smashed. Moreover he and other independent producers who followed him westward discovered that in southern California nature made it possible to produce movies in an entirely new manner. With sunshine almost the year around, interior scenes could be photographed outdoors without the need for electric lights. And California offered every type of landscape—mountains, desert, fields, sea, lakes, islands—much of it unoccupied. These were the factors that brought to Los Angeles, in 1910, the man who was to initiate most of the changes that soon took place in the motion-picture industry.

In David Wark Griffith, a sensitive, intelligent Southerner who was the son of a Confederate officer, the industry found the director who made the American public take films seriously. Within a remarkably short period he turned out more than four hundred one- and two-reel pictures, filled with innovations. He made the camera a roving eye instead of a static piece of equipment. He originated such techniques as the long shot, the vignette, the close-up, the fade-in and fade-out, and the angle shot. He was the first to try night photography, and one of the first to insist that the public would accept pictures that ran longer than one reel, or fourteen minutes.

In the fall of 1914 Griffith began work independently on a film based on a novel called *The Clansman*, by Thomas Dixon, a melodrama about the Reconstruction period, depicting the Ku Klux Klan as chivalrous heroes. He visualized it in a dimension unheard-of in the industry—twelve reels, which would take six months to film, at a cost of a hundred thousand dollars. Released in February 1915 as *The Clansman*—the title was soon changed to *The Birth of a Nation*—the film aroused immediate and intense excitement. It was shown at the White House; it was hailed by the press, denounced in Boston, and became an overnight sensation wherever it played.

Meanwhile a former actor named Mack Sennett, who had worked with Griffith and absorbed many of his ideas, was directing one- and two-reelers which poked fun at the conventions of American society: the successful businessman suffered an ignominious pratfall or received a custard pie in the face; the innocent American girl was portrayed as a beautiful, dumb bathing beauty who had eyes only for a man's bankroll; the romantic lover was seen as cross-eyed Ben Turpin or Fatty Arbuckle; imbecilic Keystone Kops revealed the underlying contempt of the country for its law officers; and Sennett's cynical view of the almighty automobile took shape in the impossible adventures of the Model T, which inevitably came to an explosive demise.

The gifted comedians Buster Keaton, Harry Langdon, and Charlie Chaplin (whom Sennett called the greatest artist who ever lived) all worked for Sennett, and millions of Americans began crowding into theaters to see their comedies.

About the time the Vitascope was unveiled at Koster & Bial's, a couple named Mr. and Mrs. H. H. Wilcox purchased one hundred and twenty acres of land northwest of Los Angeles, subdivided the property into lots, and named the development Hollywood. In 1910, when D. W. Griffith began filming a picture there, residents were dismayed by what happened to their town. Soon actors and actresses were everywhere; and as other companies followed Griffith, streets were roped off to stage parades or gun battles or automobile accidents; once-quiet hotels were filled with painted women, noisy cavalrymen, Indians, and cowboys; vacant land was gobbled up and turned into studios and movie lots.

In 1913 three partners arrived from the East, rented a barn near the corner of Sunset Boulevard and Vine Street, and began filming a motion-picture version of the stage play *The Squaw Man*. The three were Cecil B. DeMille, a former actor and playwright; Jesse L. Lasky, a vaudeville producer; and Lasky's brother-in-law, Samuel Goldfish, who had been born in the Warsaw ghetto and had made his way to the United States, later joining Lasky and DeMille.

In quick order DeMille made three successful movies, and the company was on its way. In those days everything about the making of a picture was highly informal. Scripts were rudimentary, not much more than a three- or four-page synopsis of a plot line which the actors and producers improvised on. While this casual approach was all very well for slapstick comedies, novels and plays that were translated into movies usually lost something in the process. The action tended to be static, and something clearly had to be done.

Samuel Goldfish, who was about to call himself Goldwyn, was a pioneer in the effort to improve the quality of scenario writing. Having formed his own company, he hired a group of novelists to whom he gave the resounding name of Eminent Authors. Among them were Mary Roberts Rinehart, Rupert Hughes, Gertrude Atherton, and Rex Beach. Beach's wife was the sister of Fred Stone's wife, and a friend of Will Rogers'.

Beach had sold Goldwyn one of his books, *Laughing Bill Hyde*, and his wife had the idea that Will was the ideal person to play the lead. Goldwyn came to New York to see Will and told him that

The primitive nature of early Hollywood cinematography is suggested by the shooting of this scene from Jubilo, *a Rogers silent movie, in 1919.*

the picture could be shot in a Fort Lee, New Jersey, studio during the summer, when the *Follies* was not playing. Will agreed to do it.

When *Laughing Bill Hyde* appeared, in September 1918, *The New York Times* greeted it enthusiastically: "Those inclined to believe that all of the magnetic Rogers personality is in his conversation will realize their mistake if they see this picture. The real Will Rogers is on the reels." Goldwyn was pleased with the box-office receipts and offered Will a two-year Hollywood contract. Will was drawing a good salary from Ziegfeld, but Goldwyn offered to double it for the first year and triple it for the second. There was a fourth child now—Freddie, named for Fred Stone— and according to Betty, they were attracted as much by the prospect of moving to California as by the generous salary terms. In

the spring of 1919 Will headed alone for Los Angeles and located
a house on Van Ness Avenue that would accommodate the family. When Betty and the children joined him he met them at the
station in a big black Cadillac driven by a chauffeur.

His first picture under the contract with Goldwyn was *Almost
a Husband*, in which he played opposite Peggy Wood. He was
on location when the three boys, Bill, Jimmy, and Freddie, came
down with diphtheria. No antitoxin was available in Hollywood,
and Will drove all night to find some; Bill and Jimmy recovered,
but the baby died.

That tragedy spoiled the house for them, and they bought another in Beverly Hills. They had decided to make California
home, and the new property was spacious enough so that they
could have a stable, a tanbark riding ring, a swimming pool, and
two log cabins for the children.

Will was not only acting in his pictures, he also had a hand
in the scripts and wrote the titles used as descriptive clues and
as dialogue. He couldn't take himself very seriously as an actor and liked to tell about a letter he had received which said, "I
understand you have never used a double in your pictures—now
that I have seen you I wonder why you don't." He missed the
presence of an audience, but he thoroughly enjoyed the work; he
could go to bed early, arise early, and spend much of his time
outdoors. All in all, it was "the grandest show business I know
anything about, and the only place an actor can act and at the
same time sit down in front and clap for himself."

By the time his contract expired, Will had made twelve pictures for Goldwyn, six in 1920 alone. In most of them he played
romantic parts. The films were pleasant, amusing, and reasonably successful, but the expiration of Will's contract in 1921
came at a time when the industry was in the throes of reorganization. Goldwyn left the studio, and Will was suddenly on his
own, without a contract.

Some of the leading actors and actresses in Hollywood had recently established their own independent companies; in 1919,
when Griffith, Mary Pickford, Douglas Fairbanks, and Charlie

Chaplin formed United Artists, word circulated through the movie colony that the lunatics had taken over the asylum. Will, following their lead, decided to go it alone and write, produce, and direct his own films—starring himself. He and Betty read innumerable books and scenarios, and they mortgaged the house to raise capital.

In this manner he produced three movies—*Fruits of Faith, The Ropin' Fool,* and *One Day in 365,* the story of a day at home with his wife and children. *The Ropin' Fool* was and is a delight, a highly amusing film for which Will wrote the titles and which showed him at his best, performing over fifty of his remarkable rope tricks. And *Fruits of Faith,* according to *The New York Times,* was a charming picture, unpretentious and with a slender story line, but made human and humorous by the skill of Will Rogers.

Everything Will owned—life insurance, Liberty bonds, savings, real estate—was tied up in those pictures. But none was a financial success, and soon the Rogers family was on the brink of bankruptcy. Finally he had to borrow money on the films themselves, depositing them at the bank as security. He was beginning to understand how Hollywood operated: "If the loan is made for a Moving Picture," he wrote, "the President of the bank wants to write the story for you. The Directors want to know who the Leading Lady is, and if they could, they would keep her as collateral."

Knowing there was work for him in New York, he went back to play in the *Follies.* What Betty remembered about that year were the countless train trips she made across the country to be with him. As for Will, she said he worked as hard "as he ever did in his life, and without a break or vacation of any kind." He missed his children and his favorite ponies. By the following summer, when he came home to accept a new movie contract, much of his indebtedness had been paid.

That was accomplished in large part because of his boundless energy. He had embarked on two new professions, in both of which he succeeded simply by being himself.

7

"Well, all I know is just what I read in the papers."

DURING a long, full career Will Rogers' best character part, as so many film reviewers pointed out, was playing himself. That is what he did to perfection in the two activities in which he now engaged: after-dinner speaking and writing a syndicated newspaper column.

Will had made after-dinner speeches before, mostly for theatrical friends at the Lambs and Friars clubs in New York. Now, to recoup the money lost in Hollywood, he began scheduling luncheon and dinner appearances at the rate of three or four a week all over Manhattan, usually for a fee of a thousand dollars. As a banquet speaker Will relied on the techniques that were so popular with *Follies* audiences. His act was completely personal, based on firsthand experience or observation. As he put it, his gags had to be based on facts. "Now rumor travels faster, but it don't stay put as long as truth."

Surprisingly, considering his years on the stage, he suffered from stage fright before every performance. "I never saw an audience that I ever faced with any confidence," he once admitted. The first few minutes in front of a crowd were agonizing for Will; he would fumble around nervously, half-muttering his lines, and he never did learn to hide his discomfort.

For a year, starting in 1922, he spoke at banquets of automobile dealers, hat- and dressmakers, leather and shoe men, corsetmakers, newspaper women, rug merchants, even New York City's Board of Aldermen. Each organization—to its delight—got the typical Will Rogers treatment.

Instead of opening with the usual formalities, he began by startling or insulting his audience. He told the automobile dealers they were "old time Horse-trading Gyps with white collars on." He addressed a group of advertising men as the "Robbing Hoods of America"; he advised the Association of Woolen Men to stay in-

Will began writing a weekly commentary on events of the day for The New York Times *in 1922, and the column was quickly syndicated all over the nation.*

doors in case of rain or there would be "about five hundred men choked to death by their own suits."

A roomful of astonished bankers heard that borrowing money on easy terms was a one-way ticket to the poorhouse. "If you think it ain't a sucker game," Will asked, "why is a banker the richest man in town?" He wished Congress would pass a bill forbidding any person to borrow from another, even if that put all bankers out of business. And as for their future: "Go to work, if there is any job any of you could earn a living at. Banking and after-dinner speaking are two of the most nonessential industries we have in this country. I am ready to reform if you are."

In April of 1923 Will was once again seeing Betty off to California—he wasn't sure, but he thought it was her eighth trip since the previous June. He remarked that every time she heard a locomotive whistle she stuffed a kimono into her suitcase and started running; and when they went out to dinner in New York, she would ask, "How many cars ahead is the diner?"

As much as he liked to make jokes about it, their life must have been almost unbelievably hectic. By mid-June of 1923, after a year and a half on the banquet circuit, he had had enough: "I have spoken at so many banquets that when I get home I will feel disappointed if my wife or one of the children don't get up at dinner and say, 'We have with us this evening a man who, I am sure, needs no introduction.'"

One talk Will gave during the frenetic period led to the offer to write a newspaper column. He appeared at a rally in New York's Town Hall on October 26, 1922, to speak in support of Ogden Mills's reelection to Congress. Had the candidate or his backers known what Will would say, it is doubtful they would have requested his assistance. Will told the audience that he didn't want his speech to go over; if it did he was afraid it might lead him into politics, and up to now he had tried to live honestly. He said he did not know his candidate's opponent, but assumed he must be a scoundrel and a tool of the special interests. Then he admitted that he hadn't met his *own* candidate: that was the reason he was "more apt to say something good of him than anyone else." Most people, he thought, took up politics through necessity or as a last resort, but Mills (whom he kept referring to as "this guy") was wealthy before he went into politics —"not as wealthy as now, but rich." Unfortunately, Will continued, Mills was handicapped by having been educated at Harvard, but he was the only candidate who owned his own silk hat and the only politician other than Henry Cabot Lodge who could get past the front door of a Fifth Avenue residence without delivering something. Mills, Will recalled, sat through the talk without the suggestion of a smile, not knowing "whether I was for him or against him." He was reelected either because of or in spite of Will's support.

Will's speech was reported in *The New York Times*, where it was read by the founder-proprietor of the McNaught Syndicate, a man named V. V. McNitt. With his partner, Charles V. McAdam, McNitt arranged to meet Will and suggested that the *Times* might be interested in his writing a weekly column.

By now Will had already done some writing for publication. His little books of jokes about the peace conference and Prohibition had appeared in 1919, and that same year, en route to California, he had written an amusing political commentary for the Kansas City *Star*. The *Star*'s theater critic had sat up until three a.m., listening to Will tell story after story, and begged him to put them on paper.

Will agreed to write the column for the *Times*, and there never was a contract; McAdam and McNitt shook hands with Will and agreed to pay him five hundred dollars a week. Sometime later Will came into the McNaught offices and mentioned that a rival syndicate had offered him eight hundred dollars a week, to which McAdam replied that they would give him a thousand dollars. Will told McAdam he was nuts, but he loved him for it.

Charles Driscoll, a McNaught editor, was responsible for coping

On American generosity: *"I have . . . heard lots of appeals, but I have yet to see one where the people knew the need . . . that they didn't come through. I don't know anything about 'America' being fundamentally sound and all that after dinner 'Hooey,' but I do know that America is 'Fundamentally Generous.'"*

with Will's spelling, punctuation, and grammar, and one of his first admonitions to the new columnist was to refrain from using the word ain't. That produced the response, "I know a lot of people who don't say ain't, ain't eating."

On December 24, 1922, the first column appeared in the *Times*, and a week later it was syndicated by McNaught—beginning a series that would continue for nearly thirteen years and become a familiar feature of America's Sunday newspapers.

The times were ripe for what Will Rogers had to say about the country and the world at large. Prohibition was turning out to be virtually impossible to enforce. The Ku Klux Klan, whose membership was said to be five million, was terrorizing minority groups in the North and Midwest as well as in the South.

There were also reports that President Harding, unlike his predecessor in the White House, did not care for Will Rogers' brand of humor—particularly the way Will poked fun at the nation's most sacred cow, Warren Gamaliel Harding himself. When Will was playing in the *Follies*, he heard that Harding wouldn't come to the show and concluded that it was "on account of the humorous relations between the White House and myself being rather strained."

In April 1923 those relations were strained further by a column Will wrote in the form of an open letter addressed to the President. In it Will applied for the job as ambassador to the Court of St. James's, citing his accomplishments as a speech-maker (which he said was ninety percent of the work), his motion-picture experience (he would never be caught in the background during the photographing of a big event), and his movie appearance in knee breeches ("we haven't had a decent looking leg over there in years"). While this was all bland enough, Harding may have been stung by the last line of the letter: "Now, as to Salary, I will do just the same as the rest of the Politicians—accept a small salary as pin Money, AND TAKE A CHANCE ON WHAT I CAN GET."

There were ugly, persistent rumors that things were not as they should be in the administration, but as yet few Americans were aware that Harding was a distraught and desperate man—betrayed by venal cronies he had put into positions of responsibility. Only after Harding's death, following a trip to Alaska, were the sordid scandals revealed.

On August 19, 1923, when Will wrote a tribute to the dead President, there was no way he could know that Harding's widow and a trusted assistant were at that very moment consigning case after case of the chief executive's papers to the flames—to "preserve his memory." Years later Will wrote that Harding was, in his opinion, the most human of any recent President. "If he had a weakness, it was in trusting his friends, and the man that don't do that, then there is something the matter with him. . . . Betrayed by friendship is not a bad memorial to leave."

WILL'S SYNDICATED COLUMN was a gently amusing, common-sense, down-to-earth approach to the problems, large and small, that bedeviled the American citizen and the people of the world. Initially it was Will's habit to turn from one subject to another in quick succession, but over the years the column became less staccato, with longer anecdotes and fewer punchy gags. Yet while the format changed, the tone of voice and the personality behind it did not.

Hardly a week went by without an entertaining story or joke about prominent men and women: kings and queens, presidents and prime ministers, congressmen, sports heroes, big business-men, movie stars—no one escaped. But no matter how Will might disagree with their principles or their politics, he never resorted to malice. There was something about the way he could turn a phrase that removed the sting from his criticism.

What he said, or what he might say, was nevertheless a matter of continuing concern to Betty, who was often embarrassed by the informality of his approach to important people. She worried that he would go too far or that someone would take offense. Life with Will had, as she put it, an "explosive" quality, be-cause neither she nor anyone else ever quite knew what he was going to say or do. The Rogers' two sons, long after their parents' death, remembered vividly the "civilizing" effect their mother had on their father. As Will, Jr., observed, his father came out of the world of Wild West shows, rodeos, the circus, and vaude-ville—all "harum-scarum" activities that were not held in uni-versal esteem—and it was Betty who "tamed him" and led him in a more respectable direction. Jim Rogers added, "And she was a censor. When Dad would come out with something a little raw, she would tell him, 'You just can't say that!' "

Fifty years later the weekly articles hold up astonishingly well. Topical as much of it is, the humor is still fresh, and contains nuggets of enduring wisdom and rare understanding. His com-ment about James Cox, the unsuccessful candidate for the presi-dency in 1920, is characteristic: "I don't know of any quicker way . . . to be forgotten in this Country than to be defeated for President. A man can leave the Country and people will always remember that he went some place. But if he is defeated for President they can't remember that he ever did anything."

Will formed the habit of opening his column with the line which began his *Follies* act: "Well, all I know is just what I read in the papers." All over the country Americans were turning every Sunday to those weekly asides on the news which were so distinctively Will Rogers. His exposure to the public was not only continuous, it was ubiquitous. He was appearing annually in the *Follies* and performing at frequent benefits; Americans were reading his weekly column and hearing him on the radio (he made his first broadcast over Pittsburgh's pioneer radio station, KDKA). And in 1923 he returned to Hollywood, at a salary of three thousand dollars a week, to make twelve comedies for producer Hal Roach. The films were successful enough as far as Roach was concerned, but they were not especially gratifying from Will's point of view. The problem, essentially, was that silent pictures lacked the dimension of conversation, the vital aspect of his stage act. So when the contract with Roach expired in 1924 Will headed east again.

IT WAS 1924, a presidential election year, and since Will had no set act in mind for the *Follies*, he informed his readers that he would stop off in Washington en route to New York to pick up some new jokes. "Congress," he explained, "has been writing my material for years."

Actually most of the politicking was going on outside the capital, and Will headed for Cleveland, where the Republicans were holding what he called the "Coolidge Follies—a one-star show." This was the first national political convention he attended, as a commentator for the McNaught Syndicate, and he was disappointed; it was altogether too tame. Coolidge, who had succeeded Harding upon the President's death, "could have been nominated by post card." As far as Will was concerned, the sole memorable moment was a lunch he had with William Jennings Bryan. The old Democratic war-horse was a correspondent covering the convention for the same syndicate, and when they first met in the press box Bryan said to Will, "You write a humorous column, don't you?"

Will admitted that he did.

"Well," Bryan remarked, "I write a serious article, and if I think of anything comical or funny I will give it to you."

"I thanked him," said Will later, "and told him, 'If I happen to think of anything of a serious nature, I will give it to you.' When he said he wrote seriously and I said I wrote humorously, I thought afterwards: 'We may both be wrong.' "

After seeing Coolidge nominated on the first ballot, Will left for the *Follies* rehearsals.

On elections: *"Every time we have an election, we get in worse men and the country keeps right on going. Times have proven only one thing and that is you can't ruin this country ever, with politics."*

The show opened on June 23, the same day the Democratic convention began at Madison Square Garden. Typically, Will was involved in both shows.

He had agreed to cover this convention for McNaught, too, and for a flat fee, which proved a costly mistake. The meeting lasted from June 24 to July 9, during which time the names of sixty candidates were placed in nomination for President.

As the convention dragged on endlessly, Will observed that the people in the hall heard the identical speech given by one man after another, each extolling the virtues of "the man I am going to name." Young Franklin D. Roosevelt had an opportunity, Will thought, to make a nominating speech that would have lived through the ages—if only he had had the sense to say, "Delegates, I put in nomination Alfred Smith; try and find out something against him."

By July 2, the ninth tedious day of the convention, Will decided to place his own candidate in nomination, and wrote a speech in his behalf. The man he was about to name, he said, never saw Wall Street, was not a member of the Klan, and had no connection with oil. He was the only man who would win in 1924. His name, Will stated, was Calvin Coolidge.

On July 5, to his astonishment, two Arizona delegates, with half a vote each, cast them for Will Rogers. (He had never heard of the men before, he said, but he had heard of Arizona.) A few days later the by-line of thirteen-year-old Will Rogers, Jr., appeared on the column, which stated, "Papa called us all in last night and made his last will and testament. . . . He put in the will that I being the oldest was to take up his life's work, that of reporting the Democratic National Convention." Finally, on the 103rd ballot, John W. Davis was chosen as the nominee, and William Jennings Bryan's brother Charles was later nominated for Vice-President. Will could remind readers that he had predicted Davis' nomination. (A visit with Davis on July 1 had convinced him that he was "a political dark horse turning white.")

In one of his articles Will remarked that if Mrs. Davis got into the White House, no titled European visitor would ever embarrass her, since she knew all the rules of etiquette. "She will never tip her Soup plate even if she can't get it all," said Will.

When the results of the presidential election were in, Will wrote that they were "just as big a surprise as the announcement that Xmas was coming in December." Whatever he may have felt about Coolidge's victory, he could rejoice in the return of one of his favorite targets to the White House. The first time Will had mentioned Coolidge in his weekly column was a few weeks after Harding's death, when he discussed Coolidge's "failure" as the new President, enumerating all the problems Coolidge had failed to solve during his several weeks in office: he had not produced rain for the farmers, he had not come out against boll weevils, he had not raised the price of wheat, he had not made France pay its war debt, he had done nothing for capital or labor, and he had not taken a stand on what size baseball bat Babe Ruth should use.

During the next four years there were frequent mentions of Calvin Coolidge in Will's column—most of them sympathetic in tone. It was no accident that Will liked, admired, and was amused by the thirtieth President. Both men came from a plain, rural background, both had a simplicity of expression, a subtle, dry wit, and both frequently employed exaggeration or understatement to make their points.

THE 1924 edition of Ziegfeld's *Follies* was the last one for Will. After eight years he had had enough, and only when Ziegfeld promised that he could quit after the New York run did Will reluctantly agree to join the cast once again. As soon as the show went on the road, as it always did, Will was to leave; but this time Ziegfeld altered his traditional schedule. He kept the show in New York for over a year and held Will to his word, much to the latter's annoyance.

When the show closed he returned to California. Except for the period in 1928–29 when he filled in for his friend Fred Stone in *Three Cheers*, it was Will's last Broadway season.

During this period he made occasional radio appearances, but he was never entirely at ease behind a microphone, especially in a studio with no audience, for many of his best lines were spontaneous, impromptu reactions to the mood of a crowd. "That little microphone that you are talking into," he wrote, "it's not going to laugh, so you don't know . . . whether to wait for your laugh, or just go right on."

Not long after he finished at the *Follies*, Will began playing to another kind of audience and, according to Betty, he got more satisfaction out of this experience than anything else he did in the 1920s. The idea of becoming a lecturer was proposed to him by Charles L. Wagner, probably the best-known lecture manager in this country at the time. Wagner offered to arrange a tour in which Will—backed up by a male quartet, the de Reszke Singers—would deliver sixty or more lectures between October 1 and November 30, 1925, for a fee of a thousand dollars each plus travel expenses. After December 1 he was to receive fifteen hundred dollars per appearance, which meant that it was possible for him to earn almost the same amount of money in eleven weeks as he had been making for twenty-six weeks' work in the *Follies*. (In 1924 his total earnings had been $157,428, of which $83,000 came from the *Follies*; the rest came from movies and his weekly articles. In 1925 he earned $235,000, of which the lecture tour accounted for $75,000.)

From October 1925 to mid-April of the following year, he gave a hundred and fifty-one lectures—speaking to women's clubs and social groups in theaters, school auditoriums, concert halls, lodge rooms, churches—in places he hadn't seen since the old vaudeville days. If the community had "a railroad and a Town Hall," he promised, "we will be there sooner or later."

Will was having the time of his life. On arrival in a town that was unfamiliar to him he would go to the newspaper office to collect what he called "the dope," material to work into the opening of his lecture. He inquired about traffic problems, the city council, the police force, the bond issue. "What about the mayor?" he would ask. "What's he doin' now?" He would write snippets of information on an old envelope, stuff it into his pocket, and just before going onstage read his notes to be sure he had the names right. Once on, he never looked at them again.

Notes and typewritten sheets, headed Lecture Routine, survive to indicate the type of material Will was using at this time. He had heard that we wanted to raise the guns on our battleships, but were prevented from doing so because of treaty commitments. All we asked, he said, was to be able to point the guns in the general direction of the enemy; the way they were pointing now, if the boat rocked we would shoot ourselves.

He would move on to discuss such topics as New York's subways, rumrunners, college football, and Coolidge. Often there was something of a personal nature to pass along. A congressman had read part of one of Will's articles into the *Congressional Record*, at which another legislator jumped to his feet and objected to the remarks of "a professional joke maker" being included in that august journal. As Will saw it, congressmen were the real comedians. "Every time they make a law it's a joke and every time they make a joke it's a law."

Will taught his children (from left, Bill, Jim, and Mary) to ride soon after they learned to walk. In 1925 he embarked on the first of several lecture tours (below). Betty frequently went along.

UNLIKE THE TRADITIONAL lecture fare, these performances were so informal and casual that it was virtually impossible for an audience not to warm to Will immediately, and he could play on his listeners the way a talented musician performs on an instrument. "You're doing fine," he would say when they roared with laughter. "We'll get out early tonight. It takes twice as long to get out when you have to explain the jokes." Frequently an audience kept him talking until he was exhausted and sat down on the edge of the stage with his feet hanging into the orchestra pit. He would grin at them and say, "I'm tired. Now, you folks go on out of here and go home—if you've got a home."

A nephew, Bruce Quisenberry, who managed Will's company for three seasons, remembered with a sense of awe his incredible energy. He never seemed to mind the killing pace of his schedule. He never worried, never asked to see the books or requested an accounting, and never disappointed an audience. Once a packed house of Texans kept him talking well past the appointed closing time, with the result that Will and his nephew missed the train they had planned to catch to Wichita, Kansas. He called the station agent to ask if he could hire a private train, and when told it would cost him eleven hundred dollars, said, "Tell 'em to saddle her up." And off they steamed, arriving in time to make the Kansas date. On another occasion he was driving through Arkansas, hurrying to a benefit performance, and came to a little town where twenty or thirty children were standing on the sidewalk holding a sign that read WELCOME WILL ROGERS. Will told the driver to stop, explaining, "They may have been here all morning"; and although it made him late for the benefit, he got out one of his ropes and did a few tricks for the children.

IN THE spring of 1926, at the conclusion of his first lecture tour, Will was asked by George Horace Lorimer, editor of the *Saturday Evening Post*, to go to Europe and write a series called "Letters of a Self-Made Diplomat to His President." Will agreed, and at the end of April he and Will, Jr., sailed on the *Leviathan*. In one open letter to Calvin Coolidge, published in the *Post*,

Will explained that he had had some difficulty obtaining a passport—a little mixup over the fact that he had no birth certificate: "You see, in the early days of the Indian Territory where I was born there was no such things as birth certificates. . . . We generally took it for granted if you were there you must have at some time been born. . . . Having a certificate of being born was like wearing a raincoat in the water over a bathing suit."

In England, as the self-appointed ambassador of the President, he managed to meet nearly everyone of any consequence—including the Prince of Wales,

Before Will spoke to the Old Trail Drivers' Association in Texas in 1926, a smiling Mrs. R. R. Russell of the Ladies Auxiliary pinned a membership button on him. Her smile faded as Will remarked, tongue in cheek, "You Old Trail Drivers . . . did all right. You'd start out down here with nothing, and after stealing our cattle in the Indian Nation, you'd wind up in Abilene with two thousand head or more." By the time he sat down, Mrs. Russell was steaming. "My husband was no cattle thief," she told Will. "Don't insinuate that he was."

Lady Astor, Sir James M. Barrie, Sir Thomas Lipton, Sir Harry Lauder, and George Bernard Shaw. Then he and young Will were off to Paris by plane, and once he recovered from his initial nervousness about flying he realized that this was the way he wanted to get around from now on. Airplane travel precisely suited his passion to get from one place to another in the quickest possible way. Traveling around the Continent, he visited the preliminary conference on disarmament in Geneva; he met the king of Spain; he had an interview with Mussolini; and he went to Russia, hoping (but failing) to talk with Trotsky.

Perhaps nothing illustrates the man's sheer animal energy so well as his activities during the summer of 1926. Not only did Will take his wife and children on a rigorous sight-seeing trip through Europe (Betty, with Mary and Jim, joined Will and their older son in June), but he found time for a dizzying number of other projects. He was writing articles regularly for the *Post*— enough to make a fair-sized book when they were all complete. The material from his Russian trip became another book— *There's Not a Bathing Suit in Russia*. He returned to London and made a motion picture called *Tip Toes* with Dorothy Gish. He made twelve travelogues, for which he also wrote the humorous lines that appeared on the screen. He played in a musical review produced by Charles Cochran, whom Will called "the British Ziegfeld." He continued to write his regular weekly article for American newspapers. He made a radio appearance. He went to Dublin to play a benefit for the families of victims of a theater fire. And on July 29 he sent a cable to *The New York Times* which resulted in his writing a series of daily telegrams that would continue for the next nine years, making the name of Will Rogers a household word throughout the United States.

What prompted the cablegram was Lady Astor's imminent visit to New York. Will and Betty had lunched with her one day, and after she sailed for the States he wired Adolph Ochs, the publisher of the *Times:* NANCY ASTOR, WHICH IS THE NOM DE PLUME OF LADY ASTOR, IS ARRIVING ON YOUR SIDE ABOUT NOW. PLEASE ASK MY FRIEND JIMMY WALKER TO HAVE NEW YORK TAKE

GOOD CARE OF HER. SHE IS THE ONLY ONE OVER HERE WHO DON'T THROW ROCKS AT AMERICAN TOURISTS. YOURS, WILL ROGERS.

Ochs printed the message in a box on the front page of the second section and wired Will, requesting more of the same. So for the rest of his stay in Europe, Will sent the short items to the *Times*. He had no particular thought of going on with the series, but when he returned to the States he discovered that readers were clamoring for more, and he decided to oblige.

The McNaught Syndicate dispatched the daily telegrams under the by-line "Will Rogers Says," and eventually they were featured in more than five hundred newspapers in the United States, reaching forty million readers.

From October 16, 1926, until the day of his death Will filed his telegram every day except Sunday, no matter where he was or what he was doing. Bruce Quisenberry described how they were produced while Will was on a lecture tour: "His newspaper dispatch . . . had to be filed by half past one. He would watch the time, then at the last possible moment, he would put his portable on his knees, stare into space for a few moments, then begin to peck. His hands—so amazingly skillful with a rope—were all thumbs when he tackled a typewriter. *Peck-peck-peck!* Sometimes he would stop, turn up the page and scowl at it for a minute. Then peck-peck-peck! When the telegram was finally ready, I would hop off the train at the first stop and file it. Sometimes I would have to run to catch the train. When I would finally get on he would say, 'I'll bet we lose you some day.' "

Written under every conceivable circumstance, while he was on location for a movie, in a hospital bed, or traveling about the world by steamship, airplane, automobile, or train, this concise expression of Will Rogers' philosophy cheered the American reading public. At the time he began it he was known as a popular comedian; now Americans began to realize that what he had to say was an authentic reflection of what most of them were thinking. Through this medium, more than any other, he emerged as a philosopher as well as a humorist. In the end he became a national institution.

THROUGHOUT THAT SUMMER of 1926, while the family toured Europe, Will gave Americans a view of it unlike anything they had read since Mark Twain's *Innocents Abroad* in 1869. England, he said, "has the best Statesmen and the Rottenest coffee of any Country in the world." In France, he learned, Nice is "pronounced neece. They have no word for nice in French." From Italy he reported that San Francisco Bay would make the Bay of Naples look like the Chicago drainage canal. Until he got there he didn't know that "Rome had Senators. Now I know why it declined."

Interspersed with all the open letters to the President were special cablegrams, addressed to CALCOOL WHITEWASHHOUSE, and signed WILLROG, summarizing what Americans thought about Europe. The final cable to CALCOOL ended, BACK HOME AND BROKE. WILLROG. When he landed in New York, Will actually did send the President a telegram and was invited to the White House to make his "report." His summation of the summer's experience was that America "don't stand as good as a Horse Thief" in Europe. "The only way we would be worse with them was to help them out in another war."

When his collection of letters from the *Post* appeared in book form in October 1926, a *New York Times* reviewer commented, "There has rarely been an American humorist whose words produced less empty laughter or more sober thought." And Franklin D. Roosevelt remarked later that "the first time I fully realized Will Rogers' exceptional and deep understanding of political and social problems was when he came home from his European trip in 1926. . . . Will Rogers' analysis of affairs abroad was not only more interesting but proved to be more accurate than any other I had heard."

Will was now forty-seven years old and had entered upon the most productive and creative phase of his life. With the possible exception of films, he had succeeded magnificently at everything he had tried and was known not only in the United States but in most countries of the Western world. The man who used to sign his letters to Betty "Injun Cowboy" had come a long way.

8

"If your time is worth anything, travel by air. If not, you might just as well walk."

THE summer of 1926 was a fair sample of what Will Rogers' life was to be like from then on. As if driven by some inner demon, he was actively pursuing half a dozen careers simultaneously, without pause. Each day was a new adventure, launched with a spur-of-the-moment decision to go somewhere and see something he might otherwise miss. There were no vacations, in the usual sense of the word. "It's always a bird that never does anything that enjoys a vacation," he observed. "There's nothing in the world as hard as playing when you don't want to."

Although some of this bustle can be laid to that old restlessness that had been with him since he was a young boy, the continuous need for material for his newspaper articles also played a part. Never satisfied with secondhand information, he wanted to see things for himself, to talk with the people involved, and whenever the mood took him he hopped an airplane and was off. "I got one little old soft red grip," he said, "that if I just tell it when I am leaving it will pack itself. A few white shirts, a little batch of underwear and sox. All I take is my typewriter and the little red bag, one extra suit in it. It's always packed the same, no matter if I'm going to New York or to Singapore."

In a day when comedians and columnists rely on gag writers and researchers for much of their material, it is difficult to fathom how Will Rogers could have written everything himself, but that is precisely what he did. Much of it was composed hurriedly and carelessly, but it was all his own, and considering the circumstances under which it came to life, the overall quality is astonishingly high. Will's copy was enough to give an editor fits. He never retyped anything, never made a carbon, didn't bother to correct spelling, grammar, or punctuation. Frequently he didn't even read his articles over. "When I write 'em I am through with 'em," he admitted. "I am not being paid reading wages." Yet in the same way that his easy, relaxed manner took the bite out of certain remarks he made about people, the spelling, grammar, and construction of his written work had a curious softening effect.

If ever a man's office could be said to be in his hat, Will's was. Even when he finally did rent space in an office building in Beverly Hills, it was no more than a mail drop. Mrs. Daisy Tyler, a public stenographer hired to help with the daily accumulation of mail, recalled that during the eight years she worked for Will he probably never dictated more than eight replies. She would select the letters she thought would interest him, take them to his home, and on weekends he would type the answers himself, never making a carbon copy. As often as not he would fire off a telegram in response.

On American intervention: *"I don't care how little your country is, you got a right to run it like you want to. When the big nations quit meddling, then the world will have peace."*

WILL's frantic pace in 1926 is suggested by the fact that he set off on his second lecture tour the day after he visited Calvin Coolidge at the White House, following the frenetic summer in Europe. He was enlivening the talks now with fresh material from his travels on the Continent, and his lectures and his daily telegrams reflected an increasingly jaundiced view of the international situation. Wherever he looked, the United States seemed to be interfering in the affairs of other nations: "Our gunboats are all in the Chinese war, our marines have landed in Nicaragua. . . . If Nicaragua would just come out like a man and fight us, we wouldn't have to be hunting away off over in China for a war." He concocted slogans for the Central American adventure. One was "Stop Nicaragua while there is still time."

When he embarked on the lecture circuit Betty returned to California to enroll the two youngest children in school. Will, Jr., the oldest, was sent to Culver Military Academy; there, on his fifteenth birthday, he received a letter written by his father in

Spartanburg, South Carolina. Will was planning to be home for Christmas, he said, and would see his son then. Meanwhile he was heading for Oklahoma, a new project in mind. He was going to buy some more land and "fix up the old ranch place."

On Will's part there was more sentiment than business sense involved in this decision. His roots—along with the family and friends he cared for deeply—were there and were never far from his thoughts. "I'm just an old country boy in a Big Town tryin' to get along," he said. "I been eatin' pretty regular, and the reason I have been is because I've stayed an old country boy."

In May 1925 he had made a sad journey to the town of Chelsea for the funeral of his sister Maud Lane, following which he wrote one of his few entirely serious weekly articles. "I am out in Oklahoma, among my People, my Cherokee people, who don't expect a laugh for everything I say. . . . I have just today witnessed a Funeral that for real sorrow and real affection I don't think will ever be surpassed anywhere. They came in every mode of conveyance, on foot, in Buggies, Horseback, Wagons, Cars, and Trains, and there wasn't a Soul that come that she hadn't helped or favored at one time or another. Some uninformed Newspapers printed: 'Mrs. C. L. Lane sister of the famous Comedian, Will Rogers.' . . . It's the other way around. I am the brother of Mrs. C. L. Lane, 'The Friend of Humanity.' And all the honors that I could ever in my wildest dreams hope to reach, would never equal the honor paid on a little western Prairie hilltop, among her people, to Maud Lane. If they will love me like that at the finish, my life will not have been in vain."

They were a close family, the old ties ran deep; and as Will's niece Paula McSpadden Love wrote, the greatest excitement in the lives of relatives in Oklahoma was to hear that Uncle Will was coming home, which he often did when crossing the country. If Betty was with him, she would play the piano after dinner while Will sang the latest musical hits in his high tenor voice. He impersonated other actors, told jokes and stories, and showed the home folks some of his new routines.

What Will liked to do best was to get on a pony and ride

around the ranch or rope some goats, then have a plate of beans with ham hocks. He could always get good beans in Oklahoma. His nieces, wrote Irene McSpadden Milam, were taught "to cook navy beans as he liked them, with plenty of soup. Then there would be ham, hickory smoked, cured just the same as it was on the old ranch, and cream gravy with hot biscuits." And in the springtime there would be tiny wild onions, scrambled with eggs.

Yet as much as he loved Oklahoma, the homeplace, and the informality of life there, his commitments and interests simply would not permit him to return to the ranch near Oologah for any extended period. As a substitute for what he felt he was missing, he began turning over in his mind the possibility of selling the Beverly Hills house and building on land he had acquired in the Santa Monica Mountains.

That was easier said than done. Just before Christmas of 1926 the daily telegram began to be signed Hon. Will Rogers. On December 21, when he returned home for the holidays, the residents of Beverly Hills turned out en masse—movie actors, a corps of motorcycle police, two brass bands, and people carrying banners—to see Will presented with a five-foot scroll honoring him as mayor. "They say I'll be a comedy mayor," he said in his acceptance speech. "Well, I never saw a mayor yet that wasn't comical. As to my administration, I won't say I'll be exactly honest, but I'll agree to split fifty-fifty with you and give the town an even break. I'm for the common people, and as Beverly Hills has no common people I won't have to pass out any favors."

Fortunately for Will's other interests, the mayoral term was brief. According to California law, in sixth-class cities like Beverly Hills the president of the board of trustees was constitutionally the mayor, so Mayor Rogers was deposed. "I ain't the first mayor that's been kicked out," he wrote. "If I'd knowed Beverly Hills was a sixth-class town I wouldn't made the race."

He began to concentrate with a vengeance on the Santa Monica place. He had purchased a hundred and fifty acres, which he eventually increased to three hundred—nothing to compare in size with the Oklahoma property, but he referred to it as a

*After 1919 the family made California home. In 1926
his Beverly Hills neighbors appointed Will mayor, though
by law the head of the board of trustees automatically
held that office. Will "resigned" gracefully.*

ranch. ("It sounds big and dont really do any harm.") There
were no paved roads in the vicinity, the land was brushy and
steep, laced with canyons, and the only open space in the sea of
greasewood and sagebrush was a small clearing made by a truck
gardener. This lay on a mesa that was accessible only by means
of a virtually impassable road, but the view was worth all the
trouble of reaching it—in those days before smog one could see
off in the distance Santa Monica Bay, the Pacific Ocean, and
Catalina Island.

Things started to hum: Will hired men to clear away the
brush and build a corral and stables; then the ground was lev-
eled for a polo field. He had been introduced to polo years
earlier, while the family was living on Long Island. He taught all
three children the game, and the four Rogerses made a family
team until, as Will said sadly, "Mary went social on us."

IN THE SPRING OF 1927, during his lecture tour, one of the worst floods in history laid waste the Mississippi Valley. Hundreds were dead, hundreds of thousands were homeless, the damage ran into millions of dollars; but the federal government showed a curious reluctance to do anything. The Coolidge administration was convinced that private relief agencies could handle the immense task of feeding and clothing the destitute. Will thought otherwise; the Red Cross was appealing for five million dollars, but almost a million people had been victimized. "That would be only five dollars a head," Will said. "Five dollars ain't much good to you, even if the water's just up to your ankles."

In daily and weekly articles he plugged away at the need for assistance and donations. "Look at the thousands and thousands of Negroes that never did have much, but now its washed away," he wrote. "That water is just as high up on them as it is if they were white. The Lord so constituted everybody that no matter what color you are you require about the same amount of nourishment." He wired Florenz Ziegfeld to say that he would put on a benefit for flood victims if Ziegfeld would donate the theater, and Will and the tenor John McCormack raised nearly eighteen thousand dollars for the Red Cross. Another performance in New Orleans produced forty-eight thousand, and Will kept hammering away at his readers to open their pocketbooks.

ON MAY 21, 1927, the daily telegram expressed what was on the mind of every American. "No attempt at jokes today," it read. "An old slim, tall, bashful, smiling American boy is somewhere out over the middle of the Atlantic ocean, where no lone human being has ever ventured before." From that day on Will was one of Charles A. Lindbergh's most ardent fans. Almost half a century after the event, it is difficult to describe the worldwide outpouring of joy, excitement, and admiration that resulted from Lindbergh's twenty-seven-hour solo flight from New York to Paris in *The Spirit of St. Louis*. What somehow caught people's imagination was the American's exceptional integrity and courage, his indifference to the usual hallmarks of success. Lindbergh, Will

Rogers said, was our biggest national asset and ought to be allowed to spend his time promoting aviation instead of making an "exhibition out of himself"—a message few Americans would heed. The flier not only fulfilled Will's concept of a hero, he was also a member of a fraternity Will had come to admire enormously: the barnstorming pilots of the twenties.

After World War I aviation had fallen on evil days in the United States. There was almost no demand for planes, military airfields were deactivated, and only a few adventurous young men and women would have any part of flying. They piloted surplus DH-4s and Curtiss Jennies, hopping from county fair to carnival to give exhibitions of wing walking, stunting, and parachute jumping. For a time they were very nearly the only non-military aviators around.

In Europe, by contrast, commercial aviation had prospered. One reason for this was that European governments were subsidizing commercial airlines, while the U.S. government avoided anything that smacked of federal control over private enterprise. What changed this attitude was the Post Office Department's disastrous experience in flying the mail.

After establishing airmail service from Washington to New York, it made plans for a route from New York to Chicago, but almost at once the hazards of crossing the Allegheny Mountains proved too much. Because of prevalent storms, the absence of navigational equipment, and the use of inferior, open-cockpit, rebuilt warplanes, thirty-two of the first forty pilots hired by the Post Office were killed before the operation was turned over to commercial fliers. Though in 1925 Congress finally passed legislation encouraging commercial aviation, there remained more profit in carrying mail, and few airlines were interested in attracting passengers. Only after 1926, when the landmark Air Commerce Act was passed, did the new Bureau of Aeronautics begin licensing American planes and pilots and setting up standards for aircraft, landing fields, and navigational aids. So it was little wonder that Will's was a lonely voice advocating public acceptance of flying.

IN 1927 WILL BEGAN TAKING planes whenever and wherever he could. Not that air travel was easy to arrange in those days. The only way he could fly to some out-of-the-way places was on a small commercial plane carrying the U.S. mail. His son Will, Jr., remembers that his father would come into his bedroom at the Beverly Hills house at two a.m. and shake him awake. "Come on, boy. Get up. I got to go to the airport," he would say, and they would drive through the darkness to a landing field on the edge of Los Angeles.

There Will would pull on a fleece-lined leather flying suit, a helmet, and goggles, and then get on the scales. "They didn't put stamps on him," Bill says, "but he paid for his own weight as if he were a package." As soon as Will climbed into the forward cockpit of the open plane, the ground crew would pile sacks of mail around him and on top of him. Usually it was still dark when the plane taxied onto the runway and warmed up at the end of the field; then it would roar down the strip, and young Bill, driving home, would see it climb into the dawn sky.

Will flew with most of the outstanding aviators of the time, and although he occasionally made a pretense of concern, it was clear that he had little, if any, fear of flying. Captain Frank Hawks said Will "never paid any attention to the weather or the flying procedure while he was in the air. He read most of the time. . . . He placed all his confidence in me, figured that I knew my business, and would always get him to his destination." Flying was simply one of his great enthusiasms, and he never lost his love for it.

HE WOULD be in several plane crashes; but in the early summer of 1927 Will had his first close brush with death, and it had nothing to do with airplanes. He was in Bluefield, West Virginia, lecturing, when he began to suffer intensely from what he said was nothing more than a bellyache. He had a recurrence of the symptoms a few weeks later, while visiting the ranch in Oklahoma, and when he arrived in Beverly Hills, Betty called in the family physician, Dr. Percy White, who diagnosed the problem as gallstones and advised that a specialist be consulted. As Will told the story, the doctor then "phoned for what seemed like a friend, but who afterwards turned out to be an accomplice." This man, a surgeon named Dr. Clarence Moore, advised an operation. ("Imagine asking a surgeon what he advises!" Will commented. "It would be like asking Coolidge, 'Do you advise economy?' ")

Although Will was seriously ill following the operation, he managed not to miss a single one of his daily columns (he wrote no weekly article, however, between June 19 and July 17); just before he was wheeled away to the operating room he dictated the daily wire: "I am in the California Hospital, where they are going to relieve me of surplus gall, much to the politicians' delight." On Sundays his wire did not appear, so he could skip Saturday, but on the next day he dictated his Monday message, just six words long: "Relax—lie perfectly still, just relax."

While he was still hospitalized, hundreds of telegrams poured in from well-wishers, including Coolidge, and as Will remarked, "People couldn't have been any nicer to me if I had died."

With an uncanny ability to put experience to good use, Will not only wrote about the operation in his daily and weekly articles, but published several stories about it in the *Saturday Evening Post*. These were brought out later as a book, *Ether and Me: or, Just Relax.*

Back on his feet again, he began shooting what was to be his last silent film, *The Texas Steer*, in which he played the part of a Texas rancher who was elected to Congress. When the company arrived in Washington, D.C., to film some political scenes against the backdrop of the Capitol, the National Press Club gave him a reception and appointed him "congressman-at-large for the United States of America." Will was pleased, but said it was "the poorest appointment I ever got. I certainly regret the disgrace that's been thrust on me here tonight. I . . . have lived, or tried to live my life so that I would never become a Congressman."

While the Press Club's title was bestowed in fun, the next one Will received was intended seriously. He was invited to become the nation's "unofficial ambassador to Mexico."

9

"I'd rather be right than Republican."

RELATIONS between the United States and Mexico had never been serene. Following the war between the two countries in the 1840s, the United States had acquired from Mexico the territory that now comprises Arizona, Nevada, California, and Utah, parts of New Mexico, Colorado, and Wyoming, as well as its claims to Texas north of the Rio Grande. Mexicans had neither forgotten nor forgiven. In 1927 President Coolidge named his Amherst College classmate Dwight Morrow, a partner in J. P. Morgan & Co., as ambassador to Mexico. There were those—including Will Rogers and a good many Mexicans—who looked on the appointment as a mixed blessing.

Will had a genuine affection and sympathy for the Mexicans, many of whom he had met in roping contests and rodeos, and he had decided views about the U.S. policy toward their country. "Up to now," he said, "our calling card to Mexico or Central America had been a gunboat or a bunch of Violets shaped like Marines." Mexico had her problems, he concluded, "and we are most of them."

Shortly after Ambassador Morrow arrived at his post he had an inspiration: to invite Will Rogers and Charles A. Lindbergh to visit the country on a goodwill mission. Already, Morrow had gotten off on the right foot with the Mexican man in the street by touring the country for several weeks with the popular President, Plutarco Calles. Will joined the two men aboard the heavily guarded presidential train.

On the second day of the trip he was late for dinner, and a member of Calles' party who found Will talking with the troops suggested that it was impolitic to keep Calles waiting. "You tell him," Will said, "that I've been in Mexico only a few days and I have found out that it's better down here to stand in right with the soldiers than with the President." Fortunately, Calles' interpreter was an American named Jim Smithers, who had a gift for reproducing Will's comments in Spanish. And Will's candor endeared him immediately to Calles, as did his love of close-harmony singing, which he and Morrow performed to the accompaniment of the president's guitar. He attended a bullfight, and to the amusement of the crowd buried his head in his arms to avoid seeing horses gored by the bull. He played polo, flew over the volcano Popocatepetl (he called it Popocatepillar), and was guest of honor at a banquet given by Morrow and attended by President Calles.

As a contribution to the goodwill mission, Lindbergh had agreed to fly nonstop from Washington to Mexico City, but lost his way somewhere over Mexico. Two hundred thousand people, including President Calles and his cabinet, waited patiently for eight hours and then gave him as tumultuous a welcome as he had received in Paris. As Will described it, "the streets were two inches thick with flowers." He and Morrow were resigning as ambassadors, he said; Lindbergh was taking over.

On bankers: *"[Bankers] are likeable rascals, and now that we are all wise to 'em, and it's been shown that they don't know any more about finances than the rest of us know about our businesses . . . why they are getting just as human as the groceryman, the druggist or the filling station man."*

Seemingly the only person in the country who didn't care about seeing the aviator was Dwight Morrow's twenty-year-old daughter Anne, who had just arrived for the Christmas holidays and considered Lindbergh no more than a newspaper hero—of the baseball-player type. She was certainly not going to worship Lindy ("that *odious* name," she called it); but when she met him at the embassy she found him much more poised than she had expected, and quite unlike the grinning Lindy pictures she had seen. A year later she was writing to a friend to say, "Apparently I am going to marry Charles Lindbergh."

Mrs. Morrow worried about the effect Lindbergh's arrival might have on Will Rogers' popularity, but speaking at a dinner that very evening, "he held the whole room in the hollow of his hand," she recalled. Like audiences everywhere, when the Mexicans were exposed to the typical Will Rogers performance they loved it. "I dident come here to tell you that we look on you as Brothers," he said. "We look on you as a lot of Bandits and you look on us as one Big Bandit."

He also offered some views on diplomacy: "A Diplomat is a man that tells you what he don't believe himself, and the man that he is telling it to don't believe it any more than he does. So Diplomacy . . . always balances." Morrow, he said, was different; he recognized that the only way for people to get along was to be honest with each other and get to understand one another. "He knows we don't hate you and that you don't hate us."

From the point of view of relations between Mexico and the United States, Will's visit was a triumph, and he carried away a lasting attachment for Ambassador Morrow, whom he described as "Wall Street's sole contribution to public life."

The meetings with Lindbergh in Mexico served only to whet Will's appetite for flying. Sometime before, he and Betty had flown with Lindbergh to California, with Will in the copilot's seat, asking innumerable questions. "How can you tell where to land when you don't know which way the wind is blowing?"

Lindbergh pointed to a clothesline on which laundry was flapping in the breeze. "That tells me," he said.

"Suppose it ain't Monday?" Will asked.

"I just wait till it is," Lindbergh responded.

Will flew part of the way home from Mexico to be with his family for Christmas, and on December 29 he was in the air again, this time courtesy of the U.S. Navy, in a plane catapulted from the battleship *Pennsylvania*. "Just watch your head," he advised, "and see that you don't leave it behind you." And to President Coolidge he said, "Keep after this air stuff, Calvin. Let's get all the planes we can, do all the commercial aviation we can to keep the boys in training."

THE YEAR 1928 WAS ANOTHER presidential election year, and politics, naturally, was beginning to dominate the news. The Democrats' Jackson Day dinner in Washington, D.C., brought to Will's mind all that the Cherokees had suffered at Old Hickory's hands, and he remarked, "I am not so sweet on old Andy. He is the one that run us Cherokees out of Georgia and North Carolina. I ate the dinner on him, but I didn't enjoy it. I thought I was eating for Stonewall."

He began another lecture tour, and both his talks and his newspaper columns emphasized his growing concern about the nation's economic health. What he said came across in the good-humored Rogers style, but there was no mistaking his worry over the situation. His trips around the country had convinced him that the good times Americans were enjoying were only on the surface. The attitude of most people was, "We'll show the world we are prosperous, even if we have to go broke to do it."

Two weeks before the Republican National Convention, Will made his own debut as a presidential candidate. The humor magazine *Life* announced that it was sponsoring a new political movement, the Anti-Bunk Party, with Will Rogers as its nominee. In the same issue Will stated that his acceptance was based on one pledge: "If elected I absolutely and positively agree to resign [and] that's offering the Country more than any Candidate ever offered it in the history of its entire existence." From then until the election in November, the opening editorial pages of the magazine were devoted to Will's "campaign."

No Anti-Bunk candidate for the vice-presidency was chosen. As for a platform, the candidate promised that "whatever the other fellow don't do, we will." There were no commitments: "We want the wet vote, and we want the dry vote. We are honest about it." There would be no party leaders; no slogans ("slogans have been more harmful to the country than Luncheon Clubs, Sand Fleas, Detours and Conventions"); no "baby kissing, passing out of cigars, laying cornerstones, dodging issues."

While the voters were absorbing all this, Will was en route to Kansas City, where the Republicans were gathering. After Herbert Hoover was nominated for President, Will was tickled to see that Charles Curtis was picked for the second spot on the ticket. Curtis' mother had Kaw Indian blood, and thus he was "the only American that has ever run for that high office. Come on Injun," Will pleaded, "if you are elected let's run the white people out of this country."

Will was in Houston, Texas, at the end of June for the Democratic convention. He listened to Franklin Roosevelt, who at the 1924 convention had nominated Governor Alfred E. Smith of New York, "do his act from memory. Franklin Roosevelt could have gotten far in the Democratic party himself. But he has this act all perfected, and dont like to go to the trouble of learning something else. So he just seems satisfied going through life nominating Al Smith."

When it was all over, he considered that the party had nominated its best possible ticket: Governor Smith and Senator Joseph Robinson of Arkansas. One of the principal issues was Smith's Catholicism, and Will had something to say about that: "What do we care about a . . . Presidents religion. They dont do any business on Sunday anyway. Its week days we want to use him. Its one relief to find somebody mentioned for President who we do know what their religion is before they get in. There is not 2 out of 10 that can tell me what religion Coolidge is."

He liked and admired both presidential candidates, but he was disturbed during the campaign by the way the two parties tried to influence voters on the issue of prosperity. "How a speaker can convince a man that he is prosperous when he is broke, or that he is not prosperous when he is doing well, is beyond me. If a voter can't feel in his pockets and see if he is doing well without having some total stranger tell him, then his Government shouldn't be in the hands of the people."

As the campaign drew to a close, Will was disgusted with the whole thing. He predicted that Hoover was a shoo-in—had been, in fact, since the GOP convention in June. Smith's problem was that he was a Democrat.

The day after Hoover's election Will's daily telegram appeared in the form of a want ad. FOR SALE, it read, WOULD LIKE TO SELL, TRADE, DISPOSE OF OR GIVE AWAY FRANCHISE OF WHAT IS HUMOROUSLY KNOWN AS DEMOCRATIC PARTY. As the year came to a close he was depressed by the state of the Democratic Party, but more so by the state of the nation. In an unusually bittersweet column that is Will Rogers at his best, he told his readers why:

> The nation never looked like it was facing a worse Winter—birds, geese, Democrats and all perishable animals are already huddled up in three or four States down South. We are at peace with the world because the world is waiting to get another gun and get it loaded. Wall Street is in good shape, but Eighth Avenue never was as bad off. The farmers are going into the Winter with pretty good radios, but not much feed for their stock.
>
> Yours,
> *Will Rogers*

IN THE summer of 1928 Will had come to the aid of an old friend in his typically generous way. The actor Fred Stone had learned to fly, and he was critically injured when his plane crashed. Stone was to open on Broadway that fall with his daughter, Dorothy, in a musical called *Three Cheers*. The show was already in rehearsal, the opening date was set, costumes and sets were made. When Will heard about the problem he immediately wired his friend to say that he would go into the show in Fred's place, "just to sort of plug along till you are able to rejoin, and I will do the best I can with the part." Will didn't even want any billing, though he would have to cancel his lecture tour at some financial sacrifice.

Will had only two weeks of rehearsals before the opening, but it didn't seem to matter. *Three Cheers* opened on October 25 and was an immediate smash hit. Will, of course, was playing himself—not the part written for Fred Stone. He simply used the part as a vehicle for the kind of routine he had done in the *Follies* for years—commenting on the news in the latest editions of the papers. One critic suggested that what was unique about Will was a public platform manner that made it possible for him to

Unlike many silent-movie stars, Will adapted easily to talkies, which he called "noisies." These are stills from his Hollywood years.

With Mickey Rooney in
The County Chairman

With Shirley Temple, another top box-office attraction

talk to an audience privately and confidentially. "Even before he opens his mouth to speak, the barrier of the footlights is down and we are in the same room with him."

This was to be Will's final Broadway performance. After a successful New York run, *Three Cheers* went on the road in April, 1929, and closed in Pittsburgh on June 1. The following day Will flew to California to launch another career: playing in talking pictures.

THOMAS EDISON had originally planned to combine his Kinetoscope with a phonograph to produce a moving picture with sound accompaniment. He lost interest in the scheme, but other inventors did not. Lee De Forest, originator of the triode or three-terminal tube that had made long-distance broadcasting feasible, synchronized sound and moving images on film, and his first "phonofilms" were shown in New York in 1923, but without causing much of a stir. Hollywood displayed no particular en-

With Myrna Loy in
A Connecticut Yankee

On the set of
Down to Earth

thusiasm for talking pictures until 1926, when William Fox brought out something called a Movietone, and the nearly bankrupt Warner Brothers company agreed to take on the Vitaphone produced by a subsidiary of the Western Electric Company.

The first sound films were shorts, but in 1927 the Warners produced the first feature with dialogue and music: *The Jazz Singer*, starring Al Jolson. It was an immediate and stunning success, and the rest of Hollywood realized that the old silent days were gone for good (only Charlie Chaplin held out into the thirties). Like all revolutions, this one left a cluster of pathetic derelicts in its wake—those once-popular stars whose voices were not suited to the new medium. Pola Negri and Clara Bow, the "It" girl, disappeared, and John Gilbert, the great lover of the silent screen whose high-pitched voice was incongruous in the roles he played, was doomed to oblivion.

But to Will Rogers talkies were quite another matter. He had never been as successful in silent pictures as on the stage or the lecture platform, simply because his act was so dependent on what he had to say and the way he said it. When he went into talking pictures he had something else going for him, too—a personality already familiar to millions of Americans.

From the beginning Will took a relaxed, amused view of what he called the "noisies." Yet when his first one, *They Had to See Paris,* opened in September 1929 he felt the old nervousness and lack of assurance that accompanied each new venture he attempted. As the time approached for the picture's preview, Will became increasingly apprehensive, and finally he announced to startled studio executives that he had to go to Oklahoma and would not attend. Not until a few days later was his mind set at ease; in Tulsa he received a telegram from Betty reporting that the picture had opened and he could come home.

The talkies he made ran to a pattern. He usually played a thinly disguised version of himself: a rustic, somewhat seedy common man, an underdog speaking out against wealthy, unscrupulous characters. He was the kindly, impractical philosopher, a sort of surrogate for the American conscience, reflecting the innate honesty and idealism of the plain folks of the land. To see any of Will's pictures—*A Connecticut Yankee, David Harum, The County Chairman, State Fair, Life Begins at Forty, Steamboat 'Round the Bend*—is to be transported suddenly into another world, a world that was gentle, kind, and thoroughly predictable, where the simple virtues and homely truths were opposed by easily discernible villainy, and where good would always triumph at the end. They were pictures that children wanted to see, and that their parents wanted them to see; in some towns school was dismissed so that students could attend special matinee performances of a Will Rogers film.

Will was a thoroughly untypical Hollywood star. Although a considerable portion of his income came from making movies, he never quite took it seriously, and it never became more than a sideline as far as he was concerned. Yet every tourist who visited Hollywood wanted to see him, and he was continually badgered at the studio by people who dropped by to meet him.

Despite his growing fame, his dress remained as casual as his personality—as often as not he wore blue jeans and boots and a small cowboy Stetson or well-traveled felt hat. He drove his own car to the studio, the back seat filled with the paraphernalia of his trade: portable typewriter, a stack of newspapers, telegraph blanks, ropes, some old clothes, and an extra pair of boots. When he arrived, it was evident that he was the most popular person on the lot; everyone said good-morning to Will Rogers.

Will's approach to making a picture never failed to astound old hands in the business. The night before shooting was to begin he would take the script home and read it through, just to get the gist of it, and the next morning would appear on the set with no idea whatsoever of his lines. Oblivious to all the hectic activity around him, he would slouch in a canvas chair, eyeglasses down on his nose, reading the morning papers. When called to play a scene he would ask the script girl to read what he was supposed to say and that, as often as not, would remind him of a story which he would proceed to tell while the director and other players waited.

At last they would begin, and those actors who were unused to playing opposite Will Rogers suddenly realized what it meant. Most of them, Joel McCrea remembers, were scared to death, because no one knew for certain what he would say or how long he might talk. As one of Will's cameramen described an actor's dilemma, "He waits for a certain cue in a speech. The cue doesn't come. For Will ad-libs his lines. . . . It isn't because he's too lazy to learn them; it's because each time he rehearses a scene he thinks of a better way of delivering a speech."

At the end of the morning's shooting, Will would call out "Lunchee! Lunchee!" and head for the studio cafeteria trailed by the cast and crew, who knew they would be entertained by a running barrage of jokes throughout the meal. Afterward he would walk out to his car, climb in, and thumb through the newspapers again, marking items that interested him with the stub of an old pencil. When he had what he wanted, he would put the typewriter on his lap and sit with his feet on the running board, pecking away at the daily article. Frequently he read the finished copy to the studio crew, and if they didn't get what he was trying to say he would change it. Then he would send it by messenger to the telegraph office. Afterward, to the director's dismay, he might disappear to the car again for a nap.

Will seemed to have none of the usual professional jealousy about scene-stealing. In fact, he made a point of seeing that minor or bit players got more of a part than the director had planned for them. Bill Robinson, the great Negro dancer, recalled that Will "put me in fifteen or sixteen scenes in [a] picture that I wasn't written in for. . . . He wouldn't let them hide my face."

Romantic parts were not for Will. As he once told a scriptwriter, "Hollywood park benches are filled with ex-actors who didn't know they were too old to make love." But something else—an innate modesty and sense of propriety—kept him from playing love scenes. In one film the script called for him to kiss his wife, played by Irene Rich, but Will kept putting off the scene. Finally the director took Miss Rich aside and told her to give Will a kiss when the time came, and she did, taking him completely by surprise. Embarrassed, he grinned sheepishly, and said, "I feel as if I'd been unfaithful to my wife."

Although he was completely natural on the movie set, never using makeup, never seeming to act when he was before the camera, there was something about him that baffled those who thought they knew him well. Whenever people were around he was the Will Rogers of the stage—easygoing, wisecracking, friendly with everybody, seemingly a wholly uncomplicated person. But beneath the surface, one scriptwriter said, the private man was "vastly reserved; there was a wall that no one went beyond; and there were dark chambers and hidden recesses that he opened to no one." Spencer Tracy said Will was "at the same time one of the best-known, and one of the least-known, men in the world. By inclination, he is a grand mixer; by instinct, he is as retiring as a hermit."

Frank Borzage, a director who worked with Will on several movies, claimed that it was his ability to make audiences forget

Though the Fox studio provided him with an ornate Spanish bungalow as a dressing room, Will preferred relaxing—or writing his column—in his car.

that he was a comedian from time to time that made him so popular. He was capable of portraying simple, human emotions with sincerity and conviction, and people seeing his films realized that he was more than a comic who cracked jokes. He was basically a man of many causes, and the humor which came so naturally to him was the most effective means of getting a message across to people, whether he was putting ideas on paper or acting them out in motion pictures.

According to a chart of the top ten box-office stars compiled by *Motion Picture Herald*, Will was in ninth place in 1932. In 1933 he was second (behind Marie Dressler); in 1934 he reached the top of the ratings; and in 1935—the year of his death—he was in second place behind the sensationally popular child star, Shirley Temple. At the outset he received $110,000 for each picture he made, and he averaged three a year. In 1930 he signed a new contract with the Fox Film Corporation calling for payment of $1,125,000 for six pictures, or nearly $200,000 each.

He thoroughly enjoyed making a picture, and there were few dull moments when he was around. During the filming of *State Fair*, the plot of which centered around a prize boar, the film company bought Iowa's grand champion boar to use in the movie. Known as Blue Boy, it was a mountainous creature with huge tusks and a vile disposition, and when it arrived the director, Henry King, cautioned Will to keep away from it.

The first time a scene was to be shot with Blue Boy, King sent for Will, but he was nowhere to be seen. King and the other actors found him stretched out on the ground beside the sleeping Blue Boy, head pillowed on the hog's side and hat over his eyes, apparently sleeping. What Will knew and King did not was that as long as he didn't disturb the animal he was quite safe. As soon as he saw King's horrified reaction to the gag and had his laugh, he got to his feet and climbed out of the pen.

When the picture was finished, Will was asked if he would like to buy Blue Boy, as meat for the family. Will declined. "I wouldn't feel right eatin' a fellow actor."

10

"We are continually buying something that we never get, from a man that never had it."

IN THE fall of 1929 Will was invited to Detroit to speak at a celebration honoring the inventor Thomas Edison, who was nearing the end of his long, productive life. Henry Ford had built a museum devoted to the history of industry and invention—about a third of it memorializing Edison's achievements—and decided to combine the dedication of his Dearborn Village with a commemoration of the fiftieth anniversary of the lighting of Edison's first electric lamp. To this grand occasion he summoned the nation's most eminent figures, including President Hoover, a number of prominent businessmen and financiers, Orville Wright, and his friend Will Rogers.

Will had a good time at the Edison affair. The inventor, he remarked, "had no idea when he invented that all-day lantern that it would lead to so much glory and confusion. He just invented it because he needed it to work by," and Ford had honored him because another of Edison's inventions had enabled people to start a Model T car without breaking an arm cranking it. There were so many wealthy industrialists present, Will said, that every time he spilled some coffee out of his saucer, it landed on a millionaire—John D. Rockefeller, Jr., numerous railroad presidents and automobile executives, Julius Rosenwald, the head of Sears, Roebuck, and others.

Those big men had something rather more pressing than the good old days on their minds in the autumn of 1929, however, for the economic storm cloud was directly overhead now and threatening to burst. Since the armistice, unprecedented changes had shaken the nation's economic structure. Merger after merger had taken place, and the holding company, which Will described as "a thing where you hand an accomplice the goods while the policeman searches you," was now the accepted means of assembling a complex pyramid of stockholdings. By 1929 fifteen companies controlled ninety percent of all the power produced in the country; U.S. Steel owned more than half the nation's iron-ore deposits; the Aluminum Company of America was a virtual monopoly.

Yet statistics and statements by men in the know assured Americans that this was for the nation's good. Between 1923 and 1926 trading on the New York Stock Exchange had doubled, while the average price of twenty-five representative stocks was up fifty-four percent. There seemed no limit to the money that could be made in the right securities. The radio industry, for one, was clearly here to stay, and Radio Corporation of America rode the heady tide. The stock's low in 1928 was 85½; the next year it reached 549. Everyone in New York talked stock prices. Bootblacks and barbers, shoe clerks and cabbies—all had a tip to pass on. As Will put it, "There had never been a time in our history when as many fools are making money as now."

Inauguration Day—March 4, 1929—produced a confident message from the new President, Herbert Hoover: "I have no fears about the future of our country. It is bright with hope." Like Coolidge, he opposed government controls and meddling in the stock market, and the speculative spiral went on unabated. Despite temporary lapses, the listed value of stocks more than doubled during the six-month period between March 3 and September 3, 1929. But what no one at the time realized was that that final day, Tuesday, September 3, was the dying effort of the great bull market.

On September 5 came unwelcome news. The economist Roger Babson, speaking to the National Business Conference, stated flatly, "Sooner or later a crash is coming, and it may be terrific." This was the signal for the so-called Babson break in the market, and from then on the trend was down.

BABSON was by no means the only prophet of doom. According to a biographer of Calvin Coolidge, when someone pressed Grace Coolidge to explain her husband's reason for not "choosing" to run for reelection, she replied simply, "Poppa says there's a depression coming." Others saw portents in the continuing agricultural woes, with farm surpluses growing while prices went steadily down. There were waves of labor unrest, an increasing number of bank failures, exposures of cruelly low wages. (Congressional investigators heard in 1929 from a fourteen-year-old girl who received $4.95 a week for sixty hours' work in a Southern textile mill.) The thing was there, if anyone cared to heed the warning signs.

Yet on October 17, while the industrialists were on their way to Dearborn to honor Edison, there were some optimists. The political economist Irving Fisher of Yale asserted that the market was on a permanent high plateau. Less than a week later the president of New York's National City Bank said there was "nothing fundamentally wrong with the stock market or with the underlying business and credit structure" of the country. That remark preceded by just two days the landmark known forever after as Black Thursday, when the whole house of cards collapsed. Despite efforts of New York's most highly placed bankers to stem the tide, an angry, half-hysterical crowd of brokers on the floor of the exchange fought to unload their stocks before it was too late. On that day thirteen million shares were sold, and the ticker was four hours late at closing time. The following Monday was even worse: in a single day the value of stocks plummeted fourteen billion dollars, and no bottom was in sight.

Will was in New York City on Black Thursday, or "wailing day," as he called it, when "you had to stand in line to get a window to jump out of." The following Saturday he was in Oklahoma, musing about the contrast between the canyons of Wall Street and the lovely, pastoral countryside he had just flown over. "Why, an old sow and a litter of pigs make more people a living than all the steel and General Motors stock combined." A few days later, back in California, he was more rueful. What irked him was the talk about how Rockefeller and other financiers were "stabilizing" the market: "Sure must be a great consolation to the poor people who lost their stock in the late crash to know that it has fallen in the hands of Mr. Rockefeller, who will . . . see that it has a good home. . . . There is one rule that works in every calamity," he added: "Be it pestilence, war or famine, the rich get richer and the poor get poorer."

Toward the close of the year he tried to sum up what had gone wrong. People had been carried away by the fever of speculation, he wrote, and they had to get over the idea that they could live by gambling: "Somebody has to do some work."

What he neglected to say was that Wall Street was not so much a cause as a symptom of a far more serious and widespread disorder. And it is doubtful whether Will Rogers was fully aware just then how grave conditions in the country really were.

This is not to suggest that he was insensitive to the plight of most Americans—far from it, as his tireless efforts to help the unfortunate during the next few years were to demonstrate. But as 1929 drew to a close it must have been almost impossible for a man of his circumstances to comprehend the difficulties facing millions of his fellow countrymen. In 1929 the average family income was about $2300; three years later it would fall to $1600 or less. At the same period Will's annual income from movies, radio, and other appearances, and daily and weekly columns exceeded $500,000. He had never invested in the stock market. He had substantial capital in land, endowment policies totaling $200,000, nearly $500,000 in life insurance, plus annuities and U.S. bonds.

In 1930, when he signed a $72,000 contract for fourteen radio talks, there was criticism over the fact that he was being paid the unprecedented fee of $350 a minute to tell jokes. It was not generally known that he donated the money to charity.

IN 1930 THE Depression gnawed at the vitals of American society—on farms, in factories, small enterprises, and enormous industrial concerns. That year nearly four and a half million people were unemployed as compared with one and a half million in 1929. The figure would rise to eight million in 1931, twelve million in 1932, and thirteen million in 1933.

No one seemed to know what to do. The government in Washington did not fully comprehend the extent or the nature of the disaster. Hoover had no answers for the jobless, who were lining up outside soup kitchens waiting for something to eat; he approved an appropriation of forty-five million dollars to feed cattle affected by the 1930 drought while opposing the expenditure of twenty-five million to feed farm families. The latter, he believed, were the responsibilities of local governments or the Red Cross. He was convinced that the Depression was merely a passing interlude in the nation's life.

Drought seared the farm country. In a bountiful land breadlines were everywhere. During the second winter of the Depression, after five hundred farmers marched up to a country store in the little town of England, Arkansas, and demanded food for their wives and children, the Senate appropriated fifteen million dollars for food, but the House turned it down. A week later the same legislators voted the same amount of money to improve entrances to the national parks, and Will regarded it as a clear indication that "You can get a road anywhere you want to out of the government, but you can't get a sandwich." In two years, he supposed, there wouldn't be a poor farm that didn't have a concrete highway leading to it.

In January 1931 Will met with the President, exploring Mr. Hoover's proposal that the Red Cross should meet the crisis. Dubious of that approach ("I don't think we have anybody in Washington that don't want to feed 'em, but they all want to feed 'em their way"), Will determined nevertheless to help raise funds for the Red Cross.

He set out on a trip across the country to see at first hand the farm communities most seriously affected by drought. "You don't know what hard times are till you go into some of these houses," he wrote. Later in the month he embarked on a charity tour for the benefit of the Red Cross, flying in a navy plane piloted by Frank Hawks, giving performances in several towns each day, paying all the expenses for himself and whatever additional talent he could scrape up, and adding his personal check to the contributions received. In eighteen days he visited fifty cities or small towns in Texas, Oklahoma, and Arkansas, raising $225,000 in cash, plus an additional amount in pledges. His only requests were that every cent of the proceeds go to the needy, to be

On manners: *"Manners are nothing more than common sense, and a person has no more right to try and get every drop of soup out of his plate than he has to take a piece of bread and try and harvest all the Gravy in his plate. You must remember . . . that the question of the World today is, not how to eat soup, but how to get soup to eat."*

divided equally between those in urban and rural areas, and that a portion of the $90,000 he had raised in Oklahoma be set aside specifically for the relief of Cherokee Indians.

The effects of Will's whirlwind tour went far beyond the money he raised. Suddenly people became aware that at least one prominent man in the nation cared deeply enough about them and their troubles to try to help. Their reaction was an outpouring of affection and love the likes of which few men are privileged to receive.

The most vivid record of it is in newsreel films from the time. On the edge of a desolate prairie landing strip outside a tiny Texas or Oklahoma town a crowd of people stands, looking off into the distance. Then the camera pans around to catch a small aircraft approaching, its wings wobbling in the wind as it comes in for the landing. Before the wheels touch the ground the crowd surges forward—men, women, and children running, overcoats flapping behind them. The camera picks up the blurred faces; they are laughing and cheering out of sheer joy, oblivious of everything but getting to that airplane as fast as they can. And then there is Will Rogers, climbing out of the plane, somewhat startled to see the size of the crowd, grinning, waving, shaking hands with hundreds of strangers who are his friends.

When he had to return to California in February to make a picture, he read that the government had finally appropriated twenty million dollars for drought-stricken farmers. But the money was to be loaned against security put up by the farmers. "Now the man and his family that are hungry down there have no security," he explained. "If he had any security he wouldn't be hungry." Given the prevailing mood in Washington, there appeared to be no alternative to private assistance through the Red Cross, and in an unusually bitter column Will suggested that there were certain people the Red Cross couldn't reach— people so far back in the woods that the rest of the world had almost forgotten them: "I am speaking of the Senate and Congress of these United States."

Noting that the stock market had picked up a bit, he observed that U.S. Steel might go to a thousand, "but that don't bring one biscuit to a poor old Negro family of fifteen in Arkansas who haven't got a chance to get a single penny in money till their few little bales of cotton are sold away next fall." He was sick at heart over the attitude of the Republicans, who were claiming that business was getting better "because there is fewer apples being sold on the street. Lord that only means it's getting worse."

In the fall his active help was sought by the President—a remarkable request, all things considered, which indicated the extent of Will's hold on the American public. On October 31, 1931, in a nationwide hookup, Herbert Hoover and Will Rogers spoke over the radio on the subject of unemployment.

On Presidents: *"We shouldn't elect a President; we should elect a magician."*

Will's talk was basically an appeal for the type of public-spirited generosity and private support on which Hoover counted so heavily. What effect it had on the unemployment situation is difficult to ascertain—the situation having gone well beyond the thumb-in-the-dike measures Hoover was requesting. But it did cast Will Rogers in his most important role by far and produced the memorable line: "We are the first nation in the history of the world to go to the poorhouse in an automobile."

Meantime conditions were growing worse. In 1931 twenty-three hundred U.S. banks went under. In 1932 Detroit's unemployed auto workers, who had stood in line for days hoping for a few hours' work, confronted Henry Ford's factory guards in an ugly battle, leaving behind four dead and a number of wounded. And in May 1932 a band of World War veterans, determined to collect the bonus Congress had voted but had not appropriated, began moving eastward from the Pacific Northwest, picking up supporters in every city along the way.

These men were angry and desperate, but they were remarkably peaceable in their intentions. They were led by a veteran who had been out of a job for eighteen months, and who imposed on the Bonus Expeditionary Force the rules of "no panhandling, no drinking, no radicalism." When they arrived in Washington they were permitted to camp on the flats along the Anacostia River, where they waited patiently for Congress to deliver their bonus. The administration did little, a bill for immediate payment was voted down, and the thousands of increasingly restive men threatened to remain until they had seen Hoover and received their money. Toward the end of June the President called out the army. The chief of staff, General Douglas MacArthur, assisted by Major Dwight Eisenhower, Major George Patton, and other officers, led tanks, machine gunners, and a column of infantry with fixed bayonets along Pennsylvania Avenue to scatter the veterans and burn their camp in what was called the battle of Anacostia Flats.

While Will did not approve of the bonus march, he conceded that veterans had as much right to put pressure on Congress as any other lobbyists, particularly since they were acting only in their own behalf. He especially admired their conduct throughout the long, sordid mess. "They hold the record for being the best behaved of any 15,000 hungry men ever assembled anywhere in the world. They were hungry, and yet they remained fair and sensible. Would 15 thousand hungry bankers have done it? 15 thousand farmers? 15 thousand preachers? And just think what 15 thousand club women would have done to Washington even if they wasn't hungry. . . . It's easy to be a gentleman when you are well fed, but these boys did it on an empty stomach."

Further trouble was mounting in the farm belt. In the Plains states drought and erosion had turned thousands of acres to hardpan or dust, and the topsoil blew away on the summer winds or ran off in spring floods. In the early thirties the dust storms began—thick brown clouds, sometimes five miles high, that forced families to huddle indoors or tie handkerchiefs around their noses and mouths when they went outside. Thousands of debt-ridden tenant farmers packed up their pitiful belongings and drove away. In Iowa farmers armed with clubs and pitchforks blocked the roads, barring the movement of milk into the cities. (Dairymen were then receiving two cents a quart for their milk.)

Violence broke out before the "strike" was called off, but nothing was accomplished; it only dramatized the critical situation in America's breadbasket.

Will sympathized with the farmers in Iowa, who were "stopping the trucks and eating what the other farmers send to town." It impressed him as a pretty good scheme; if farmers would eat all they raised, not only would they get fat but the price of farm products would undoubtedly rise. "Course," he added, "on account of this not being an economist's idea it might not work."

As often as Will criticized President Hoover and his method of dealing with the Depression, he had considerable sympathy for and understanding of the man. He once remarked, "Nobody ever asked Coolidge to fix a thing. We just let everything go, and everybody grabbed off what he could. . . . Now Mr. Hoover is elected and we want him to fix everything. Farm relief . . . Prohibition . . . Prosperity—millions of people never had it under nobody and never will have it under anybody, but they all want it under Mr. Hoover. If the weather is wrong, we blame it on Hoover."

Luck, he thought, had been against Hoover all the way. "He arrived at the picnic when even the last hard-boiled egg had been consumed. Somebody slipped some limburger cheese into his pocket and he got credit for breaking up the dance."

11

"A Man that don't love a Horse, there is something the matter with him."

SOMETHING so untypical of Will Rogers' normal behavior occurred during 1931 that his wife Betty went out of her way to record it: after returning from a tour of Central America and the Caribbean he spent six months at home.

Home, by this time, was the Santa Monica ranch—and the move, Betty explained, had been prompted initially by their daughter Mary's lack of a bathroom. In the Beverly Hills house she shared a bath with her parents, who decided in 1928 that she ought to have one of her own. An architect was consulted, and remodeling began. Then termites were discovered, and Will, in disgust, finally had the workmen tear down the house. By then the Santa Monica place was finished and that, in any case, was where he wanted to live. He liked a lot of room to move around in, and he wanted more space for the horses.

The entrance to the ranch was off to the right of the road that eventually became Sunset Boulevard. A long curving drive—dotted with hundreds of eucalyptus trees set out by Will—wound up the hill. At the top was the long green sweep of a polo field. Beyond were the house, a garage and other outbuildings, a large horse barn, corrals, a cage for practicing polo, an oval-shaped roping ring, and a tennis court. At one side of the house were several golf holes for the use of friends. Will never had cared for the game (he couldn't understand why anyone would walk when he could ride), and when visitors were playing he would ride around on a horse and with a polo mallet hit the balls back to the unnerved golfers.

The house, which Anne Morrow Lindbergh described after a visit as "so quiet and far away and protected" that she and her husband felt "completely private and free," looked as if it had always been lived in and loved—relaxed and comfortable, with a casual, unpretentious beauty. The original building included three small bedrooms, a large living room, and a patio built around two live oaks; later this structure was enlarged piecemeal—becoming, at last, a long, rambling house. There was no dining room, since Will hated formal dinners and preferred to eat or entertain on the patio, where he often did the cooking himself at a barbecue grill.

With all his nervous energy he found it almost impossible to sit still throughout an entire meal, and between courses he would get up from the table and throw a rope—keeping up a steady flow of conversation all the while. If Fred Stone was there for dinner, the two men would leave the table and begin swinging lassos while they talked and joked—sometimes aiming at a

*Souvenirs of the Old West and of Will's career
decorated the living room of his Santa Monica ranch
house. The stuffed calf was for practicing roping.
The large spread also had a horse barn, polo field,
roping ring, tennis court, and a small golf course.*

chair, sometimes throwing a loop over another dinner guest. One
friend, the artist Ed Borein, finally tired of being roped and presented Will with a stuffed calf on casters.

The big living room overflowed with the mementos he loved:
over the stone fireplace was the head of a Texas steer; a light
fixture in the ceiling was made from an old wagon wheel; there
were spurs, riding quirts, and beautifully worked saddles from all
over the world; Navaho blankets and rugs; Western paintings by
his friends Charlie Russell and Ed Borein; skins of a tiger and a
black leopard sent him by the sultan of Johore; the model of a
covered wagon; a barrel full of his ropes; and, for a couch, a porch
swing hanging from the exposed beams.

At one end of the living room was a big picture window, the gift of Florenz Ziegfeld. The producer had always admired the view from the house but didn't like having to go outside to see it, so one day when Will was not home he sent his chauffeur to take measurements, and the next thing the Rogers family knew, workmen were tearing out the wall and installing the window. At a table in front of it, Will ate breakfast, read the morning papers, and planned his daily article.

Now in his early fifties, Will had begun to experience some difficulty in reading; the old "Injun eyes" weren't quite as good as they had been. One day in The Lambs, a club in New York, an actor friend saw him holding a newspaper at arm's length and offered his glasses. Will put them on and left the club with them in his pocket. He never had his eyes tested; Betty simply had the friend's prescription duplicated and ordered a dozen pairs at a time, since Will was so hard on them. When talking to someone he would twirl them in his hand or chew on the earpieces until they were twisted and gnawed out of shape.

WHEN he was at home Will was outdoors constantly. If he was not roping calves—a small bunch was always kept on the ranch for this purpose—or riding or playing polo, he was having new fences built, buildings altered, new roads or bridle paths cut into the hills. Several Mexicans were employed for this type of work, and to help around the house there was a butler named Emil Sandmeier, as well as a former cowboy, turned chauffeur, whose principal qualification in Will's eyes was that he could teach the children how to rope.

The two boys, Bill and Jim—and, for a time, Mary—played polo with Will, and since each rider needed five or six mounts for an afternoon's game, the stables and corrals were usually full. All this exercise kept Will in superb physical condition (he still did the Texas skip, jumping back and forth through a vertically spinning loop, every morning). And the result, his son Jim remembers, was that "he was *tough*, physically."

Active as he was, he also had the ability to relax completely.

Coming into the house after roping or riding, he could sit down and be sound asleep within minutes; then he would wake up, restored, and start on another project. He was, Jim says, an extremely nervous person who always had to keep moving, "and like so many creative people, he had days when he was riding high, on the crest of the wave, and the next day he would hit bottom. Mother always knew when to jolly him along and how to play to his moods." She was also the calming influence, "the balance wheel," Will called her. As he wrote on their twenty-fifth wedding anniversary, "The day I roped Betty, I did the star performance of my life."

Disciplining the children was evidently Betty's job; she once told an interviewer that Will had never spanked them—she took care of that. Even so, Jim retains a vivid recollection of his father's quick temper—his "short fuse." Whatever tension may have flared up occasionally between parents and children, Will's feelings on the matter were expressed in a letter he wrote Mary on her nineteenth birthday: "Sometimes we old ones dont see eye to eye with you Kids. But its *us* that dont stop to see your modern viewpoint. Times change. But Human Nature dont."

THE pattern of the Rogers' homelife was directly traceable to Betty's and Will's upbringing and background. "Our parents were wholesome country people," Betty once said, "and that's the kind of life we like. And the kind we want our children to like." All three children were given music and dancing lessons, but Will didn't want them in show business. He was content to have Mary play in summer stock, but he didn't want her career to go further than that.

His sons recall that their parents were away from home continually; there never seemed a time when their father, in particular, was not involved in something that took him away. While the children were young, Betty Rogers had had to make a choice: to be with her husband as much as possible or to stay at home with them, and she chose the former, after arranging for her unmarried sister, Theda Blake, or "Aunt Dick" as the children called her, to be with Bill, Mary, and Jim. For several years, while the family was in Beverly Hills, Will's niece Paula Mc-Spadden also lived at the house, helping the youngsters with their lessons, riding with them, and taking them to plays, ball games, and picnics.

In the fall of 1931 both boys were away at school, and there must have been some discussions between their mother and father about their failure to write home. Will brought the matter to his readers' attention in his column on October 29, brightening the day for many an American parent: "Early in the autumn," he wrote, "Mrs. Rogers and I sent two sons away supposedly to schools (we got tired trying to get 'em up in the morning). One went north here in this state, another to New Mexico. Since then we have received no word or letter. We have looked in every football team all over the country. Guess they couldn't make the teams, knew their education was a failure and kept right on going. Any news from any source will be welcome. I am flying to Mexico City today. The big one spoke Spanish so maybe he is there. The little one didn't even speak English but he loved chili and hot tamales so he may be there too."

In 1932 Bill accompanied his father to the Democratic convention and shared a hotel room with him in Chicago. He never got any sleep at night because Will was constantly on the telephone, and during the day it was Bill's job to keep people away from his father as much as possible, since everyone seemed to want to meet him. At one point a man dressed in an old sailor suit approached, and Bill dutifully began to fend him off. The sailor called out to Will, who hurried over, greeted him with open arms, and introduced him to his son as the poet Carl Sandburg. One of Bill's colorful recollections was a late night in the hotel room when Will, Sandburg, and Groucho Marx sat together playing guitars and singing. Will had a high regard for Groucho, who "can play as good on the guitar as Harpo can on the harp, or Chico on the piano, but he never does. He is really what I call an ideal musician. He can play but don't."

Despite considerable evidence to the contrary, by his own account Will was not much of a reader of books. As he put it: "I just got started in wrong. All educated people started in reading good books. Well I didn't. I seem to have gone from Frank Merriwell and Nick Carter, at Kemper Military Academy, right to the Congressional Record, just one set of low fiction to another."

There are occasional glimpses of his pride in having succeeded without benefit of college or degree, but he regretted not having taken advantage of the opportunities to acquire a good education. In May 1931, hearing of plans to give him an honorary degree, he fired off a telegram:

WHAT ARE YOU TRYING TO DO, MAKE A JOKE OUT OF COLLEGE DEGREES? THEY ARE IN BAD ENOUGH REPUTE AS IT IS, WITHOUT HANDING 'EM AROUND TO COMEDIANS. THE WHOLE HONORARY DEGREE THING IS THE "HOOEY." I GOT TOO MUCH RESPECT FOR PEOPLE THAT WORK AND EARN 'EM TO SEE 'EM HANDED AROUND TO EVERY NOTORIOUS CHARACTER. I WILL LET OOLOGAH KINDERGARTEN GIVE ME ONE—D.A. (DOCTOR OF APPLESAUCE).

ALTHOUGH he belonged to no church and rarely attended services, he was a deeply religious man on his own terms. He had been raised a Methodist, he once told a clergyman, but having traveled so widely and seen so many types of people, "I don't know now just what I am. I know I have never been a nonbeliever. But I can honestly tell you that I don't think that any one religion is *the* religion. Which way you serve your God will never get one word of argument or condemnation out of me."

His whole outlook on living was relaxed and casual. He disliked plans intensely, Betty said, and "would not make an engagement two weeks ahead of time if he could possibly help it." His idea of heaven was to have a free day when he and Betty could get in the car and drive without any preconceived notion of where they were going, and she recalled those trips as some of their happiest times, when she had him all to herself.

"Come on, Blake, let's get going," he would say, and they would drive until it was time to file his daily article. He would pull off the road and sit on the running board with the type-writer on his knees while she worked at her knitting, and then they would drive to the nearest telegraph office. If they had no sandwiches with them, Will liked to stop at a small-town grocery store and wander from shelf to shelf, collecting cans and boxes of food for lunch; then he would chat for a while with the store-keeper before they went on.

He had a rule about clothes. "He dressed only once a day," Betty said. "After his bath in the morning he put on a clean shirt, and that bath and that shirt had to last him through the evening, no matter what came up." On the ranch he wore work clothes—blue jeans, boots, a cowboy shirt and sometimes a hand-kerchief around his neck, and a small, light-colored Stetson. For more formal occasions he had a reliable double-breasted blue serge suit which, with a white shirt and black bow tie, had to do also for evening wear. He did not dress up for anyone.

It occurred to Betty now and again that she had four chil-dren, not three, and that Will "was the greatest child of all." He was not unaware of this himself. Speaking to a radio audi-ence he alluded to "the mother of our little group," saying that she "has been for twenty-two years trying to raise to maturity four children, three by birth and one by marriage. While she hasn't done a good job, the poor soul has done all that mortal human could do with the material she has had to work with."

DESPITE the Depression, there was little concern about the family fortunes in the Rogers household. If ever his father did feel the need of ready cash, Bill remembers, he used to say he could always make another lecture tour; there was more money in that than in anything else. Will's own attitude toward money was simple; he liked making it, he wanted to make a lot of it, but once he had it he disposed of it prodigally. Money was for trips, and he liked to travel in style; it was also something to be given away, and he was extraordinarily generous to relations less fortunate than he, to charities, and to friends.

Will was never comfortable in smart shops, but he liked to

do his own Christmas shopping. Putting it off until the last possible moment, he would hurry out alone and buy a staggering number of presents for everyone. He never asked the price of anything, and when he had finished he would carry his bundles to the car, drive home, and spend the remaining hours of Christmas Eve wrapping his packages.

For Florenz Ziegfeld the country's economic plight had brought the golden days to an end. He was faced, in the early thirties, with failing health and mounting debts, but still he would come over to Will's ranch, immaculately attired in riding habit, looking for all the world as if nothing had changed. In 1932 Ziegfeld died, a bankrupt, and Will—after delivering a moving tribute to his old boss in a newspaper article—quietly paid his medical and funeral expenses.

IN SPITE of the immense amount of time Will Rogers devoted to his career, it was rarely discussed within the family circle. What success he had achieved he viewed largely as the result of luck or accident, and he suspected that the public would "catch onto" him sooner or later. When people did, he figured, he and Betty might go back to Claremore, Oklahoma, where he had purchased acreage on a hillside at the edge of town. That would be the site of their house.

When some people began giving serious thought to the possibility that Will might run for public office, he was both annoyed and embarrassed. He had gotten a kick out of having his name put in nomination at the 1924 Democratic convention; he had rejoiced in the Anti-Bunk candidacy of 1928. However, in 1931 matters took a different turn. A committee called on him to urge that he run for senator from California, and that overture was followed by talk of his running for President.

He dealt with this matter firmly. "I hereby and hereon want to go on record," he wrote, "as being the first Presidential, Vice-Presidential, Senator, or Justice of Peace candidate to withdraw. I not only 'Don't choose to run,' I won't run. . . . Who will be the next to do the public a favor and withdraw? . . . It's one year away but the candidates will be Hoover and Curtis versus Franklin D. Roosevelt and some Western or Southern Democratic Governor."

Roosevelt's running mate was a Southerner *and* a Westerner. He was the Speaker of the House of Representatives, John Nance Garner of Texas. The campaign—which came at the bottom of the Depression—was as bitterly contested as that of 1928.

Fifteen million people were out of work. In New York City alone, a hundred thousand meals were served each day to destitute people waiting in bread-lines. Huey Long, the vulgar, self-styled "Kingfish," was promising the confiscation and redistribution of wealth to make "Every man a king, every girl a queen." A radio priest named Charles Coughlin was preaching about social justice to thousands of rapt listeners; and on the West Coast, Dr. Francis E. Townsend was giving elderly Americans a vision of a society in which anyone over sixty would receive two hundred dollars a month.

On Democrats: *"The Democrats are having a lot of fun exposing the Republican campaign corruptions, but they would have a lot more fun if they knew where they could lay hands on some of it themselves for next November."*

Not everyone took Franklin Roosevelt's candidacy seriously when it was announced in January 1932. The best that columnist Walter Lippmann could say was, "He is a pleasant man who, without any important qualifications for the office, would very much like to be President."

Will had regarded Roosevelt as the Democrats' likeliest candidate since 1930, when he wrote of his reelection as governor of New York, "The Democrats nominated their President yesterday, Franklin D. Roosevelt." But the presidential nomination was by no means a sure thing. The party split into factions supporting one candidate or another; it was divided along religious and sectional lines, by disparate views on Prohibition, and by a host of other ideological disputes. When Will arrived in Chicago late in June he was astonished to see so many smiling delegates; he wondered if they were going to "degenerate into a party of agree-ment and mutual admiration." But the next day "They fought, they fit, they split and adjourned in a dandy wave of dissension." That was the old party spirit he was accustomed to.

During those dead hours while the platform committee was meeting, Will was called upon to address the convention dele-gates. For a quarter of an hour he kept them laughing. Then he got to his point: "Now, you rascals . . . no matter who is nominated, go home and act like he was the man you came to see nominated. Don't say he can't win. You don't know what he can do until next November. I don't see how he could . . . not win. If he lives until November, he is in!" He left the rostrum to an enormous ovation, with the crowd standing and whooping in the aisles, begging for more.

On Republicans: *"You can't make the Republi-can Party pure by more contributions, because contributions are what got it where it is today."*

When the nominations began, Will received Oklahoma's twenty-two votes as a favorite son on the first ballot, but as he said, "Politics ain't on the level. I was only in 'em for an hour but in that short space of time somebody stole 22 votes from me . . . didn't even leave me a vote to get breakfast on."

By the time the convention settled down to more serious busi-ness, Roosevelt had an almost certain majority, and by the fourth ballot it was all over. The band struck up "Happy Days Are Here Again," the tune that was to become the perennial anthem of the "Squire of Hyde Park."

WHAT Will Rogers called "the same old vaudeville team of Hoover and Curtis" had been renominated without opposition earlier in June, and Hoover was quick to announce that he perceived in Roosevelt's philosophy elements of the poison that had already spread through Europe and "the fume of the witch's caldron which boiled in Russia." Will took a fairly relaxed view of things: "This is not an election of parties or policies," he wrote. "It's an election where both sides really need the work."

Midway into September, Roosevelt was scheduled to make a campaign speech in Los Angeles, but he learned that the city's Republican mayor would not welcome him. FDR's managers got in touch with Will, who assured them he would greet their candidate; as a former mayor of Beverly Hills, he thought he was entitled to welcome the man to southern California. On the night of September 24 he introduced the Democratic challenger to a huge crowd at the Hollywood Bowl. "Now, I don't want you to think that I am overawed by being asked to introduce you," Will told Roosevelt. "I'm not. I'm broad-minded that way and will introduce anybody." Apologizing for his lack of floweriness, Will said, "Come back as President and I will do right by you. I'm wasting no oratory on a prospect." Roosevelt led the laughter.

The following Monday, Will commented on Roosevelt's obvious cheerfulness. "That is one thing about Democrats," he said. "They take the whole thing as a joke. The Republicans take it serious but run it like a joke. There's not much difference."

His daily article of November 1, advocating a moratorium on speeches by the candidates, stirred up a first-class rhubarb. Stating that these two ordinarily fine men had been goaded by their political advisers to say things that "if they were in their right minds they wouldn't think of saying," he pointed to Hoover's remark that any change of policies would bring disaster to every fireside in America. That was ridiculous: "This country is a thousand times bigger than any two men in it, or any two parties. . . . This country has gotten where it is in spite of politics, not by the aid of it." He advised both candidates to go fishing until the election the following Tuesday instead of calling each other names.

"You will be surprised," he told them, "but the old U.S. will keep right on running while you boys are sitting on the bank," adding that when they came back the day after the election, "we will let you know which one is the lesser of the two evils."

A few days later he was in a more philosophical mood. Even though the candidates had lost their tempers, he advised voters not to be too critical. Neither man was going to save the country; neither would ruin it. And if the Depression continued, the loser was going to be the winner: "This President business is a pretty thankless job. Washington or Lincoln, either one, didn't get a statue until everybody was sure they was dead."

Will was attacked for his remarks by partisans of both sides. His reply took the form of a letter to the editor of the Los Angeles *Times*, which had been one of his severest critics. He was surprised, he wrote, that people were so exercised over his suggestion that the candidates go fishing. There was not a man in public life he didn't like; most of them were his good friends—"but that's not going to keep me from taking a dig at him when he does something or says something foolish." Hoover knew better than to say grass was going to grow in the streets if Roosevelt's tariff proposals were adopted—"You can't get it to grow on your lawns." And it was foolish for Roosevelt to blame the Depression on Hoover because he knew it was not so. Will meant what he said about the United States being bigger than any two men or any two parties.

IN THE wake of the election he offered solace to Mr. Hoover. "It wasn't you, Mr. President, the people just wanted to buy something new, and they didn't have any money to buy it with. But they could go out and vote free and get something new for nothing." The people, he wrote, had simply lost their taste for the Republican Party, which proved only that "There is something about a Republican that you can only stand for him just so long. And on the other hand there is something about a Democrat that you can't stand for him quite that long."

Then he had some advice for the incoming chief executive. In a personal telegram he told Roosevelt that to see a smile in the White House again would be "like a meal to us." As for handling congressmen and senators, "don't scold 'em. They are just children that's never grown up. Don't send messages to 'em, send candy."

In the month following the election a number of daily telegrams voiced his thoughts on Europe's war debts to the United States—an old and favorite topic. "Don't ever lay the fault on Europe for not paying us," he advised. "They would start tomorrow if we would just loan 'em the money to do it on."

Perhaps the mood of the country was changing; perhaps Will's comments were slightly more acerb. Whatever the reason, he received an increasing amount of criticism from readers and editorial writers—notably in *The New York Times*, which published a spate of letters from readers who took him to task for what they considered his destructive criticism, lack of taste, and general mischief-making on the crucial issue of war debts. There were letters in his defense, but the *Times* took a hands-off posture, while harrumphing in an editorial about the importance of publishing views that differed from its own.

On foreign relations:
"There's one thing no nation can ever accuse us of and that's Secret diplomacy. Our foreign dealings are an open book . . . generally a check book."

Will's response to that was to dish out some of the same medicine: "I would like to state to the readers of the *New York Times* that I am in no way responsible for the editorial or political policy of this paper. I allow them free rein as to their opinion, so long as it is within the bounds of good subscription gathering. . . . Every paper must have its various entertaining features, and their editorials are not always to be taken seriously, and never to be construed as policy."

There were signs that incessant travel and the demands of his complicated life were beginning to tell on Will. Increasingly sensitive to criticism, he was now defending his opinions by replying to letters that he might have ignored in earlier years.

One tragic occurrence in 1932 had had a profound effect on him. On March 1 the twenty-month-old son of Charles and Anne Morrow Lindbergh was kidnapped from their home in Hopewell, New Jersey. Only two weeks earlier Will had visited them and watched in delight as the aviator played with the child, and in the days following the crime his columns reflected the nationwide feeling of horror and outrage. Deeply troubled by his friends' tragedy, he lashed out at the society that had somehow permitted it to occur. "120 million people cry one minute and swear vengeance the next. A Father who never did a thing that didn't make us proud of him. A Mother who though only the wife of a hero, has proven one herself. At home or abroad they have always been a credit to their country. Is their country going to be a credit to them? Will it make him still proud that he did it for them? Or in his loneliness will . . . a thought creep into his mind that it might have been different if he had flown the ocean under somebody's colors with a real obligation to law and order?"

In January of 1933 he bade farewell to an old friend. "Mr. Coolidge," he wrote, "you didn't have to die for me to throw flowers on your grave. I have told a million jokes about you but every one was based on some of your splendid qualities. . . . By golly, you little red-headed New Englander, I liked you." After a ceremony was held in the House of Representatives to honor the memory of the former President, Will's comment had a bite to it: "The lawmakers . . . can pay more homage to a President in death and deal him more misery in life than happens in any civilized nation."

As WINTER and the Depression deepened, America's banks faced a new crisis. Over the past three years, despite Hoover's reassurances that the credit system was sound, five thousand banks had closed, and despite the President's efforts to resuscitate them with aid from the Reconstruction Finance Corporation, in mid-February Michigan's banks began closing their doors. As Inauguration Day, then March 4, approached, the bank panic spread to other states.

When Roosevelt proclaimed in his inaugural address that "the only thing we have to fear is fear itself" and almost immediately declared a national bank holiday, many Americans felt there might now be an end to the uncertainty that had plagued the country. In an almost springtime mood, people made the most of a common plight, accepted scrip, and joked about it.

According to Will, "America hasn't been as happy in three years as they are today—no money, no banks, no work, no nothing." He was confident that the entire nation was behind the new President. "Even if what he does is wrong they are with him, just so he does something. If he burned down the capitol we would cheer and say, 'Well, we at least got a fire started, anyhow.'" The Republicans had never voluntarily closed a bank— "Their theory was to leave 'em open till they shut." It was astonishing, he thought, how little money people really needed to get by on; even if the banks never reopened, "it's such a novelty to find that somebody will trust you that it's changed our whole feeling toward human nature." He couldn't recall when the country had seemed more united, and suggested that "The worse off we get the louder we laugh, which is a great thing."

He admired the way the new occupant of the White House was dealing with Congress, making them act for the first time in their lives like U.S. citizens and not like senators or representatives. "Roosevelt just makes out a little list of things every morning that he wants them to do that day (kinder like a housewife's menu list)," and they were doing it. And Eleanor Roosevelt immediately endeared herself to Will by making it plain that she was air-minded—"no maid, no secretary, just the first lady of the land on a paid ticket on a regular passenger plane."

12

"I never met a man I didn't like."

THE public's regard for Will Rogers was never higher than in the spring of 1933. The twenties and early thirties had seen a succession of heroes flash like meteors across the national scene— polar explorers Richard Byrd and Roald Amundsen; aviators Charles Lindbergh, Amelia Earhart, and Wiley Post; athletes "Big Bill" Tilden, Jack Dempsey, Babe Ruth, and Red Grange;

and a host of others—but none managed to retain such constant, unwavering affection as Will Rogers. He was the one man, people seemed to believe, who was above fame and success. His consuming interest and involvement in the nation's affairs were such that no man's importance was quite confirmed until he had been kidded by Will Rogers—and no event was complete unless it drew the gentle barb of his wit. His brief commentary was the first item to which millions of Americans turned in their daily newspaper. His motion pictures were so successful that he now ranked as the number two box-office attraction in Hollywood. And soon another string was added to his bow.

Will started in radio in 1933 and for three seasons was heard in millions of homes from coast to coast.

In May it was announced that he had signed a contract to make seven nationwide broadcasts for the Gulf Oil Company. He would be paid fifty thousand dollars for the series, and immediately said he would donate all the money to unemployment relief—half to be distributed by the American Red Cross, half by the Salvation Army.

FOUR decades later it is difficult to suggest the powerful hold radio had on Americans, when the voices of Amos 'n' Andy, Rudy Vallee, Kate Smith, Jack Benny, Fred Allen, Eddie Cantor, George Burns and Gracie Allen, Edgar Bergen and Charlie McCarthy, were as familiar in the nation's living rooms as those of old friends. During the Depression years listening to the radio became the public's greatest diversion—radio was one of the few mediums of entertainment that were free. On weekdays between 7:00 and 7:15 p.m., when thirty million people were listening to Amos 'n' Andy, the use of telephones regularly fell off by fifty percent. And listening to Will Rogers on Sunday nights at nine became a ritual that people still remember with a smile.

Will's success in show business, as he readily admitted, was the result of a happy coincidence of talent and timing. He had appeared on the scene with a highly original act when vaudeville and the *Ziegfeld Follies* were at the height of their popularity; his arrival in Hollywood coincided with the heyday of the silent films; his personality and manner were precisely right for the advent of talking pictures; and although he was never as comfortable in radio, his style was superbly suited to the format of the variety show, which offered a half hour of humorous comment sprinkled with light music.

His first broadcast for Gulf, in the spring of 1933, established a pattern for those that followed. After a medley by Al Goodman's orchestra and a song from the Revelers (the quartet that had accompanied him on many benefit performances), Will came on to deliver a monologue that ran about fifteen minutes. It was a variation on the familiar *Follies* routine, of which audiences never seemed to tire. He drew on the headlines and news of the day for his commentary, so it was no accident that Franklin D. Roosevelt dominated the programs. In the opening broadcast Will proclaimed it to be President's Day: "We have apple week, and potato week, and don't murder your wife week. . . . If prunes are worth a week, the President ought to be worth something anyhow."

Roosevelt had been in office for seven weeks, and "That bird has done more for us in seven weeks than we've done for ourselves in seven years. . . . He was inaugurated at noon in Washington, and they started the inaugural parade down Pennsylvania Avenue, and before it got halfway down there, he closed every bank in the United States." Jokes followed about Republicans,

Mahatma Gandhi, Al Smith, the repeal of Prohibition, and presidential commissions.

Will's act, perfected over the years, involved rambling from one anecdote to another, with no real concern for the length of time he talked. But radio was geared to split-second timing; if a program was scheduled to end at 9:30, that was when it ended, even if the star performer was in midsentence. Characteristically he took advantage of the situation to extract a few additional laughs from the audience by bringing an alarm clock to the studio. "The hardest thing over this radio is to get me stopped," he announced during his second broadcast. "So tonight, I got me a clock here. . . . When that alarm goes off, I am going to stop, that is all there is to it. I don't care whether I am in the middle of reciting Gunga Din or the Declaration of Independence, I am going to stop right when that rings." And every Sunday night thereafter the alarm would ring when his time was up; he would quickly tell the listeners what was in store for them next week, and sign off.

When the Chicago World's Fair opened in 1933 Will asked his listeners if they agreed with its theme—a "Century of Progress." One hundred years earlier, he reminded them, we had had only thirty-six senators, "and the evil has grown now until we have ninety-six." We were on the gold standard in 1833; there was no golf except in Scotland; there were no chamber of commerce luncheon speakers; and you lived until you died and not until you were run over by an automobile.

On the final program of that series he discussed the pros and cons of working on radio. He admitted he did not like the microphone, which put him in mind of an automobile radiator cap; he had feared that the listeners weren't much interested in politics, but had discovered that they knew more about it than a congressman; and he had thought he might have to speak as well as an announcer did, but found that "you don't have to speak correctly at all, and you are understood by everybody." Having relieved his mind of those worries, he concluded that the only trouble with radio was that "you never know how good you are."

The studio audience might applaud; but the real test was whether Gulf sold more gasoline.

Actually there was little risk that Will would give up radio once he had made a success of it. As with so many enterprises, he was filled with doubts at the beginning, and only after he realized that he was good at it did he regain his self-confidence. He signed up to make six additional broadcasts for Gulf in the fall of 1933; the next year he was on the radio every Sunday night for twenty-four weeks; and in 1935 for sixteen more.

Nor did this perceptibly tax his phenomenal store of energy. In the spring of 1934 he made three motion pictures while continuing to write his daily and weekly articles, and in July he and his family sailed from San Francisco for a trip around the world to celebrate Will's and Betty's recent silver anniversary. It was in the nature of a second honeymoon, with the boys, Bill and Jim, accompanying them. (Will had tried to interest Mary in going along, but she was playing in a summer theater in Maine and turned him down.)

The preliminaries to a family expedition, Will realized, were far more complicated than they were when he was traveling alone and carrying only the "old soft, flat red grip that packed itself." Betty packed and repacked. Will wanted to be outside roping calves, but Betty and the butler, Emil Sandmeier, insisted that he try on some white shoes and new Palm Beach suits. The last straw was to find that someone had packed his bathrobe: "You only wear them when you are getting well from an operation."

Their arrival in Honolulu coincided with Franklin Roosevelt's visit to the islands, and the President and the comedian were honored at a dinner at which Will was kept speaking by an enthusiastic crowd for two hours. He and the President had an opportunity to chat about something that was very much on FDR's mind; when he learned that the Rogerses were going to Japan, he said, "Will, don't jump on Japan, just keep them from jumping on us."

From Japan, Will and his family went to Korea and then to

Siberia, where they boarded a trans-Siberian train after laying in a supply of food for the long trip, including a big basket of oranges, a canned-heat cooker, and plenty of beans for Will and the boys. They were cooped up in a tiny compartment, with their luggage and supplies stacked around them, for nearly eight days. The wild, unspoiled country made a deep impression on Will, reminding him of his youth in Oklahoma. "It's exactly like the Indian Territory was when I grew up in it as a boy. And if you can find a finer one than that was before they plowed and ruined it, I don't know where." Siberia was ideal cow country: "Not a fence, all you would need would be one drift line between you and the Arctic Ocean."

On diplomats: *"A diplomat is one that says something that is equally misunderstood by both sides, and never clear to either."*

Moscow, when they arrived at last, was something else—"a town on a boom," with buildings going up everywhere, a new subway being built, the excitement of a horse race, and stimulating talk with experts on Russia—Maurice Hindus, Walter Duranty, and Louis Fischer. From Moscow, Will and Betty went to Leningrad, leaving Bill to go to Germany and Jim to Paris. Before leaving the States, Will had announced his intention of "finding Finland." If Finland could go to the trouble of repaying its war debts,. he said, "I can certainly take the time to try and find them," and he was happy to arrive in the land of "integrity's last stand." Then he and his wife toured the Scandinavian countries, Austria, and the Balkans before going to the British Isles.

In Will's first radio talk in the fall—broadcast while he was still in England—he gave listeners a report on what he had seen on his travels. He had learned that England, which he described as the first country to recover from the Depression, had "the highest income tax rate of anybody in the world; they are the nation that first give the dole to unemployed." Russia was getting along better than he had expected because "there is no Communists or Reds there"—no agitators, no one trying to start a strike. Each country, he concluded, had its own form of government peculiar to it—"Russia has her Soviet, Italy her dictator, England her king, Japan her Son of Heaven, China her various bandits, and us, we don't know what form of government it is. But whatever it is, it's ours. . . . And as bad off as we are we are better than anybody else I have seen."

Probably the statement most frequently associated with Will Rogers, and the one that endeared him most to the American public, was his remark, "I never met a man I didn't like." This was the attitude that characterized all his trips abroad; in Moscow, Dublin, Hong Kong, or Mexico City he talked to everyone with whom he could strike up a conversation—in the streets, in restaurants, wherever he went—and his inclination was to believe that the world was basically a family in which all would be well if man's native instincts were allowed to prevail instead of being gummed up by the politicians. This old-fashioned confidence in the virtues of the common man, seasoned with a benevolent tolerance for the human condition and mankind's frailties, was suspected by some critics of his day as being a pose. They refused to believe that anyone as successful or as wealthy as Will Rogers could possibly remain the eternal homespun cowboy.

WILL's success as a humorist was constructed, as are all such successes, upon a formula. But the formula was concocted out of real elements and was an extension of a personality that had not altered substantially since he was a boy in Indian Territory. What had changed was not Will Rogers but the world, and something of what audiences responded to was the aura of nostalgia that his manner suggested—a trace of the days when life had seemed far less complex, confused, and phony. In a curious way, his radio broadcasts came closer to suggesting what Will was all about than did his stage or movie appearances, because what he said to an audience that could not see him was not obscured by gestures or mannerisms. No shuffling about, no pulling the forelock, no sheepish grins or sly winks or glances from under his eyebrows intruded on the talk.

More original than what he said was the peculiar twist he gave it, with the result that the listener—hearing Will say pretty much what he himself had thought or known all along, but hearing it placed in an entirely different context—suddenly found himself thinking that Will had uttered some eternal truth. For example, in 1934 everyone knew about Austria's troubles with Hitler's Germany, but it was left to Will to say that "If ever a nation lived in the wrong place it seems to be them."

In much of what he said there was a strong element of compassion, as when he remarked that "we are the last civilized nation, if you can call us that, to do anything for old people. All we do is just watch them get older." Or, on the subject of government relief programs, "Now is this thing of havin' millions of people . . . workin' for the government—is that a good thing? Well, no, it's not a good thing, but it's better than starvin'."

When not discussing politics or the international scene he frequently dealt with God, family, mother, honesty, common sense, the underdog, just plain folks—contriving to do so in a way that was neither maudlin nor cloying. On Mother's Day in 1935 he reminded the audience that "it's a beautiful thought, but it's somebody with a hurting conscience that thought of the idea. It was someone who had neglected their mother for years and they figured out, I got to do something about mama, and then they says, 'Well, we'll give mama a day.' . . . You give her a day and then in return mother gives you the other 364."

BEFORE Will and the family left on their round-the-world trip he said he had hit on a formula for avoiding wars. Most friction between countries, he stated, was caused by proximity. "Now Germany and France, they fight every forty years, you know—just as true as history. Every forty years they just come around, and they look at the calendar and start fighting. Well, it isn't anyone's particular fault, but it just seems to be habit." So he had devised a scheme to move neighbors away from each other if they couldn't get along. "Take Germany, for instance, and place it where Mexico is." And once Mexico was transplanted to Germany's place, "France and Mexico would get along fine."

Since England and Ireland were always fighting, he would swap Ireland and Canada, being careful not to let England know where the Irish were going.

The trip somehow convinced him, despite the ominous rumblings from Europe, that there would be no war. In his travels, he said, he had found one surefire thing to say when he arrived in a country: " 'Folks, I bring you no good will.' The whole world is fed up on somebody bringing good will in. . . . Nations don't want to have any good will, and all that. They want to be let alone, the same as we do. Let 'em alone and let 'em work out their own plans and their own salvation."

Unhappily events were getting out of hand, beyond the control of the ordinary man in whom Will had such faith. In March 1935 Hitler tore up the Versailles treaty, which, as Will said, "wasn't a good treaty, but it was the only one they had." Mussolini would soon pounce on Ethiopia, and civil war was about to erupt in Spain. Will, saddened by the course of events, could only mourn, "England's got a gun, France has got a gun, Italy's got a gun, Germany wants a gun, Austria wants a gun. All God's children want guns . . . going to buckle on the guns and smear up all of God's heaven."

The state of the world was not the only thing on his mind that spring, fortunately. He had three pictures to make, and when they were finished, he thought he might take another trip—maybe fly someplace he had never been before.

13

"This Alaska is a great country."

TO WHAT extent chance plays a part in human affairs is beyond all knowing. Certain actions are taken on the basis of sudden whim; others result from a chain of interrelated factors that, like the pieces of an intricate Chinese puzzle, fall into place one by one. The latter seemed to be the case with the trip Will made to Alaska in 1935.

The year before, while he was playing the lead in a stage production of Eugene O'Neill's *Ah, Wilderness!* in California, he received a letter from a clergyman who had taken his fourteen-year-old daughter to the show. After watching a scene in which Will lectured his "son" on the subject of immoral relations with a woman, the minister left the theater, taking his daughter with him, and in his letter told Will that he had not been able to look her in the face since.

Will was stunned. He had regarded the play as just an "old family affair," but if it struck even one person as improper, he wanted nothing further to do with it. He not only quit the play but decided he would not accept the role in the screen version. Because of a letter from an indignant clergyman, he would have the summer of 1935 open and would be free to travel.

Another factor in the equation was the state of Will's mind in the spring of 1935. At fifty-five, for the first time in his life, he was showing signs of weariness. In addition to the radio broadcasts, he had recently given speeches or played benefits all over the country. The daily and weekly articles consumed their usual share of his time. His contract with Fox obligated him to make three movies annually, and he crowded all three into the first half of the year in order to have the remaining six months to himself. The plain fact was that he was worn out and, Bill Rogers remembers, increasingly nervous, restless, and tense. He longed to be on the wing. He considered making a long trip, but his plans were vague. Then another piece of the puzzle dropped quickly into place with a visit from a famous aviator—a fellow Oklahoman who had started life with nothing and had gained a worldwide reputation.

WILEY POST was born in Texas, the son of an itinerant farmer, and had spent much of his boyhood in Oklahoma. He first saw an airplane in 1913, and from that day on he was determined to become a pilot. He took a job with a flying circus as a parachute jumper and acquired some flight training. He worked for a time in the oil fields, where an accident occurred that made it possible for him to purchase his first plane. An iron chip from a sledgehammer lodged in his left eye, which became infected and had to be removed. Wiley was awarded $1700 in compensation, with which he immediately bought a damaged aircraft. He worked for months on training his vision, learning how to calculate distances by guessing how far it was to a tree or building, then pacing it off to see how nearly right he was.

He married a Texas girl, became a barnstormer, took passengers on rides for $2.50, and gave flight lessons. He was a natural pilot, one of his students said. "He didn't just fly an airplane, he put it on." When barnstorming failed to provide enough income he landed a job as personal pilot for two Oklahoma oilmen, Powell Briscoe and F. C. Hall. Briscoe remembered vividly that

On government: *"Lord, the money we do spend on Government and it's not one bit better than the government we got for one third the money twenty years ago."*

Post didn't have a nerve in his body. "When other people were scared, Wiley just grinned."

After some months of braving the wind in an open cockpit, Hall was ready for a novel craft developed by the Lockheed Aircraft Company that became available in 1928. It was a cabin ship called the Vega, with plywood fuselage and no exposed struts or braces. Hall bought one, named it the *Winnie Mae* for his daughter, and had Wiley fly it until the stock market crash of 1929 forced him to sell the plane.

For a year Wiley worked as a Lockheed test pilot; then Hall bought another Vega, to which he gave the same name, and in 1931 he decided to sponsor Post and an Australian navigator named Harold Gatty in a round-the-world flight. In one of those dramatic air exploits of which the twenties and thirties were so full, Post and Gatty flew around the globe in eight days, fifteen hours, and fifty-one minutes, arriving in New York to a wild heroes' welcome. "This Post and Gatty," Will commented, "are making this world of ours look like the size of a watermelon."

(Later Will flew to Tulsa to participate in the celebration for the Oklahoma boy, and rode with the fliers in the *Winnie Mae* to Claremore.)

Two years later Wiley, flying solo, bettered his round-the-world record, making it in a little under eight days. Howard Hughes, who made the same trip in 1938 in less time, but with a crew of five, called Post's feat the most remarkable flight in history. "What did I tell you about that little one-eyed Oklahoma boy?" Will crowed. "He is a hawk, isn't he? He holds the doubles and singles championship now."

In 1935 Wiley acquired a new airplane. Because he was short of funds he had to settle for a hybrid craft assembled from the parts of two previously damaged ships. To a Lockheed Orion he added wings taken from a Lockheed Explorer and some flight instruments from the *Winnie Mae*. The Lockheed company did not encourage this amalgamation of parts, but Post applied for a restricted license to operate the ship for experimental cross-country flights and other special tests. Post discovered that he was going to have difficulties with the unconventional craft. When the plane was operated at low airspeeds and reduced power, it had a definite heaviness in the front end and a tendency to pitch forward.

At the time Post visited Will in California it was rumored that the aviator was about to make a flight to study the feasibility of an air route between Alaska and Russia. Will was thinking of going along. In August, when Post flew to Seattle to have a set of pontoons installed in place of landing wheels, Will asked that he telephone from there; at that time Will would let him know whether he was coming.

"There was nothing unusual about this vagueness," Betty recalled. "Our trips were nearly always made that way, and we didn't plan beyond the first stop." She had not fully reconciled herself to Will's departure, because she dreaded his flying across Siberia. Yet she could tell that "Will wanted me to want him to go. And so I tried to be happy about this."

BY AUGUST 3 WILL WAS fairly certain he would make the trip. That morning he and Betty went for a long ride over the ranch, discussing what he wanted done while he was away, and stopping to see a little log cabin that had just been completed in a canyon back in the Santa Monica hills, away from the ranch house and its steady stream of visitors. When Betty suggested that he put off his trip for a few days so they could camp out there, Will said, "No, let's wait till I get back."

Early in the afternoon, while he was packing, Betty came into the room several times, and once he called her back, gave her a sheepish look, and said, "Say, Blake, you know what I just did? I flipped a coin."

Betty said she hoped it came out tails. Will laughed, held out his hand, and replied, "No, it's heads. See, I win."

That evening their son Bill had dinner with them, and then they went to a rodeo at Gilmore Stadium in Los Angeles. As usual, Will knew most of the performers, and a number rode over to shake hands. During the evening someone gave him a small wood-and-paper puzzle, and Betty watched him toy with it unconsciously while he watched the riders in the arena. "It was a mannerism I knew so well," she said. "His restless hands could never stay still. Then, when the show was over, I saw him stuff the puzzle in the pocket of his coat." In with it went the rodeo program. His pockets, Betty said, were always filled with trinkets, like those of a little boy.

Will had a reservation on the eleven-o'clock flight to San Francisco. They drove to the airport, and it was time to say good-by. Will, with an overcoat slung over a shoulder and a stack of newspapers clutched under an arm, climbed the steps and boarded the plane. Betty caught a last glimpse of him in the window, smiling, and she and Bill watched until the plane's green and red wing lights vanished in the night sky.

IN SEATTLE, Wiley Post was having his problems. He had ordered a set of Edo pontoons, similar to those used by Alaskan bush pilots, but they had not arrived by the time Will got there.

*In 1935, at fifty-five, Will was overworked and tired out.
With the veteran flier Wiley Post (second from right)
he set out on a trip to Alaska. As they took off for
Barrow on August 15 the plane (inset), equipped
with oversized pontoons, seemed nose-heavy.*

Since Will was financing the trip and was impatient to be off,
Wiley settled for what he could find: a pair of pontoons from a
Fokker trimotor, much heavier than he required. When he took
the hybrid plane up he discovered that the big pontoons accen-
tuated the nose-heaviness; landing or takeoff would be quite
hazardous unless the plane was operated under a good deal of
power. Will asked about the pontoons, thinking they were "awful big looking things," but Wiley replied laconically, "None
too big." The pilot, Will was learning, was "kinder a Calvin
Coolidge on answers; none of 'em are going to bother you with
being too long."

Post decided that if Will rode as far aft in the plane as possible, his weight would compensate slightly for the heaviness of the nose. It would have been possible to correct the condition more scientifically by installing a new stabilizer-elevator on the plane, but since the change would delay their departure further, it was not made. In the front of the plane was a single seat; Wiley had removed the other to provide as much room as possible for their baggage, a rubber boat and canoe paddle, some life vests, several coils of rope, sleeping bags, and Post's rifle and fishing tackle.

At 9:20 a.m. on August 6, after loading two precious cases of chili aboard the plane and dodging a reporter's question as to whether they planned to fly around the world, Wiley taxied out onto the waters of Lake Washington, made a short run, and "took off like a bird," in Will's phrase, pointing the ship's nose in the direction of Juneau, Alaska.

EN ROUTE Will's enthusiasm for the beauty of the scenery was equaled only by his admiration of Post's skill at navigating; the maze of channels and islands along the coast all looked alike to him, "but this old boy turns up the right alley all the time." In Juneau, where they were grounded for several days because of bad flying conditions, Will met the governor of the territory and spent a nostalgic evening with Rex Beach, who had written his first silent movie, *Laughing Bill Hyde*.

Before taking off the next morning Will bought a red-fox fur, took it to the post office in Juneau, and mailed it to Betty. As the plane made its way north he sat in the rear seat, typewriter in his lap, pounding out his columns, which were chatty, newsy observations on the scenery, on the vastness of Alaska, and on the Eskimos and their way of life.

Flying east into Canada, they traveled over the Yukon and the Klondike region, then headed north along the MacKenzie River to the Arctic Ocean, then west to Fairbanks. "Was you ever driving around in a car and not knowing or caring where you went?" Will wrote on August 12. "Well, that's what Wiley and I are doing. We sure are having a great time. If we hear of whales or polar bears in the Arctic, or a big herd of caribou or reindeer, we fly over and see it."

The next day, with nothing pressing to do, they went down to Anchorage in a different plane, piloted by two local fliers, one of whom, Joe Crosson, was known as Alaska's best bush pilot. They flew over Mount McKinley on a brilliant sunny day, and Will said it was the most beautiful sight he had ever seen. They also visited the Matanuska Valley, to which some seven or eight hundred pioneers from the States had recently migrated, hoping to find good farm country. The settlers swarmed out to see Will.

"Where you boys from?" he asked, surveying the group. "Anybody here from Claremore?"

At the end of an hour and a half's inspection, during which Will had the crowd laughing most of the time, they were climbing into the plane when a construction-crew cook rushed up with half a dozen fat cookies. "They're good!" Will called, taking a bite. "But I'll toss 'em out if we can't get off the ground." And on a wave of laughter the plane taxied down the strip.

On conferences: *"There is one line of bunk that this country falls for, and always has. 'We are looking to America for leadership during the conference: She has a great moral responsibility.' Why, they didn't discover us till 1492 and the world had had 1492 wars. 1492 peace and economic conferences, all before we was ever heard of."*

"A conference is a place where countries meet and find out each other's short comings and form new dislikes for the next conference."

One man Will wanted to see while he was in Alaska was Charles Brower, an old-timer known as the "King of the Arctic," who was U.S. commissioner in Barrow, a little settlement three hundred miles north of the Arctic Circle. When Will spoke to Crosson about going there, the flier, who had observed the excessive nose-

heaviness of Wiley's aircraft, advised against it until some altera-
tions could be made to correct the problem. As an experienced
bush pilot, he was concerned about the possibility of engine failure. He realized that if Post had to make a forced landing somewhere without power, he might not be able to prevent the plane
from nosing over into a dive.

FROM Fairbanks, Post radioed the government weather station
in Barrow for a report on conditions and was told that snow,
sleet, and zero visibility made a landing impossible; but after
waiting a day he decided they could make it. Crosson, who knew
what the weather could be like five hundred miles to the north,
didn't like the sound of this. But when he realized that Post was
determined to leave, he advised him to fly directly north until he
sighted the Arctic Ocean; then he should turn west, hugging the
coast until he reached Point Barrow, an easily identifiable penin-
sula that was the northernmost reach of the North American
mainland.

About twelve miles south of Point Barrow lay the village of
Barrow, a fishing community inhabited by about three hundred
Eskimos and nine whites. Dr. Henry W. Greist and his wife, a
nurse, were in charge of a Presbyterian mission and hospital there.
The Signal Corps operated the weather station, and Commissioner Brower described his own work as recording births and
deaths, performing marriages, and trying to play Solomon in settling disputes. The surrounding region was bleak, treeless tundra,
one of the most desolate places imaginable.

Before leaving Fairbanks about eleven in the morning on August 15, Will handed his daily article to Joe Crosson and asked
him to take it, with a telegram he had written to Mary, to the
telegraph office. He wired her:

GREAT TRIP. WISH YOU WERE ALL ALONG. HOW'S YOUR ACTING? YOU
AND MAMA WIRE ME ALL THE NEWS TO NOME. GOING TO POINT BAR-
ROW TODAY. FURTHEST POINT OF LAND ON WHOLE AMERICAN CON-
TINENT. LOTS OF LOVE. DON'T WORRY.   DAD

Mary was in Skowhegan, Maine, performing in summer stock. That week she had the lead in *Ceiling Zero*, a play in which her stage father was killed in an airplane crash.

Post decided not to take off with a full load of fuel from the narrow, winding Chena River in Fairbanks. He arranged for enough gasoline for the hop to Barrow, and headed north. The little red plane made its way through the notch in the mountain barrier, and somewhere beyond the north face ran into a bad storm. Ninety miles from the settlement some natives tending a herd of reindeer heard the sound of a plane overhead. A trader named Gus Masik heard it while he was crossing Smith's Bay; so did an Eskimo at Point Tangent; and from these reports it appeared that Post, flying blind after losing his way in the storm, had at some point turned due west. Providentially about three o'clock in the afternoon he spotted a break in the dense cloud cover and caught sight of land and a stream. Flying low along the stream, he came to a lagoon and went in for a landing.

The body of water was known as the Walakpa lagoon, and there was an Eskimo fishing camp on the shore. Wiley taxied over, cut the engine, and he and Will climbed out onto the pontoons and spoke to two of the natives—Claire Oakpeha and his wife, who knew English fairly well. Wiley asked how far Barrow was (it was no more than a ten-minute flight); Will inquired what the Eskimos were fishing for (they were after seals). Following a brief consultation, the two Americans climbed back into the plane, waved, and taxied to one end of the lagoon to begin their takeoff.

Watching from the lonely shoreline, the Eskimos saw the plane begin moving faster and faster across the water—the pontoons throwing twin sprays behind. It lifted off, started to climb, and banked to the right. Then suddenly the engine misfired, sputtered, and went dead. The red plane turned nose down, hurtling like a stone into the shallow lagoon, spewing a geyser of sand and gravel and water into the air as the fuselage split open on impact. One wing broke off, the plane flipped over on its back, and at the same instant there was a dull explosion and a quick flash of fire, which went out immediately. Then silence. There was only the soft lapping of waves on the shore as ripples from the shattered plane broke, ebbed, and finally died.

The terrified Eskimos' first instinct was to run away; then Claire Oakpeha took courage and went as close to the plane as he could and shouted, again and again. There was no answer.

He told his wife that he must get word to the Americans, and leaving the others behind to stare in disbelief at the spectral, broken hulk in the water, he started running toward Barrow.

14

"A smile has disappeared from the lips
of America. . . ."—John McCormack

FIVE hours after the crash Claire Oakpeha, having run for sixteen miles through the tundra grass, finally staggered into the store in Barrow. Gasping for breath, he told the owner, a man named Bert Panigeo, about the crash he had seen, and Panigeo called Frank Dougherty, the local schoolteacher, on the telephone. There was some immediate speculation that it might be a party of American hunters or possibly a Russian plane that had gone off course. It occurred to nobody that it might be Will Rogers and Wiley Post, since they were not expected for several days.

Dougherty sent Oakpeha to tell Commissioner Brower what had happened, while he phoned Sergeant Stanley Morgan, the man in charge of the Signal Corps weather station, got a launch into the water, and rounded up a rescue party. Dougherty, Morgan, and a group of Eskimos headed out at once. Brower, who had loaded a launch with blankets, sleeping bags, and medicine, sent it after them, with his son David in charge. Dave's boat also towed an umiak, a large, light, open boat made of hides stretched over a wooden frame, which could be portaged across the sandbar surrounding the lagoon.

On the long voyage through the fog and ice Oakpeha gave Sergeant Morgan some additional details about the catastrophe. "One mans big, have tall boots," he said. "Other mans short, have sore eye, rag over eye." And suddenly it dawned on Morgan who must be in the plane.

At the lagoon the Eskimos from the sealing camp had removed Will's broken body from an opening in the side of the fuselage, but Post was wedged between the engine and one of the big pontoons. After Dave Brower arrived with a block and tackle, they pulled off the pontoon and the remaining wing, and with great difficulty got his body out. They placed the two corpses in sleeping bags they found in the plane, loaded them into the umiak, and headed for open water and the long trip to Barrow.

It was three o'clock in the morning when Charles Brower and Dr. Greist, who had been detained at the hospital by an operation, heard the launches returning. They knew at once that the worst had happened: the doctor could hear the voices of the Eskimos, chanting the "plaintive song they sing when the headman in a village dies. . . . Once heard it is never forgotten."

Dave Brower came ashore and told his father, "Dad, it's Will Rogers and Wiley Post."

THE two bodies were carried to the hospital, where the badly shaken Greist, his wife, and Brower removed the men's clothing and began to prepare the corpses for burial. When the contents of the pockets were examined, it was noted that Wiley Post's gold watch had stopped at 8:18 p.m., the time of the crash. (He was still carrying Oklahoma time, which meant that it was 3:18 at Barrow.) In Will's clothing Dr. Greist found cash and traveler's checks, a newspaper clipping with a picture of his daughter, a stub of a pencil, a pocketknife, a pair of eyeglasses, a magnifying glass, and a pocket watch that was still running. The doctor also noticed that there was a program from a rodeo in Los Angeles and a curious little puzzle made of paper and wood. To Charlie Brower the watch somehow symbolized "all that made Will the simple, beloved man of the people he was. It couldn't have cost over a dollar and a half. He wore it tied to the end of an old string."

In Will's badly smashed typewriter was the third page of his latest weekly article. There was a description of their departure from Fairbanks only hours before and several stories about Alaskan dog teams. He had started to tell a yarn he had heard about Joe Crosson's partner, a Swede, and a wirehaired terrier who had the unfortunate habit of barking at bears. The article ended in the middle of a sentence; the last word he had typed was "death."

PRECISELY what happened between the time the plane lifted off the lagoon and the moment, a few seconds later, when it banked and crashed will never be known for certain. Dr. Greist,

who talked with Joe Crosson and others, had his own ideas about what had caused the engine to fail. The plane was equipped with two gas tanks, one in each wing, which meant that when one tank ran low, the pilot had to turn a hand control to open the other. Perhaps, the doctor thought, Post heard the engine misfire, realized the tank was empty, and quickly turned the hand control. But he was too late; the plane was only about fifty feet off the ground, and before the gasoline could reach the engine the nose-heavy plane plunged into the lagoon.

Charles Brower was more positive than anyone about what had occurred. In a book describing his fifty years in Alaska he told what his son Dave had found that night on Walakpa lagoon after the bodies had been removed from the wreckage. "Before leaving, Dave examined the plane carefully to try and discover why

As the plane carrying Post and Rogers passed overhead, a party of Eskimo seal hunters heard the motor die, and as they watched in horror, the ship nose-dived into a shallow lagoon. Both passengers perished.

it had crashed. That was easy. Not only did none of the tanks contain so much as a drop of gas but there was no sign of any on the surface of the landlocked lagoon. . . . It seems certain that the men were entirely out of gas. Perhaps they thought they had enough for a bare twelve miles or more. Perhaps they didn't even check their gauge. We shall never know."

As soon as the bodies were brought to Barrow and positively identified, a radio message from Sergeant Morgan went out to Seattle. Communications between the northern outpost and the outside world were so tenuous that it took nearly two hours for news of the tragedy to reach the continental United States.

Betty Rogers was in Skowhegan, Maine, visiting Mary. The last word from Will was the telegram he had given Joe Crosson to send to Mary; it had gone out from Fairbanks on August 15—the day of the crash. What disturbed Betty was Will's reference to Nome, the point from which Wiley intended to fly to Siberia. She was still hoping that Will, after flying around Alaska for a week or two, would have had enough and would return to the States and join her in Maine.

Bill Rogers was working that summer as a wiper in the engine room of a tanker, and his brother Jim and a cousin were driving east from California. On August 16 Betty was talking with a friend outside her cottage when she saw a car coming up the road and recognized the driver as the manager of the theater where Mary was working. When he got out of the automobile and spoke to her sister, Theda, something about his manner alarmed her.

She ran to speak to him. "Has something happened to Jimmy? Tell me," she pleaded.

There was no answer from the theater manager, but Theda told her, "No, Betty, it's Will. Will has had an accident."

For an instant, Betty remembered, she felt only relief, knowing that nothing could possibly happen to Will—nothing more serious than mechanical trouble or a forced landing. Then she was told of Sergeant Morgan's message from Barrow.

PERHAPS NOT SINCE the death of Abraham Lincoln had a tragedy touched so many Americans as did the loss of Will Rogers and Wiley Post. It overshadowed everything that was going on in the world. Four full pages of *The New York Times* were devoted to the event on Saturday, August 17, and for a week the newspaper and radio coverage continued. From every city and hamlet across the land came stories of people shocked and heartbroken. In a grocery store in a small New Hampshire town, customers were waiting to be served when a little boy came in and told them Will Rogers was dead. People walked out silently, their errands forgotten. In Locust Grove, Oklahoma, half a dozen Cherokees were building a fence when they received the news. Again, there was only stunned silence—people could find no words to express themselves. After a time some of the Indians spoke of how they had known Will, or remembered a favor he had done for someone. Then one said, "I can't work any more today," and all of them stacked their tools and quietly walked away.

On inflation: *"I have been accused of being worried over this 'inflation.' I wasn't worried. I was just confused. . . . When you are worried, you know what you are worried about, but when you are confused you don't know enough about a thing to be worried."*

Some of the most poignant messages of sympathy came from countries Will had visited and helped in one way or another— from Ireland, where he had put on the benefit in 1926 for victims of a theater disaster; from Puerto Rico, where he had aided victims of the 1932 hurricane; from Nicaragua, whose president recalled how Will "made me cry one minute and laugh the next during the bitter days following the 1931 earthquake."

It was extraordinarily difficult then, as now, to describe the hold Will Rogers had on so many millions of Americans. "A peculiar sense of national loss will be stirred by the tragic death of Mr. Rogers," a *New York Times* editorial read. "He had a unique career, which we all like to think could have been run only in America. He came to hold such a place in the public mind that, of his passing from the stage it might be said, as it was by Dr. Johnson of Garrick's, that it will 'eclipse the gayety of nations.' "

It was left for John McCormack, whom Betty and Will had heard sing at the St. Louis Exposition so many years earlier and who had become their friend over the years, to sum it up. "A smile has disappeared from the lips of America," he wrote, "and her eyes are now suffused with tears. He was a man, take this for all in all, we shall not look upon his like again."

SHORTLY after Betty Rogers learned of Will's death, Charles Lindbergh called to say that he would take charge of bringing the bodies home and that Pan American Airways, for which he worked as a consultant, would make its facilities available for this purpose. Joe Crosson flew to Barrow to pick up the bodies, and on August 17 Will and Wiley began their journey home. In Fairbanks the next morning hundreds of Alaskans saw Crosson off when he left for Vancouver. In Seattle people had waited all night for a glimpse of his airplane; flags were at half-mast, and planes overhead dipped their wings in salute.

On the nineteenth Crosson landed in Burbank, California, just as darkness was falling, and as the plane moved slowly through the twilight into the hangar, the throb of its idling motors reminded thousands of onlookers of muffled funeral drums.

While arrangements were being made for Will's funeral, Post's body was put aboard another plane bound for Oklahoma City. Without telling anyone, his elderly parents drove to the Oklahoma City airport, parked their car among the thousands of others, and waited, unrecognized by anyone, to see their son's body arrive. "We didn't want to create a stir," Wiley's father said.

On the day before Betty was due to reach the coast by train, a parcel arrived at the ranch. It was addressed in a familiar, rambling scrawl to Mrs. Will Rogers, and inside was Will's final gift to his wife—the small red-fox fur.

On August 22 the last rites for Will Rogers were held in Los

Angeles. Prior to a simple service at the Wee Kirk o' the Heather, his casket lay in state in Forest Lawn Memorial Park, where fifty thousand people—many of whom had been standing in line since the previous night—filed by in silence under a scorching sun. Other memorial services were held in the Hollywood Bowl, in Beverly Hills, and in Claremore. In many towns the flags were at half-mast; the nation's motion-picture theaters were darkened; the CBS and NBC networks observed a half hour of silence; and in New York a squadron of planes, each towing a long black streamer, flew over the city in final tribute to the hero and the friend of aviation.

Across the nation Americans were pausing to take Will Rogers' measure and to think what a different place their world would be now that he was gone. None of the descriptive labels—cowboy-philosopher, humorist, star of stage, screen, and radio—suggested what was in the hearts of most Americans when they learned of his death. Damon Runyon hinted at it when he called Will "the closest approach to what we call the true American."

IN THE years following his death many memorials to Will Rogers were established. In 1944 Will's children gave the Santa Monica ranch to California for a state park. On a high cliff above the Walakpa lagoon, facing the Arctic Ocean, is a marker of Oklahoma stone in which these words are cut: "Will Rogers and Wiley Post ended life's flight here, August 15, 1935." Clem Rogers' old ranch in the Verdigris valley was flooded when the Oologah dam and reservoir were built by the Army Engineers; but not before the Rogers ranch house was moved to high ground about a mile west of its original location. In 1959 the family donated a hundred-acre tract to the state, with the understanding that the house be relocated.

In 1938 Betty Rogers gave twenty acres of land in Claremore to Oklahoma for a memorial to her husband. It was a hillside Will had purchased in 1911, with the thought that he would come back there to live one day. Here, in 1944, his remains were brought from California, and a month later, when Betty died, she was buried at his side. In the rambling limestone building are all his letters, his newspaper articles, films, broadcast transcriptions, and the personal memorabilia of fifty-five restless, energetic years.

This is the place to which more than half a million Americans journey each year to pay tribute to the man they have never forgotten. In the center of the towering hall is a bronze statue of Will that bears the epitaph he wrote for himself: "I never met a man I didn't like."

The statue, by Jo Davidson, is a deep brown color, except for two gleaming bright spots on the toes of the shoes. Nearly every one of those millions of Americans who have come here since the Will Rogers Memorial was dedicated in 1938 has paused before the statue, looked up at the face, and then, before moving away, silently reached out to touch the tip of one shoe in a gesture of love. As it did in life, a little of Will Rogers has rubbed off on each of them.

W. A. Sonntag

Richard M. Ketchum

A few years ago, Will Rogers, Jr., approached the editors of *American Heritage,* a magazine he had long admired, and suggested that they publish a full-length biography of his father. They agreed, and requested their former book editor, Richard M. Ketchum, to write it.

Betty Rogers, Will's widow, had died in 1944, but Will, Jr., a former United States congressman now living in Tubac, Arizona, was enormously helpful in sharing with Mr. Ketchum his memories of his father. So was his brother Jim, who breaks horses on his ranch near San Bernardino, California. Their sister, Mary, has lived for many years in Europe, and transatlantic interviews proved unfeasible. But the staff of the Will Rogers Memorial at Claremore, Oklahoma, made available copies of Will's diaries, correspondence, radio and movie scripts, lectures, newspaper columns—over two million words in all—and many photographs, a selection of which accompany this condensation.

Mr. Ketchum, a native of Pittsburgh, is a Yale graduate and a former editor for the U.S. Information Agency. Among his other writings are two books and a number of magazine articles on the American Revolution. He lives in Vermont, where he and his wife, Barbara, operate a cattle-breeding farm which is also home to—at last count—five goats. The Ketchums have a son, a married daughter, and one grandchild.

Last May, in partnership with William S. Blair, a former publisher of *Harper's,* Mr. Ketchum started a new monthly magazine aimed at people who own farms or vacation homes in the New England area. *Blair & Ketchum's Country Journal* now reaches nearly fifty thousand readers, and circulation is climbing. The overworked proprietors intend to combine their January and February issues "so we can get a vacation."

Mr. Ketchum has a new text-and-picture biography of George Washington coming out, and is at work on an account of the critical period between Munich and Pearl Harbor.

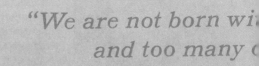

"*We are not born wi*
and too many o

How to Be
Bes

a condensati

MILDRED NEWMAN

wi

e secret of how to live,
never learn it"

Your Own
Friend

the book by

ERNARD BERKOWITZ

an Owen

- What if I can't achieve all the things I'd like to achieve?
- How can I be sure that those I do achieve will make me happy?
- Why do I often act so immaturely?
- How can I find peace in this uncertain world?

These and other questions all of us ask ourselves from time to time are answered by two eminent psychoanalysts in this wise and helpful book. "We can all help ourselves," the authors write, "to change, to grow, to become the person it is in us to be. We can learn to be our own best friend."

"There is no pill made that is as simple, effective and fast-working as this book. If I'm gloomy, I read it twice a day with a glass of water. It has never failed to uplift me."

—Playwright Neil Simon

Introduction

WHEN Thoreau remarked that most men live "lives of quiet desperation," he could not have foreseen how noisy that desperation would become. Modern man may suffer, like his forebears, but he does not suffer in silence. More and more, what's bothering us is up for discussion.

We talk, of course, about what's wrong with the world, about war and welfare, prices and pollution. But we also talk more frankly than ever before about what's awry in our inner world, about frustration and boredom and anxiety, about difficulties with marriage and sex, about the lack of fulfillment in our lives. We may not be any unhappier than our ancestors, but one thing is clear: we do not accept misery as our natural state. If we are unhappy, we feel cheated, displaced, left out; and we protest, either individually or collectively—as in the cry of women's liberationists—our right to meaningful work and satisfying lives.

We readily locate the causes of our grievances: our jobs, our husbands, our unhappy childhoods. Many take steps to remove the offenders—change careers, divorce, and go to psychoanalysts. Yet the rising decibels of our complaints make one wonder. Are we really doing all we can to make our lives more rewarding? Granting that we live in a time of social upheaval and dissolving values, where man's chances of survival are anybody's guess, we also have open to us more options than any previous generation. To put it mildly, we don't seem to be making the most of them. Why don't we, and how can we?

These questions were posed to two Manhattan psychoanalysts, Dr. Bernard Berkowitz and Mildred Newman, a husband and wife who separately and together (working with groups) are engaged in helping people do better with their lives. Our probing conversation follows.*

---

* For the purpose of coherence, the responses are a composite, as if only one psychoanalyst were speaking.

The Conversation

People say they want to be happy; yet real happiness seems like the impossible dream. What are we doing wrong? Why are so many people dissatisfied in so many ways? Is it the times we live in? Do we expect too much? Do we want the wrong things?

Well, it's not as bad as all that. There are plenty of people who are living to the hilt and loving every minute of it. But they don't talk about it much; they are busy doing it. They don't usually write articles or go to analysts. Yet it's true; not enough people have that sense of zest in their daily lives. Too many people have just not mastered the art of being happy.

You call it an art. Do you think it is something that can be learned, like dancing or making pottery? I don't see how you can make *happiness. You can go after the things you hope will make you happy, but you really don't know until after you get them whether they will.*

In a sense that's true. But the way you put it is part of the problem that many people have. They think there is something that will make them happy if they can just get hold of it. They expect happiness to happen to them. They don't see it's something they have to *do*. People will go to a lot of trouble to learn French or physics, or how to operate a car. But they won't be bothered learning how to operate themselves.

That's a funny idea. You make it sound as if we should be standing at our own controls and pushing buttons. Shouldn't the art of living be more natural than that?

Maybe it should, but for most of us it's not. We are not born with the secret of how to live, and too many of us never learn it. There is nothing cold-blooded or mechanical about it, but there are many things we have to learn to do.

For example?

The first thing is to realize that we've probably been looking in the wrong place. The source is not outside us; it is within. Most of us haven't begun to tap our own potential; we're operating way below capacity. And we'll continue to do so as long as we are looking for someone to give us the key to the kingdom. We must realize that the kingdom is within us; we already have the key. The choice is ours; we are accountable only to ourselves for what happens to us in our lives.

It still seems like a strange idea. If it is up to us, if we can push a magic switch and turn on happiness, why doesn't everyone just do it?

There is no magic switch. But there is an attitude. To take responsibility for our lives means to make a profound change in the way we approach everything. We do all we can to avoid this change, this responsibility. We would much rather blame someone or something for making us feel unhappy. We even talk about our own feelings as if they were visitors from outer space. We say, "This feeling came over me," as if our feelings changed from sunny to stormy, like the weather, over which we have no control. This meteorological view of our emotions is very useful; it takes us off the hook for the way we feel.

You know, I really find that hard to accept. If I am angry or upset about something, I can stop myself from breaking dishes or maybe from breaking into tears, but I can't just stop being upset or miserable. I'm not sure I would even want to. After all, if something has hurt me, I have a right to feel that hurt.

You certainly do. You have as much right to your painful feelings as to your happier ones. To feel all that you can feel is to be truly human. But too often people cling to unpleasant feelings; without fully realizing what they are doing, they actually do things that make them feel bad and then they say, "I couldn't help myself." What most people mean when they say that is, "I *didn't* help myself." But we can all help ourselves.

Can we really? That's an exciting and lovely thought. I would like to hold on to that. How can we do it?

In so many ways. First, you have to make a very basic decision: do you want to lift yourself up or put yourself down? Are you for yourself or against yourself? That may seem like a strange question, but many people are literally their own worst enemy. If you decide you want to help yourself, you can choose to do the things that make you feel good about yourself, instead of those that make you feel terrible. Why should you do what gives you pain when it is just as easy to give yourself joy? Yet for many people, finding out what helps them feel good is a real challenge. It's as if they had blinders on that shut out all the bright spots.

But there are plenty of people who see nothing but their bright spots. They think they're quite satisfactory as they are, and if anything is wrong, it is with somebody else, not them.

Of course. But they don't really believe that. They can't see their faults because they're afraid they've got nothing else. They think their choice is between being perfect and being the worst person who ever lived. The trouble is, it's very hard to give up that way of looking at yourself, because it is based on refusing to look *into* yourself. You must be able to see the ways you're pulling yourself down and decide that that isn't what you want to do. Then you can start doing the things that give you pride and pleasure in living.

Such as?

Such as being aware of your own achievements. When you do something you are proud of, dwell on it a little, praise yourself for it, relish the experience. We're not used to doing that for ourselves or for others. When things go wrong, they call attention to themselves. When things run well, we must actively bring them to our own attention.

It is up to us to give ourselves recognition. If we wait for praise to come from others, we feel resentful when it doesn't, and when it does, we may well reject it. Have you ever noticed how quickly the glow from a compliment wears off? When we compliment ourselves, the glow stays with us. This is the tragedy of some marvelous performers, who need endless applause to tell them how great they are, but who feel a chill as soon as they enter their dressing rooms. They have never applauded themselves.

I suppose it's like the people who have to prove something over and over again because they never really believe it, or buy things over and over because of something they feel, inside, that they don't really possess—the people who can never get enough of anything.

Yes, they're still looking in the wrong place. It's supposed to be what Don Juan was doing in all those beds. We can see the craziness of it clearly when we look at such extreme examples. But we all fail to appreciate ourselves enough. If someone is on a diet for a week and goes off it for a day, the overeating is nothing compared with the orgy of self-recrimination he then indulges in. What about the week he was on the diet? He should give himself credit for that and go right back on it. The pitfall is this: very likely it was not so much the food he couldn't resist as the temptation to tear down the wonderful self-image he was building all week long. That's something many of us find hard to take: really feeling good about ourselves.

But what if you do feel lousy about yourself? That's a real feeling, too, isn't it? How can you tell someone to do things to make him feel good if he really thinks he's a terrible person?

I suppose if someone said, "Look, I'm a terrible person and I like it that way, leave me alone," there wouldn't be much I could tell him. But chances are he wouldn't mean it. Most people are quite unhappy about making themselves miserable; there is usually a severe inner struggle going on. Part of the person is pushing himself down, but another part is crying out that that's not where he belongs. It's a question of having some compassion for yourself.

So when you do something that makes you feel bad inside, ask yourself whether that's the way you want to feel. If not, stop doing what makes you feel that way. Instead, do the things that make you feel good about yourself.

Since you seem to know so many secrets, what are some of the other things that people can do?

They really aren't secrets. People know so much more than they're willing to admit. They're keeping secrets from themselves. Some of them are so simple. One fundamental thing, for example, is to meet your own expectations. If you have housework or homework to do and you are tempted to let it slide, ask yourself how you will feel if you put it off. If you sense that you will be a little disgusted with yourself, then go ahead and do the job and let yourself savor the feeling you get from having done it. Enjoy the experience of being in charge of yourself. It's quite exhilarating. Housework and homework may be a small part of life, but how you feel about yourself throughout the day is life itself. And this process of imagining how you will feel about doing something can turn up some surprises, too. You may discover that doing something else will make you feel even better about yourself that particular day. You may decide to write a poem instead.

Isn't that encouraging people to be awfully self-centered? I have this vision of a woman greeting her husband with a possessed gleam in her eye when he comes home at night. He looks around in dismay at crying babies and unmade beds and asks, "Where's dinner?" and she says, "I wrote a poem instead!"

I think very few women would genuinely feel better about themselves if they wrote a poem at that price—at least not more than once. People rarely feel good about themselves for being unkind to others. If something like that happened, I suspect the woman would feel elated but also distressed. And if her poetic urge continued, she would have to make some other choices. Could she manage to write poetry and take care of her family, too? If not, how important was the poetry to her? If it turned out to be something she very much needed to do, she would have to get help with her other responsibilities. Maybe her husband would be willing to do more. And, of course, some artists find that marriage and a family just aren't for them, and they choose their art. That's all right, too. I think one of Katherine Anne Porter's husbands said to her about the failure of their marriage, "But you were already married." We must establish our priorities.

You know, a lot of women's liberationists argue that day care should be widely available so that mothers aren't forced to stay home with their children and stagnate. I'm not against day care or careers for women. But having children is—or ought to be—a choice. If women want to have babies, they should. If they don't, they shouldn't have them. But once they do, they have a certain responsibility. If they want to have both a family and a career, they are taking on a tough challenge, and it's up to them to meet it. They can lobby for day-care centers if they like, but they shouldn't feel like victims.

But what if you can't manage everything you'd like to do— few of us can—and you have to make choices? When does doing good things for yourself become pure self-indulgence?

Doing what makes you feel good about yourself is really the opposite of self-indulgence. It doesn't mean gratifying an isolated part of you; it means satisfying your whole self, and this includes the feelings and ties and responsibilities you have toward others. Self-indulgence means satisfying the smallest part of you, and that only temporarily.

You should be self-centered enough to care for yourself. If you don't learn how to do that, you can never care properly for others. The Bible says, "Love thy neighbor *as* thyself," not "better than" or "instead of" thyself. If we cannot love ourselves, where will we draw our love for others? People who do not love themselves can adore others, because adoration is making someone else big and ourselves small. They can desire others, because desire comes out of a sense of inner incompleteness. But they cannot love others, because love is an affirmation of the living, growing being in all of us. If you don't have love, you can't give it.

Charity begins at home.

Yes. You can see the difference between love and what looks like love very clearly in relations between parents and children. Parents always claim that they are acting out of love for their children, but it's easy to see when they're not. When a parent "sacrifices" for a child, you know there's something wrong because of the way the child reacts. The child feels guilty, not grateful, because what he's getting comes to him not out of love but out of self-denial. Self-denial is one of the worst kinds of self-indulgence. It is feeding the part of you that feels worthless. No one benefits from that. You can sometimes decide to give things up, but that is a choice you make, and it is done out of self-regard, not self-hatred.

In other words, it's not what you do but why you do it. And you keep coming back to the concept of choice. You seem to be saying something about freedom.

You are free when you accept the responsibility for your choices. And when you choose your own best interests. It's not as hard to do as it sounds.

It's hard enough. I can think of hundreds of times I've wanted to be wise and thoughtful and mature and gracious and all those lovely things, and ended up acting like a brat.

But that's just what everybody does. Why don't you think about the times you were wise and kind? Why remember and dwell on defeats instead of victories? Many people are under a sort of negative self-hypnosis. They put labels on themselves. They say: I am (a) a terrible person who (b) always does awful things and (c) can't possibly do better. Instead of convincing ourselves beforehand that something we want to do is impossible, we should spend those energies looking for ways to do it. When you insist you're not the kind of a person who can climb a mountain or make a speech, all you are saying is that up to now you haven't done it. Sometimes even that's not true, because if people want to see themselves as unable to do something, they manage to forget the times they actually have done it. But even if they haven't, who knows what they will do in the future? That's what growth is: doing things you've never done before, sometimes things you once didn't even dream you could do.

I really never climbed a mountain, and I'm sure I never will!

I don't suppose you ever wanted to. Of course, difficult things are a lot of trouble, and you have to want very badly to do them. But when you don't set limits on your efforts, great things can come out of them.

Sometimes the limits are set by others. Schoolchildren who are classified as low achievers tend to become low achievers; they sense that is what their teachers expect of them, so they learn to expect little of themselves. Many low achievers are simply slow growers or children with problems that interfere with learning; they could do very well, given the right encouragement. As the warden of the Federal House of Detention in Manhattan said recently of his prisoners, "If you treat an individual as he is, he'll stay as he is. But if you treat him as if he were what he ought to be or could be, perhaps he will become that."

We can all do much more than we think, but first we have to believe it. We should try some positive hypnosis for a change.

That sounds like positive thinking, perhaps with a bit of Coué thrown in: "Every day in every way I am getting better and better." That kind of pep talk is very popular in this country, but I wonder whether it's done more harm than good. Denying difficulties isn't the way to overcome them; it just helps people avoid facing them. People may have smiles on their faces, but they're dragging the same old anchors around.

It's unfortunate. Positive thinking has more than a grain of truth in it, but it goes too far. Or maybe it doesn't go far enough. When you rely on willpower, on making up your mind, you're using only one of the tools you need to make a change. Good things don't come out of forcing yourself. When you try to do it all out of willpower, you are not treating yourself with respect. You are making the assumption that change has to be imposed from above, that your *self* doesn't have its own impulse to do better. But it does. You need to learn to work with yourself, to use your willpower on the side of yourself. But your self must come willingly.

Your will must be enlisted to help you accomplish what you really *want* to do. We are all limited by our actual capacities and interests. It would be futile for me to make up my mind to be a painter if I had no talent in that direction. But the truth is, if the talent is lacking, the desire will be absent, too. Your genuine self does not want to do things that are utterly foreign to it; it wants to realize its own potential.

When we use our willpower to achieve goals that do not

spring out of us, but which we set for the sake of pleasing others or fulfilling a fantasy about who we are, we create a kind of monster, a mechanical man in which our living self is trapped. We have all seen people who are held together by sheer willpower; the effort is enormous, but the result is hardly worth it. They aren't people we enjoy being with—or who enjoy being with themselves.

Yet ex-alcoholics often give that impression. You can sense a terrific strain in them; it's costing them a lot. But you can't say the effort isn't worth it or that it doesn't come from a real desire for liberation.

Yes, that's true. Their tragedy is that many of them don't release their energies from the struggle against what they *don't* want to be, to spend those energies on becoming the person they *do* want to be. They have taken an important step forward, but they have to go on from there.

What I am trying to say is that if we want to become all that is in us to become, we have to use everything we've got— our feelings, our intuition, our intelligence, and our willpower —our whole self. If we do, the payoff is enormous.

Then why don't we do it? Why do so few of us live that way?

Because there's also a hidden payoff in continuing to suffer. For one thing, it's familiar; we're very comfortable with it. It gives us a sense of security to keep on in the same old self-defeating ways, letting one bad action lead to another. We know what to expect. It makes our world comprehensible, predictable— in some sense manageable. One of the things people need most is a feeling of living in a world they understand; that's one of the deepest appeals of religion. That's why people are so disturbed today: it's not only the violence around us, but also the feeling that life doesn't make sense. Nothing seems to hang together anymore; the old explanations don't seem to apply.

People don't know what to count on anymore. Things seem more and more uncertain.

Social chaos is terrifying, but personal chaos is even more horrifying. From a very early age we are all looking for ways to organize that chaos. We all start out as scientists of a sort. Gradually we build an inner view of the world, which helps us sort out the overwhelming flood of stimuli that come our way, and calls some of them good and desirable and safe and others bad and dangerous. We decide that certain actions will get us the results we want, while other actions are likely to get us into trouble.

How does that come about?

Each of us creates a kind of working hypothesis which says, "This is what life is about." We do that when we're very young, and these theories are often very ingenious and really help us to survive. The trouble is that too often we don't revise them as we grow older and gain more experience. We keep fitting new experience into the old slots.

I'm sure most people would deny they had anything as sophisticated as a theory.

Most people don't know they have one, because they have never put it into words. These theories are made up of vague feelings, unspoken apprehensions, the things we didn't dare talk about or even admit to ourselves as children. They deal with the most powerful and problematic forces in human life, like sex and aggression, which most families find too formidable to discuss. So we develop complex ideas about the nature of reality, which we never communicate and never examine. Someone said that God created the world in a fit of absentmindedness. We do almost as well. We build world views half asleep and let them, like tinted lenses, color our lives.

You mean our most important ideas about life are ones we are not even aware of, and we've been carrying them around since childhood?

Yes, and their impact can be very powerful. Often when we think we're responding to actual people and events, we're merely assigning them parts in the inner novel we've been writing all our lives. For example, if someone has felt deserted as a child by an important adult, and this becomes a key experience in his way of seeing the world, there are several ways he can continue to have that experience. One way is to seek out the kind of people who are likely to desert him as an adult—and we are all very clever about that. Another is to drive people away by his own behavior. Or he can imagine he is deserted by people who really haven't mistreated him at all. Whatever way he chooses, he confirms his theory, and this is very gratifying.

Come on! That certainly doesn't sound like any way to have fun.

You'd be surprised. Being right is one of the most satisfying experiences in the world. Or let's say, rather, that being wrong is one of the most unsettling. It's an awful blow to the ego to feel you've made a mistake. That's why people don't want to change. It would mean admitting they were wrong.

A patient once burst out at me indignantly, "But that would mean I wasted the first forty years of my life!" Some people would prefer to go on making the same mistake for another forty years rather than to admit it and cut their losses. People are very stubborn. Sometimes they secretly believe that reality will conform to their views, rather than vice versa. They're still trying to get their parents to give in. They haven't given up their anger over what they didn't get when they were five years old.

People feel very justified in that anger; they can give you all the details on how unfairly they were treated. They are usually right: they did get cheated as children. But what they don't see is that they are now cheating themselves as adults. As long as they spend their energies being angry at the people who deprived them once, they won't spend them on getting what they need now. Their rage isn't hurting their parents, but it's crippling them.

Damn it, that doesn't seem fair. You mean we should just let them get away with it? After all they put us through?

Life is not fair. And they did get away with it. There's no way to even the score. Hamlet eventually evened the score, like a lot of other tragic heroes, and he died. Life, on the other hand, lies in letting go, in giving up your grievances.

So we just have to write off all that suffering, all those years, all we believed in as children? We have to accept that none of it ever was what we thought it was?

But in a sense it was what you thought it was, then. What people rarely understand is that they were not wrong at the time they made up the theories.

You don't mean that that bundle of unspoken apprehensions gave an accurate picture of the world?

No, but it was the best way we had of dealing with our corner of the world. We all start out being the smallest, least powerful person in our immediate world, the family. Our helplessness is not a theory, it's a fact. In the early stages of coping with our world, we have to work through others. At five, we need our mother. We must please and pacify her to get the things we need; our life literally depends on doing so. To accomplish our own thing as children, we must be able to manipulate adults. So it is appropriate in childhood to look to others; we can look to ourselves only secondarily.

The mistake lies in carrying this sense of helplessness, this need to placate others, into adulthood, making a fantasy out of what was once a fact. Our success as adults doesn't depend on pleasing others. What others once did for you, you can now do for yourself. When you're thirty, you don't need your mother to love you the way she did when you were three. You don't have to fear her anger anymore. You can stop wearing the ties she likes or dating the women she would approve of. That's all over; it's ancient history. You're your own man—or woman—now. But many people will not realize that.

Why not? Why don't they grab that freedom?

They're terribly afraid of losing something they think they cannot do without. You know, the French philosopher Rousseau said, "Man is born free, and everywhere he is in chains." It is closer to the truth to say, "Man is born in chains, but each of us has the potential to be free." Too often people cling to their chains even after they've outgrown them.

Well, yes, I guess it's obvious that some people do that. But what are we so afraid to let go of?

It's actually a childlike sense of security we're holding on to. As long as we feel small and helpless, we feel we're in the presence of invisible, all-powerful adults. They may not be very nice adults; we're always expecting them to blame us or yell at us. But as long as they're there, we're not alone. That's the thing we fear most: if that disapproving parent goes away, we will be all by ourselves. But that feeling, too, is a leftover from being five years old. To be abandoned is a terrifying prospect to a child; he literally couldn't survive it. But an adult not only can survive aloneness; he often needs to be alone to grow, to get to know himself, and develop his powers. Someone who cannot tolerate aloneness is someone who doesn't know he's grown up.

It takes courage to let go of that fantasy of childhood safety.

The world may never seem so certain again, but what fresh air we breathe when we take possession of our own separateness, our own integrity! That's when our adult life really begins.

When you say it, I can feel it. It sounds wonderful, and yet frightening, too, and somehow bleak. It means being so on your own, so exposed. Something in me pulls back from it.

Not only you. Many people hold themselves back from taking that step. The reason is that they have some very distorted ideas about what will happen if they go ahead. It's another childhood myth. When we were small, there was one man and one woman in our world, our parents. They were the big ones, the adults. What a child experiences is, to him, the only way things can be. So he gets the idea that there can be only one man and one woman, and if anyone has the audacity to set himself up as an adult, he must knock someone else down. He is imbued with a competitive sense of life—to pay Paul you must rob Peter. If we take our lives into our own hands, it feels like taking life away from someone else. We feel literally as if we are dealing a death blow to our parents, so we back down. But we have to face that feeling and go ahead anyway. It's the price of self-assertion.

But I don't blame people for backing down. I wouldn't want to feel like a killer. People have enough guilt without that.

You have to live through those feelings if you ever want to grow up completely. What you're killing is not your parents but your fear of them and their power over you. In a very ruthless, primitive way, you have to choose yourself over them. If you do make that basic assertion, you will see that no one will end up dead in the process—except old ghosts. Unless, of course, you wait too long, and then reality may accommodate itself to your fantasies.

I know someone who imagined that if she ever had a child, it would kill her mother. So she waited until she was forty-five, and, in fact, her mother did die at about the same time. But the outcome is usually much less dramatic.

What you achieve doesn't take anything away from anyone else. Whatever you do, the world will continue to go about its business. People must compete for real things in the real world, like jobs or scholarships, but they don't have to compete for their own good opinion. If you become more, it doesn't make me less.

There is room for many marvelous people in the world and many wonderful achievements. When we really grasp this, we take pleasure in what others are able to do; we do not feel diminished. And we are able to do our own thing without feeling anxious or guilty toward anyone.

We actually live in an atmosphere of emotional abundance. Developing our human resources doesn't use them up; it only enlarges our possibilities. But those resources do not keep. If you do not mine them now, they are lost forever.

That's something else people don't face. They think they have eternity before them, that what they don't do now, they can do tomorrow or the day after. They think they're playing a game and that if they hold out long enough, the other side will surrender and give them what they want. But it is not a game; there is no other side. And we don't have eternity; we only have time. There are no limits to how much we can grow and develop, but time limits us. People are often obsessed with aging, with what time does to them. Instead they should be concerned about what they do with time.

It sounds so wise and so beautiful. I would like to wrap it up and take it home with me. But isn't it asking too much of people? Who has the power to keep that steady an eye on reality? I think I know a few things about life, but I often lose track of them. I get discouraged and impatient and in need of reassurance, and I worry about the future. Can people expect to be that mature?

They don't have to be totally mature. That's still another thing people don't understand. They envision adulthood as a door that opens only out. They think that once they step through it they can never return. Growing up is not a one-way trip. The two states aren't mutually exclusive, which is lucky; otherwise the generations would have more than a gap. They would face an unbridgeable abyss.

It's all right to be immature at times; people who are totally adult are a little intimidating. That's the wonderful thing about marriage. A good marriage is a very adult relationship. But husbands and wives can be all things to each other. You can be parents and playmates, as well as lovers and partners. You can be babied when you need it, and we all do.

That's very reassuring. I do feel better knowing I don't have to be a superadult. I think I used to, try to do that and it made people feel I was looking down on them; they didn't like it at all.

Perhaps because you didn't feel good about being a child. But there's a child in each of us, and we should be kind to that child. Nobody can take away what happened when you were four years old. What you can do is to be compassionate to the four-year-old who is still within you. Adults can often be tender toward a four-year-old, but when they find themselves feeling or behaving like one, they become disgusted with themselves, and they disclaim the child they in part still are.

They probably started doing that very early. Somehow in the process of growing up, which should be basically a reaching out to new ways of handling experience, the emphasis shifts to feeling bad about the old ways. This is really the beginning of self-hatred. Genuine growth means having the courage and confidence to try new things and, in the process, to let go of old ones. But this doesn't mean you have to despise the self you were. You let go of what you don't need anymore because you are on to something better.

That sounds easy, like things just falling into place and appearing when they're needed. But growing isn't easy. It's painful to grow, and terribly difficult. You're not sure of where you're going or whether you can get there. There's so much uncertainty and so much ambivalence.

Of course, of course. Growing pains are very real. And when children are struggling with an important new step forward, they sometimes have to push away their old habits rather violently. They don't need them anymore but partly they still do, so their behavior can be quite contrary and unsettling to those around them. Any parent knows what I am talking about.

What is it someone said? That the only way to true adulthood is through a real childhood.

Yes. A good childhood is liberating; good parents help their child move on. The tragedy of a bad childhood is that people tend to get hooked on it. They go through life looking over their shoulder at something they once had, or thought they had, or wanted. They waste years trying to recapture the bliss they had too little of as infants, instead of capturing the joy they could have as adults.

That's what addicts are often looking for in drugs, isn't it?

Yes. They want to go back for happiness. But it doesn't work. You have to go ahead. It's much harder. Going ahead means taking chances, trying things you've never tried. Of all you said earlier—about not being sure of whether you can get there—the hardest thing is when you must give something up and you don't see what you'll get if you do.

That's why some people don't want to stop suffering; they know they've got that, and they really don't believe there's anything else. One of Faulkner's characters said, ". . . between grief and nothing I will take grief." But our choice is between grief and a full life. To take the first steps toward that life may be painful, and you may have to endure sharp pangs of loneliness and loss. But you were lonely anyhow and your loss happened long ago. What you are losing now is only a dream.

It must be a strange awakening. Like opening your eyes for the first time. Like being born. What are those first steps? How does one start?

You start by paying attention. If things keep turning out the way you don't want them to, ask yourself what you are doing to make them come out that way. See the connection between what you do and how you feel. You may have to sit yourself down and demand some answers. Why do you go on being unkind and unfriendly to yourself? Why do you trip yourself up? What are you getting out of it? What kind of vision of yourself are you holding on to? Do you secretly think that if you act helpless enough, someone will come and take over for you? Do you really think failure will make you lovable?

You talked earlier about the inner novel we've been writing all our lives. This sounds like a form of playacting, going through our part in a private drama, hoping someone will play the other characters we've cast. But if it's all a fantasy, why do we give ourselves such thankless roles?

That's just the point. They're not as thankless as they seem. In all the bad things we do to ourselves, there is usually an expectation of some kind of reward. Punishment, after all, can be a very real reward. Some children feel loved only when they're being punished. The only other thing they get from their parents is indifference, and that's the worst of all. So, as adults, we put ourselves through all kinds of hell, just to feel that the people who once mattered to us are still around. But we've been communing with ghosts—even if they're ghosts of people still alive.

I suppose ghosts can seem better than nothing.

That's the tragedy of it. We think that if we give up the reassurance of those unseen presences, we'll have no one. And it is true that if we let them go, we will have to experience the pain of separation, that sense of aloneness that every mature individual must know. But if you have the courage to endure that wrench, it will pave the way for something far better than the childlike dependence you gave up: the true intimacy that is possible only between equals, between adults.

That's when the fun really begins. When people really know who they are and *are* who they are, that's when they can really open themselves to others. When you stop trying to get from people what they can't give you, you can begin to enjoy what they can offer. People can share whole worlds with each other, but first they must have access to their own.

You mean for adults intimacy is something quite different from the intimacy a child knows or wants?

And far more enjoyable—for an adult. When the only kind of closeness you can imagine is that of a child to a parent, you may want that closeness desperately, but you have to fear it, too, because in its ultimate form it reduces you, literally, to a gibbering idiot. If you seek closeness by feeling small and finding protective shelter in someone big, there is always the fear of disappearing altogether. But adult love does not diminish the lover. It enhances us; it makes us more.

You mean the risk of love is not as great as we think.

No one can take the risk out of love. When you expose your being to someone, you inevitably take the chance of being hurt. That's why some people prefer not to love at all; they would rather live enclosed in themselves than risk the pain of that exposure, that nakedness that love implies. But an adult, when he loves, does not risk his whole identity. That he already has, and will keep, however the other responds. If he loses his lover, he will still have himself. But if you look to someone else to establish your identity for you in some way, losing that person can make you feel destroyed.

You mean that even in the deepest love, you keep a sense of separateness?

At moments of great closeness, there is no consciousness of separate selves. But that deep sharing of self is different from being swallowed up.

I wouldn't want a life without love in it.

Who would? Everything you do is richer and fuller when love is there. But love is not always there, and how you feel about yourself at those times when there isn't someone around to receive and return your love has a lot to do with how rewarding the experience of love is when you have it.

I think of a great-aunt of mine, now in her mid-eighties, who lives alone on the edge of the California desert. I once asked her what she did with her time. Her answer was, "There are not enough hours in the day." We visited her recently and found out what she meant. When we were there, she entertained her literary group, so there was the weekly selection to read in advance and a cake to bake. She also takes a course in creative writing, and between her cultural activities she raises things in the garden, visits people, and carries on a voluminous correspondence with friends, relatives, and people on radio talk shows. She isn't just making busywork for herself, either; she genuinely enjoys everything she does. A few years ago she took a trip abroad, by herself, and had a wonderful time. She stayed with us awhile on the way back and was a pleasure to have around. She was always glad to spend time with us, but she was perfectly happy when we were busy elsewhere. We never had the feeling she was waiting for us to come and entertain her. She never had that look that says, "Feed me." She had found ways to feed herself.

So we're back to the question of how we go about it. How do we learn to feed ourselves?

It's important to learn to listen to ourselves. Most of us learn to tune ourselves out. We start out receiving our messages loud and clear; babies know when they're hungry and when they hurt. But when we're small, other people's voices are so much louder and surer than our own. It's easiest to go along with what others say. They've got it all figured out already, and we're just starting to put the pieces together. Besides, it's their side the bread is buttered on. If we listen to them, we get room and board. What can we offer ourselves to compete with that?

Tuning in again takes practice; we have to encourage ourselves to speak up. If we've stopped listening to our own voice for a long time, that voice may be very faint; it may have half given up. It may also be pretty angry for having been shut up so long. But it's there; we have to give it a chance. If we learn how to listen, we will find out a lot and hear some wonderful things.

I suspect we may hear some terrible things, too. Isn't there a lot hidden in us that would be pretty hard to take? That would be too much for people to handle by themselves if it did surface? Isn't that what psychoanalysts are for? To help people dig it up, sort it out, and maybe, eventually, be free of it?

Analysts can help people a great deal, of course, in delving into the reasons they mistreat themselves. Some people are so caught up in doing harm to themselves and have so little understanding of why they do it that analysis is the only way they can begin to break out of their self-destructive spiral. It can help them get around the roadblocks that stand in the way of growth.

Analysis is a great tool of liberation. When the first patient lay down on the couch, that was truly a giant step for mankind. But there is so much people can do off the couch. And there is so much people have to do for themselves, even with an analyst's help. One reason analysis sometimes takes so long is the refusal of many people to realize that, at bottom, change is up to them. No matter how many insights they may gain, no matter how much emotional catharsis they may achieve, change does not just happen.

But I have the impression that sometimes change does simply come. I know that has happened to me. Suddenly you feel very different about someone or something; burdens are lifted; doors open; something you were struggling with becomes easy all at once.

Miracles do seem to happen, and it's a good thing, because they help people keep going. However, the struggles must come first. A lot of plugging goes into the making of miracles. They happen to people who are ready for them. But it takes more than these sudden leaps to change a life. It takes a conscious act, a decision to take our life into our hands and shake free of comfortable habits. A lot of people don't want to face that decision. They think their analyst is the good father or mother they never had and that from now on they'll be taken care of. They're partly right, and one of the most important things an analyst can give is his loving interest. But people forget that a good parent is one who helps the child take care of himself. Someone has said that if you give a man food, you feed him for a day, but if you teach him how to grow his own, he can feed himself for life.

When you decide to take care of yourself, there is still a big job ahead. It takes thought and effort to shake free of bad habits. A part of you may well be quite indignant at the changes you're trying to make. That part of you that is quite comfortable in the old ways can put up quite a fight.

But change must go much deeper than just getting rid of comfortable habits. There's more at stake than that, surely.

All the things we've been talking about are at stake: our illusions, our fantasies, our sense of being right about our world and about ourselves. In a profound sense, a part of one's self feels that its very existence is threatened. But that's a misunderstanding. What are under attack are truly the bad habits of thinking and behaving that have poisoned our lives.

Getting rid of them takes a lot of perseverance. It's not enough to want to change. You must want to *want* to. You have to watch what you're doing. Every time you catch yourself putting yourself down, just stop and turn around and push yourself up.

It takes realism, too. People often want to be perfect and become discouraged when they're not. They have to give that up. Perfection is not for human beings. A perfect person—whatever that would be—would be unbearable. Judging yourself by superhuman standards is another way of mistreating yourself and a good excuse for giving up. Don't judge yourself at all; accept yourself and move on from there.

Accept the messiness and the mistakes? But I thought the point was to stop making them.

If you do, you'll be the only one.

You know, there's another thing that bothers me—all this watching and working at it all the time. It makes me kind of tired to think about it. It certainly doesn't sound like fun. Where is that zest we were talking about at the beginning? Where does spontaneity come in?

People often talk about wanting to be spontaneous, to live out of their feelings. They have locked themselves into intellectual boxes, where they hardly know what they feel anymore. They become desperate to experience plain, simple emotion.

They think if they could throw away their minds, they would be free.

But neither freedom nor feelings are that simple. We have in us a catchall of programmed reactions—remembered scoldings, schoolbook maxims, nostalgia, and old wives' tales—all mixed up with our own true feelings. So, in practice, spontaneity usually means grabbing the first thing that floats to mind and taking it as if it were a message from our depths. But there's a lot of pollution in those depths. We have to examine the reactions that surface to see where the messages really come from, and which represent our true interests.

This doesn't mean you have to watch yourself every minute. You don't have to become as self-conscious as the centipede who forgot how to walk. But living out of your own true feelings does take work. If you're willing to invest the effort, the zest will come.

People say they want to "let go." What they really need to do is take hold. Only when you're really in charge of yourself can you afford to let go, to be spontaneous, and expect good to come out of it. That's why sex is more satisfying for adults. Only mature people have the self-possession to abandon themselves and know they'll come out of it intact. It sounds like a paradox, but it is one of the secrets of love.

You're convincing me; it sounds better and better. I'm not sure I know enough yet. What else can I do?

You must also learn to talk to yourself. That's very important. You need to explain things, to reassure yourself. You need to establish an ongoing dialogue. It can help you through all kinds of tough situations.

When the child in you is up to mischief, you can stop and discuss it first; you can tell him no. There is usually a moment when it could go either way. If you pay attention, you can take that moment and consider what you really want to do. You have the power to stop yourself; this is a good thing to know. At first it's hard, but it gets easier.

It sounds as if a man's freedom may hinge on just that little pause. What a narrow margin it is.

You won't always use it well, either. And when the child in you does misbehave, don't punish yourself; you've done that enough. Forgive the child in you. Most of the things you feel terrible about weren't so bad to begin with. We often go on doing things against ourselves just to prove we are the terrible person we imagined we were as a child. Don't glorify your lapses. Just try to understand why they happened and steer yourself back on the right track.

All the loving help you would give a living child, you can give yourself. When you know a child well, you have a feel for when to put on pressure, when to offer comfort, and when to leave him alone. If you come to know the child in you, you can get that feel for yourself. You can know when to be easy, when to make demands. You have to get on familiar terms with yourself. Embrace the child in you; make friends with yourself. It gives such a reserve of strength to call on.

I once was seeing a man who was grieving deeply. The person he had been closest to had died, and he felt utterly desolate. I sat with him and could feel the depths of his sorrow. Finally I said to him, "You look as if you had lost your best friend." He said, "Well, I have." And I said, "Don't you know who your best friend is?" He looked at me, surprised. He thought a moment, and tears came into his eyes. Then he said, "I guess it's true—you are your own best friend."

If we do all of this, if we understand all of these things, will it really make such a difference in our lives?

If we can learn to love and nurture ourselves, we will find ourselves richer than we ever imagined. We will still be beset by real problems and suffer real defeats. Life is not a picnic— or a rose garden. There is no escaping the human condition, which involves pain and difficulty and loss. But we can bring everything we have to bear on the challenges life presents and make the very most of what it offers us.

People often have a need to see themselves as worn out, having tried everything, exhausted their resources, as if they have given up on themselves. Yet when we begin to make available to ourselves our own possibilities, it is like drilling a well to an untapped energy reserve, like finding a bank account we haven't yet used. It's the cheapest form of entertainment there is. You never run out; you are never bored. It is also old-age security. When the art critic Bernard Berenson was almost ninety, he said, "I wish I could stand on a busy street corner, hat in hand, and beg people to throw me all their wasted hours." He never lost his capacity for enjoying each moment to the full. You can say, "Well, he was an exceptional man." But we can all do it.

It sounds like the secret of living. I wish I could believe we can all learn to live like that.

There is no question that we can. I have seen so many people do it, really come to life. We can all help ourselves to change, to grow, to become the person it is in us to be. We can learn to be our own best friend. If we do, we have a friend for life.

I feel that I have learned many secrets from you, and heard many wise words. I hope I can remember them.

Of course you'll remember them; you knew them all the time.

*Mildred Newman and
Bernard Berkowitz*

Husband and wife for more than twelve years, Mildred Newman and Bernard Berkowitz have a unique and special relationship—so close that they often have the same dream. In a sense, *How to Be Your Own Best Friend* grew out of this closeness. When a friend, Jean Owen, suggested they collaborate with her on a book, ideas they had exchanged over the years took shape under her questioning, "and before we knew it," Mildred Newman recalls, "we had a book." While its outstanding success caused a sensation in the literary world, the authors never doubted its impact, for in it, Dr. Berkowitz points out, "we talked about what we deal with daily in our respective practices—the nitty-gritty that brings people to consult with us."

Both psychologists were born and educated in New York, and both have been practicing psychoanalysts for more than twenty years. Mildred Newman worked for a number of years after college with the eminent Austrian-born psychologist Theodor Reik and was trained at the National Psychological Association for Psychoanalysis. Dr. Berkowitz attended the Alfred Adler Institute and the Postgraduate Center for Mental Health.

In private life, they enjoy traveling and often spend summers navigating their converted barge along the waterways of Europe. Last summer, however, they remained at home to work on a new book, to be entitled *How to Be Awake and Alive*.

Illustrations by William Hofmann

The dramatic first eyewitness account of
life inside China's forced-labor camps

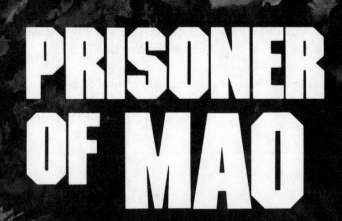

PRISONER
OF MAO

A condensation of the book by
BAO RUO-WANG (JEAN PASQUALINI)
and **RUDOLPH CHELMINSKI**

At Ching Ho farm in northern China the work was hard, the rations almost nonexistent. Many of the prisoners died. But Bao Ruo-wang's companions were determined to keep him alive. As a foreigner (his father was French), there was a chance that he might someday be released. He was, in the words of a cellmate, the only one who could tell about it afterward.

Miraculously, he lived to see that day. By then he had spent seven years in Chinese jails and work camps. He had known horrors and privations, but humor and friendship too. And he had undergone the extraordinary process of "reform" that actually makes a man grateful to his captors.

Now he has fulfilled his fellow prisoners' hopes. While *Prisoner of Mao* is his story, it is also the story of uncounted millions whose release will come only with death. It has justly earned for its author the title of "the Chinese Solzhenitsyn."

> "A unique, vivid and dispassionate picture of an extraordinary aspect of life in Mao's Marxist state."
>
> —Buffalo, New York, *Evening Globe*

Chapter 1

O N THE afternoon of Friday, November 13, 1964, a political prisoner was released at the Chinese border checkpoint of Shumchun, the principal land entrance to Hong Kong. There were no delegations to meet him, no reporters, no relatives. Only the usual English colonial policeman was there, at his post on the other end of the Lo Wu Bridge.

The prisoner was a French citizen, and his name was Jean Pasqualini, which was odd, considering his Asiatic appearance. He had a typically Chinese face and appeared to be in his late thirties. His gray woolen suit was obviously government issue, and the collar of his white shirt was absurdly large for him. Along with a single companion he walked across the bridge in a busy, hunching gait, face expressionless, never looking back.

That prisoner was myself. I was about to start my new life in the West with six Hong Kong dollars (one U.S. dollar) in my pocket. I was on my way to France, which was my father's country, even though I had never set foot there. France and the People's Republic of China had just officially recognized each other, and it was as a "gesture of extraordinary magnanimity" that I, a French citizen, had had the remainder of my twelve-year sentence remitted. By then I had spent seven years in Chinese prisons and forced-labor camps. As I crossed that bridge I was leaving behind the culture into which I was born, every friend in the world, a wife who had had to divorce me, and two sons whom I shall probably never see again.

But I had learned about *Lao Gai*.

Lao Gai—short for *Lao Dong Gai Zao*—is an invention of the Chinese Communist theoreticians. It means Reform Through Labor.

In our fair and pleasant world there is no shortage of modern civilizations built on a foundation of concentration camps and prison farms. The Soviet complex of forced-labor camps, impressively vast in its prime, was brutal, unsophisticated and inefficient compared with what the Chinese Communists developed after they came to power in 1949. What the Russians failed to understand is that convict labor can never be productive if it is extracted by brutality. The Chinese were the first to grasp the art of motivating prisoners. That's what *Lao Gai* is all about.

Those seven prison years constitute my own story, of course. But far more important, they are the story of the millions upon millions of Chinese who endured the camps with me and are still in them today.* For these prisoners, I am the only spokesman. The story of *Lao Gai* has never been told before.

THERE is a simple basic truth about the Chinese labor camps: for all but a handful of exceptional cases such as mine, the prison experience is total and permanent. Those sentenced to Reform Through Labor spend the rest of their lives in the camps, first as prisoners and then as "free" workers after their terms have expired.

Labor camps are far too important to the Chinese economy to be run with transient personnel. It is convicts who have made the vast Manchurian wastelands productive; convicts who run some of China's biggest plastics factories and agricultural stations;

---

* Estimates of the number vary widely, though sixteen million is probably a reasonable figure. At least as many more are undergoing the three-year terms of *Lao Jiao*—Education Through Labor. In theory these persons, who have committed "mistakes" rather than "crimes," maintain their civic rights while in the camps.

convicts who grow the very food Mao eats. At branch farm number three of the Ching Ho State Farm, northeast of Tientsin, I raised that food with my own hands. To achieve these successes one thing was indispensable: a stable supply of hardworking manpower.

"A living hell" is the popular image conjured up by the idea of Communist labor camps. There is truth in the image, of course, but it is distorted. The reality I discovered was the same one that had already been testified to by the survivors of Stalinist camps: not only is the society within the camps in many ways purer than the larger one outside, but it is also freer. It is in the prisons and camps that the notions of friendship and personal freedom are the most highly developed in China.

In spite of the doors recently opened, there is much misinformation in the West concerning China, especially with regard to her prison system. Many Westerners—journalists, priests, businessmen, soldiers—have spent some time in confinement on the mainland and written books about the experience. As reporters, almost all were handicapped because they spoke little or no Chinese. Even more important, as foreigners, they received special treatment—private cells, different rations, isolation from Chinese prisoners. No Westerner has ever been allowed to visit the regular camps, and certainly none has ever won the doubtful honor of being selected for Reform Through Labor.

I did because the police authorities considered me as Chinese—a foreigner born in China, speaking the language like a native, with the face of a Chinese.

MY NAME, Pasqualini, comes from my Corsican father, an adventurous character who left his native island (part of France) at the turn of the century (in something of a hurry, as I understand it), joined the French army and eventually found himself on garrison duty in Peking. In those days just about every Western power had a piece of poor, humiliated China. With demobilization at the end of the Boxer Rebellion my father elected to stay on there. He went into business for himself and took a Chinese wife.

As their only child, I grew up first as a Chinese with my play-mates and then as a Westerner when I attended Peking's French elementary school and Catholic mission schools run by the Marist brothers and the Salesian fathers. It was, my jailers pointed out later, a rotten and reactionary bourgeois education.

English, the tongue I now prefer, came to me by a funny boy-hood accident. At an age when I already spoke Mandarin Chinese and French, my father sent me away to a Catholic boarding school in Tientsin. On opening day I got into the wrong line and found myself in a section where they were speaking English instead of French. That was all right—I preferred those kids.

When I returned to Peking for vacation, my father met me at the station. *"Comment vas-tu, petit?"* he asked affectionately.

"Oh, fine, Dad, how are you?" I answered. When he had re-covered from the culture shock, he decided to let me stay on where they spoke that strange language.

To the Salesian fathers I was Jean Pasqualini; to the Chinese, Bao Ruo-wang, a name roughly derived from the P sound in Pasqualini and the Chinese appellation for Saint John. Very early I faced the classic dilemma of the *métis*, the half-breed who par-ticipates in both societies but feels truly at home in neither. My closest friends were half Chinese like me and a multinational cocktail on the other side: Irish, Russian, Polish, Czech, Italian, German. Of us all, I was the one who looked the most completely Chinese.

Throughout my adolescence China was swept by great events: some natural, like the floods, droughts and famines; and some man-made, like the Japanese invasion and occupation; World War II; and the civil war between Chiang Kai-shek's Nationalists and Mao Tse-tung's followers, which ended in total victory for the Communists. It was a confused time, often dangerous but unde-niably exciting.

My own life was influenced by personal tragedy: both my par-ents died while I was still a minor. I became a ward of the Church and the French embassy, living in the French hospital, watched over by nuns.

There was no money for the university. On graduation from an industrial school just after V-J Day in 1945 I began looking for work. By instinct I gravitated toward the Western diplomatic and military missions, where my training as a machine-tool technician, my biracial background and my command of four languages could be useful. I was nineteen that September, when I started driving a jeep for the U.S. Fifth Marine Division.

I quickly rose to interpreter and civilian specialist for local affairs with the division's military police. My experience with these easygoing Americans was overwhelming. In my youthful enthusiasm I regarded the Marines' life as ideal—I even asked once if I could enlist. At twenty I was a big wheel in China—a uniformed civilian with the privileges of an officer, earning good money and shopping in the PX.

LIFE would have seemed rosy if it hadn't been for my second job. At that time the French had vested interests in the Peking streetcar company, and they were looking for foremen. I could do that during the day, I thought, since most of my work with the Marines was in the evening. Through my mentors at the French embassy I was introduced to the Chinese director, who immediately made me an inspector, first class, a position that might take an ordinary Chinese twenty years to reach.

My education began the first morning I reported for work at the depot and saw the people who were soon to bring Mao to power, huddling around little coal stoves, coughing, dressed in rags and eating meager bits of corn bread. They were the motormen, ticket takers and maintenance crews. After a few weeks I fell into the habit of bringing them antiseptics, sulfa pills and aspirins I had wheedled from the Marine medical corpsmen. They began calling me *ban mei shih*—the one who does things the American way. I wonder if Americans realize how much goodwill there is toward them in China among the older people.

Late one afternoon in December I was taking a streetcar home. In the chilly, swaying car I was shocked to see the ticket taker dip into his till. Without a second thought I strode over and denounced him. The missions had taught me that stealing was a terrible sin. But I hadn't learned much about compassion. The poor ticket taker was weeping in his corner.

A Chinese inspector—an older man still wearing his uniform—had boarded the car. "If you're going to write a report," he said, "you'll have to do it right. Here." He handed me a printed report form. Then, as if suddenly changing his mind, he motioned for me to follow him off the car. "I want to show you something," he said.

I plodded along with him in the dark, deeper and deeper into Peking's mazelike poorer quarter, where people slipped past us like shadows. Finally my guide thrust open the door of a low wooden shed. A woman, an old man and seven children regarded us in surprise. No one said a word. The inspector closed the door.

"That's that ticket taker's family," he said. "He feeds them all on four dollars a month. Do you still want to write that report?"

"I was off duty," I said. We walked out of the slum together.

I quit the streetcar job after a few months and went to work full time for the Americans. Several years later, after the victory of the Communists, I caught sight of that same inspector on a busy Peking street, in the uniform of the People's Police. Obviously, he had been a Communist all along. To spare him embarrassment, I turned away, but he hurried over and shook my hand.

"Don't worry," he said. "You'll always be in our good graces. We haven't forgotten what you did for us once."

A YEAR after I began working with the Marines I got married. It was a typical Chinese union. The story started in 1937, when the Japanese invaders were openly looking for pretexts to take control of China. My father had become friendly with a large and powerful mandarin family who owned a sprawling, 270-room palace in the northern part of Peking.

In July of 1937, after the Marco Polo Bridge incident,* some

---

* Japanese garrison troops maneuvering near Peking deliberately provoked a battle with the Chinese army to use as an excuse for full-scale war.

of the affluent in Peking paid huge sums for the privilege of holing up in foreign legations. Others found reasons to place their residences under foreign protection. Old man Yang, the patriarch of the clan with the huge palace, made my father a lush proposition: if he would live on Yang's grounds, he would be given elegant quarters rent free, plus two hundred Chinese dollars a month. His French citizenship would entitle Yang to fly the French flag on the roof. Never one to turn down a good offer, my father took us to live with the mandarin.

What a fantastic person old Yang was! His life was like a melodramatic Chinese film—adventure, intrigue, elegance, violence, sex, even murder. A Manchu by birth, he had been a close confidant of the last emperor and held the high ceremonial position of master of the clocks. Every day, wearing the proper gown and followed by a retinue, he would go from clock to clock in the imperial palace, winding each with a gold key that hung from a chain at his waist. It was with the treasure acquired from his years of royal service that Yang built himself one of Peking's most splendid private residences.

I have a clear childhood memory of playing by a little pond in one of his courtyards with his granddaughter, Yang Hui-min. After my parents died, old Yang called me to him. Would I marry his granddaughter? There would be a dowry and a nice house. My part of the bargain would be to help the family through my connections with the Americans. Working for them, the Chinese said, was like having a tiger skin—no one dared touch you.

I accepted—more because of the advantages and because of my respect for the old man than out of love for the granddaughter. Unions in China are much less emotional and the rapport between spouses much more distant than in the West. My wife and I got on correctly, no more.

After our marriage we moved into a little three-room Chinese house, by tradition facing auspiciously south, with gray brick walls and a pointed roof. My first son, Mow, was born in 1947, and a daughter, Mi, two years later. She died of typhoid when she was only three. Our second son, Yung, was born in 1953.

WHEN THE FIFTH MARINES withdrew from Peking, I moved over to the U.S. Army, first as a technician with the Signal Corps and later as civilian liaison with the Criminal Investigation Division (CID). That job counted heavily against me later. The Chinese Communists tend to view all foreign diplomats and journalists as spies; my job with the CID convinced them that I was a full-time agent of imperialist aggression. In reality, my duties were far more mundane: keeping track of the Chinese whom the army hired and fired. I stayed on with the U.S. military in Peking until their hasty departure in November 1948, less than a month before the city was invested by the Communists.

The siege of Peking was carried out in a manner that probably only the Chinese could have accomplished. The Communists wanted no bloodshed or destruction in what was to be, after all, their own capital. They waited patiently in the surrounding countryside, allowing food and other normal civilian supplies to pass through their lines into Peking. They held the powerhouse twenty-five miles out, but continued supplying electricity—now and then cutting off power for an hour or two to remind the people of who really ran things.

We inside the city lived, worked and ate normally; the only signs of conflict we saw were distant reflections. The Nationalist Army was evident everywhere, but it was surrounded and desperate. It was only a matter of time before the city fell like a ripe fruit.

Liberation Day, as it came to be called, was January 30, 1949. The top Nationalist brass had fled, and the Communist vanguard moved methodically through the city that morning in their padded winter uniforms. In the afternoon the full besieging army marched in through the Yung-ting Men and Hsi-chih Men (two of Peking's famous gates), the armored units driving old Japanese tanks and towing American howitzers captured in battle. The soldiers carried portraits of Mao and Chu Teh, head of Mao's armed forces. The citizens lined the streets waving homemade red flags in the cold wind and crying, "Welcome to the People's Liberation Army!"

On October 1, 1949, the People's Republic of China was officially proclaimed, and gained immediate recognition from the Soviet Union. At the time it seemed the dawn of a bright new era for Communism. The most populous country in the world had joined with the biggest to bring a new way of life to mankind. Waves of technical and military advisers arrived from Moscow. People were encouraged to refer to Russia as Elder Brother.

Strangely enough, though, the Soviets botched the job as the years went by. They fancied themselves as the leading force against imperialism and began treating China with an arrogance that bordered on scorn. In spite of all the new revolutionary teachings, the Chinese remain a profoundly prestige-conscious people, and the Russian advisers became objects of disdain. "Poor bald eggs," the Pekingese used to call them—a Chinese image signifying the third-rate style the boorish Russians uniformly projected. They always arrived at night, it was said, and were whisked by bus to their hotel, so that the Chinese populace would not catch sight of their poor clothes.

The Russians had lost face. What a contrast to the American "tiger skin"! One of the most popular moves Mao ever made—and a good part of the reason the Chinese follow him as lovingly as they do—was kicking the Soviets out of the country. This coincided with the Great Leap Forward that took place in the years 1958–59.

There was some rapid housecleaning when the Communists took over the new China. The first victims were the obvious criminal elements and exploiters of the people. Yang, my grandfather-in-law, was arrested as a degenerate, money-hoarding rascal and died in a Peking prison camp. The city's numerous prostitutes were rounded up and witnessed the execution of their pimps and madams by firing squad. In 1951 came the first campaign for the suppression of counterrevolutionaries. The proceedings of the People's Courts were broadcast in public places, where the crowds shouted for death. In one day 199 were shot.

Some of my foreign and *métis* friends were arrested for their foreign ties. As for me, I had been out of work for two years. A short stint as interpreter and legman for an Associated Press correspondent had ended six months after the fall of Peking. I passed the time making myself inconspicuous and reading in the public library.

When the pitch of Communist retribution rose to near hysteria, I applied for an exit visa. Every time I queried the foreign ministry about it, I was curtly informed that my application was "still pending." It continued to pend right through to 1955, when the second campaign for the suppression of counterrevolutionaries began, and more of my friends were taken away.

I had finally found work in 1953, as an assistant to an officer in a Western embassy. The work I did was routine. I would report to my boss on the latest rationing measures or pass an afternoon in a teahouse listening to the workers gossip, to help him assess his country's relations with the young republic. That my work was regarded as espionage by the "new order" I learned in November 1954, during the census of foreigners.

Because we were about to be issued resident permits, we were summoned to the headquarters of the Peking Bureau of Public Security. First we filled out detailed forms on our personal resources and everything we had ever done in China. Personal interviews followed. I was led to a comfortable sitting room where three men in gray uniforms met me.

"How are things going with you?" the oldest asked pleasantly. "How's your work? How's the family? We apologize for those shortages that still continue, but that situation will improve. However, if you need anything special, don't hesitate to ask us."

"Thank you," I said warily, "but everything's fine."

"You're doing all right then?" he continued.

"Oh, yes."

"Well, if I were you, I'd keep it that way." Now there was the hint of an edge in his voice. "You see, Bao, we know all about you. And you should know that we don't tolerate people doing things against us. We're not threatening you. We're simply stating a fact. The eyes of the masses are as bright as snow. They report to us everything that is suspicious. If you act in a law-abiding way, you will be allowed to stay on in China with your family. If not, you will stay on in China away from your family. We are generous, Bao Ruo-wang, so be generous with us."

"Thank you for your kind advice," I answered, "but I'd like to assure you that I'm not doing anything against you—"

He didn't let me finish. His face revealed exasperated impatience. "Look, don't make statements like that. Don't make yourself guilty of another sin. We've warned you. That's all."

Now that I look back I can see the events that led to my arrest unreeling like a film. It all began there at the Peking Bureau of Public Security.

For the international Communist movement, 1956 was like a string of firecrackers going off. In February, Khrushchev made his famous anti-Stalin speech. The Chinese leadership reacted cautiously, with an article published in newspapers and magazines throughout the country: "On the Historical Experience of the Dictatorship of the Proletariat." The authors, presumably Mao and Teng Hsiao-ping, the vice-premier, admitted that Stalin had committed some serious mistakes, but reiterated the good he had done the socialist cause. The Hungarian revolution against Soviet domination in October only proved to the Chinese that the de-Stalinization campaign had been ill-conceived. At the end of the year Mao published another article maintaining that the uprising could have been prevented and cautioning the Communist world to take a lesson from it. It was Mao's bid for ideological leadership.

But his forwardness made problems at home. Students and intellectuals started asking questions, and the Party hierarchy felt the first stings of criticism.

Let us go to the masses, Mao decided. If the criticism is constructive, we can learn from it. "Let a hundred flowers bloom," he said. "Let a hundred thoughts contend." The campaign got under way in March 1957. The criticism—expressed in public debate, articles, posters and even song—was overwhelming. Ordinary citizens found the courage to demand lower prices and an end to rationing. Scholars and teachers heaped odium on the party hacks who controlled education. Students demanded that Communists resign from their unions. Many even called for the outright dismantling of the government structure.

There is still debate as to whether the Hundred Flowers campaign was an error on Mao's part or a coldly calculated ruse to entrap the regime's enemies. In any case, Mao reacted swiftly. By June criticisms were no longer regarded as welcome commentary but as rightist provocations. The Hundred Flowers was replaced by the struggle against the rightist bourgeois elements. This campaign did not end until December 1957, the month of my arrest.

Chapter 2

IT HAPPENED on a Friday night two days after Christmas. Six weeks earlier the police had ordered me to remain close to my house until further notice, and I had been waiting for the other shoe to drop. It came down with only a polite knocking at the door. I was reading in bed and my wife was asleep. I jammed on my old slippers and shuffled to the door.

"Yes, who is it?"

"Lao Chia, from the police precinct." *Lao*, when used with a person's family name, is a friendly greeting, comparable to the British "old chap" or the American "ol' buddy." And so, for an instant, I felt a surge of optimism.

As I swung the door open, however, I was propelled backward by five grim visitors—Chia himself, a dour woman from the street security committee, and three large armed cops in padded blue winter uniforms. Their theatrical entrance woke my wife, who asked what was the matter. All I could mumble was, "Nothing." It was the understatement of my life.

The tallest policeman planted himself ceremoniously in front of me and another stood by my side. The third sat gingerly on the bed. Chia and the security woman barred the door.

"What is your name?" asked Chia.

"Pasqualini."

"What is your *Chinese* name?"

"Bao Ruo-wang."

"Your nationality?"

"French."

He opened his briefcase and extracted a printed card with my photograph stapled to one corner. "Bao Ruo-wang, known also as Pasqualini, you have been discovered to have been engaged for a long time in counterrevolutionary activities and to have violated the laws of the People's Republic of China. This is the warrant for your arrest."

At the word arrest, the cop at my side seized my wrists and the one on the bed bounded forward and snapped a pair of steel cuffs over them. The tall one standing in front of me thrust the warrant at me to sign, which I did, awkwardly. They frisked me, checked my papers and hustled me out.

My terrified wife cried, "Go, and learn your lessons well!" She had certainly learned *her* first lesson in a hurry. But what else could she say? In China one is expected to react correctly to every situation. What counts is not what a thing is, but what you call it. Prison is not prison but a school for learning about one's mistakes. Had she failed to show the proper spirit, my wife could have been imprisoned herself—for having knowingly lived with a counterrevolutionary. Our two children were still sleeping as the door closed.

I was jammed in the back seat of a black Russian Pobeda between two Sepos—security police. There was no traffic, and we sped past the Drum Tower and into a small, twisting road that led to the famous Tsao Lan Tse Hutung—Grass Mist Lane. Through a side door of the prison we swept into a reception office, where I was left with a surly young guard who gave me my first lesson in humility.

"Squat!" he ordered. "Head down!"

He shoved my head roughly down to my chest. After five minutes of silence he whistled and gestured for me to stand. He searched me meticulously, taking my papers, my ball-point pen and my identity card. He put them all in a little heap, then drew up a list, which I signed. Another guard trotted me across the compound to a prison block, where a fat little warder was waiting for us at a desk. We padded down a corridor lined with wooden doors. The warder stopped at one and pulled back the latch.

The cell was about eight feet deep by twenty feet wide, and was lit by a single, dim bulb. I could make out a long row of men sleeping on pallets, under thin cotton quilts, on a communal shelf bed along the back. Set in the whitewashed brick walls were two small barred windows with frosted panes; on the ledges underneath were two neat stacks of books, pamphlets and newspapers. A pair of tar-lined iron buckets sat in the far corner. The warder shook a prisoner awake and told him to make room for me; somehow, pushing around him, he managed to clear a space not more than a foot and a half wide. The warder went out.

The prisoner who had been awakened put a finger to his lips and motioned me to lie down. I took off my shoes and clambered up onto the shelf. The warder appeared again with a quilt. He tossed it over me and left.

I lay staring at the ceiling, too confused and depressed to sleep. My wife might be able to find a job; what worried me most was the children, who would have to face their schoolmates with the stigma of a counterrevolutionary father. I huddled miserably under the quilt as the north wind swept past the windows. The only heat came from a stovepipe across the ceiling. Finally I crept over to the tar buckets to urinate. Just as I started, a chorus of angry shushings arose. Apparently I was breaking the rules. I shuffled guiltily back and drew the quilt around me.

I must have dozed off, because it seemed only a minute later that a whistle blew furiously out in the corridor and everyone leaped to his feet. Astonished, I witnessed the incredible precision of reveille in a Chinese prison. Two men folded the pallets and quilts into neat triangular stacks. Another dragged a glazed terra-cotta jug from under the bed and ladled cold water into six enamel washbasins. While six prisoners washed their faces at the basins, four more brushed their teeth over the slop bucket in the far corner. At precisely the right moment four of them changed places with four of the face-washers and received a fresh scoop of water. The silence was total, except for the spittings and splashings. Not knowing what part I was to take, I simply watched.

After everyone had finished, the basins were emptied into the buckets, which were carried to the door. My seventeen cellmates fell into line behind the buckets. Automatically, I joined them. We marched silently out onto a pathway along the prison's high wall. At the end was the latrine—two cement trenches, very clean. From a watchtower a Sepo stared down at us.

Back in the cell, we sat cross-legged on the bed and began the meditation period, in which we were to ponder our sins, exactly like a flock of Buddhist monks.

"What's your name?"

It was the man whom the guard had awakened the night before to make room for me. When he asked me if I knew why I had been arrested, I answered cautiously, "I'm not sure."

He regarded me with immense calm. "You are a counterrevolutionary, like all of us. Do you know where you are?"

Curious to see how much he could tell me, I pretended complete ignorance. There followed a perfect example of the admonitory discourse, in which prisoners reform prisoners.

"This is the interrogation center of the Peking Bureau of Public Security. Some of us are here because of things we did before the liberation. These individuals are called persons with a counterrevolutionary past. Those who have been arrested for things they did since the liberation are called active counterrevolutionaries. But all of us have committed our crimes because we had bad thoughts."

He gave a sweeping glance around the cell. "We must reform these thoughts and become new men again. This morning you will be interrogated. When they come for you, you must walk briskly, with your head bowed. The guard will give you directions and tell you when to turn. At the interrogation confess your crimes frankly and sincerely. Your salvation lies in the attitude you adopt. Your interrogation room will always be the same, so remember the number. You will have to send all your written reports and confessions to that number."

I felt familiar emotions welling up in me, confusion, anxiety, but also a certain excitement—the same feelings as when I first went away to mission school. Already I was slipping into the role of the pupil eager to reassure the teachers of his good behavior.

"Soon we'll be having our morning meal. There are two meals a day, one at eight o'clock and the other at four. Each of us gets one *wo'tou* [a rough corn bread], a piece of salted vegetable and a bowl of corn gruel. My name is Loo Teh-ling, and I am monitor of this cell. Here we call each other either by our full names or *tung-hao* [cellmate]."

Carefully, he unfolded a slip of paper and handed it to me. I looked ignorantly at the ideograms as he spoke them, since at the time I could speak but not read Chinese. "This is the policy of the government: leniency to those who confess, severity to those who resist; expiation of crimes through gaining merits; reward to those who have gained great merits."

Loo folded the paper and put it inside his shirt. He was serious, relaxed, pleased to have done his duty well. Was that a product of brainwashing? As a Chinese I recognized the desire to display good faith. It is a national characteristic. But this man, and the others, too, apparently felt a need to display a permanent zeal. And this, of course, is the gist of brainwashing: submission of your will to that of another. Once submission has been obtained, it is not difficult to increase it from begrudging to fanatic.

Two prisoners picked up big earthen basins and waited for the warder to open the door. Someone passed out bowls and chopsticks; a few men had little individual bags of salt. When the breakfast detail returned I saw that the *wo'tou* was not half as big as those I had eaten at home. Each of us received only one half-inch slice of boiled turnip. And the corn gruel was watery. My God, I thought, if that's how it's going to be . . . It was.

After the meal Loo took me aside. "Some of the cellmates have

a criticism to make against you. Last night you awakened everyone when you got up to urinate. You must learn to do things
silently at night." I nodded. Loo turned to the others. "The newcomer didn't know the way we do things. He has accepted your
criticisms with humility. I suggest that we excuse him."

I was beginning to like this odd man. Beneath his portentous
manner he was human and generous.

At 9:00 a.m. a whistle blew and everyone assembled on the
bed once again in Buddha position. It was study time. Loo was
reading aloud from the *People's Daily* when the latch clunked
back. The tall cop who had arrested me was there.

"Bao Ruo-wang!" he called. I dashed outside.

The big cop handed me over to a Sepo in a yellow-green
padded uniform who slowly drew a monstrous Browning .45
automatic from his holster. He told me to get moving. "Keep
your head down!" he screamed. "Left! Get a move on! Right!"
Terrified, I trotted along, blindly doing as he said. We moved
out through a courtyard and passed a long row of doors. I could
hear shouts and threats from other interrogations. Left, right,
left, right. Finally my man brought me to a dark green door with
a wooden plaque reading 41.

"Report your arrival!" I made a modest try. "Louder!" This
time I shouted, but my voice was strangely squeaky.

A quiet voice invited me to come in. I found myself in a large
room with tile floor and fluorescent lights. On one of the whitewashed walls was a gigantic color poster of Mao. A desk faced me
below a large red star. Behind it sat a young man in the dark-blue
flannel uniform of a Party functionary. He, it turned out, was my
interrogator.

The interrogator made a gesture toward a low stool in the
center of the room. "Your name? . . . Address before arrest?" As
he questioned me he showed no signs of animation until he
reached the point where he could begin making speeches. Interrogators are born speechmakers.

"Now, then. In front of you are two paths: the one of confessing everything and obeying the government, which will lead you

to a new life; the other of resisting the orders of the government and stubbornly remaining the people's enemy. This path will lead to the worst possible consequences. The better your confession, the quicker you will rejoin your wife and children.

"You need not worry about your family. You are the guilty one, not they. If they are in difficulties, the government is there to help them. So set your heart at ease and confess your crimes thoroughly. Do you understand me?"

I nodded, relieved by what he said about the government taking care of my family.

"There are two types of confessions. We call them Toothpaste and Water Tap. The Toothpaste prisoner needs to be squeezed every now and then, or else he forgets to keep confessing. The Water Tap man needs one good, hard twist before he starts, but then everything comes out. You are an intelligent person. I don't think we need resort to persuasion. Do you understand me?"

I nodded again and waited for him to go on.

"Good. Now, do you know why you were brought here?"

I made my first mistake. "When I was arrested they told me that I was a counterrevolutionary."

My interrogator leaned forward angrily. "*Told* you that you are a counterrevolutionary? You *are* a counterrevolutionary! You will have to be frank or things will go badly for you."

It must have been his arrogance that raised what was left of my hackles. For the last time in China, I acted like a wise guy. "How can I be a counterrevolutionary if I am not Chinese?"

He stared at me, dumbfounded, then exploded in rage. "How dare you ask questions? Your activities have caused great losses to the government. You are a counterrevolutionary through and through. We have plenty of proof. Now, start again."

"Where shall I begin?"

"Before the liberation, when you started working for the American imperialists."

I began the long list—the Marines, the Signal Corps, the Associated Press—but the interrogator broke in. "We know where you have been working. What we want is a confession of your crimes. You are a loyal running dog of the Americans. Tell us all the dirty work you did for them. We have complete records, and we have formal accusations from people you victimized. Tell us about your duties for the Marine military police."

It was easy to see I was in trouble. The Communists had always regarded the military police as an organization of repression against the Chinese people. I had been along on raids, confiscations, all sorts of vice-squad dealings. There were black marketeers, nightclub operators and pimps, who could have poured out tales of suffering under the Americans. I talked about the Marines until past noon, when a guard returned me to the cell.

"How did it go?" Loo asked me.

"Well, I don't know. They told me I'd be called again."

"Of course you'll be called again. Perhaps dozens of times. The sooner we end the interrogations by being open and frank, the sooner we will leave here."

I was really liking Loo a lot by now, but it mystified me why he talked like a Communist functionary. That was cleared up for me in time. At the end of my interrogation, a full fifteen months, I, too, was speaking like Loo.

Mao's police have perfected their methods to such a point that I would defy any man to hold out against them. Their aim is not so much to make you invent nonexistent crimes as to make you accept your actual life as rotten and worthy of punishment. I know of a man who was imprisoned by mistake—right name but wrong man. Finally, in despair, he confessed all the crimes of the other. When the mistake was discovered, the prison authorities had a terrible time persuading him to go home. He felt too guilty.

At 8:00 p.m. that same day I was called for a second interrogation. It was pitch-dark when they led me away through the maze of corridors. This time I had four armed guards. I found myself descending a flight of dimly lit steps, boots creaking behind me. One of the guards unlocked an iron gate. I could make out more steps twisting steeply downward. The walls were closer, barely leaving a passageway the width of my shoulders. With each step the air seemed to grow damper and warmer. My mouth was dry. I felt as if I were walking into a plague. At the end of the passage was a wooden door sheathed in iron.

"Baogao!" someone ordered behind me. "Report!"

I shouted out my name and the door flew open. Two men locked my arms behind me and jerked me inside. I found myself in a torture chamber.

I don't think a person really screams when he is terrified. The first instinct is to freeze up. It's not possible, I thought.

There was a "tiger bench" before me. It is a simple device, a sort of articulated board. The subject is tied firmly to it in several places, and then the bench is raised in different and interesting ways. It is the hip bones that crack first, I have been told.

Next to the bench were water and towels, indispensable for that great classic, the water torture. The towel goes over the prisoner's face, the water is poured gently on it and the man drowns. It is a handy little torture, because it is light and portable.

I also saw bamboo splinters and hammers, even a set of chains heating over a coal fire. I think I would have sunk to the floor if the guards hadn't supported me.

The interrogator stepped before me with his scribe. "This is a museum," he said. "Don't be afraid. We wanted you to see how the criminal Chiang Kai-shek reactionaries questioned their prisoners. Now we are living under the humane regime of Chairman Mao. We do not use such crude and inhumane methods. Our methods are a hundred times more efficient." He looked at me for a long moment, then ordered the guard, "Take him away."

Long live Chairman Mao, I thought as I shuffled out.

The next time I saw the interrogator I asked him, "What do you want me to confess?"

He looked pained. "We don't tell people what to confess. We already know everything about you, Bao. If what you tell us tallies with that, then I can give you my word that you will be leniently treated. But if you tell us only five or ten percent, then you'll never go home."

"Where do I begin?"

"It's up to you, Bao. We know we will get it all eventually. We have lots of time."

I began the story of my life, from age eight. The interrogator hardly interrupted again. The scribe took it down in Chinese characters with admirable speed. That session lasted six hours.

As the sessions continued, the gaps between them gradually grew longer. I had plenty of time to think, to observe my new home and to slip into its routine.

THERE had once been a Buddhist monastery on Grass Mist Lane; it had been razed by the Nationalists to make way for the prison. The great square area was divided into the south, east, west and new compounds, each with its own courtyard. The whole thing was surrounded by a wall about twenty feet high, topped by electrified barbed wire. Each compound was divided into blocks, each block into cells, offices, storerooms and so on.

I was amazed by the organization of life in Grass Mist Lane.

Every man had a daily housekeeping job. Confessions and inter-rogations occupied five days of the week. Sunday was free for political study. Tuesday was cleanup day; two cellmates would scrub the concrete floor, while the rest washed windows, curtains and walls, mended clothing, or took the cotton quilts to the courtyard to be aired.

Tuesday was also the day for shaving and nail trimming, both jobs being performed with the same little pair of nail clippers. (Toenail parings were collected for sale to the outside, as one of the exotic ingredients in traditional Chinese medicine.) It took me an hour to take off my beard, whisker by whisker, but it was as close a shave as if I had done it with anything as dangerous and forbidden as a razor. About once a month the barber, a freed worker, made his rounds.

There was an accepted form for requesting whatever we needed. When the warder passed, Loo might chant, "Cell number fourteen reporting. We would be grateful to have four clippers, two big needles, six small needles for quilts, twenty white threads and forty black ones."

The requested gear would be shoved through the spy slot in the door. Everything had to be returned by nightfall. If a needle had been broken, both pieces had to be returned: prisoners had been known to commit suicide by swallowing needles.

For the rare free time, each cell had a deck of cards, a box of checkers, two penholders and a bottle of ink. Paper and pen points had to be requested.

Every second Tuesday was bath day. The bathing area was a rough, walk-in swimming pool in the next building, and it serviced about a thousand men each time it was filled. If our cell happened to be called early, it could be a healthy and even pleasant experience. But if we went toward the end, it was revolting to wade through the greasy water up to our chests.

For half an hour every day we were herded outside for exercise, and we ran in tight little circles in the narrow space between the buildings and the wall, beyond which we could often hear squeals and laughter from an adjoining children's school. We lined up and ran in the same order in which we were arranged on the bed while sleeping, so that the guards could identify any prisoner by looking down at the cell charts they carried.

And then there was the food—the watery corn gruel, the hard little loaves of *wo'tou* and the slivers of vegetable. Six months after my arrest I had grown so thin that my stomach was entirely caved in, and I had the characteristic bruised joints from simple body contact with the hard communal bed. The skin hung loose on my backside. My vision became unclear and I lost my power of concentration. My hair began falling out.

Thoughts of food obsessed us so completely that we were insane, in a way. We were ready to admit anything. It was the perfect climate for interrogations.

Chapter 3

As the weeks slipped past I gradually grew accustomed to the environment and cell 14 became my world. The rules governing my new existence were posted on the wall:

1. The instructions of the government must be obeyed in all things.
2. All conversations must be conducted in a normal voice and within the hearing of at least two or three other persons. Conversations in a foreign or secret language are strictly forbidden.
3. The exchange or lending of objects between prisoners is strictly forbidden except upon the approval of the warder.
4. Prisoners are not permitted to seek sympathy among themselves, nor are they allowed to shelter criminal activities. Mutual surveillance must be practiced at all times, and reliance upon the government should be cultivated.
5. Prisoners may make requests of the government either in writing or orally; in the latter case the prisoner must stand over three yards away from the warder he is addressing.
6. Good behavior during the period of interrogation will be taken into account when one's case is dealt with.

Loo and the others introduced me to the weekly examination of conscience, in which we all promised to be good-natured with fellow prisoners, cooperative with the interrogators and reliant on the government. At this time work assignments were discussed and volunteered for. My job in the cell was floor sweeper.

I was startled to see that the prisoner who had been cleaning the urine buckets—the most repulsive job—volunteered enthusiastically to continue. I learned that he was only trying to give evidence that he was on the road to self-reform.

Shang was his name. He had been a Communist cadre,* but had made the common mistake of talking too much during the Hundred Flowers period. The former Communists I met in the prisons were a special breed. Disciplined by their years with the Party, they were model prisoners, always ready to explain the latest convolutions of the official line. But they were good friends to fellow prisoners. Never did I know a former Communist to turn informer or denounce a cellmate.

Shang was always trying harder. One day he devised cardboard covers for the slop buckets. Loo was pleased, and gave him a written citation for his concern for the communal welfare.

Loo was vigilant in ensuring our ideological soundness. When talk lagged he told us stories with guiding moral principles. Everything else that might make the mind wander—home, food, sports, hobbies or, of course, sex—was absolutely prohibited.

Another personality was the prison doctor, a tall, white-haired, scholarly type who had been around Grass Mist Lane for years. Even though he was a civilian he wore a blue uniform and cap and everyone called him Officer Wang. He had a good heart, but when a prisoner came to him with a physical complaint he almost always responded with a speech. "Study," he told us. "Study what the government tells you or you will never learn."

---

* A person who holds any position in the Chinese Communist bureaucracy, but especially one who has been fully indoctrinated in Party ideology and methods and is employed in ways that make use of this training. [Editor's note.]

EVERY CELL HAD ITS DAILY study session, and every man had to participate. At an ordinary session an extract from the Peking *People's Daily* might be read by the cell leader and commented on by the cellmates. One of the prisoners, appointed cell clerk, would note each man's words, then make up the résumés that would be placed in the individual dossiers. Unusual or criminal remarks were quoted in full, and later the prisoner paid: he would get a stretch in solitary or have years added to his sentence. He quickly learned to talk in noncommittal slogans. The danger was that he might end by thinking in slogans, and most did.

Whenever an important event occurred in the world outside, the ordinary study sessions were replaced by prison-wide meetings to present the government's interpretation. The first such special study session I experienced concerned Mao's pamphlet *On the Correct Handling of Contradictions Among the People*. This session was absolutely typical of the postrevolutionary Chinese mentality.

It began in the afternoon, when the interrogations were finished and we were seated cross-legged on the big bed around Loo.

"Now listen carefully," he warned, "because afterward everyone will have to speak."

Mao's pamphlet, like the later famous little red book, *Quotations from Chairman Mao Tse-tung*, is divided into small, readily digestible portions. Loo read a passage slowly, then looked around. "Is everything clear? Good. Now let's meditate for a few minutes." After a long silence he cleared his throat. "Before we start our discussion I will explain a few things for those who are on a lower cultural level." (Some prisoners were barely educated peasants.)

"What we are reading today," he went on, "is a famous report made by Mao during the Hundred Flowers. It is now being used to settle all the differences and misunderstandings among the people. It is the basis of the struggle against the bourgeois and rightist elements.

"There are two kinds of contradictions: those among the people, and those between the people and the enemy. The second kind is more dangerous—disagreement over policy, counterrevolutionary activities, willful acts against the state. As far as we prisoners are concerned, we have been given a chance to redeem ourselves and realize the errors of our ways."

Loo's calm rhetoric was tremendously persuasive for a cell full of dejected men who knew their fates were utterly dependent on a bureaucracy's judgment. Every day the prisoner was taught to believe that it was not judicial process that would mitigate his sentence but rather *the way he behaved.* Our relationship with the state was that of child to parent.

"All right, now," he continued, "let's get started with the discussion." He motioned to a thickset, fiftyish peasant named Wu, who was serving time for agricultural counterrevolutionary activities. Wu had owned land, but he farmed it entirely with his own family, exploited no workers, bothered no one and, so far as he knew, committed no crimes. But he had refused to join the cooperative movement.

"I was arrested," Wu said, "because someone accused me of obstructing the cooperative movement. But when the Communists came, they told us that the farmers were free to work for themselves. So what am I supposed to think when they accuse me of not joining?"

Loo asked the rest of us to comment. The litany began.

"Wu is looking down on the workers," someone piped up.

"Wu has bad ideas," barked out another cellmate. "We have to help him realize this so he can make a good confession. We don't want to see him shot or given a life sentence."

The accusations flew. Each prisoner was expected both to help the guilty one and to expiate his own crimes by personal enthusiasm. And, of course, these comments looked good in the dossier.

"Wu doesn't care about the rest. He just wanted to make a fortune for himself."

"Wu doesn't have a place in our society. Certain landlords must be eliminated and he is one of them. Lenin taught us that."

It was probably the half-knowledgeable reference to Lenin that persuaded Shu Li to break into the talk. "Let's not be so drastic there," he said. "Let's look at it from another angle."

Like Shang, Shu had been in the government, and he also came to his downfall during the Hundred Flowers. He was an economist in Shansi Province; his scheme to reward individuals' higher production with bonuses got him into trouble during the rectification campaign. He was arrested and charged with materialist molestation. Now in his mid-forties, thin and ascetic, he spoke with all the authority of a professor who had spent years studying "Party-think."

"The cooperative movement is a mass movement," said Shu. "Millions of pieces of land are being joined together. Instead of thirty- or forty-acre plots, we have hundreds and thousands of acres now. So what happens if right in the middle you have ten acres owned by a private farmer? If the rest decide to plant rice and he wants to plant corn, he disrupts the entire system. They can't plow through his fields, so they have to detour around them. And he is a bad example who may have given the others second thoughts about sharing their crops. But the most important thing is that the cooperative movement was decreed by Chairman Mao himself, so Wu was disobeying the directives of Mao."

Shu was getting hot now, ready to make his point. "Classmate Wu," he asked, "how much food did you have in the days before liberation? What was your yearly yield?"

"About five hundred and fifty pounds a head," Wu answered respectfully.

"And what was it afterward, at the time you were arrested?"

"About seven hundred."

"How is it you produced a hundred and fifty pounds more?"

"Irrigation used to be bad, and we were robbed by the Nationalist soldiers."

Everything was falling into place, as Shu knew it would. "Don't the soldiers come and ask for food now?"

"Of course not." Wu seemed almost indignant. "The people from the provisional army don't do that sort of thing."

"And how is the irrigation now?"

"Improved since the irrigation movement of 1953."

"So instead of being grateful to the Communist Party, you try to throw a monkey wrench into their system. Do you see what a bastard you've been?"

Loo cut in, his voice tinged with anger. "Don't call him a bastard. We can't use that sort of language toward cellmates."

Shu retreated one step. "All right. Rotten egg, then."

"Not even that." Loo shook his head. "You may call him a bad element, or a reactionary, or a stinking landlord." He turned to Wu with all the dignity of a superior-court judge. "Do you see the trouble you have caused?"

Overpowered and a bit frightened, Wu said cautiously, "Yes, I am beginning to see my error. I didn't realize how much damage I was doing by not joining the cooperative movement."

No one else had anything to say. Wu was finally off the hook.

Loo next signaled to a bald, skinny little man with a gray beard. His name was Wei I-sha. (I-sha is the Chinese transliteration of Isaac.) Wei was a Methodist pastor, and used to addressing crowds. "I am a missionary. I joined the Church in my early twenties and I have been with it now for over forty years. I make no secret of the fact that I worked for the Americans."

"Imperialists!" shouted a couple of cellmates.

Wei went on. "There's something I still don't understand. When Peking was liberated by the People's Government, they said they would grant freedom of religion. All right. Then they said that in order to liberate the Church from the influence of the foreigners they had decided on reforms that would keep the Church Chinese. Well, I was all for that. As a matter of fact, I was on the first reform committee.

"I began to worry when they appointed a Communist Party member to supervise the committee's activities. Pretty soon we weren't allowed to teach children religion anymore. Then the committee began warning us to pay less attention to religion and more to our means of livelihood. What they had in mind was a church without preaching. What is the use of a church when you can't preach in it?"

Hostile faces studied him, but no one answered his question.

"So at the next committee meeting I told them that while the Communists said they tolerated the principle of religious freedom all their actions aimed at doing away with it. The committee told me my views were harmful to the government. The next day they arrested me. Here I am."

Wei was labeled a running dog of the foreign powers. Like so many Chinese men of religion, his faith made him difficult to break down. "Up to now, I don't understand my interrogators," he continued. "They say I was a spy. But I never spied."

Wei's simple affirmation may sound mild to the Western reader, but in the Chinese Communist context he was being strongly defiant. "Shut him up!" one of the prisoners cried.

Loo intervened. "This is a special case," he said. "It is up to us to help Wei as best we can. Today I am going to break custom and start asking him questions myself." But instead of interrogating the pastor, Loo rolled into a surprisingly passionate denunciation. "The trouble with you, minister, is that you're no longer Chinese. For forty years you have been carrying out the orders of a foreign religion without even questioning them. You don't even think like a Chinese anymore."

This low blow brought forth indignant cries of agreement. Wei sat silent. "No wonder you haven't confessed yet," Loo continued. "All you are doing is getting deeper and deeper into the mess you've made. One day they're going to take you out and shoot you. But don't think you'll end up a martyr. You're only a traitor. Tell me—do you think like a Communist?"

"No."

"Do you act like one?"

"No."

"Then you shouldn't be surprised to be here." As if he were snapping a book closed, Loo ended the questioning of Wei and moved on to the next man. The session ended at 4:00 p.m.

THE natural complement to the study meeting is the "struggle." It is an intellectual gang-beating of one man by many, sometimes thousands. The victim has no defense, not even the truth.

The first struggle I ever witnessed took place in the cell adjoining ours a few months after I arrived at Grass Mist Lane. The entire cell was working over a newly arrived prisoner, and the din of their shouts was so passionate that our peaceable study session was derailed. The technique, as I heard it, was a fierce and pitiless crescendo of screams demanding that the victim confess. Any answer he gave was greeted by hoots of dissatisfaction.

The din continued for a couple of hours. Then, as the man was being led away to solitary, a guard slammed open the slot in our door. Loo beckoned us over one by one to get a glimpse of the prisoner. He could barely move. His ankles were fettered with a foot-long iron bar joined by chains to his wrists, which were also chained together. In all, I learned, the outfit weighed thirty-two pounds.

The struggle was born in the 1930s, when the Communists began making headway in the great rural stretches of Nationalist China. It became the standard technique for interrogating enemies. There is a very real rationale behind it. The Communists are extremely formalistic: a man must be made to confess before he is punished, even if his punishment has been decided beforehand. In those early days the victim—say, a captured landlord—was shoved to an open area and forced to kneel and bow his head as dozens or hundreds or thousands of peasants surrounded him. Screamed at, insulted, slapped, spat upon, sometimes beaten, the victim could not hold out for long.

Struggles also became prevalent in ordinary civilian life in the 1950s. A man might be trapped by one of the denunciation boxes which proliferated in every city. They were painted bright red, slotted at the top like mailboxes, and padlocked. On a shelf underneath were forms on which the denunciator supplied information about the person he was denouncing. The police collected the forms from the boxes daily.

If a denunciation led to a struggle, the process could go on indefinitely. At the end of the first day the victim was locked up, with the promise that the next day would be worse. After three or four days the victim might begin inventing sins, hoping that a monstrous enough admission might win him a reprieve.

The struggle is one of the most effective weapons for weaseling into a man's mind to control his thoughts. I was given a vivid reminder of this years later, when our cell was assigned to struggle a prisoner who had stolen two pieces of bread. We worked him over for three evenings. Finally I went to the warder.

"Look, warder," I said, "we've been at him for a total of ten hours now. He *admits* he stole the bread. Do we have to make him say he is a dirty bourgeois because he was hungry?"

The warder reached over to a bottle into which he had stuck some flowers. Pulling out the flowers, he emptied the bottle of its mucky water and handed it to me. "Fill it from the teapot," he said. "Don't rinse it out."

As I replaced the bottle, it was murky once more because of the thick sediment that had swirled up from the bottom.

"The water won't be clear as long as there are dirty things in the bottle, will it, Bao? And your cellmate has dirty things in his head that he doesn't even know about. As long as they remain, none of our friendly criticisms will be able to sink in."

So we went on struggling our cellmate until he realized the ideological implications of two pieces of bread.

Loo, our impeccable spiritual leader, began his trip to Grass Mist Lane after being struggled. A government functionary and Party member in good standing, he had the bad judgment to open his mouth during the Hundred Flowers. After several months his words returned to haunt him. Locked in his office at night, struggled during the day, he gradually made a full confession to his fellow office workers, even admitting that he had once served in the Nationalist Army. He was allowed to return to work, but three weeks later his local Party secretary gave him some heavy news: "You must undertake some serious study. The Party is concerned about your political welfare." Three days later he was arrested.

Loo was the model prisoner—humble, energetic in carrying out orders and positive in his thoughts. He believed that his behavior would earn him a lighter sentence. He was wrong.

I SPENT THE ENTIRE year of 1958 in Grass Mist Lane. It was the year of the Great Leap Forward, a memorable period for China. An enormously unrealistic enthusiasm gripped the country during those months. Production was supposed to rise dramatically. Newspapers publicized new techniques for fantastically increasing the yield of the rice crop, with pictures of stalks growing so closely together that a man could stand on them. (The same papers neglected to report later that the miraculous rice suffocated before it was ready to be harvested.)

Every little village had a jerry-built furnace with which the people hoped to make steel. Personally, my finest symbol of the campaign was when my wife wrote to tell me she had donated our iron bed to the steel drive.

Coexisting with the Great Leap Forward was the People's Commune Movement. These two campaigns were mutually defeating, but no one could realize that until it was all over and the poor Chinese had to start from scratch again.

The Chinese peasants cheerfully supported the commune idea. They built community mess halls and ate their fill of free meals. Home kitchens went out of style; many peasants broke their clay vessels and donated their metal pots and pans to the little furnaces, which roared and glowed and produced trickles of what they all took to be steel. Marveling at their own ingenuity, the peasants concluded joyfully that engineers were mere parasites. But as time went by, the production of both foodstuffs and the useless steel began to fall.

The Great Leap, meanwhile, had created an insatiable demand for construction projects. The peasants, especially the young ones, flocked to the cities, where they found instant employment at prime rates, and the farms began suffering from lack of hands. This became a governmental problem; the nation's crops were in jeopardy. Party secretaries pleaded fruitlessly for peasants to return home. Finally the government confiscated the ration cards of the families whose young men refused to return home. The threat was clear and simple: either get your sons back to the land or you won't eat.

Slowly, the young peasants returned and took up their work again, but only halfheartedly. Their sulky lassitude paved the way for the disastrous agricultural years of 1960, 1961 and 1962.

DURING the Great Leap, we in Grass Mist Lane were treated to double doses of study sessions. The only way we could demonstrate our revolutionary ardor was to confess well. We chattered away our platitudes like parrots.

After my fifth interrogation I was allowed to write my confession—in English, since I was a foreigner. Three days a week I was led, head down, to a tiny room where there was a typewriter and paper. The guard who watched me spent the time working on a fabulously detailed map of Hong Kong. Every traffic light and police box was marked. God knows who had ordered it.

The two of us worked in silence as a kettle simmered on the stove. I was permitted to drink as much hot water as I wanted—an indulgence, but one I had to be careful with. Water drinking is the prisoner's standard answer to the perpetual pangs of hunger. I later heard of starving prisoners who died from edema. Disciplining myself away from excessive water consumption was as tough for me as when I finally quit smoking.

It took me over two months and seven hundred typewritten pages to tell the story of my life. One night in March I was summoned before a panel of three interrogators. "How are you doing, Bao?" one asked. "You've been here quite a while, haven't you? I've been reading your confession. So far there's not much to it. There are lots of names you don't mention. Do you remember Linda Lee?"

Linda was a Chinese friend who taught painting and who, I knew, had had affairs with diplomats. "You might be happy to know that she's not far, Bao. In fact you are in the same compound. I thought that might help you with your confession."

It did, indeed. Linda knew all about my connections with the Western embassies, and obviously had told them everything.

Still, I made my modest little efforts at dissimulation. I was certain that no one but the Americans knew about my work with the CID, so I omitted mention of it. I finished my confession and awaited word from the interrogators.

It came on the night of June 4. The interrogation room was dark except for a weak lamp illuminating my questioner's face. The arrangement was deliberately theatrical. The interrogator flipped indolently through my seven hundred pages and asked if I had anything to add. For an hour he questioned me; still I told him there was nothing more.

Then a voice rang out. "Turn around, Pasqualini."

The interrogator switched on the overhead light. Before me was my friend Robert Chen, a CID colleague, now in the uniform of the political police. So he had been their agent all along.

I broke down and told them absolutely everything. In the end they indeed got their "full and frank admission of sins."

In mid-September the warder called me in; it was time for me to write my self-accusation. In this document the prisoner builds the case against himself as skillfully as he can, for an unsatisfactory statement will be bounced back and he will continue to wait in the interrogation center. When he is done, the government holds a document with which, depending on interpretation, it can sentence him to any number of years it desires. The self-accusation is a prosecutor's dream.

It took me four hours to write my sixteen-page statement. The next day I was called in by the scribe who had been present during all my questionings. "Have you anything more to add?"

"I might have forgotten some minor details," I admitted, "but everything important is there."

"Good. Stand up." He assumed the proper manner for such situations. "We hereby announce that your period of interrogation is over. Have you anything to say?"

I certainly did. I was ready with the standard phrase which every prisoner learns for this very moment. "I hope I will be leniently dealt with by the People's Government."

Now the scribe had *his* ritualistic words. "You will be leniently treated if you behave well, but if you do not behave well, no amount of requests will earn you an ounce of leniency." Then he surprised me. "Tell me, Bao," he asked, "did you ever feel that we tricked you into confessing things you didn't need to tell us? Or made a case against you where there was none?"

"No, not at all," I answered quickly. What else could I say?

Still, he insisted. "Don't say that so easily. What we're saying now is very important. It will affect your behavior later on, when you are undergoing Reform Through Labor. I am here to dispel any doubts from your mind. So tell me truthfully, did you ever have those sorts of thoughts?"

"All right," I admitted. "Sometimes during the past year I did wonder whether I went further than I really had to."

"Very good. Now look at this." He pulled from the drawer a folder about the size of a Sears, Roebuck catalogue. "These are accusations and denunciations concerning you. You will see that your confession tallies with them almost perfectly. We want you to read this, Bao, not to give you vengeful feelings about these people who did their duty to the state, but rather to prove to you that we have had a case against you for years."

As I couldn't read Chinese then, the scribe read it to me. It took several hours. On those hundreds of pages were handwritten denunciation forms from colleagues, friends, people I had encountered only once or twice. When I returned to the cell my head was spinning—how many persons whom I had trusted without a second thought had betrayed me!

Next morning I was summoned for one final ceremony. My interrogator was there. His voice was almost friendly. "Confessing your own sins doesn't make you perfect, Bao. There are also the sins of other people to be denounced. Do you understand?"

Of course. Now it was time for me to do in my friends.

"We're not asking you to be a stool pigeon," he assured me, "only you weren't alone in your crimes and errors. How can we consider you to be truly on the good road unless you tell us about your associates? You still have some time here before you will be transferred to the transit center. Here are some denunciation forms. I hope you will show your appreciation by helping the government to ferret out its enemies."

For the next two weeks I filled out the forms, trying to be certain that the people I mentioned would already have far worse accusations against them. It was exhausting. Throughout, I was obsessed with leaving Grass Mist Lane and being able to eat again. I lost myself in reveries of food.

OUR first move, however, was no farther than the eastern compound. This happened in early November, when the last member of our cell had finished his full confession. At nine o'clock on a chilly, sleety morning a warder bustled in and ordered us to get our things together. Heads down, the eighteen of us tramped the five hundred yards across to the eastern compound, stopped, squatted by the entryway and awaited orders.

I was disappointed when our group was broken up, but my new cell turned out to be something of a family reunion. When I trotted in, the first man I laid eyes on was Anthony Liu, a good friend who had worked as liaison in another Western embassy. And then, four days after that, Johnson Wong was led in. An overseas Chinese, Johnson had worked in a Western embassy as I had, but later turned informer to the political police. When he was of no more use to them, they put him away.

The cellmate I liked best, though, was Bartek, the first non-Oriental I had seen in prison. He was a Pole in his early fifties, with brown hair and beard and a fine, long face. His deep blue eyes were set in a mass of smile wrinkles. "Welcome to our cell," he called out jovially in perfect Mandarin. He was lying against his bedroll, thick glasses perched on his nose, glancing over an English edition of *The Peking Review*. As a foreigner, he was allowed to have approved reading matter not printed in Chinese. After the briefest of conversations I fell upon Bartek's books and magazines like a starving man.

The euphoria lasted three days. I was called into the warder's office and reminded that the reading matter was for the foreigner only. Anthony Liu and I, who had committed the sin of speaking English, were removed to another cell.

The next day I discovered that there were American prisoners

among us. On the floor of the latrine I found an empty American cigarette pack! I had known for years that two American airmen were being held in Peking; this proved at least that they were receiving Red Cross parcels. I learned that they had three meals a day—soup, Chinese dumplings, rice, meat, vegetables. Compared to us they were fantastically well off, but they had to endure the crippling isolation and solitude that we were spared.

THE days dragged by. No exercise, no games, no reading. We stared witlessly at the walls, waiting for mealtimes. That week we discovered to our horror that the soup was becoming thinner and the bread loaves smaller! I was desperate. The next day, when I went into the mess hall to pick up our ration, I snatched two extra pieces of bread when the guard wasn't looking. Liu gave me a long stare when I handed him his unexpected bonus. But he held his tongue.

Twenty-four hours later I tried again, but the warder caught me and denounced me for stealing from the government. That night I was called in for a scolding. "It's hard to be good on an empty stomach," I told the warder.

"Don't be impatient, Bao. You won't be here long."

He sounded strangely reassuring. The next morning the guard told me to take three loaves for each of us. "Orders from the ideological warder," he said. To this day I feel grateful to him.

LESS than a week afterward Liu and I were transferred back in with Bartek. The guard told me I might read his magazines and books provided we conversed only in Chinese. Bartek's collection included a Soviet literary magazine and Russian editions in English of *A Tale of Two Cities, Nicholas Nickleby* and *Oliver Twist*. In the Moscow *New Times* I read that Boris Pasternak had slandered the Soviet people with his new book, *Doctor Zhivago*.

During breaks from reading I joined Bartek and Liu in working our old iron stove. The prison-issue coal balls were meager things of compressed coal dust, bits of wood and dry dirt. They had to be watched over like a sickly newborn child to keep them from going out. We sat around the stove toasting our pitiful little corn bread, drinking hot water and talking. On one of those bone-chilling winter days Bartek told us how he landed in jail.

Bartek was from a wealthy Polish merchant family in Harbin. He had a lucrative stamp business and dabbled in real estate. Everything considered, he was happy to be living in China. He married a White Russian girl (who was now keeping him in rela-tive luxury by sending Red Cross packages from Australia). When the civil war came to Shanghai and the American forces cleared out, they contracted with Bartek for the use of one of his ware-houses. It wasn't until 1953 that the police decided to have a look around. Fearing nothing, he showed them the invoices covering the dozens of heavy wooden crates: curios, clothing, machine parts. But when the Communists pried the lids off, they found high-quality Yankee rifles, grenades, five thousand American dollars, bolts of rich cloth and forty bars of gold.

The matter was brought to the central authorities in Peking, who accused Bartek of preparing a guerrilla action. They refused to accept his plea that he knew nothing of the contents of the crates; he was sentenced to five years in prison, and all his prop-erty was confiscated. Bartek was prepared to take the five years, but balked at losing everything he had worked for. He appealed. Evidently he could not accept the elementary truth that any wise prisoner learns: in China an appeal means the prisoner is not repentant for his crimes. Therefore it is a demand for further punishment.

At the appeal trial the government exhibited an old photo-graph of Bartek posing with a samurai sword in Harbin in 1934, when the area was occupied by the Japanese. The photograph was taken at the scene of a recent skirmish with the Chinese rebels, to which Bartek had been invited by a Japanese officer. Now he was charged with having participated in a massacre of Chinese patriots, and his sentence was changed to life.

Our cellmate Johnson Wong was in Grass Mist Lane because he, too, had appealed. He had not served the first year of his twenty-year sentence when he decided he had been unjustly treated. After about one week with us, Johnson left to face his new interrogation and trial. I saw him again two years later, in the camps. His sentence, too, had been changed to life.

LATE in December I was summoned back to the interrogation center for my "trial." I was only one of many to be tried, and the atmosphere in the room, around the huge, dossier-covered table, was one of bustling efficiency.

"This is not an interrogation," the prosecutor announced. "You are not obliged to say anything. You will answer only when you are told to. We have chosen someone for your defense."

The trial took only a few minutes. The prosecutor read aloud my self-accusation and his official charges:

1. Collecting information for imperialist powers.
2. Engaging in illegal activities and transactions prejudicial to the economy of the state.
3. Spreading rumors with the intention of creating confusion among the masses.
4. Slandering, calumniating and insulting the Chinese Communist Party, the Chinese People's Republic and its leadership.
5. Distributing imperialist propaganda with the intention of discrediting the Chinese People's Republic . . . and in a vain attempt to corrupt Chinese youth.
6. Undermining the good relations which exist between China and various friendly nations.

I admitted that the accusations were just. The prosecutor called on my defense lawyer, a young fellow of about thirty in a Mao-style suit. His plea was to the point: "The accused has freely admitted to these crimes. Therefore no defense is necessary."

The prosecutor sent me back to my cell and urged me to devote my time to studies before sentencing.

About a month passed before anything happened. During that dreary time the only thing I remember with clarity was a struggle session in which about a thousand of us were huddled, shivering, in a big courtyard next to the main building. Up on the roofs the guards were silhouetted against the pearl-gray February sky.

Our victim was a middle-aged prisoner charged with having made a false confession. He was an obstinate counterrevolutionary, a cadre shouted out to us through a cardboard megaphone. I never did learn the man's name. He sat in a little open space, head bowed. We surged around him and began.

"Down with the obstinate prisoner!" we screamed. "Confess or face the consequences!" Every time he raised his head to say anything, we drowned him with cries of "Liar!" "Scum!" or even "Son of a bitch!" As the struggle continued, a strange, animal frenzy built within us. I almost think we would have been capable of tearing him to pieces. Later I realized that we had been struggling him and ourselves at the same time, mentally preparing to accept the government's decision in our own cases.

After three hours our victim could bear no more. He cried out to the guards, "Don't waste their time any longer. Punish me according to the regulations." It was a request that was defiance at the same time. The guards came forward with the chains.

A week later the warder called me in to show me a document in which I formally requested the honor of going to a labor unit. I signed instantly. In a few days Anthony Liu and I were sent to the transit center. We had joy in our hearts.

Chapter 4

In a convoy of closed trucks led by police jeeps, the shipment of prisoners including Liu and me arrived at the transit center, known to its guards as the detention center and to the outside world as the Peking Experimental Scientific Instruments Factory. Assembled in the yard, we had a chance to inspect the place. In front of us was the great, gray, four-story main building shaped like a K. Behind it was the three-story technical building, which housed prisoners who were engineers, architects, physicists, translators—the intellectuals who did the paperwork for the transit center. But there was one building that drew the attention of all of us: the central kitchen. Great clouds of steam—the live steam used to cook the cornmeal *wo'tou*—billowed up from the vents. We regarded it with hungry fascination.

Next to the kitchen was a smaller, L-shaped building, death row, and adjoining it, rows of solitary-confinement cells. The whole ugly complex was known as the northwest corner.

Walking into K Building, we found ourselves in a book factory. A vast, drafty central hall rose past four open stories to a glass ceiling. The air reeked of creosote. On one wall was a monstrous poster picturing a worker gazing down sternly with a sheaf of paper in his left hand and pointing at the viewer with his right. Underneath was an admonition in large black ideograms:

TO DAMAGE A BOOK LEAF IS TO RUIN AN ENTIRE BOOK.
TO RUIN AN ENTIRE BOOK IS TO DEPRIVE ONE PERSON
OF THE CHANCE FOR EDUCATION.

Everywhere there was frenzied, antlike activity. Men rushed back and forth toting stacks of printed sheets three to four feet high. To the din of hammering and footfalls was added the piercing voice of a man who moved up and down the stairways with a megaphone, encouraging production. "Cell number seventeen has issued a challenge to cell number one," I heard him shout.

Anthony Liu and I were assigned to B section of the third brigade, and a guard led us to the third floor. Along both walls of the corridor prisoners sat on their haunches, some folding the printed sheets, others binding them into packets. The only noises here were the grunts of the workers and the slap of the bamboo folding rods against the paper sheets. The cell doors were open. Inside each cell the communal plank beds had been dismantled to form two large worktables. Each table had eight men to a side and everyone was feverishly folding pages. Each sheet, about three feet by two, had to be folded three times and then stacked to one side. On the wall of each cell was a printed notice:

The target set by the government is 6000 sheets. The average output is 4500. The beginner's norm is 3000. All must strive to surpass their targets.

Mealtime was announced as we stood in the hallway. We each got three warm corn-bread loaves, smaller than the *wo'tou* in the interrogation center but heavier. The soup was richer: in with the potato peels were little chunks of potato and even some fat! Sitting on our bedrolls, Liu and I gobbled it down.

A warder brought us long forms to fill out. I spent almost two hours writing another history of my life, arrest and interrogation. When we had finished, another warder assigned us to our cells. Mine was number fourteen. The cell leader motioned me to the worktable and told my neighbor to show me what to do. Bamboo stick in hand, I laboriously started folding.

We worked until 6:00 p.m., broke for the evening meal (as at lunch) and then continued to 7:30, when we stacked the sheets we had folded, labeled them with our numbers and put them out in the corridor for pickup. I had managed only three hundred.

With practiced precision my cellmates hefted the table planks and replaced them to form two communal beds with a narrow aisle between them. Then we all sat cross-legged on the beds for the nightly study session. Tonight a cellmate explained the ration system.

A prisoner's ration depended on his production and, equally important, on his attitude. There were four categories of rations: beginner, light labor, heavy and punishment. My portion as a beginner—one who could not fold a minimum of three thousand sheets—would be two bowls of corn mush in the morning, vegetable soup with three *wo'tou* at lunch and the same for supper. The light-labor ration, for three thousand sheets, amounted to three extra *wo'tou* a day, and the heavy-labor ration—six thousand or more sheets—to five more *wo'tou* per day than the beginner received. The expert folders also got one meal of wheat-flour bread and one of rice every month. The punishment ration could be anything the warders decided.

When the study session was finished and it was time for lights-out, the forty of us shoehorned ourselves into our spots. Twelve slept on each big bed, four more on the floor between, then four more on planks laid over them, making the aisle a double berth. The remaining eight slept in the corridor.

We were awakened at 5:00 a.m. "I didn't think we got up until six," I remarked to one of my cellmates.

"Shao shuo hua"—"shut up"—was his answer as he began dismantling the bed. Quickly the workbenches were formed up. Groggily I started folding. By the time I had finished my first sheet the man next to me had done a dozen. At 6:30 the trusty came by with breakfast. To a man, my cellmates continued working while they slopped down the corn mush. The only thing that mattered was to fold and fold.

We knew it was 10:00 a.m. when we heard music from the loudspeakers in the yard: the guards were doing their morning calisthenics. If a prisoner hadn't finished a quarter of his daily quota by then, it was assumed he wouldn't make it. At lunchtime we drank down our soup with hardly a hitch in the rhythm. By the end of the day I had folded only fifteen hundred sheets. My arms were so stiff it hurt to move them, and my back felt as if it had been sledgehammered.

Three days later I was called for a routine medical exam. For the first time since my arrest I saw myself in a full-length mirror. I was appalled. My weight had dropped to 110 pounds. The skin hung loosely on my frame, blue and callused where it had been in contact with the benches. I couldn't sleep that night.

AFTER the medical exam I had the luck to be transferred to a less crowded cell containing only twenty-two men. The leader was a handsome young man named Howe, who came from a good bourgeois family and had a girl friend in Canada. He knew as many American tunes as I did, and we would break the monotony of folding by humming along together. I suppose the irony of "My Old Kentucky Home" and "Swanee River" wafting out of a cell full of Oriental jailbirds was lost on the guards.

Howe paid only lip service to the didacticism that old Loo took so much to heart, and aimed only at getting us all first-class rations. He had us start each day with a personal goal, announce it and deliberately commit ourselves to it. By the end of March I was up to thirty-five hundred sheets and was put on the light-labor ration.

We folded quite a selection of material over the months: *The Farmer's Dictionary*, a simplified manual of history and ideo-logical terminology; textbooks on electricity; politically oriented spy stories; a deluxe edition of *Don Quixote*; and Mao's works.

Our folding operation was, of course, only one of several steps in the entire book production. Each man's daily output of book sheets was carried up to the fourth floor, where a machine punched three holes in the margins. After that the sections were sorted into proper order for sewing. At a long table one prisoner clamped the pages for an entire book into place and with a powerful stapling machine rammed a temporary staple through. His partner, the sewer, then ran a line through the three holes and removed the staple.

The sewing sometimes did terrible damage to a prisoner's hands, but the worst job in the transit center belonged to the runners who carried the folded pages upstairs. Each man ser-viced two binders, and each binder had a daily quota of seven hundred books. A runner toted fourteen hundred books a day on his back, thirty or forty at a time, stacked on planks tied to his shoulders. He had to run up the stairs to make his quota, and if he fell, the man behind would run over him.

Our output was sent to the state-run New China Bookstore in downtown Peking, for sale to the general public.

DURING this period of apprenticeship I saw my first live enter-tainment in prison, on International Women's Day. At 6:30 p.m., just after supper, we bundled up in our warmest clothes and filed out to the courtyard, each with a bit of cloth to sit on.

Like everyone else, the man next to me lit up as soon as he sat down. "How come you're not smoking?" he asked.

When I told him I didn't have any cigarettes, he handed me a Big Fortune. It was one of the cheapest Chinese brands, but it was the first cigarette I had smoked since my arrest and it tasted fine. "I have nothing I can give you in exchange," I said.

"That's all right." He handed me four or five more. "Maybe I'll see you again someday. You can pay me then."

The evening's spectacle told the story of the Hsing Kai-Hu labor camp in Manchuria, and it was entitled *The Dam*. It was the opening salvo of the campaign to attract volunteers to the camps on the Sino-Soviet border.

The Barren Lands, as they were called, were one of the greatest challenges the Party had ever tackled. For centuries it had been known that the Manchurian steppe had the potential for fabulous agricultural production, but no one, including the Japanese invaders, had been able to withstand the climate. The first *Lao Gai* prisoners—four thousand of them—arrived there in 1954. By the time of the Great Leap in 1958 enough food was coming from the Barren Lands to feed a million people a year.

Hsing Kai-Hu inspired mixed emotions in us. The eating in Manchuria was rumored to be good—soybeans, wild-boar meat now and then, plenty of fish, poultry and eggs, even milk. Also, the earlier prisoners had been permitted to take their families with them as nuclei for future settlements. But life in the north was harsh. The winter temperatures dropped to forty below. And since the whole area was marshland, summer brought not only heat but plagues of mosquitoes.

Someone had figured that a good way to generate enthusiasm was to produce a show. The result was the New Life Theatrical Troupe: the one hundred members of the cast were prisoners themselves, and had honed their spectacle to such perfection that I am convinced it could make money on Broadway.

THE stage darkened and the narrator came forward under a spotlight—a true Chinese hero in a splendidly tailored Mao suit. "Schoolmates," he shouted, "we come here from the great barren northeast. The show tonight tells of the beginnings, struggles and future of the Hsing Kai-Hu camps. We need your collaboration. These camps are testimony to the greatness of the program of Reform Through Labor. This is a success story!"

The lights came up on an old couple in traditional peasant work clothes trudging wearily over a marsh. They both began to sink; the more they struggled, the deeper they sank. Presently only two gnarled hands showed above the surface.

The second tableau brought optimistic settlers during the years of the Great Famine. Their efforts were doomed, though, and the tableau ended with a field of bones bleaching in the sun.

The third tableau illustrated the war year of 1931, with the fiendish Japanese wielding bayonets and whips over teams of Chinese slave laborers plowing the soil. Occasionally a team would sink into the marsh, their Japanese overseers with them.

The fourth tableau showed the failure of the Nationalists, who took over in 1945, leaving the lands untouched, wild as a moor.

Then we saw the unmistakable rays of a rising sun. The red glow grew stronger and lifted slowly from the horizon to become Mao, rising in the east! The liberation was upon us.

"But what sort of liberation is this," asked an actor, "when a land reputed to be so rich is left untilled and barren? The land must be liberated, as well as the people. But who can do it?"

It was a loaded question. Who else but prisoners?

Now the tableaux succeeded each other majestically, showing how the prisoners at first lived in holes in the wintry ground, covered with branches. Teams of surveyors and agronomists spread out; and engineers made plans for the dam that would tame the waters of the marshy steppe, form an artificial lake and dry up the fields below it so crops could be planted. It was eight months before the dam was finished, and three dozen workers had drowned when the earthworks gave way and the waters came flooding through. They were all given the exceptional honor of posthumous rehabilitation. Their families in the villages were no longer required to "wear the black hats marking them as relatives of enemies of the people" and could thenceforth refer to themselves as "families of heroes."

Once the dam was completed, other teams were depicted fertilizing the fields by spreading dried wheat stalks and setting them afire to provide the soil with rich ash. Here, too, ten men died when a sudden change of wind engulfed them in the flames. Like the others, they were upgraded to heroes.

Subsequent tableaux showed the arrival in 1955 of the construction battalion. The construction battalion! It is the most perfect Orwellian triumph of Chinese scientific socialist thought. Its nearly five hundred supervisors and technicians were prisoners themselves, and their raison d'être was to travel around China building prisons for others. Touched by the trials of the Barren Lands settlers, the construction battalion set new records. In four months they built a thousand cells in prison houses of red brick, with hollow walls for heat flues.

The last scene brought us the sixty-four villages, peopled by smiling, well-fed prisoners and their families, that were now infusing life into Hsing Kai-Hu. Then we poor paper-folders shuffled back to our overcrowded cells, wishing we could be up there with the heroes in Manchuria.

The following day we were herded to lectures extolling the joy and virtue of life in the northeast. The state urgently needed fresh hands to man new villages and farms, two thousand from our transit center alone. But the night's sleep and the blatant recruiting talks had dampened our enthusiasm. The camps did sound splendid, but every prisoner knew he would never return from them. If we could at least bring our families . . . ? The recruiters cut these illusions short; only the government would decide who could bring his family—after everyone had volunteered.

Volunteered? We soon found that the show and the pep talks had been only a demonstration of the Party's passion for the form of things. Early the next morning we were all lined up in the courtyard. A tough, businesslike character strode rapidly down the rows. "I'll take this one, and this one, and you, and you . . ." He passed me over. I was too thin for his taste.

That evening the "volunteers" selected were promptly marched to another part of the compound. Twelve went from our cell.

The rest of us were locked in. Next day life resumed as usual.

On April 1 the warder called me into his office to announce that my wife had left three packs of cigarettes and the equivalent of $1.50 in Chinese money for me. I was bitterly disappointed at the gift. It wasn't until May, after I had been sentenced, that I learned how much it had represented to her.

THEN I saw Loo again. I had left the cell to go to the latrine and there he was, shuffling quietly down the corridor.

"Loo," I said, "what a pleasure to see you. How are you?"

"Not good, Bao," he answered, and he did look terrible.

"Have you been sentenced?"

"Very heavy, Bao." He shook his head. "Everything's finished. My wife's divorcing me. They gave me life."

After that meeting I feared I would never get out of prison. If they were so harsh with Loo for his Nationalist past, how would they judge my association with the Americans?

Around this time the Chinese army had taken over Tibet. Howe dutifully read us the newspaper accounts, and my cellmates trotted out the old atrocious tales, repeated for centuries, concerning the Tibetan aristocracy's penchant for killing Chinese. I tried to present things more honestly. "I think that these stories are pretexts to justify our annexation of Tibet. But why invent reasons? We have been taught that Tibet is part of our national domain. We are simply annexing our own land."

Howe even congratulated me. "Bao," he said, "it was good that you got rid of the thoughts in your head."

I felt proud, but I got the bill for my words later.

ON APRIL 13, 1958, my big day finally arrived—my sentencing. I was folding forty-five hundred sheets by then and dreaming of making it to six thousand so I would get heavy rations. In the warder's office I met a young man in an olive jacket and blue pants. "This is a representative of the People's Court," the warder said.

The young man opened his briefcase, brought out a sheet of

paper and began reading from it. "The accused is charged with participating in the repression of the Chinese people by being a faithful running dog of the imperialist powers, with engaging in illegal activities and black=marketing, with slandering the Chinese Communist Party and calumniating its leadership, and with distributing imperialist propaganda with the intent of corrupting the Chinese people.

"The accused having admitted all these crimes by himself of his own free will, the People's Government hereby sentences you, Bao Ruo-wang, to twelve years' imprisonment, counting from the date of your arrest on December 27, 1957. You will carry out this sentence in units of Reform Through Labor."

Long live Mao, I thought. It could have been life or twenty years, and I was getting only twelve. What a relief! Probably because of my partly foreign past, the Party decided I had earned twelve years and that is exactly what they gave me. The ordinary sentencing procedure is quite different. If, as in my case, the prisoner's actual sentence is twelve years, the Party may tell him it is twenty, or even life. And he will be told that he can lighten his sentence by making the necessary efforts. After perhaps a year of furious effort he may be rewarded by a reduction of his sentence from life to twenty years. Radiant and grateful, he becomes the perfect prisoner, and after three more years the sentence is reduced to only fifteen years. Since he has already served four, and continues to behave with zeal and gratitude, they wait until he has served eight more—making a total of twelve years, his original sentence. Twelve years instead of life! It is at this moment that the government generously decides on an amnesty. The man becomes a free worker with a song in his heart, thinking only of helping to build socialism.

Another Chinese Communist invention is the suspended death sentence—the execution to be carried out only if the prisoner misbehaves. That, too, tends to make model prisoners. Lo Jui-ching, formerly China's number-one policeman, explained the system in the *People's Daily:* ". . . Capital punishment with suspension of execution gives a last chance for reform. . . . Where in the capitalist world can such a humanitarian law be found?"

"Do you wish to appeal?" the court representative asked me.

"*No!*" I said. Bartek and the others had cured me of that. "I am happy with my sentence. I only wish to sign my name."

"Raise your right hand," he ordered me. "Do you hereby accept that you were given a fair trial and a just sentence?"

"I do."

"Sign."

When I got back to the cell I was bursting with joy. The soup tasted good that night. Only after the lights went out did I begin thinking of what lay before me. Ten more years. It began to seem longer and longer.

Chapter 5

A FEW evenings later the warder hauled about five hundred of us out into the corridor to hear him announce that we were being given the honor of "launching a satellite." A satellite signifies the highest production possible. The very best workers were classified as rockets. The slower ones, regressively, were airplanes, locomotives, automobiles, bicycles and finally oxcarts. I knew one character who was below that: he was only a turtle! That was a double humiliation, for a turtle is also the traditional Chinese symbol of the cuckold.

The production warder stood on a stool haranguing us through a tin megaphone. "You all know," he began, "that the laboring masses are taking part in the Great Leap Forward. Filled with revolutionary enthusiasm, they are carrying out the directives of the Party and the government, determined to match the industrial capacity of England within fifteen years. Working sometimes sixteen and eighteen hours a day, they have accomplished brilliant results that are almost miracles. Do you think that you, who are traitors to the new society, should do any less?

"With the first of May approaching, the government has decided to make tomorrow a satellite-launching day. Tomorrow you will increase your targets by a hundred percent. Laggards will be treated to solitary as saboteurs, and all cells which fail to attain the targets will go on a diet of corn mush for one week. Before you go to bed tonight each of you will declare his norms for tomorrow."

That night Howe pledged us to something like two hundred thousand sheets. We all went to sleep as rapidly as possible.

At precisely 3:30 a.m. a trusty shouted, "All right, everybody up!" Within seconds the building was echoing with the din of hundreds of men restacking their plank beds and chucking the bedding into stowholes. Every second counted. Within minutes we were all seated, blinking and half asleep, ready to fold.

A cellmate flopped a stack of book sheets down beside each of us. We laid out our toilet kits—the square of toweling, the enamel mug, the toothbrush, the sliver of soap—and started folding each sheet, once, twice, thrice, four times. Back and forth went the bamboo sticks. The more machinelike we were, the quicker it went.

When our latrine call came, we scrambled to the door and trotted double time to the washroom, meeting the next cell on our way back. Before we started folding again, we went through a little ritual—the gluing of three cigarettes end to end to make one superking-size smoke, for we were allowed to light up only one a day. The paste gave a weird taste, but a smoke was a smoke.

"Here comes the light," Howe warned us. A warder handed a single match to the trusty, who lit his own cigarette, then worked his way down the corridor, passing his cigarette to each cell leader. The chain grew until the entire brigade was smoking.

By breakfast at 7:00 a.m. I had folded just over eight hundred sheets, but most of the others had gone beyond a thousand. (By the time I left the transit center I could do ten thousand on satellite days.) We gobbled the food feverishly. The day passed in a dreamlike haze of endless motion. There were no rest breaks, no studies. We drank as little as possible, to avoid having to squander a few minutes on trips to the latrine.

I did not contribute my announced share, but the experienced hands made up the difference. So everything was all right. We would hold on to our rations. We went to bed at 11:15, absolutely dizzy from exhaustion but, I suppose, happy.

THE trick to folding book pages was matching up the black dots along the borders. We also, obviously, had to keep the page order straight. And woe to the man who damaged a page! At the end of each day a warder called off our names; one by one, we reported our personal counts of damaged sheets. Three or four were considered inevitable, but more could bring serious trouble.

One of the most skillful folders in our cell was a man named Hu. Even on normal days he turned out about eight thousand sheets. He went so fast that his folding was sometimes sloppy. But Hu's problem was that he was illiterate. One evening in May, Howe, our cell leader, was called away urgently. He returned looking grim and mean, a folded sheet in his hand.

"Hu, you're going to get it," he said bleakly.

Hu was startled. "What do you mean? What did I do?"

"What you did is terrible, Hu. You have caused grave losses to the state."

"Don't try to frame me, Howe." Hu was angry now. "You know I didn't damage more than five sheets all last week."

"It's not a question of five or six sheets. It's three hundred."

Hu blanched. "That's not possible."

"No?" Howe held out the sheet. "Look at the bottom, Hu. The numbers start at twenty-five, instead of sixteen." Long silence. "Do you still say you didn't make any mistakes?"

Hu got a week in solitary for that. Jailers in China will give a man free time to learn to read and write, so Hu had no one to blame but himself. When he rejoined us after solitary his face was gray. He'd lost eight pounds.

"If it's any consolation," Howe told him, "the guy who cut your paper and lined up the numbers got two weeks."

After that I began studying written Chinese, and by my release I could read and write the language as well as I spoke it.

AT INTERVALS THROUGHOUT the year the cells had ration-voting sessions. One by one, each of us made a little speech describing his past work, outlining his plans for the future, and finishing with a request for the level of rations he thought he should have. The others then commented and voted. One early session I experienced will give an idea of how the system works.

"My name is Bao Ruo-wang," I began. "I am here for counterrevolutionary activities. The government has assigned me to folding book pages and at present I am on the light-duty ration. Since I am now up to about five thousand sheets a day and since I don't think I'll be able to reach the target set by the government in the near future, I guess I should stay on my light ration."

Two cellmates commended me for my positive attitude, but it was too much to expect that I would get off without negative comment. "Bao Ruo-wang is commendable in his attitude," someone piped up, "but rations are not awarded on the basis of attitude alone. His production figures are low. If he doesn't make it to the target, the warder will probably punish him. So wouldn't we look bad if we voted him such high rations now?"

Even worse was to come, from a real sour guy with a high-pitched voice. "I think Bao should be demoted," he squeaked. "Does he think he's here to enjoy himself? He came in the middle of February and we're now into May. Should he still be entitled to light rations? Other prisoners who arrived a month ago are already up to seven thousand a day."

Howe looked around, but no one had any more to say. "I have nothing to add," he finally said, "except to ask that when you feel compelled to throw out accusations, keep in mind what your own production figures are. Let's take a vote. Light?"

Everyone but the sour guy and myself (the prisoner whose case is being considered never votes) raised his hand. So I was all set: light rations until the next session—providing the warders agreed.

The saddest case I ever came across was a ruddy-faced prisoner who came the closest to speaking the truth. "My production figure is around forty-five hundred sheets," he said in a weary monotone, "but because the government thinks I can do better, I am still eating the beginner's ration. The government may think I can fold more than forty-five hundred, but I can't do it on the beginner's ration. So if you ask me if I want the light-work ration, I will say yes; not because I think I can fold more, but because I am hungry."

We all looked down in embarrassment. We knew he would pay for his words.

And then there was Lo—a champion folder, one of the best. "I have been here for six months," he said. "My production figure is around nine thousand a day. I've been on the heavy ration for four months. By next week I might be up to ten thousand sheets— I've discovered a way to make it go faster. But anyway, I think this heavy ration is unfair. The guy who folds six thousand a day gets as much food as I do and I fold fifty percent more than he does. Shouldn't I get fifty percent more food than he?"

He spread his palms out, a reasonable man asking for an obvious answer. "Of course, I realize that I'm asking for the impossible. There's a limit, isn't there? Therefore I'd like the classmates to vote me the light ration. I feel like taking it easy for a while."

It was a bombshell that left us all speechless. The best Howe could do was to lightly admonish Lo not to make jokes.

"I'm not joking," Lo protested. "I don't think the light ration will hurt me for a month or so. I feel quite fit now. If I went down to folding five thousand a day, it would be a nice break."

"Do you know what the consequences of your action might be?"

"Sure I do. But all I want is a little rest, schoolmates."

We decided to let him have his way. He had scored a victory.

UP TILL now I had not been allowed to see my wife. The law permitted her to come to the place of my imprisonment only once a month, and to deposit small parcels, perhaps a letter, or photographs of the children. Her letters were optimistic; otherwise they never would have been delivered and she might have been prosecuted for disseminating antigovernment propaganda. I had let myself be lulled into an unreal sense of security. My jailers had assured me that the state takes care of a sinner's family.

I finally saw her in May 1959—a year and a half after my arrest. The evening before her visit I trotted over to the barber for a shave and the regulation crew cut. I doubted it would help my appearance, though. Some boils that had developed on my neck still hadn't healed, and I wore my standard folding uniform —gray shorts, sandals and dirty gray shirt.

At 5:30 p.m. those receiving visitors were marched downstairs. I carried a quilt that I planned to give Hui-min to wash. Roll call. The personal body search. The warders even slit open the linings of our jackets. Inspected and passed, standing at attention with faces to the wall, we heard the final directives: "Make your visits brief. Prisoners must refrain from dramatics. Speak in a loud voice so the guards can hear you. No dialects allowed—only official Mandarin. If there are any infringements, the warders will end your visits on the spot."

About face. We tramped out into the courtyard, where waist-high plank barriers had been set up, with guards posted at intervals. Among the families on the other side, Hui-min was standing with our younger son, Yung. Yung was my favorite. He reminded me of poor little Mi, who had died of typhoid fever. Yung barely knew who I was; I wondered what he was thinking now. My wife had never had the heart to tell the children what had happened to me. She had said I was away working somewhere and that I'd bring them candies when I came back.

Hui-min had put on her best flowered dress. She looked much too thin. Yung was wearing a white shirt and a pair of khaki pants. He looked at me with big eyes, then started crying. Hui-min was shocked, too. I guess I really looked like hell.

"How come you're like this?" she asked.

"No dramatics!" the guard said.

"How are you, Yung?" I asked.

The poor boy was too scared to speak. He thrust a little parcel toward me, still looking away. There were a handkerchief, a couple of packs of cigarettes, a newspaper and toilet articles.

I told Hui-min not to worry about me. She said the same for the family. The older boy was in school. Everything was all right.

"I heard about the sentence," she finally said. "How can I take care of the kids alone for twelve years?"

"You must not talk about that subject!" shouted the guard.

I gave her the quilt and asked her to wash it. The visit was over. It had lasted six minutes. Yung waved back at me as they left.

A few days later I received a letter from Hui-min apologizing because she had no money to send me. As she explained the situation briefly, I realized what she had gone through to make that visit. When I was in the interrogation center she had come quite regularly to bring parcels for me, because our house was less than a mile's walk away. But the transit center was on the other side of town, and Hui-min hadn't had even enough money for the bus fare. She had walked eight miles to the prison, carrying Yung whenever he became too tired to walk, and had started the same trek home—with the quilt.

But on the way home, as Hui-min was trudging along, a bus driver stopped to pick her up. My wife said she had no money. The ticket taker, a young girl, waved her aboard anyway. "I'll pay your fare, comrade. You can take my number and reimburse me if you ever get up the cash." The bus dropped her fifty yards from our door. That restored my faith in humanity.

As NIGHTMARISH as the paper-folding operation could be, I experienced a little interlude that showed me even worse ways to pass time in the transit center. For one week in April, I had been transferred to the fourth brigade—the technical brigade. Because of my shop training I was sent in to help fill a personnel shortage in the machine-tool production section.

The technical brigade was so obsessed with output that their study sessions eschewed politics entirely and dealt only with ways to increase production. Early the first morning I picked up my set of tools from the supply room and walked over to the lathe that had been assigned me, a tired, rusted old thing dating from World War I. Everywhere around me prisoners were filing and cutting in a confusion of metal chips, smoke and dust. Ting, the superintendent, gave me a six-foot length of old steel pipe three inches in diameter. I was to make rings from it, of precise measurements—discouragingly precise, considering the state of the machines. From my length of pipe I should be able to make 110 rings, Ting warned. No less. My daily quota was to be 600.

That day I managed only 450. The next, I made 600, but I had wasted pipe, averaging only 85 rings per pipe instead of 110. Within a few days I was holding the norm, but still averaging only 95 rings per pipe. I lived in an atmosphere of perpetual scolding. At the end of the week my cutting tool snapped.

Ting blew up and sent me back to folding pages. "You're lucky to get off this easy," he growled. "Prisoners have gone to solitary for breaking tools."

Back in the book division I was sent to a new cell. The leader was a thickset northeasterner named Yen, who had been a doctor before his arrest. Our paths would cross again later on.

ON APRIL 28 we were marched out of our cells for haircuts. The occasion was the approach of May Day—one of the great national holidays in China, as in the entire Communist bloc.

April 30 was a holiday, too—an extra meal, and in the cell we could play games and talk of subjects unrelated to politics or production. After dinner there was an entertainment, but first a speech from the head warder. "We are here to celebrate May first. In spite of the fact that you prisoners have no right to such a celebration, it is the government's opinion that the constructive work you are doing should be rewarded. Therefore, in recognition of the presents you have made to the state, tomorrow you will receive a bonus of two [Chinese] dollars."

The show that followed was called *On the Tracks of the Snowy Mountains*. It was presented by the New Life Theatrical Troupe and was the story of a commando unit of the People's Liberation Army in Manchuria, which defeated the resident bandits by infiltrating their headquarters. It was a fine show.

For May Day the morning meal included steamed white bread made from wheat flour, a stew of pork, vermicelli and potatoes, and two ounces of candy. To digest it we were called to the great central hall to listen to a radio broadcast of the big parade in Peking. We knew it by heart already and it was a bore to be assailed by the same stock phrases. Here came the workers, marching with firm step. Then the peasants, the schoolchildren, the athletes. On they came in seemingly endless bands, everyone chanting, "Long life to Mao!" Two and a half hours it lasted.

That evening we watched a movie, *Fire on the Frontier*, about how the Nationalists persecuted the ethnic minorities and the new order treated them like brothers.

The following week the prison swung into the ideological reform campaign, our own mini-Hundred Flowers. It began in the courtyard at 8:00 p.m. on Friday evening with an announcement from the prison director, a tall, bearded native of Shensi Province.

"Most of you," he began, "have the mistaken idea that you are here only to work. Well, to reform yourselves you have to get rid of your bad thoughts as well. You mustn't be afraid to speak your bad thoughts—we know you have them, or you wouldn't be here. Therefore, beginning next week, each of you must write down all his bad thoughts. The cell leaders must make sure that each prisoner gives a true account of what is really in his head."

Like a fool, I followed orders. I wrote that my experiences in the transit center had led me to conclude that the government's concern for our spiritual well-being was a sham. All it really wanted from us was slave labor. I even felt a perverse pride when my cellmates praised me for having such truly bad thoughts.

On June 15 I got the bill for them. That evening the director announced, "In order to ensure that you all receive the proper instruction, we are now going to open a denunciation campaign. Every one of you is expected to denounce others for what they have said or done against the government. Do not be afraid to speak. It is better to offend a cellmate than the government."

Back in our cells, we started in a low key: "I saw so-and-so stealing bread from the food trough."

"When?" asked the cell leader.

"Two months ago."

"Why didn't you report him?"

"Because he gave me half."

Things quickly worsened. One man was accused of trading food for cigarettes; that was black-marketing. Someone said he saw me using code in my letters home and writing in a foreign language. I was shaken. It was weird and unhealthy.

A week later we were assembled in the courtyard at 7:00 p.m. for the climax of the campaign. We sat in the warm evening sun and looked up at the stage, where the director sat at a green baize table with his fifteen assistants around him. Behind them was a large poster of Mao and a fresh banner with a slogan:

PUNISHMENT TO ALL THOSE WHO REFUSE THE
GOVERNMENT'S REEDUCATION

The director rose to make his speech. I held my breath.

"The denunciation campaign has been a great success. The results show that the majority of you are truly concerned with ideological reform. But a few of you have launched attacks against the Party and the government."

A dramatic pause. "Bao Ruo-wang, counterrevolutionary, thirty-three years old, sentenced to twelve years—on your feet!"

My dear cellmates shoved me upward with remarkable fervor.

The director continued. "This individual has attacked the state's glorious program of Reform Through Labor. What is worse, he has dared to insult the Chinese People's Liberation Army by saying that the pacification campaign in Tibet was imperialist aggression." He had twisted my words from that early study session in the cell with Howe. Nothing, I realized, is ever forgotten.

"For these and other insults the government has decided to place him in solitary confinement until he has shown signs of repentance."

The courtyard erupted in applause. "Long live the Chinese People's Government!" "Punish the agent of imperialism!"

It was an impressive din. My fellow prisoners shook their fists in the air. I saw faces full of hatred turned toward me. I was cer-

tain that my schoolmates would have torn me to bits if the director had suggested it. Two guards grabbed me, pushed my head
down and dragged me toward the dreaded northwest corner.
There a warder awaited us. "Put him in cuffs," said the guard.

Presently I found myself in a long, dank corridor lined with
small doors, as if made for midgets. The place smelled like a
lion's cage. A guard swung open one of the doors and another
pushed me forward. Bent double, I squeezed into my hole.

The cell itself measured about four by three feet and the
ceiling was four and a half feet high. I would be able to sit or
squat, but it was impossible to stand or lie down. My escorts
threw in a dirty blanket and slammed the steel door shut. The
door had a peephole for the guard near the top, and a smaller hole
for the food spout to fit through. There was a wooden bucket for
my latrine, and an electric bulb that stayed lit permanently.

I felt despairing and bitter. They had ordered us to speak our
minds, and evidently I had been the only one to take them at
their word. My arms, bound behind my back, hurt like hell. I
dozed and nodded through the first night.

The next morning a guard opened my door. "The government
has decided to be lenient with you," he announced. For an instant
my hopes soared. Was I to be freed? The guard unlocked the
cuffs. "Put your arms out in front of you."

He snapped the cuffs back on. So that was the leniency. At
least now I could sit in relative comfort. Half an hour later another guard opened the door and thrust in a bowl. At what must
have been around 9:00 a.m. a voice outside gave me an order:
"Get ready to take your meal."

I held the bowl under the bottom hole. A spout pushed through
the opening and slopped in scalding corn mush, some of which
spilled onto my hands. In pain, I dropped the bowl. That was
just what he had been waiting for.

"You fool!" he bellowed. "That's wasting food—blood and
sweat of the people. I shall make a note of your attitude."

Furious, I licked up what was left in the bowl. In five minutes
the guard returned for the bowl, followed by the turnkey, who

handcuffed my arms behind me again. Having them in front for eating was something, though. Some prisoners had their arms always behind them and had to lap up their food like dogs.

Hunched in a corner, I daydreamed until I could avoid reality no longer: I had to pee. I lurched over to the bucket, turned around and took off the cover with my joined hands, then turned again to face the bucket. But there was no question of pulling my shorts down. So I peed down my leg.

Some time in the late afternoon a guard came to change my cuffs around to the front again.

"I'm sorry," I said. "I wet my pants. Can't I change them?"

He looked at me as if I were a caterpillar. "*Change* them? Don't you know where you are?"

He handed me another bowl and closed the door. This time I was ready for the food and didn't lose a drop. To my surprise, the turnkey didn't put my arms behind me after supper. From then on this was the rule only during the day.

That night and for the next several days I could hear someone singing a demented song. Why couldn't the guards shut him up? I brooded about it, then decided it must be coming from the death cells down at the end of the corridor.

On the third day the guards were heaving buckets of water into the cell next to mine. The floors were sloped slightly downward, so they could be sluiced of their filth. My neighbor began shouting abuse. I was stunned at his daring.

"I don't need a shower. I just hope I get my hands on you someday. You call yourselves Communists? You're no better than the Nationalists!"

"If you don't shut up, we'll gag you," warned the guard.

"Kill me, you bastard."

Afterward he was silent. I suppose they did gag him.

ON THE fifth day I was taken to the warder in charge of the solitary block. "What have you got to say for yourself?"

"I want to talk to a representative of the Ministry of Public Security."

"Why him?"

"His department sent me here."

I was thrown back into the cage, but three days later they led me to a meeting room where I met a uniformed officer of the Peking Bureau of Public Security. I respected them for that. The form on which Chinese Communists insist can often be used to a prisoner's advantage. "What is it?" the officer asked.

I figured I had to hit hard. But above all I had to protect myself by staying within their ironclad logic. "I have been told a bunch of lies by the People's Government."

He raised an eyebrow and waited for me to continue.

Carefully I outlined my point of view. I quoted the director's exhortations for us to put our worst thoughts on paper and his assurances that honesty would be rewarded. Having obeyed, I had been rewarded with solitary. Where was my sin? The officer assured me that he would look into the matter.

I am certain today that my accusations had an effect on the bureaucrats in Peking. The Maoist order is inordinately proud of its special sort of integrity. But since the Chinese are also face-conscious, it would be inconceivable for them to simply release me from solitary. They found a compromise.

On a Sunday evening, ten days after my arrival in solitary, I was dragged up, handcuffed, filthy and teeming with lice, to my wing of the K Building and dumped on the floor before five hundred of my chosen classmates to be struggled. Most of my own cellmates were there.

"Bao Ruo-wang has come back to make a public confession," announced the warder.

I spoke. "In the past I have used various study sessions and campaigns to spread unfavorable ideas."

The catcalling began. "You're not being sincere!"

"You are not telling the truth!"

Again I tried to explain myself, but the warder ordered, "Stop talking!" (He had not said, "Shut up." He was being fairly polite; it was beginning to look like just a pro forma struggle.) "All right, you people," he went on. "Start criticizing him."

One character set the tone. "Bao Ruo-wang is a fox who could no longer hide his tail. He was condemned as an imperialist spy and now he dares to carry out his imperialist duties right here in prison! We demand that the government punish him severely!"

After only about forty-five minutes the warder intervened. "It's getting late," he said. "You people have to get back to your cells. Thank you for the help you have given Bao Ruo-wang."

I went back down to solitary, but the next morning the guards eliminated my cuffs, allowed me to wash, and gave me two *wo'-tou*. The following day I was put back on the light-labor ration.

Early in July I was returned to the cell, where I was warmly greeted. "Good to have you back, Bao," said the friends who had struggled me. "Have a cigarette."

HUI-MIN VISITED ME once more in the transit center a few days after my release from solitary confinement. It was what in prison terminology is called a dishonorable visit. A warder led me to the empty courtyard. There, next to the door from the main building, were my wife and our sons, Yung and Mow. Little Yung was crying again. The warder allowed me to touch them both.

Hui-min began reciting her speech. "I have been told that lately your behavior has been bad."

The bastards, I thought. Couldn't they have spared her this?

"Your behavior has not made things easy for me," she went on in that unnaturally loud voice. "All the children's classmates know their father is a counterrevolutionary prisoner. But there is a difference between a counterrevolutionary who is genuinely trying to reform and one who is not. I beg you to work and study hard. Then maybe the government will forgive you."

The visit lasted maybe ten minutes, and I heard nothing but that speechifying. Yang Hui-min left me a political pamphlet and two packs of cigarettes. Yung and Mow were too intimidated to say anything. Neither of them waved as they left.

Chapter 6

IN SEPTEMBER 1959 thirty of us were transferred from the overcrowded transit center to Prison Number One—Peking's model jail. It was to be the happiest part of my incarceration.

Prison Number One had been built around the turn of the century, during the reign of the dowager empress, as a model for Chinese progressiveness in penal theory. Known officially as the Ching Ho—Clear Stream—Combined Factories, it consists of five three-story octagons (the factories) connected by eighteen wings containing cells, offices and storerooms. The cell windows are unbarred, the wooden doors left permanently open. The danger of escape is virtually nil; only a madman would exchange this paradise for another place of detention.

In the courtyard a squad of Sepos eyed us while the warders went through our belongings. "Are those all the clothes you have?" one of them asked me with a hint of surprise.

"Yes, sir."

"I see you have some very good cigarettes."

That was true. A few days before, I had received a carton of Chien Men Grandes from the consular agent who was representing France in Peking at that time. I had known him for years.

"You may smoke if you want," the warder said. He leafed idly through the dictionary and the few other books in my bundle. "Are these the only books you have?"

"Yes, sir."

"We have a library here." He made a gesture of approval. "Everything's all right. You can put your gear back now."

It was almost shocking to be treated like a human being. As we started toward the dormitories, another warder picked up my bundle—not to search it, but to carry it for me!

THE cell I was led to was about ten by twelve feet, with the usual raised wooden bed, luxuriously topped with a Japanese-style tatami mattress. A stranger who later became one of my friends—Tang Yung-ming was his name—was propped up on the bed with his bedroll behind him, reading and smoking.

"Hi, schoolmate," he called out. "Good to see you. That's your spot, but if you want to be over here by the wall, I'll change with you." As he explained the sleeping layout, I realized I would have more than three feet to myself. Unbelievable!

"What sort of rationing do you have here?" I asked.

"Rationing?" Tang had a nice laugh. "You can eat as much as you like. But sometimes you newcomers overdo it and get sick."

In a cloud of euphoria I stowed my gear and took my enamel basin down to the washroom. Tang appeared as I was drying my face. "Hey, the warder wants to see all you new guys." I ran back to the cell. By the time Tang got there I was trotting out the door. I bumped into him. He smiled indulgently. "Take it easy. They can wait a minute." I actually walked to the assembly point.

Warder Chao was the finest jailer I ever knew. Having come from the transit center, I expected slave drivers; instead, Chao was a man who respected honesty and morality. I was led to an admiration for him that bordered on love. If all Communists were like him, the movement would sweep the world effortlessly.

He was almost six feet tall, about forty, with high cheekbones and a dark complexion. In his light blue jacket, blue pants and Chinese slippers, he looked pleasantly unmilitary.

"All of you here are assigned to work in the Clear Stream plastics factory," he began. "We are very proud of this factory, because it was the first one of its kind in China. I know what you've been through. First you will all get a medical checkup and rest for a few days. You'll be eating in two hours. We're starting you on a diet of corn mush, for your own good. Maybe tomorrow you'll be able to try something solid. That's all for now. Dismissed."

In the afternoon a trusty came with word that Warder Chao wanted to see me. Chao's office was opposite our cell. He had a little desk and a bed of rough planks. Everything was immaculate. On the wall was a portrait of Mao on tasseled silk and a color photo of Chu Teh, commander in chief of the Red army. The small night table held a picture of Chao's wife and children. A plaster bust of Mao was respectfully placed in the center of the desk.

The warder invited me to sit and gave me a low-key speech. "Don't be discouraged. You will be given every opportunity here to gain merits, but unless you have confidence in us, we can't make any progress toward your redemption. I am here to reason with you. The fact that you had bad ideas and committed crimes means that we have to see to it that you start getting good ideas and never sin again. If you ever have any problems, come and see me. My door's open twenty-four hours a day."

He opened my dossier. "I see that you don't have many clothes. If your family's financial situation is bad, the government can give you some. Meantime, keep making efforts to reform, and maybe you'll be released sooner than you think. You may go."

At my first meal that evening I followed Warder Chao's orders and stuck to mush. After four bowls I couldn't fit any more inside me. I wonder how many people know how good it feels to have a stomach full of corn mush.

AFTER three days of rest I was assigned to the maintenance section of the plastics factory, responsible for keeping the machines in good running order. I was a member of *di erh tzu*—team two. Twelve of us, all specialists, lived in the relative luxury of three cells. There was no actual cell leader, but the one who performed that function on ceremonial occasions was a squat, smiling character named Hu Ting-wen. Although he was only twenty-seven, he had already served eight years of a ten-year sentence for jeering at soldiers of the liberation army.

Our team also included a Muslim from Peking, who was in charge of setting the norms for the entire plastics factory, a team orderly, and an accountant in the head office. One who became a special friend was Dai You-ling, a prison veteran whose wise advice pulled me out of trouble more than once. Square-Jaw Dai we called him.

The day began at 6:00 a.m., when a trusty awoke us with a shout. Between 6:00 and 7:00 we had time for washup (an orderly had filled our basins during the night) and a breakfast of mush or millet cooked with vegetables. I discovered that if I squirted soy sauce over the food, it became a passable imitation of the canned American soups I had eaten in Peking.

At 7:30 we went to our jobs, and lunch break was at noon—thick vegetable soup and corn bread. We were allowed fully forty-five minutes to eat, smoke and rest. No hurry. At 6:00 p.m. the next shift took over and we headed back to our cells for supper. At 7:30 we held a group discussion of production problems: "putting the heads together." From 8:00 to 9:30 was study period, at the end of which flags were issued for productive output. Our day ended with a talk from Warder Chao.

"I want you to fulfill your norms in an ordinary working day," he was fond of telling us, "and not by launching you-know-what." He was too correct to speak critically of satellites.

ALTHOUGH PRISON NUMBER ONE was the model for Chinese penal institutions, it was not without its bittersweet folklore. There was the translation brigade, for example. It could have sprung directly from the pages of Solzhenitsyn's *The First Circle*.

The brigade was made up of a hundred and forty specialists. The individual norm was four thousand words a day. They were a smart and versatile group, translating many languages.

As the tenth anniversary of the founding of the People's Republic approached, speeches had to be prepared in many languages for the benefit of visiting dignitaries and the press. With the deadline almost upon it, some government subdepartment realized too late that it had several important untranslated speeches on its hands.

In desperation someone thought of the boys over in Clear Stream. There was, the story goes, some hesitation about handing over state documents to a band of counterrevolutionaries. But it was the translation brigade or nothing. The speeches were delivered to Clear Stream on the morning of September 29. The anniversary falls on October 1.

"I've got good news for you," the chief warder announced, and the translators shuddered. "For months I've been worried over what gift this brigade could give the government for the anniversary of the founding of our state. But now our glorious task will be to translate six speeches by high officials into twenty foreign languages. Let us approach this task in the spirit of the Great Leap Forward."

They did it. Everything was ready by October 1, and the translation brigade was awarded a red flag. But the branch that did the most for the honor of Clear Stream was the electrical division, which won a red flag for putting together the two-hundred-watt amplifier that Mao himself used for his tenth-anniversary speech in Tien An Men Square.

During those giddy days of the Great Leap Forward, the official line was that socialism must be constructed by achieving better, faster and more economical results. A cook in our central kitchen decided to apply this to food production.

One of the great staples of Chinese prison fare has always been the *wo'tou*. The molded lumps of dough were placed on a perforated tray above a large water-filled wok—that ancient oriental cooking pot—and steamed until ready. Since the operation was slow and had to be repeated over and over again, our cook came up with a bright idea: why not speed up the process by using the live steam from the factories and knitting mills? He went to the warder with his idea. Cautiously, the warder said he feared it wouldn't work. But the cook trumped him with a Mao quote: "Dare to think, dare to speak and dare to do."

After talking it over with the machinists, the cook dismantled the section of the stove where the wok had been seated and replaced it with a rack of six iron pipes. From the shop he ordered square steaming trays. On the first try he put six dough-laden trays on the rack, but when he opened the valve, the blast of steam sent them flying. So he installed a more modern valve that allowed him to control the flow of steam. The result was six trays of bread cooked in fifteen minutes instead of one in half an hour. The kitchen was presented with a red flag.

The cook soon added more racks, so that forty-two trays could be cooked at one time. He was proclaimed an activist of labor, named chief cook and given a scroll. His system spread throughout the camp network. Then he invented a stamping machine that turned out *wo'tou* twice as fast as hands could.

In addition to various specialist corps, Clear Stream housed a brigade of juvenile delinquents, who would be eligible for the adult camps when they were eighteen. They worked at grinding lenses for cameras and optical instruments. Their raw material was Coca-Cola bottles. The eyeglasses I wear today have one lens ground from the bottom of a Coke bottle. Since the glass is tinted, my right lens is a shade darker than my left.

MY PRISON paradise had unexpectedly turned sour toward the end of September 1959 when the warder in charge of education and discipline gave me a long form to fill out.

My heart sank when I read it. "The government desires detailed information on the following persons: Dr. A. P., Mrs. A. P. (I am withholding their names.) Relate their personal history and dealings, their friends, activities legal and illegal, connections with foreign embassies and time spent in these activities."

At study time I filled out the form: "Dr. P. is an Indian physician. His father was a Parsi and his mother Chinese. He was educated in England and France. He returned to Tientsin in 1939 as a doctor on the Chinese railways. He married a Chinese girl and they have four children. They live in Peking. He is one of the physicians for the Western diplomatic corps."

I returned it to the warder. The next day I was called back to his office. Standing by the desk was an officer from the Ministry of Public Security—epaulets, decorations, briefcase, the works. He spoke in dry, clipped tones. "What do you take us for, Bao Ruo-wang? We are aware that Dr. P. is an Indian physician. You have been acquainted with the P.'s since 1955. You used to visit their house nearly every day. You know very well the sort of information we want from you."

Of course I did. Only they weren't going to get it. "I don't deny what you say. But I have already made my confession."

His eyes narrowed. "Be careful, Bao Ruo-wang. I wouldn't like to add five years to your sentence—"

He had given me a beautiful opening. I hit him with the catechism. "Five years for what?" I asked innocently. "I know by heart the eighty-seven articles concerning the punishment and handling of counterrevolutionaries, and the four articles concerning foreigners. Since I am not a Chinese citizen, I am not obliged to divulge everything I know for the good of the state."

"Very well," he said. "I forgot you were a foreign national. But if you help the Chinese People's Government, it won't be ungrateful. Wouldn't you like to shorten your sentence?"

"My crimes are so heinous that I consider my sentence more than just. I can only defer to the government's decision and accept it as it is."

"As you wish. But remember—I made you an offer." He zipped up his briefcase and went out.

I never saw him again. But he had been quite right: I knew enough to put Dr. P. in jail for years. He left China in 1961 or 1962 and is safe in Hong Kong now.

A FEW days after the Mid-Autumn Festival my family paid their first visit to me in Prison Number One. It was still sunny and warm in the courtyard. This time I finally had something to give the children. With the pocket money I had earned in the maintenance shop, I had bought candy and two moon cakes, the little round delicacies associated with the festival. As I approached the visiting table, a guard made a move to take the sweets from me. I gave him a ferocious look, and he let me go. My children got their moon cakes.

That evening I went to see Warder Chao. "Warder," I announced, "I hereby confess that I committed a grave mistake today. I gave one of the guards a very dirty look. I forgot that I was a convicted prisoner and that he was a representative of the People's Government. I would like to apologize."

He heard me out. His answer was a pleasant surprise. "I know what you did today. I already have the report. But you seem to think we're not human. Most of the prisoners ate their moon cakes themselves, but you gave yours to your children, even though they can buy them on the outside. I am glad you came to see me, Bao Ruo-wang. You are making your first steps toward reform. But there's still a long march ahead of you."

AT THE end of October I experienced my first full-scale ideological review. These written reviews were demanded of prisoners every three months.

Three consecutive study sessions were set aside for writing and presenting the reports. A paper had to be rewritten until unanimously accepted by one's cellmates. What follows is typical of the sort of ideological review I submitted in Prison Number One, in the form that was expected. If the reader finds it preposterous or exaggerated, he has never been inside a Chinese prison, and he is lucky. It is typical of that country, even today.

ESTIMATION, COMPARISON AND EXAMINATION OF THE PROCESS OF IDEO-
LOGICAL REFORM FOR THE MONTH OF _____ 19 _____

Name: Bao Ruo-wang
Unit: Brigade 4, Team 2

1. RECOGNITION AND UNDERSTANDING OF ONE'S CRIMES AND SUBMISSION TO LAW AND REGULATIONS

After due reflection, assisted by the teachings of the People's
Government, I have come to realize how serious and heinous my
crimes were. They have caused incalculable losses to the Government. They have caused serious harm to the People. Lastly, they
have brought sufferings upon my own family. In spite of the fact
that my crimes are so grievous, the Party and the People's Government have shown me mercy. I am convinced that my sentence
of twelve years at Reform Through Labor is a most lenient and
just one, and I should like to express my gratitude to the Party
and the People's Government. I know very well, however, that
concrete actions must support sentiments. Therefore, I am placing
my activities and achievements of the past month before the
People's Government so that it may judge whether I have done
what was expected of me.

2. PRISON REGULATIONS AND DISCIPLINE

Generally speaking, I have observed all the regulations pertaining
to discipline. To my knowledge I have not committed any serious
mistakes over the past month. However, I did commit a number
of minor errors. I have disregarded the regulations of mutual surveillance which tell us always to move about in groups of two or
more. Several times I have left the cell unaccompanied. Further,
during study sessions I have not always sat in the regulation manner, but leaned back against my bedroll. How can one learn his
lessons well if he allows thoughts of comfort to invade him? Also,
I occasionally have talked excessively during working hours. Although the subjects I spoke of were not reactionary, the fact that
they distracted the attention of others and thus impeded production
made them harmful to reform. On several occasions, too, I have
made remarks about food. Complaining about food is a concrete act
of discontent about the treatment given us by the Government. The
vegetables and cereal that I eat were produced by the labor and

sweat of the peasants. To complain about my food is to treat these peasants with contempt. I hereby promise to mend my ways and to be more careful in the future.

3. WORK

It seems to me that I have not maintained the correct attitude toward my work, and I would like my schoolmates to help me overcome this error. First, I have come to regard the maintenance shop as a kind of elite department. Pride has blinded me to the fact that we are only there to serve the machines and to make certain that the operators have everything they need. Second, I should remember that personal relationships are forbidden, and be guided by the principle: "It is the work that counts, not the person." Partiality hampers production. Third, I have at times failed to place all my knowledge at the disposition of the Government. In assigning me to the maintenance shop, the Government was displaying a high regard for my talents. The least I can do is to make full use of them.

4. RELIANCE UPON THE GOVERNMENT

I am forced to admit that when it comes to reliance upon the Government and carrying out mutual surveillance, my accomplishments are sad, indeed. It demonstrates that I am still deeply infected with bourgeois ideology. I have been reluctant to report persons who have been good to me. Further, an evil thought tells me, Don't report others and others won't report you. These thoughts are wrong! Reporting others is a two-way help: it helps the Government to know what is going on and it helps the person involved to recognize his mistakes.

5. ATTITUDE TOWARD STUDY

This is the only category in which I have made progress. Of all the schoolmates present I am the one who received the most backward and reactionary form of education. The poison fed me by the agents of imperialism and their running dogs was particularly virulent: I became an anticommunist. However, with the education offered me by the People's Government, plus the help of my schoolmates, I now realize that it was my rotten education that embarked me upon a career of counterrevolutionary and criminal activities against the Chinese people. I hope my schoolmates will help in hastening my ideological reform.

The first time I encountered prisoners actually thanking the government for their sentences, I regarded them with astonishment and scorn. Later, as in the foregoing ideological review, I went through the same motions, with the mental reservation that I was only protecting my skin; before I left the Chinese jails, though, I was writing those phrases and believing them.

Chapter 7

BY THE time I arrived there, Prison Number One had become something of a repository for the failed espionage efforts of the Taiwan Nationalists and their American friends. One of the best examples was in my cell: Li Ming, the brigade "agitprop."

Agitprop—the word is short for "agitation and propaganda"—is an institution of key importance in China today, both within and outside of prisons. The person holding the job must be able to quickly compose elaborate texts (even poetry), and must of course be familiar with Marxist dialectics and the argot of production. Above all he must have the ability to instill fervor and enthusiasm. Li had all these qualities and more. Born and schooled in Shanghai, he had the unmistakable manner of a man of culture. He was also the most enthusiastic supporter of the government line I had met—the model prisoner.

Even though he was my cellmate, I didn't quite trust Li. My resentment finally surfaced one day when he bustled into the maintenance shop, confident and dapper. "Come on, Bao," he snapped. "The warder wants to see you."

"Who the hell are you to tell me like that?" I snapped back. "You're just a con like me, Li. If the warder wants me, he can send a guard."

Li reported me to Warder Chao, who demanded that I explain.

"It wasn't your orders I was disobeying," I insisted. "What I didn't like was the way he put it. He tries to place himself above the rest of the prisoners."

"If you have any complaints," Chao answered imperturbably, "you come to see me about them."

Later I told the story to my friend, old Square-Jaw Dai. Though Dai was technically not supposed to do it, he told me Li's story. "Li was arrested in 1955," he said, "and he's going to be a prisoner for a long time. A lot longer than you or I."

Li had been a proofreader in a state publishing house and was caught with his hand in the till. Since the sum wasn't large, his crime was considered minor. Sentenced to six years in Prison Number One, he was assigned to the stocking-knitting division and was soon promoted to activist. After three or four years a new batch of prisoners arrived. Among them was a man who had been aboard a certain transport plane. . . .

The story went back to 1952. An American-made B-25 from Taiwan was shot down near Shanghai, after it had dropped five Nationalist agents by parachute. The men were soon rounded up—all but one. He made his way into civilian life and eventually landed a publishing job. That was Li.

His charade ended when one of the new prisoners recognized him as a fellow agent aboard the B-25 and informed the police, who verified the story. They bided their time and observed their man. After a couple of months they brought the unsuspecting Li before the warder and gave him the chance to tell the truth.

"Your behavior has been very good," the warder said. "Now, tell us, Li—is your mind completely at ease about your past crimes? Do you have anything else you'd like to confess?"

Li had become overconfident. No, he had nothing to confess.

"You'd better go and think it over," the warder said.

Next day, when Li returned, there was an old newspaper on the warder's desk with the headline FOUR PARACHUTE SPIES CAUGHT IN CHEKIANG.

"There's a movie playing in town based on this incident," the warder said. "I saw it, and just wanted to compare it with what the newspapers said. You recall the case, don't you, Li?"

"Well, I remember vaguely."

"It seems that one of them escaped."

"Well, it's a big country, and Chiang's spies are cunning."

Disgusted, the warder stopped the game. He held up a photograph of Li's four companions. "Maybe you'll recognize this."

Li knew the game was up. The warder said, "You know, Li, if you had told us even five minutes ago, we would have recommended leniency. Now you don't have that chance."

Two policemen burst into the office, handcuffed Li and took him to Grass Mist Lane. Three months later he was back in Prison Number One with a life sentence.

"We have taken into consideration your past behavior," the warder told him. "Usually spies go immediately to death, Li. So you see how fair we have been. Don't betray this trust."

In Li I knew one prisoner who truly was grateful for his life sentence. Now it was clear how he could sound so genuine during the examination-of-conscience sessions.

THEN there were the tattooed men. I came across several of them in Prison Number One, on one of my visits to the bathhouse. On their arms and chests they all had similar tattoos—thick forests of apple and pine trees.

I learned from little Hu, the acting cell leader, that these men were among the Chinese "volunteers" captured by the Americans during the Korean war. While they were in the POW camps, American and Nationalist intelligence had tattooed bold inscriptions in Chinese on their bodies. "Down with Communism" and "Against Russia" were two of the most common.

That was a typically devilish imperialist trick. But why were they in prison now? After all, they had fought the war and undergone this cruel treatment as well. Hu dispelled my illusions; they were in for treason, with life sentences, and lucky at that.

They were among the small number of Chinese soldiers who had been "turned around" by American and Nationalist intelligence officers. To make the ruse more effective, the agents instructed them to act as "progressively" as possible in the POW camps. Many became leaders among their fellow Chinese captives. In a fictitious act of revenge, Nationalist guards stripped them in front of their comrades and tattooed the stigmatizing slogans on their arms and chests. This, of course, caused them to act more progressively than ever, shaking their fists at prison personnel and even spitting on them. For their intransigence they were rounded up one by one and marched off to "solitary."

Naturally, the solitary never existed. The tattooed soldiers were secretly flown to Japan for specialized espionage training. The Americans kept them undernourished and out of the sun during the training period, for at all costs they had to look as though they had been roughing it in solitary. "That was all right," one of them told me later. "They were paying us well."

When the Korean armistice was signed, a U.N. armistice commission screened all prisoners to ensure that no one would be returned to China against his will. At these sessions it was always the tattooed men who screamed the loudest about the humiliation they had undergone at the hands of their captors. The Indians who presided over the commission were shocked. They arranged for new artists to come in and tattoo lush forests over the compromising declarations. The prisoners were repatriated and received like heroes in their mainland army units.

But the Americans never realized how careful and suspicious the Chinese Communists are. They have, without question, the finest counterespionage system in the world. The political police began a systematic questioning of the newly returned heroes, keeping them separated to prevent comparison of stories. Tiny discrepancies began to merge into a pattern, and the entire ring was rounded up within a month. They were summarily court-martialed, discharged from the army and sent to Prison Number One. They were lucky not to have been shot.

IN THE beginning of November our team lived through a painful experience: the announcement of the amnesties.

To celebrate the tenth anniversary of the founding of the People's Republic, Mao Tse-tung and the Chinese National People's Congress declared a special amnesty, applying to certain categories of convicts who had served a designated portion of their sentences. A condition for amnesty was that the prisoner must have truly "reformed himself from an evil past to a virtuous present." By the end of 1959 about twelve thousand persons were amnestied, including both counterrevolutionaries and ordinary criminals; nearly four hundred were lifers or men under suspended sentences of death.

Prison Director Hsing announced that only those prisoners who had served two-thirds of their terms and had earned exceptional merits would be considered. Every cell was directed to discuss the campaign, but none of us could talk with much enthusiasm since most of us were only beginning our terms. We mouthed the usual phrases a warder expects to see in a dossier.

The only exception was little Hu. "I was thrilled when I heard the news," he said when his turn came. "I have only two more years to go. In the past eight years I've been named activist of Reform Through Labor three times. I've won dozens of special prizes, and I've committed no serious sins. I think the government will let me become a free worker."

"That's not for you to say," growled Square-Jaw Dai.

In the first week of November the Peking Bureau of Public Security announced that fifty-four inmates of Prison Number One were eligible for amnesty. On a windy morning we marched out into the courtyard for the ceremony. Director Hsing and his staff gathered before us on a stage and read the names. Hu's name was never mentioned. As we returned to the cell, Hu was in tears—a rare occurrence in the normally stoic Chinese.

Warder Chao came in. "What the matter, little Hu?" he asked.

"I've always been good, Warder Chao," Hu protested through his tears. "Why didn't I get chosen?"

That sort of question was made to order for Chao. "You seem to be forgetting, little Hu, that you have no right to question the decisions of the state. The government and the Party know much better than you do. If I were you, I'd consider this a test. I think you're failing that test, Hu. Stop your bawling and be realistic. Who knows? Maybe next March when the activist elections come around, the state might make you a present."

Hu blew his nose, shut up and went back to work. Three months later his mother died and Warder Chao made an extraordinary gesture: he wangled a three-day pass for Hu to attend the funeral. As far as any of my fellow prisoners could remember, it was the first time such special leniency had been granted.

ONE day late in February, 1960, I caused a stupid workshop incident that brought me dangerously close to trouble. I was tempering a piece of steel, a routine job that involved bathing the red-hot object first in water and then, after it had cooled somewhat, in oil. Absentmindedly I tossed the still-glowing steel directly into the oil container by the wall. A splash of burning oil spread over the wall, and clouds of blue smoke billowed up. I chucked a whole bucketful of water against the wall and the fire went out. Unfortunately, Warder Chao was away that day and his replacement was a zealot who accused me of attempting to sabotage the factory! Deliberate sabotage can mean a death sentence. He sent me back to the cell to await the government's decision. As I heard the dramatized details of my crime coming over the loudspeaker system, I was scared as hell.

It was my friend, Square-Jaw Dai, who saved me. He invented some excuse to leave his work and rushed to the cell. "Quick, Bao," he said breathlessly, "write them a confession. Tell them you were careless and overlooked the fact that the oil bath is right under those wooden rafters. Tell them you recognize how serious your action was, and all the harm it could have caused."

I wrote the confession and trotted off to the warder's office.

"It's good that you realize your serious error," he said gruffly, "but it doesn't alter the fact that it could have caused many deaths. We'll show your confession to our superiors."

For the next two weeks I lived in dread. Finally, Warder Chao appeared one evening after Li had distributed the flags for that day's production. "I know you're all tired," he said, "so I'll make this short. Your schoolmate Bao, here, sometimes forgets where he is. He very nearly caused a serious incident, but at least he recognizes he was wrong. So this time we'll let him go."

I felt a surge of genuine gratitude.

"I told you so," Dai said later. "The only way to survive in jail is to confess right away and make your sins look as black as possible. But don't ever hint that the prison authorities or the government share any of the responsibility."

Around that time I discovered that I was sick. My illness came and went, and the most uncharacteristic symptom for me was that it often cut my appetite. I reported to the infirmary. The doctor gave me some pills for my indigestion, but I still didn't feel quite right. A recurring fever nagged at me and I became a regular visitor to the infirmary for their panacea: aspirin.

As SPRING approached I became progressively weaker and my bouts of fever more frequent. One day as I was carrying a heavy steel chuck to a lathe I lost my grip and the damn thing fell on my toe. The surge of pain told me the toe was broken. With my bedroll, I hobbled to the hospital, accompanied by Warder Chao.

"This is a lousy epilogue to the Great Leap Forward," I muttered. I was genuinely upset at having made myself unproductive.

"Don't worry," Chao assured me. "They won't keep you in there longer than they have to, and you need a good rest."

An orderly showed me to a spacious room with four plank beds covered with mats. A nurse wearing a white surgical mask hurried in and made me hand over the bedroll: it was too dirty for her hospital. I was happy to comply, and for the first time since my arrest I had the luxury of lying between real sheets.

During hospitalization my fever remained, though my toe was healing normally. Clearly, something else was wrong. Eventually Dr. Tan, the head physician, diagnosed tuberculosis.

Dr. Tan was a prisoner himself. He had been arrested after a futile attempt to escape to Hong Kong. Before the liberation he had been an extremely successful private practitioner among Peking's foreign colony. Though one hundred percent Chinese, he had been schooled by French Jesuits, before studying medicine at Aurora University in Shanghai. I enjoyed speaking French with him. The big escape plot had been jointly hatched between him and a Western diplomat, who was leaving the country. On a seemingly innocent pretext—an infection or something of the sort—the diplomat officially requested permission for the doctor to accompany him as far as Canton, the last big city before the Hong Kong frontier. But the police got word of the stunt and arrested Tan in his hotel room in Canton. When the diplomat called for him later, he encountered one of those marvelous Kafka–Orwell situations.

"Dr. Tan? There is no Dr. Tan here, sir. Surely you must be mistaken. Would you like to see the register?"

Doc Tan got twenty years. He was one of the few prisoners I met who seemed unaffected by indoctrination. An unreconstructed reactionary, he could always be counted on to greet the latest loudspeaker announcement with a snide rejoinder to those disembodied voices. Of course he was a regular target for denunciations and struggles, but it was common for him to be summoned by the government when some VIP was sick.

When he told me the X rays showed TB, I asked him, in French, how serious it was.

"*On te soignera,*" he promised. "You'll be taken care of."

I was transferred to the TB ward. There were fourteen of us in big, individual beds. During my two months there I met Koo, with whom I would later share some of my worst moments. Since he was almost six feet tall, we called him Longman Koo.

ON JUNE 12 we were sitting in the sunny courtyard when the hospital administrator appeared with two warders and two officials in army jackets. They spoke quietly and took notes.

"Every time they look us over that way, it means a transfer," someone said. He was right. Four days later a trusty passed out our savings books (even in the hospital we automatically earned our five yuan a month), and the next day we were sent to our cells to clear out our personal gear.

I was eating my last lunch in Prison Number One when Square-Jaw Dai came over. "I guess it's so long, Bao. I want to thank you for all the nice things you've done for me."

I was amazed and touched.

"Just remember that wherever they send you, the thing isn't to be smart or progressive. What counts is to make people like you. It's the only way to get by in the camps."

He shook my hand and walked quickly away, solid in his blue overalls and wide leather belt. He turned around and waved once.

I felt terrible. Later in the camps a former army officer, a good Communist who got denounced, told me that what the Communists feared most was human sentiment between individuals. It was the one thing they could never entirely control, and it could make for dangerously conflicting loyalties.

The warder made the official announcement that since we needed lots of fresh air, sun and good food, the government had decided to send us to Ching Ho camp. It was exciting news. We had all heard that work there was easy and that there was plenty to eat.

At 11:00 p.m. guards marched us across the floodlit compound to a courtyard where a dozen buses were waiting. We invalids piled aboard an empty one. A warder gave us instructions: behave normally on the train. Heads should not—repeat, not—be bowed. Smoking and talking will be permitted. No funny stuff. The guards have orders to shoot.

There was pandemonium on the station platform. Thousands of prisoners had been assembled. Many were on crutches and some were blind. Rows of Sepos stood silent and impassive. The train pulled in—new, shiny green coaches. We were going to the camp in style.

Our train finally left Peking at sunrise. It was the morning of June 18. We rolled for two hours to Tientsin, then on past great expanses of carefully tended fields. When we ground to a stop our car was directly opposite a huge sign in bold red characters: FORBIDDEN ZONE.

This was Chadian railroad station. We clambered down to the wooden platform. Facing us was another sign: CHING HO STATE-OPERATED FARM. On either side were large piles of dried sweet-potato slices. I thought they were meant for pigs. I was wrong.

Chapter 8

L ONGMAN KOO and I, amid the swarming crowd of prisoners, were herded down an embankment and into a field. The sun was already unpleasantly hot—by midday the temperature would be in the nineties—and a fine, grayish dust came grittily into the mouth and nose.

A warder in shorts and a straw hat clambered onto a table brought out from the station. Since we had arrived in the middle of the wheat harvest, he announced, there would be no vehicles for us. All but the crippled would have to walk to the camp, twenty-two and a half kilometers—about fourteen miles—away. He told us to bow our heads when we passed through villages and to keep our eyes from straying right or left.

We pushed off three by three. Shortly we got our first good look at the land. Close up, the fields didn't look as lush as they had from the train. We passed vineyards with yellow, curling leaves, then huge fields of corn that stretched away to the horizon, the stalks browning and stunted. The famine of 1961 was on its way.

The sun grew hotter. I put my handkerchief over my head. There were no birds, not even an insect. In the distance I saw a shady line of trees and every now and then a mounted guard silhouetted on the road.

Shortly before noon we came to the first village. It was an agricultural commune settled by volunteers. The garish cere-monial entrance was made of two red brick columns supporting signs bearing work slogans. Little knots of children watched us silently until an old man shooed them inside. We were an army of outcasts. We refilled our water bottles at the village pump and plodded on in a stupor of heat and exhaustion. The sun shim-mered on the skimpy grain. Breathing was like inhaling fire.

We finally caught sight of our camp, dominated by a tall, red brick water tower. The overall effect was that of a nineteenth-century factory or mill. The rectangular compound was guarded by a moat and a high, brick wall topped by electrified wire. The inevitable billboard proposed: LET US MAKE A DOUBLE HARVEST, ONE OF LABOR AND ONE OF IDEOLOGICAL REFORM.

We trooped into a large, unfinished auditorium, whose roof bore a huge red star. Surrounding us were rows of single-story brick barracks, each designed to hold twenty men. On the agitprop's blackboard was chalked a disconcerting message: "In view of this year's bad crops it has been necessary to reduce food allocations. Until further notice prisoners' bread will consist of millet meal mixed with cornmeal and dried sweet potatoes."

So those piles out by the railroad station weren't for pigs, after all. At suppertime we received two ladles apiece of a vegetable soup thickened with flour, and five small loaves of the sticky, sweet bread. "Do they expect us to work on that?" Koo asked.

The ten days that followed were among the most harrowing of my life. Our trainload had obviously been rushed down to Ching Ho to help salvage the damaged crops. Awakened every

morning at 4:00, we washed and gobbled breakfast as music—ludicrous, incongruous Chinese schmaltz—blared out over the loudspeakers. We were in the fields by 5:00, where the warders passed out stubby sickles, and we set to cutting the corn stalks—bent over at the waist, three stalks at a time, eighteen stalks to a bundle, to be tied neatly. At water-break time we got the warm, greenish stuff the kitchen had used for cooking vegetables. After lunch—more soup and sweet bread—came an obligatory nap in the fields from 12:00 to 3:00 p.m. We had to keep our eyes closed, even if the sun and ants made it impossible to sleep.

Koo and I were in relatively good shape, but the weak prisoners only grew weaker. The fifth day we noticed a pile of coffins by the road, and by the tenth day one of our own cellmates was in one. God knows how many died throughout the camp.

One day, when I was flailing away with the sickle, wondering seriously if I would make it, Koo came up and pulled a little watermelon from under his shirt.

"Where in hell did you get that, old Koo?"

He *wonked* the melon in half with his sickle. "Don't ask questions," he said, his face already into the cool red pulp. We buried what was left of the rinds.

Longman was a good scavenger and one of the most loyal friends I ever had. I wouldn't have survived without him.

ON THE morning of July 1—the anniversary of the founding of the Chinese Communist Party—Koo and I and some thirty others were told by the warder, "Your health doesn't permit you to stay on here. We are going to send you to a farm where there are better treatment facilities and better rations."

Our first stop was Northern Precious Village—Bei Yuan Bao Tsun. It had, we learned later, the reputation of being a death camp. It wasn't far, and we walked there in a few hours. Our compound was a distressing sight. Little groups of old men were listlessly going through the motions of existing. Many were slapping flies and placing them in bottles. There was a national campaign on for the extermination of flies, and prisoners not otherwise engaged had a quota of fifty a day. Some men were so weak that they could only crawl; some sat in the shade staring at nothing.

Even the warder was a sorry sight. He had only one arm and he looked dirty and unkempt in his ragged clothes. "My name is Wang," he said, "and I'm one of the brigade leaders. You have been sent here to join the brigade for the old, crippled and weak. But those of you who are able will be expected to work."

He led us to a row of temporary sheds made of bamboo matting, where we dropped our bedrolls. We went to the kitchen for lunch: one bowl of vegetable soup, and black-bean bread so soggy that we spooned it up rather than holding it in our fingers.

An emaciated old man in dirty white pants shuffled up. "You guys are getting first-class rations!" he exclaimed.

Koo offered him a cigarette and the old man accepted happily. "When are you getting out?" Koo asked.

"Never, man. It's one-way traffic here." He continued emotionlessly. "This is where they send the useless ones. There's no medical treatment, so not many of us can get better. But apart from the food, things aren't too bad. We can visit each other and take it easy, until . . . well, you know."

He made a vague gesture. "You are lucky to be eating so well. They must have a reason for keeping your strength up."

He was right. We had been brought to the death camp because most of its inhabitants couldn't work. That afternoon we were assigned to carrying earth in the brickmaking compound.

Four days after we arrived, Warder "One-Arm" Wang called me to his office. "Tell me, Bao, what did you do before your arrest?"

"I was a translator for embassies, Warder."

"A stinking intellectual, huh. By the time we're through with you, you'll be a new man, Bao. I have decided to transfer you to section six."

Yeh, the leader of section six, was bald, round-faced and in his fifties. He welcomed me politely. "Attention, everyone," he said, "this is our new classmate, Bao Ruo-wang. I'd like it if we could all give him a helping hand with work tomorrow so he'll be able to learn quickly."

Incongruously enough, his polite words were followed by an invitation to join my new classmates in a little struggle. The object of our attentions was seated on an old stool. He was a tanned, skinny little character about twenty-six years old, with enormous black eyes, dressed in rags and wearing a homemade patchwork hat that resembled a baseball cap. He was Pan Fu-kang—called Small Pan, to differentiate him from others with the same common name. He had never made the adjustment to confinement and food rationing, and lived in such terror of dying that he reverted more and more to childhood. By the time I met him, he was already acting like a whimpering baby. We all liked Small Pan and tried to help him.

Our struggle that night broke up in less than half an hour, with a few perfunctory accusations concerning Pan's attitude. No one had his heart in it. Yeh had the scribe record that Pan had resisted criticism that had been sincerely offered.

THE NEXT MORNING AT 5:00 I followed Yeh to the sties, where hundreds of pigs, massive and black, were struggling to get at the garbage a prisoner was heaving into their troughs. The pig yard was floored with brick, so that none of the fertilizer would be lost, and the rows of pens were freshened up each day with shovelfuls of sandy earth. Our job was to shovel the fouled sand from the pens, toss it into a ditch, then add straw to the mixture, which fermented to make a high-grade fertilizer. We would then scoop the muck out, pile it in mounds and repeat the process. There are many ways of building socialism.

Yeh called a break at 10:00. I was about to light up a cigarette, when he stopped me. "You're wasting that," he said. He broke my cigarette open and dumped the tobacco onto a little square of newspaper. From a cloth pouch he poured out an equal amount of dried wild mint leaves, mixed it together and rolled two fat cigarettes. "Here," he said with a laugh. "Have a menthol smoke."

I was surprised at how rapidly I became accustomed to the pigs' stink. That evening I saw Small Pan was eating a rotten tomato from the pig slops. I was appalled, but I, too, would eventually eat worse things than rotten tomatoes. By the following week the farm's food supply had suffered so from the drought that a system of official scavenging was instituted. Our rations were to be stretched with wild vegetables and weeds. I remember in particular the stems we called *ma erh tsai*, which looked something like green spaghetti when they were boiled. Just to keep things fair and square, we also fed wild vegetables to the pigs.

After work that first day everyone but me changed to a set of clean clothes. I didn't have anything else to wear. Yeh took me over to the library. The librarian was a tall old man named Hsiung, quite distinguished looking in his horn-rimmed glasses, white jacket and pants, and black sandals. In a storeroom opposite the library, dozens of used shirts and pants were stacked next to a pile of shoes. I grabbed one set of everything.

Hsiung told me he had been sent up for thievery. "I stole lots of stuff," he said. He busied himself with an abacus, then took a slip of paper, entered my name and added some figures.

"What's that for?"

"Your allowance. You get two yuan on the fifteenth."

"Does everyone get allowances?"

"No. Only those who work."

I noticed a chart on the wall, filled with little squares.

"The cemetery," he said. "We enter the name in each square so we can keep track of who's buried where."

A few days later I ran into Koo, who broke into peals of laughter. "They've got me watching cows and I think I'll stay there, old Bao. I'm not a snob, but you smell worse than they do!"

THE barber in Northern Precious Village was a squat little fellow, in his forties, who stuttered. While he gave me the required military-style trim, he told me he was in on a morals charge.

"Don't spend too much time around him," Yeh cautioned me. "He's a bad example." Coming from Yeh, that was strange. He was intelligent, cultured, and scarcely bothered with doctrine.

One rainy morning a few weeks later, whistles suddenly started blowing. *"Ji ho!"* It was the call for assembly. We straggled into the steamy courtyard. I was in the front row, next to Yeh.

The first one to appear was Wang, our one-armed warder. He was followed by Yen, the production brigade leader; a dozen guards; and an official in a blue Mao uniform. In the midst of them all was the barber, his hands tied behind his back. A rope around his neck, cinched at the waist, kept his head bowed. The guards shoved him directly in front of us.

Yen had a speech. "I have something awful to speak about," he began. "This rotten egg here was jailed on a morals charge: homosexual relations with a boy. He received seven years. His behavior was bad and he stole repeatedly, so his sentence was doubled. Now we have established that, while here, he seduced a mentally retarded prisoner nineteen years old. If this happened in society, he would be severely punished. But by doing what he did here, he also dirtied the reputation of the prison and the great policy of Reform Through Labor. The representative of the Supreme People's Court will now read you his sentence."

The man in the blue uniform strode forward and read out the somber document: death, with immediate execution of sentence.

I didn't even have time to be shocked. Before the man in the blue uniform had finished, the guard standing behind the barber had pulled out a pistol and blown his head open. I looked away from the twitching figure on the ground and vomited.

Yen spoke again. "Let this serve as a warning to you. Now go back to your cells and discuss this."

Morals offenses are not treated lightly in the socialist countries, and even less so in China. Sodomy and rape can be punished by death. Females get five years for adultery or fornication. A married man who seduces a married woman gets ten years. Lesbianism has always been rare in China, and the once widespread male homosexuality is no longer tolerated.

AT THE end of July old Yeh announced that our section had been assigned to burying the dead. "I guess they figure that since we're already doing the dirtiest work," Yeh said, "we wouldn't mind taking on the burial detail, too." In return we were to draw maximum rations and an extra meal, and could keep small things we found on the bodies, like cigarettes and soap.

The next evening we had our first "assignment." We heaved him, fully clothed, into a handcart with bicycle wheels and hustled him up to the graveyard on the hill. There was a beautiful red sunset and cicadas were singing in the trees. The grave was ready. We dumped him in as he was—there were no more coffins—covered him with his sleeping mat and quickly filled the hole. Small Pan looked on in horror.

The next morning we were called again. This one, by the looks of him, was from a good family. His coat was clean, his coverlet of silk. We gathered his fountain pen and books to send to his family and heaved him into the cart. My toe ached with each step. I had hurt it several days

ago and now it was infected. Suddenly Small Pan detached himself from the others and threw himself at the feet of the guard
witnessing the burial. Two men pulled him away.

On the way back Yeh told me Small Pan had begged the guard
to send him back to Peking. He was sure he would die if he stayed
in Northern Precious Village. Back in the barracks the guard
ordered us to struggle him. We compromised by giving him a
group-criticism session, but Pan just stood there in that little
peaked cap, his shoulders heaving in grief.

The infection in my toe soon spread through the lymph
glands and formed a boil on my groin, and I had to go see the

doctor. He told me that the combination of my TB and the bad rations made the boil extremely serious, but that it wasn't yet time to operate.

One night in August I was left to carry out a burial alone. I pulled the rickshaw to the back shed. When a prisoner was in his last hours, he was carried there to expire, out of sight of the others. It was better for morale. A guard helped me load the corpse, and I had to walk more than a mile with it behind me. The moon was nearly full, but I didn't look back. The head of the corpse thumped against the side boards of the cart as if the man were alive. When I buried him, his eyes were still open. The next morning I asked One-Arm to make sure I would never again have to handle a night burial alone.

During August, September and October we buried nearly three hundred prisoners.

SUMMER was over by the middle of September. The rains came more regularly, and the cold became acute. Throughout, my pal Koo kept on as the master scavenger. He set something of a record one week by catching both a chicken and a hedgehog, which he shared with a few of us. Longman cooked the game in the classic peasant style, packed in sticky clay and hung for a few hours over a fire. When he broke the clay open, it fell away from the meat, pulling the skin with it. A little wild garlic and some salt from the horse trough, and we had a memorable feast.

In the first week of October the doctor finally lanced my boil. Since there was no anesthetic, and he was not a practitioner of acupuncture, I had only a rag to bite on. The operation was a success, though, and I could feel myself getting stronger during the five days of rest that One-Arm gave me.

On October 13 the warder sent for me. A horse cart attended by Longman was standing in front of his office. One-Arm, who had once called me a stinking intellectual, told me that because of our good efforts Koo and I were being transferred back to Ching Ho farm. We were among the few to leave Northern Precious Village to rejoin the living.

THIS TIME WE SPENT only a week at Ching Ho. On October 20 all prisoners were called into the auditorium. The deputy director announced, "I have good news. You are going to set up a new farm in Manchuria. You will have the glorious task of producing more food for the country and raising the people's standard of living."

"Come on, applaud!" demanded an agitprop. We brought our palms together in the open-handed Chinese manner.

The deputy director continued. "You may invite your families for a visit if you wish. You will be leaving in four days."

There was no way to bring our families down on that short notice, but form had been served by his giving permission. "You must volunteer," he went on, "but we can take only those who are fit."

In the days that followed we repeated the delicious hearsay of abounding food up north: the lakes full of fish; the woods of wild boars; the fertile soil which hardly needed care. But a few old hands who had been there gave us the other side. Prisoners wore handmade straw shoes in the winter, they said, because in any boot manufactured in China one's feet were bound to freeze. The trick was to line the straw shoes with a special grass called *woo la ts'ao* to avoid frostbite. In summer, huge, powerful mosquitoes filled the air.

On October 24, seventeen hundred of us piled into trucks to be driven back over the fourteen miles we had walked from Chadian railroad station. Each of us was toting a bundle containing a black, padded jacket and pants, rubber-and-canvas boots, and a fur hat with earflaps. As our train pulled away to the north, we put on our jackets. The cars were barely heated. The next morning at dawn we hit Harbin, China's northernmost major city, built by the Russians during the time of czarist imperialism. In the distance we could make out the onion domes of the Orthodox cathedral.

Our terminus was Miyun, a small city in Heilungkiang Province, where we piled into canvas-roofed army trucks for the ten-hour ride north. Two soldiers guarded the back of each truck.

At the village where we stopped overnight, the air was bracing and clear. In the brightly lit kitchen tent, smiling civilians generously scooped out our first hot meal in two days, an unforgettable noodle dish, brimming with soybeans. Though fairly shaking from the cold, we were alive with excitement. We hustled to the dormitory tents, burrowed into the straw covering the earth floor and fell into deep slumber.

The next day we followed new, well-maintained dirt roads north to Hsing Kai-Hu—Lake of Emergent Enthusiasm. All around us we saw cultivated fields, barracks, watch towers and villages, and prisoners going about their work. Everything seemed orderly and well tended. Our guards made no attempt to stop us from talking or smoking.

We reached our unit at 4:00 p.m. The brick dwellings looked solid and comfortable. As our trucks halted we were astonished to see a big paper banner bearing the message: WELCOME TO OUR NEW SCHOOLMATES. Around it were beaming faces and waving hands; the resident prisoners beat on little drums and rattled cymbals. We who were accustomed to being treated like vile, crawling things were being welcomed as heroes! When we jumped down from the trucks, prisoners offered to carry our bundles.

After a cup of tea a husky warder, wearing a sheepskin coat and a brown fur hat with a red star, said to us, "You are in number nine farm, located on some of the worst land in Hsing Kai-Hu. It was set up for people who wanted to make an extra effort and show their gratitude to the government. My name is Hsu. You may voice your problems to me whenever you like."

We had a first-rate meal and were taken to our cells. Between the walls of the brick huts were hollow spaces for fires, so the cell units were radiantly heated.

We began work the following morning—tying up the spreading leaves of giant cabbages which were about to be harvested. There were no norms; we were told that a man's rations could be cut for improper attitude, but not for low production. We responded by giving ourselves totally to the job at hand. After a few days in the fields I was truly happy to be in the Barren Lands.

FIFTEEN DAYS LATER my world fell apart. I was called in to see Warder Hsu. "It is my duty to inform you that you are in deep trouble," he growled. "I won't tell you now what is wrong, but I want you to go back to your cell and think what it could be. Tomorrow someone from Peking will speak with you."

I was horrified. "Is it something from my past?"

"No. It is something that happened since your arrest."

When I returned to the cell, I saw that Longman had been called in, too, and another classmate, Chi. What could it be?

In the morning two jeeps came for us. I was scared. We drove to the headquarters of the farm. An officer, inspecting me from beneath bushy eyebrows, said, "You are a foreigner. Why didn't you tell them at Ching Ho when they transferred you?"

So that was it. I felt relieved. "I didn't know I had to," I said. "Five months ago, when I was transferred out of Prison Number One, I told a warder I was French and he said nationality didn't matter."

"Well, it does matter," the officer said. "You're going back."

Longman Koo and Chi got the same treatment. Neither held a foreign passport, as I did, but they both came from overseas Chinese families. Apparently the Sino-Soviet border was such a delicate trouble spot that no foreigners or persons with families living abroad were allowed in Hsing Kai-Hu. We were a dejected trio as we boarded the train back south.

AT CHING HO farm we were driven to branch farm three and incorporated into team one of the fifth brigade. There were sixteen in the team. Lo was one-quarter American. Soong, who had been an apprentice at the Peking Opera, had the graceful effeminacy of some Chinese males. But he was also deadly serious and one of the best workers in the camp.

The most extraordinary-looking member of our team was Lin, a powerful old man of sixty-five who had been a warlord in the 1920s and later a general in the Nationalist Army. With his barrel chest, Fu Manchu mustache and completely bald head, he could have stepped from the pages of a Chinese adventure saga.

There were also two English-speaking intellectuals: Ku, a young student from Peking, and Jimmy Ch'in, a Cambridge graduate who became a great pal of mine. Small Pan had been released from Northern Precious Village and was back among us, too.

Longman was named cell leader, which was fine with all of us. He found himself appointed to one of the easiest but most tortuous jobs of all: kitchen worker in charge of divvying up the rations.

And then there was Lao Sun. Fair skinned and strikingly handsome, he had been a good Communist, a graduate of the police academy and a member of the new Communist Youth League. "Something went wrong with my ideology," he told me with a light laugh. "I don't know if you could call it counterrevolutionary, but I got sent up for illicit sexual relations with the wife of my boss, the police chief. It wasn't very smart of me."

Finally, there was Leong, the son of a rich Shanghai family that had fled to Hong Kong when the revolution came. He had stayed behind and eventually was arrested. The family sent him food parcels, filled with smoked delicacies, perfumed soap and the like. But the only time I saw him happy with the parcels was when he found a two-pound tin of refined lard. That was useful—he could mix it with his soup to make it richer.

I WAS assigned to the fields, picking up cabbage leaves with Lin, our own warlord. It was a pleasure to be around this cheerful, strong old soldier. He had been arrested a year after the revolution and given ten years. "At first I thought it was beneath my dignity to work," he said, "but the camps taught me the value of labor. I'm thankful to them for that."

We all liked Lin, and we looked forward to his release almost as much as he did. On Christmas Day of that year he would become a free worker and fulfill his dream of dying at home with his children and grandchildren.

A week before Lin's release our cell was directed to make a collective appraisal of him. Each of us had to give his opinion of Lin's merits and judge whether he was worthy of the government's leniency. We gave him a clean bill of health and sent the paper off to the warder.

Two days later a guard called Lin to the warder's office. He was back fifteen minutes later, and his face told us that something terrible had happened. He sat on the bed staring into space. That evening he told us what had happened. "I have something very painful to say, schoolmates. I'm afraid my graduation won't be for some time yet. When I went to see the warder, he had a man from the People's Court with him. He told me that I had never confessed sincerely. He accused me of being a mass murderer.

"I couldn't believe my ears. Then he told me that during the war against Japan, some men from my regiment had massacred the population of a Communist village. I knew that, but I hadn't even been at the scene of this massacre. I was away and had left the command of my regiment to another man. They told me I still bore the responsibility, because I was in charge."

The government sentenced Lin to twenty more years. He collapsed and was carried off to the infirmary. He came back a month later, but he hardly spoke anymore and didn't even bother to work. He used to wander around the farm mumbling to himself. They finally came and took him away.

MEANTIME, Small Pan was dying of TB. Even he knew it was terminal when they transferred him to the little hut for the hopeless cases. Late one afternoon Longman and I found him huddled in his bedclothes against the back of the shed. His face was gray.

"I'm finished," he whispered. Longman asked the ritual question: was there any last thing he'd like us to do?

To our surprise, he said, "I wish I could have a piece of cake."

All the poor little guy wanted on his last night was a lousy piece of cake, but he might as well have been asking for the moon. I was amazed to hear Koo promise we'd be right back with it. Out in the yard he explained: we would steal the cake from Warder Yang's office. Prisoners' food packages were always locked up there for safekeeping. Koo went straight to our team and talked with a man named Wong, who was in jail for safecracking.

Wong agreed unhesitatingly. "Just give me one guy for a look-out by the big gate and another outside the warder's door."

When the warder had gone to the canteen for dinner, Wong attacked the padlock on his door with bent wire. Within ten minutes he was back with a piece of almond cake. Longman and I took it to the death shed. Small Pan was barely alive, but Long-man bent down and placed the cake in his mouth. He died without finishing it.

We went back to the cell in silence. Before lights-out Wong showed up and offered us a smoke. He had fresh tobacco! We asked him where it came from.

"Well," Wong said, "when I was feeling around there in the dark trying to find the cake, I smelled this good stuff and I couldn't resist it." We had a smoke in Small Pan's honor.

As THE autumn of 1960 drew on into winter, our food situation steadily worsened. With the bad harvests, there simply wasn't enough to eat in China. As in Northern Precious Village, foraging teams were appointed, and wild plants and vegetables, dried like shocks of hay, became staples. The daily fare was the black, soggy sweet-potato bread. There was no meat or fat.

That fall was exceptionally cold. Half starved as we were, our energy didn't last long. From the remains of an old tent we fash-ioned spats to keep the mud and pebbles out of our shoes, and rough work mittens. Like the Russian prisoners in Siberia, we sealed our loose clothing by tying bits of string tightly at the ankles, wrists and waist, to keep our body heat from escaping. We were a sorry, inefficient bunch of laborers.

On December 1 our working day was shortened from nine hours to six. The result was a slower pace, with more free time and more sleep and studies; but it didn't make us any stronger or less hungry. In the last days of the cabbage harvest we were all mo-bilized to get the vegetables in before the snows rotted them. Every time a guard turned his back, whole teams of harvesters plunged their heads into the fat cabbages like bunnies and ate out the hearts.

Chapter 9

BY THE end of November I had picked up the rhythm of existence at Ching Ho. I was a professional prisoner by then, and felt that I knew how to survive. As Solzhenitsyn wrote of the Soviet camps, many better men than I broke and many stronger ones died. The strange laws of chance are always in effect.

The signal that truly desperate times were upon us came in early December, when a horse-drawn cart entered the compound. The cargo was dark brown sheets of paper pulp, and we were going to eat it. Food substitute, the prison officials called it. (We prisoners had the honor of being the guinea pigs for the various ersatzes the scientists came up with.) The warder told us that powdered paper pulp was guaranteed to be harmless, and though it contained no nutrients, it would make our *wo'tou* fatter.

Sure enough, our *wo'tou* the next day were bigger and we had the pleasant sensation of putting more into our stomachs. They tasted like normal loaves, though a bit limper. That evening I saw Ma Erh-kang, the prison doctor. He was worried about the ersatz. "If I were you, Bao, I'd try to eat some fat," he advised.

"You're joking," I said. "Where in hell am I going to get fat?"

He shrugged. "I don't know, but I wonder what that stuff will do to the digestive tract. Paper absorbs moisture."

A few days later the "health-preservation diet" was announced, for prisoners who would be holding key jobs during the winter months and whose strength would be needed for the crucial spring planting. About thirty of the almost three hundred men in our brigade won places on the list, among them our cellmates Sun and Soong. The diet consisted of millet flour without ersatz and a soup made from vegetables, often laced with horsemeat or oil.

But Sun and Soong were too embarrassed to eat their food with us. They emptied their tin mugs, brimming with horsemeat soup, into our communal soup tub. "Your health needs preserving, too," Sun growled. "You can report me if you like."

It must have been those two extra portions of fat over the next two weeks that saved our cell. By Christmas Day the whole farm was in agony. Just as Doc Ma had suspected, the paper pulp absorbed the moisture from our digestive tracts, making it progressively harder to defecate as each day passed. And painful. Men were bent double with cramps. Alarmed, the prison authorities finally gave us straight mush and instructed us to drink lots of water. But many of the older and weaker men died.

After paper pulp flopped, someone in central planning came up with the bright idea of trying plankton. Plankton was said to be almost a hundred percent protein. They skimmed the slimy, green stuff off the ponds around the camp and mixed it with the mush—it was too horrible to eat unaccompanied. Again we all fell sick, and some of the weaker ones died. That particular plankton, they discovered after a few autopsies, was practically unassimilable by the human body. End of plankton experiment.

At length our daily ersatz became ground corncobs, mixed in with the *wo'tou* flour. Afterward it was adopted as the standard food supplement for the country at large. We had been pioneers.

Two little images stay with me from that period around Christmas 1960. The most important job at that time of year was fertilizing the fields. Sun and I were watering down one of the big manure dumps one afternoon to help it ferment. We worked in silence, trudging back and forth from the water trough with yokes on our shoulders, balancing two buckets apiece. Suddenly Sun put down his buckets and stopped. A look of resignation and bitterness replaced his normally stoic expression.

"Tell me, Bao," he asked numbly. "Do you think I'll ever have a full meal again?"

"Sure, Sun," I said automatically. "Sure you will."

He gave me a dirty look. "When, Bao?"

We went back to work and never brought up the subject again.

For four or five days around the same time I was detailed to team up with Shau, a man from another cell. He had been a pedicab driver in Peking. He was tall, with broad shoulders, a head he kept shaven smooth and the musculature of a weight lifter. He was famous around the camp for his capacity to absorb work, but instead of gaining merits by overfulfilling his norms, he used to let the weaker prisoners claim part of his production so they could hold on to their rations.

As we worked together, Shau and I reminisced about places we both had known in Peking. Some of his preferred pedicab customers, it turned out, had been my colleagues in the American Marines. He remembered them as good tippers.

Shau had the best vision of anyone I had ever known. Radar Eyeballs, they called him. He had an uncanny knack for discov-

ering stray cigarette butts. A butt meant either a valuable piece of barter currency or a few luxurious moments of surcease from the despairing tedium of camp life.

On Christmas, Shau and I had been spreading manure over the wheat fields all morning long, and we took a break. "This is the foreigners' big holiday, isn't it, Bao?" Shau asked.

When I told him he was right, Shau reached inside his jacket and drew out a little square packet of neatly folded newsprint. "Here's something for your holiday, then."

I was surprised and a little embarrassed, but I took it nonetheless. Inside the packet was a lovely cigarette butt about an inch long. I automatically asked him if he would share it, but Shau said no. It was to be my present alone. I smoked it after supper that night, for my Christmas celebration.

WITH the increasing scarcity of food, we prisoners developed quasi-religious rituals around it. Persons starving and yet regularly supplied with a small quantity of nourishment eat slowly to prolong the pleasure, but I wonder how many others ever went to the extremes that we devised at Ching Ho farm. Bits of food that I now eat in two minutes I would draw out for twenty minutes then. Small, bite-size morsels we divided even smaller. Many of my friends ate only half of their *wo'tou* in the morning and held on to the rest all day long, as a supplement for supper. They carried these treasures hung around their necks, in beautifully made little bags embroidered with their names.

Everyone fashioned his own chopsticks, and the cleverer ones sharpened the ends to spear rice grains, pieces of *wo'tou* or, if it was a special day, meat. The chopsticks, too, had their custom-made cloth covers, decorated with the owner's name. Early in 1961 spoons became the rage: everyone scavenged for scraps of metal to tap out into the desired form. I still had an aluminum spoon my wife had brought me in Prison Number One.

The champion stylist of all, though, turned out to be Lo, our assistant cell leader. He began to whittle and polish a piece of cast-off bamboo with that traditional prison tool, a piece of broken glass. What finally emerged was a hybrid instrument with a delicately fashioned knife at one end and a spoon at the other. I was mad with desire to own one, but Lo's price was too high: six cigarettes. Then he and I discovered that I had gone to school with his uncle. In honor of this he whittled me a knife-spoon, and I carried it with me throughout the rest of my time in jail as my most treasured possession, after my Chinese-English dictionary. Lo spent probably twenty hours making it.

I ENTERED 1961 with what my warders would have called a high ideological level. I was convinced that if the government didn't exactly love me, it was doing everything reasonably within its power to keep me and my comrades healthy, considering the bad times. I also knew that, as a foreigner, I was the only one who stood any chance of leaving the prison and getting out of China, so it was very much in my interest to keep as close as possible to the letter of the law. For this reason I refused to forage in the fields or to steal food systematically as many did, with the result that I was growing weak and I tired easily. My legs felt like cotton and my head was always spinning. One morning, after I fainted in the fields, Sun sent me to see Dr. Ma.

Ma had already been in Ching Ho for two years when I arrived and had managed to turn a cell between the noisy kitchen and a latrine into the semblance of an infirmary. Now about forty-five, he had been a successful practitioner, with a clinic in Peking. His downfall came as the result of an abortion he performed for the wife of a Party member. Abortion is legal in China, but the husband suspected his wife of infidelity and denounced Ma for having acted without proper authorization.

When he took my blood pressure, Ma clucked his tongue with displeasure. "You're not in good shape, Bao," he said at length. "I've got to prescribe a long rest for you."

That would certainly entail a major cut in rations. I begged him not to do it.

"Your blood pressure is unbelievably low," he told me. "Excuse me for asking, but do you forage?"

"Not much," I said.

Ma gazed at me through his heavy glasses. "You're a man of honor, Bao, but as a doctor I must tell you that sometimes it's better to be less strict about interpreting regulations. I've got people here who are too far gone to help. I wouldn't like you to get that way." He pointed to an edema case I had seen before. The man's legs and feet were grotesquely swollen, the result of months of water-drinking and malnutrition. He might never walk again, Ma confided to me. I decided I would go foraging.

On my first day all I managed were two shriveled turnips and a few pieces of cabbage leaf. Soong, the opera singer, laughed when he saw them. "That ain't much, Bao," he said. "I think you need some help to get started. Come on." He grabbed his pull-cart and made straight for the hothouses. Full of apprehension, I followed. He parked the cart near the door, took a quick, expert look around, then pulled me inside.

"We're not supposed to be here," I whispered absurdly.

"Don't worry, Bao. We've just been dumping a load of manure, right? Grab yourself a turnip."

There were long rows of fresh young vegetables. I pulled one; it was big and fat and beautiful. I stuffed it quickly into the bag under my jacket and we beat it outside again. That night, while Sun and Soong kidded me about losing my ideological virginity, I ate that turnip. It was delicious.

"Good, ain't it?" said Soong with satisfaction. "Only from now on, remember to keep a few extra for a rainy day."

He laid out his store for me to see. He had turnips, cabbage leaves, some soybeans and even some garlic cloves marinating in a bottle of brine. This was scientific foraging—he could leave part of his hoard behind when he was in the fields. The men in our cell would never think of stealing from one another.

I was learning, but a few days later Warder Yang caught me red-handed. He ordered me to follow him to his office with the vegetables. I knew I was in for at least a lecture.

"I thought you were a man of honor," he began, "but now I see you're no different from the others. What you have done here"—and he began to enumerate my sins one by one on his fingers—"is, first, proof that you are discontented with what the government is giving you; second, stealing government property; third, inducing others to criminal activities; and fourth, unhygienic. You can ruin your health with dirty food. I want you to take this stuff and throw it out."

"Warder Yang," I protested miserably, "please don't say that. It took me days to find this stuff. Put me in solitary if you like, but don't make me throw away food."

There was a long silence. He watched me with resignation. "Bao, you'll outlive these temporary difficulties, but will you be able to face yourself after stooping so low?"

"Warder, it's one thing to talk about honor here, but you're on the other side."

"Yes," he agreed quietly, "but my stomach's just like yours. Go on back to your cell." He made a little waving gesture with his hand. "And take these with you."

I scooped up my treasures and trotted back, filled with admiration for my jailer, but shamefaced too.

THE most terrible collision I witnessed between hunger and petty regulation happened on the day before Chinese New Year, when I had orderly duty in the visitors' room. It was an easy job, consisting mostly of stoking the little coal stove and running errands for the guard who witnessed the meetings and weighed the food parcels visitors brought. The limit was ten pounds, but the more understanding warders rarely put it to the test. The guard that day, though, was a literal-minded bastard.

The day's first visitor was a soldier in officer's uniform, carrying two heavy parcels. The guard received him next to the long table under the portrait of Mao. At the far end of the table there were a clock and a set of scales. "I've come to visit my brother," the officer said, producing his authorization from the camp director. The guard sent for the prisoner, a handsome man named Hsu. His pants were tucked into his boots, Russian style, and his beard, black padded jacket, and scarf gave him a piratical air.

"Please open the parcels," the guard said. One bag contained canned foods—fish, meat, chicken, oil, and some preserved fruit. In the other were fifty small loaves of wheat-flour bread.

"He is permitted only ten pounds," the guard said.

As he put the bundles on the scales the soldier protested. "It's Chinese New Year. Can't you let him have more?"

"No. Ten pounds and no more."

Hsu kept his mouth shut, but his glance darted back and forth between the two. The visitor finally became angry and tried a dangerous flank attack. "In that case, comrade," he said firmly, "I would like to see your superior."

Perfectly confident, the guard left, and returned later with Liu, the warder in charge of education and discipline. "Well," Liu said with a phony smile. "What seems to be the problem here?"

The visitor was taken in by the smile. "I get to see my brother only once a year. I've come very far and I've brought him some New Year presents. I admit it's more than the regulations allow, but I thought maybe you could make an exception in this case."

Liu picked his way through the pile of food, making little grunts of displeasure. When he looked up at the visitor he let fly. "And you call yourself a member of the armed forces? What sort of ideological standards do you have, anyway? The peasants and workers can't enjoy these delicacies, can they? But because you have been given the glorious honor of protecting the fatherland, the working classes have made sacrifices to provide you with these things. They have given them to *you*—not to a counterrevolutionary! This man isn't your brother. He is your enemy!"

The soldier had been ideologically trapped and knew it.

"Comrade," Liu snapped, "you will now please give me your unit number and the name of your commanding officer."

The soldier had no choice but to comply. Liu was a member of the national security police.

"Now take all this back," Liu said. "And by the way, this prisoner would tell you himself that he doesn't need any parcels from you. He lacks nothing here. Isn't that right?"

"Yes, of course," answered Hsu obediently.

THE CHINESE DIVIDE winter into nine periods of nine days, beginning December 21. By the fourth period the temperature was dropping to around twenty below zero. According to regulations, we were not required to work if the thermometer read twenty below in still air or fifteen below with a wind blowing. Every morning we waited for the gong to tell us whether or not we would be heading for the fields. How many times have I lain with the others, fully clothed under the bedcovers, hoping against hope that one or two degrees would save us from work, while at that very moment a trusty was climbing the ladder up the big wooden gallows where a section of rail hung. When he hit it with the hammer—always nine strokes—it could be heard for miles.

"Assembly!" a warder would cry, and we would pile out.

During the days we spent indoors, our study sessions increased. The aim was to keep our minds occupied, develop our reliance on the government and make us forget as much as possible about eating. These almost never-ending studies constitute the main difference between Chinese and Soviet prisons. A Chinese prisoner is practically never left alone to think independent thoughts.

Occasionally the study sessions would turn out to be comical. One evening, after an unusually tough day in the fields, the theme was loving labor. Longman Koo, as cell leader, was directing the session. "Each of you will tell what he thinks it is to love labor," he said. "Soong will preside with me. Bao, you start."

"Loving labor is forgetting what you were in the past," I said. "It is doing your level best at all times, without complaining or asking for favors."

Soong objected. "You are speaking like a stinking intellectual."

"Loving labor is doing more than the government asks," another cellmate said.

But Soong still wasn't satisfied. "No," he insisted, "you're all wrong. You speak about doing more than the government asks, but that's just empty talk. What if tomorrow there's a force-seven wind blowing and the temperature is fourteen below? Not fifteen, but just fourteen. I'll bet neither of the two prisoners who spoke just now would go out fifteen minutes early in the morning and wait under the rail, hoping the trusty will come out and hit it. Now *that* would be loving labor. I'm sorry to say that none of us here loves labor like that."

Warder Yang, going from cell to cell, heard Soong's talk and concluded that our attitude was far from serious. He ordered us to drop labor and take up another theme: Socialism is good. We were to get our thoughts straight by meditating for fifteen minutes beforehand.

Yang should have known better. We were bone-tired. After a few minutes of meditation most of us were fast asleep. When Yang came back to check on us, he was the picture of outraged virtue. "What's this?" he exclaimed.

"We, ahh . . . were meditating on Socialism," Soong stammered.

Yang stood there glaring, hands on hips. "If I questioned you one by one," he said, "you'd swear on your grandmothers' heads that Socialism is good. But I know that deep down inside you're saying that Socialism doesn't feed you enough."

"Look, Warder," Sun said without a hint of sarcasm, "you said it, not us."

Yang sighed and left.

SOME weeks later our fifth brigade was incorporated into the fourth brigade. Our team went over intact, except for Soong, who was made leader of team seven. His place in our cell was taken by the Reverend Father Peter Hsia.

What a man he was! If all Catholic priests were like him, there would never be any crisis in the Church. Father Hsia was a Trappist monk from Yangkiaping, a small, frail, sunburned man in his late sixties, with bushy eyebrows and only a few wisps of white hair on his head. After he arrived in the cell he began asking me dangerous questions. I was extremely wary.

"John is a Catholic name," he said softly. "Are you a Christian?"

"That's none of your business," I told him.

"My name is Peter," he said, and then clammed up. He wasn't going to push it.

Father Hsia gave himself to his work with incredible conscientiousness, in spite of his frailty. He was forever apologizing if he made a mistake or carried less than the strongest ones.

To ensure that he held on to his class A rations, Koo ordered the rest of the team to help the old man with his norms. That bothered Hsia. "If I can't finish my work," he protested, "I have no right to the higher rations."

But late in April it became apparent that at least one cellmate didn't approve of the little priest. Some of us were called in one by one to see Warder Yang.

"Bao, are you withholding something from the government?" I didn't know what he was talking about and said so.

"You know Christian activities are not permitted in the cell. What's this about Hsia? I hear he's been praying in bed."

Yang was right, but I was certain he had no proof. "If he has been," I said, "I'd be the first to know. I don't practice Christianity anymore, but I can still recognize prayers."

"Well, then, what's this mumbling I have been hearing about?"

"Warder," I explained, "Hsia is an old man. Old people talk to themselves; it even happens to other people, too. Sometimes when I can't get to sleep, I tell myself stories."

"*Shen jing bing,*" he said disgustedly. "You're all lunatics."

After Longman went through the same interview he returned to the cell in a controlled fury. "I am all for confiding in the government," he said. "It means you are on the road to redemption. But if anyone makes false reports, he is committing one of the worst crimes there is." The incident was closed, and we never did discover who had told on Hsia.

The priest also used to hear confessions in the fields for some of the prisoners who had remained Christian. During breaks, when we would be resting in the sun, a prisoner would sit next to Hsia and tell him his sins while looking up at the sky. We could see their lips moving, but they never looked at each other or made any gestures. Hsia probably would have loved to make the sign of the cross, but it was just too risky. "Your sins are forgiven," he would say to the sky, and the prisoner would wander away.

Once I overheard an amazing exchange, when a devout Christian came to him troubled about the morality of stealing extra food.

"Do the guards know you people are stealing?" Hsia asked.

"Sure."

"Well, then," the old man said, "if the government lets you get away with it, then the government is pretty kind, isn't it? Do you think God will be no better than the Communists?"

Father Hsia was certainly the finest Christian I have ever met. The great Catholic martyrs may have endured more pain, but their faith could hardly have been any greater than that of this stubborn little old man. He deserves to be canonized.

Chapter 10

As WINTER gave way to spring, our slower schedule was replaced with an eight-hour workday. Tractors were still not being produced on a large scale, and horses and oxen were scarce. So all the moving of rock and loam, and the digging of irrigation ditches fell directly upon us. We were weak from malnutrition and disease, and I was among those who couldn't keep the pace.

Two incidents stick in my memory from that spring. The first was when Lei Ying-fang, a master forager, cracked up. He had been complaining more and more bitterly. When the lunch cart came out to the fields one day, he grabbed his *wo'tou* and broke it in half under a warder's eyes. To everyone's surprise, he began to curse the government loudly, first for starving him and then for forcing him to eat a *wo'tou* that was half ersatz.

"Be quiet and eat your lunch," the warder said. But Lei spat and hurled the offending loaf to the ground. That was a criminal gesture, and the warder had Lei thrown into solitary.

Then there was Lam, who was about fifty and had been in the camp since 1951; several times he had been named activist of Reform Through Labor. One day a warder found a bag of corn hidden among his belongings. What made it a serious offense was that it was seed corn stolen from the supply shack.

Warder Yang said, "That bag contained enough grain to grow an acre of corn—enough to feed a whole team for a year. Stealing food is bad enough, but this prisoner sabotaged production. And that is unforgivable."

Lam got five more years added to his sentence.

THE comical side of our life was evident more rarely, but it was there—like the morning when one of my cellmates awoke with an exultant cry. *"Pao ma!* I've been horse racing." Horse racing is the Chinese slang for having a wet dream.

"Shut up," Sun told him. "If the warders hear that, they'll cut your rations. You've got too much energy."

The question of sexuality in the camps fascinates everyone, especially Westerners, scores of whom have asked me how we endured the lack of women. Weren't we tormented by erotic fancies? The answer is no. In the first place, Chinese are less frenzied about sexual matters than Westerners. But far more than that, inadequate diet and exhaustion had made us for all intents and purposes impotent. Survival was our only preoccupation. Any one of us would have preferred an extra *wo'tou* to a woman. And one last point: sexuality is ideologically incorrect in China.

EARLY in May, Dr. Ma put me on health rations. But this did not prevent me from growing weaker every day. By harvesting time I could no longer fulfill my work norm. The team had carried me for several weeks, but it was impossible to hide my low performance forever from old Chao the peasant. I lost my class A rations.

Within two weeks Longman and Sun had to carry me to the infirmary. I had amebic dysentery, I was anemic, and my blood pressure was drastically low. Father Hsia advised me to pray and reminded me that man does not live by bread alone.

"No, Hsia," I agreed, "but it helps."

The infirmary rations were an improvement—wheat-flour noodles, bread, dried meat, sometimes bean paste—but I was feeling too terrible to eat.

That first evening, Sun appeared for a visit, still dusty from the fields. "Well, old Bao, how are you?"

"No good, old Sun. Bad." I felt utterly hopeless.

Sun leaned down. In his voice there was a bitter intensity. "You're going to die, then? You're going to let them kill you?"

"No one's killing me," I said, but I knew how his mind was working. No one is more rancorous than a fallen Communist.

"Fight it, Bao," he said, "fight it."

I was too tired to argue. "Okay, Sun," I promised, "I'll try."

"Good." Sun handed me three eggs! Scrounging a turnip was one thing, but eggs were almost unheard of.

"Where in hell did you get these, Sun?"

"They've been boiled," he said evasively. "If I were you, I'd eat the shells, too. Calcium. And there'll be no traces."

I knew that the only place where he could have found the eggs was the warders' chicken coop. The next evening Longman fed me a stew of wild vegetables, frog meat and a few grains of rice from somebody's provision sack. It was thick and hot, and as a gourmet touch he had added a pinch of salt swiped from the horses.

My team's intensive-care program continued for three weeks. By mid-July I was sitting up on my pallet. As soon as I was able to totter to my feet, I asked Warder Yang to put me back to work in the fields.

"The wind would blow you away, Bao," Yang said. "You have the proper attitude, but stay in the hospital and fatten up first." I spent the next month tidying up the infirmary and helping out in the kitchen. It wasn't real work, but it made me feel useful.

After that my recovery was rapid, and I was soon out in the fields with the others. The greatest pleasure of working in the fields (besides serving Socialism) was catching the frogs that proliferated there. We would skin them on the spot and eat them raw. Those with greater discipline would dry the meat in the sun to make a type of jerky. Roasted on a stick, they tasted like bacon. When there were wild vegetables, we would make stews of them.

Around wheat-threshing time I witnessed a terrible suicide.

As we were sitting in the shade for our midday meal, a prisoner in a tattered white shirt and blue pants ran with desperate energy toward one of the big wheat-chopping machines. Before anyone could stop him, he had dived into the blades. I never knew why he did it, but that kind of suicide wasn't rare in the camps.

In early September, Sun explained to me why my cellmates had taken such good care of me. We were taking a break and rolling ourselves a couple of vine-leaf smokes. Sun gestured broadly out at the fields. "Look at that, Bao, isn't that a magnificent sight?"

The sky was intensely blue, with rich, billowy clouds. The grain stretched to the horizon with nothing breaking the pattern except a long row of trees by the main highway. Everywhere there were men, thousands of them, bareback or in black shirts, bent to their work.

"All those people," Sun said, "and none of them will ever make it out, me included. You're the only one who might get out the big door some day. It could happen to a foreigner, but not us. You'll be the only one who can tell about it afterward if you do. That's why we wanted to keep you alive, Bao."

I was touched, but didn't quite feel his optimism. "I don't know if I'll live that long, Sun." That wasn't pessimism—in the year since August 1960, more than three-quarters of our brigade had died or been dispatched to Northern Precious Village.

Among the transfers into our team that summer was a young Chinese from Indonesia named Lu Ke-hsi, who surprised me with his knowledge of the degenerate outside world. I used to call him Luke. One afternoon in the fields I was humming "Cherry Pink and Apple Blossom White" when Luke joined in.

"Where'd you learn that?" I couldn't help wondering.

"Indonesia," he said proudly. "And I know plenty more."

We were like kids trading bubble-gum cards. I was transfixed when he gave me a rendition of "The Tennessee Waltz." It took me back to the days before my arrest. Luke had forgotten the words and asked me to help him. It was forbidden to write anything in a foreign language, but he slipped me a piece of processed American cheese, part of the booty from a parcel from his family, to refresh my memory. The cheese inspired me to let him have "Vaya con Dios" as well. Later Luke gave me a chocolate bar for the words to "I Went to Your Wedding."

WITH the corn harvest, we tried to steal as much as possible, but the guards were clever. Every day upon returning from the fields they had us search *each other,* in pairs. It was effective; they knew how much we feared that they might double-check. As a result, we quickly learned to "uncover" some contraband in every search. Each team would agree in advance to designate one man as the guilty party for the day. This way each of us took a few demerits every month for the good of the group. And as far as the warders were concerned, form had been served.

On October 1, National Day, we had a feast. But later we learned that the rumored boost in rations would not come with the harvest after all. Just before the film (it was *The Five Golden Flowers*) Liu climbed up on the stage to give us the news.

"Some people have dared to say," he observed, "that the People's Government hasn't kept its word because you haven't gotten a big boost in rations. Well, you are now eating a couple of ounces more than in the winter. And we cannot allow professional provocateurs to incite you to laziness, so we are going to give two of the worst offenders what they deserve."

The guards dragged two prisoners off for a week of solitary. It looked as if we would stay hungry for a long time.

One of the best ways to forget food was by smoking. Tobacco was just about nonexistent by then, but we found all sorts of bizarre substitutes. The men with real tobacco in their pouches were the closest thing in Ching Ho to millionaires.

The thought of smoking caused weird frenzies of voluptuousness! It finally got to me the day I heard that Gu Wen-Xuan, a smart aleck in one of the other teams, had received a parcel with sixty leaves of high-quality tobacco. Those leaves became an obsession to me. I finally had to go and ask for his terms.

"Let's make a fair exchange," he said. "How about your Roget's *Thesaurus* for ten?" He spoke some English and this would obviously be a treasure for him. I tried other propositions, but he was adamant.

"F—— you," I told him in English. He didn't need a thesaurus to understand that.

"That's all right," he said blandly. "The offer still stands."

For days, whenever I saw someone smoking, my mouth watered. A week later I went to see him again.

"I don't have much left," Gu warned me. "Tell you what, I'll make it fifteen leaves. You can choose the ones you want."

I caved in, and handed over the *Thesaurus*. I kicked myself afterward, but those smokes tasted wonderful.

A FEW weeks later my wife brought little Yung for a visit. I had not seen them in over a year and a half, and we had become virtual strangers. Yung answered my questions with the shy diffidence reserved for schoolmasters. Cowed by the guard, Hui-min and I exchanged platitudes about how well the government was taking care of us. They had brought some cakes, and we ate them together in silence.

Despite governmental rhetoric, however, she and the boys were only one step from hunger. She was "not qualified" for a skilled job, and she was then earning about six dollars a month by doing housework and watching over sick neighbors.

They missed the last train for Peking that night and Warder Yang put them up in a visitors' dormitory. The next morning I was permitted to accompany them to the main gate and say good-by. During the lunch break I went to the Warder's office and thanked him.

"Your behavior has not always been perfect," he said, "but we don't feel that that should deprive you of the pleasure of seeing your loved ones. So show your thanks by deeds."

AROUND the end of November I had an ideological problem. It was frightening, not only for me but for my fellow prisoners and for the Chinese population in general. It concerned Sino-Soviet relations.

The moment had finally arrived when the masses had to be told what the Party already knew, that the great socialist ally to the north, the one everyone had known until then as Elder Brother, was in reality an evil fraud. All of China had to readjust its thinking; it was time for white to become black.

In Ching Ho our ideological retooling began with the newspapers regularly circulated for our studies: the *People's Daily* and the *Kwang Ming Daily*. At the twenty-second congress of the Soviet Communist Party, we read, Khrushchev had attacked Stalin more virulently than ever and had ordered his body removed from the Lenin crypt in Red Square. Premier Chou En-lai had left Moscow without waiting for the congress to end.* The Russian press obliquely attacked China through Albania,** call-

---

* Delegates from Communist parties in 83 countries were present, and Premier Chou headed the Chinese delegation. [Editor's note.]
** In June 1960 Albania had publicly supported Communist China in opposition to Khrushchev's policies of de-Stalinization, and from 1961 to 1963 Albania served as the proxy through which the USSR and China carried on their polemics. [Editor's note.]

ing it dishonest and ungrateful for past Soviet aid. The *People's Daily* by indirect formulation accused the Soviet Union of letting Albania down by withdrawing technical help. In short, the world was falling apart.

We had learned our ideological catch phrases long ago and felt able to respond to almost any new situation. But now we were suddenly thrust into uncharted territory. We felt our way with desperate care, afraid that one slip could mean another five or ten years. "It is better to say little," says a Chinese proverb, and although Warder Yang constantly encouraged us to speak our minds, it was more than two weeks before anyone could bring himself actually to cast concrete accusations against the Soviets.

The ideological flip-flop may have had something to do with what happened next in the camp. Our living conditions had not improved, and our diet was still part ersatz. When winter returned to torment us and when at the same time the government suddenly directed us to make an intellectual ninety-degree turn, it was simply too much for some of the men. On the morning of December 8 I saw the only strike I ever encountered in the camps.

At the work lineup, when the warder asked about sick call, fifteen men stepped forward. Many were cell leaders or activists of Reform Through Labor. Longman was among them. The rest of us were too astonished to do anything but stand and watch.

"You have five minutes to get examined," the warder said.

"We're not sick," one replied. "We just won't go to work."

The warder put me in charge of our team and marched us off to the fields. In the evening Longman Koo's sleeping place was empty, so I became cell leader for the time being. The strikers were put in a punitive cell, with rations of corn mush and water, in an effort to compel them to work for Socialism. I saw Longman only once after that, in the presence of guards. I never learned why he had decided to take such drastic action.

THE last extraordinary experience I had at Ching Ho was the Christmas Mass of Father Hsia. That morning dawned bright and clear, with the temperature close to zero and a force-five wind roaring down from the northwest. The eighteen men under me were working in a plowed area about two miles long and a hundred and twenty yards wide. I divided my group into five teams of three men each, and sent the remaining three to gather scrap wood for a bonfire.

Around 9:30 I noticed a solitary figure hurrying toward me across the strip. I could tell from his gait that it was Hsia. The earflaps of his ragged hat danced in the wind, and his faded army overcoat and padded pants were splattered with mud. With exaggerated politeness he asked if he could have a few minutes' break. He knew we had a deadline for our job—couldn't he wait until lunch? Pained, he looked down.

"Don't you remember what day it is, John?" he asked me in English.

Of course. I had been thickheaded. "Go on, old man," I said, "but be careful."

He smiled and scurried away to a dry gully where the bonfire was burning, and where he was shielded from the wind and from the view of the warders. A quarter of an hour later, I saw a bicycle against the sky—a warder on his way. I hurried to warn Hsia.

As I looked down the embankment I saw that he was just finishing the mass. A mound of frozen earth was his altar. He was making the traditional gestures of priests all over the world. His vestments were ragged work clothes. The chalice was a chipped enamel mug; the wine, some improvised grape juice; and the Host, a bit of *wo'tou* he had saved from breakfast. I knew it was the truest mass I would ever see. I loped down the embankment, and when the warder rode past he saw only two prisoners warming their hands.

Two days later Warder Yang pulled me and a half dozen others out of the morning lineup. "The government has decided to send you back to Peking," he told us. "Don't forget that wherever you are sent, you are still undergoing Reform Through Labor. Continue to work hard and obey the government."

I asked if I could say good-by to Koo, and was pleasantly

surprised when he nodded his head. He walked with me to the punishment cell. Longman looked drawn and depressed. We had been through a lot together since Prison Number One.

"I'm glad you're leaving," he said as we shook hands. "I'll say good-by to Sun for you."

"Okay, Koo," I said, and I found that I was in tears.

"No displays of emotion!" the guard ordered severely.

"Stow it!" I said, and brushed past him out into the courtyard. Warder Yang didn't say a word.

Chapter 11

A T THREE in the afternoon a truck picked us up. All the other passengers were Koreans. I now realized that this transfer involved foreigners exclusively.

We arrived around 7:00 p.m. at Chadian railroad station. The platforms were teeming with prisoners—about seven hundred, I later learned. Most of them were *Lao Jiao* people who had served short terms in Manchuria. We lined up for tea and *wo'tou*. Then I returned to my place with the Koreans.

Their leader, Rhee, was a good-looking, lithe young man. The first part of his name, Yung Jün, most appropriately meant Ever Handsome. He had achieved notoriety as one of the rare prisoners to stage a successful escape from the camps. I had heard about him in Ching Ho.

He filled me in on the details. He had crossed over from North Korea to China in 1954, and had become a "big wheel." He rode around China with false papers and lived by stealing from trains. Rhee baffled the police for two years, but was finally arrested in 1956. He served time in Manchuria until 1960, when he became seriously ill and was sent to Ching Ho camp. During his long convalescence he became an unofficial orderly for the patients and warders, shopping at the cooperative whenever anyone had a bit of money, taking messages and the like. Bit by bit over the months he socked away quite a lot of small change.

In August 1960 Rhee took around forty Chinese yuans (about sixteen dollars), changed into his cleanest, best-repaired clothes, set off on foot for the co-op and kept on going, straight to Chadian railroad station. Everyone assumed he was a visitor, because he looked too well dressed to be a prisoner. He bought a ticket south, and he lost himself in Shanghai, where with his affable manner and good looks he quickly found a woman to take care of him. After a couple of months he borrowed fifty dollars from her and moved on to Tsingtao, where he attempted to repeat the same routine. His mistake, though, was to latch on to a married woman. He was discovered when they tried to get a hotel room and his papers were checked.

He came back to Ching Ho in chains, and they gave him a full month of solitary. It was already November, and the fact that he survived made even the guards admire him. Rhee was tough.

OUR transfer train finally pulled in around midnight. I nodded through the next several hours, but even in my stupor I couldn't help noticing that my Korean mates went to the latrine over and over again. I assumed they had been drinking too much water. At 7:30 a.m., under a bright sun, we arrived at Peking.

We piled out onto an eerily empty platform. A line of guards clutching submachine guns stared at us from behind gauze surgical masks. Orientals favor these masks to prevent the spread of colds, but those guards wearing them were like faceless automatons. Their muffled voices ordered us to form up in groups, and we climbed into beautiful red Czech buses and drove through Peking's busy streets. The housewives were firing up little stoves on their front steps, and there were vendors selling fruits and vegetables and steamed bread. Everywhere people were pedaling to work on bicycles. As we passed out of town fields appeared, and finally at around 9:00 we arrived at the red brick complex of buildings that was our prison. No sign identified the place.

The room assigned to the Koreans and me was distressingly barren. The concrete floor was bare, and half the windows had no panes. One light bulb hung from the high ceiling. The only source of heat was a stove in the hall. The warder sent us downstairs for straw, which we piled on the floor and held in place with bricks. We plugged the windows with paper. Soon there was bad news: the warder had been told of our arrival too late and had no food for us. We would have to wait until evening to eat. I stared into space and tried to make my mind a blank.

"You hungry?" Rhee's voice came crashing into my reverie.

"I don't appreciate the joke, Rhee," I answered testily.

He reached inside his shirt and handed me two small loaves of bread. They were made of wheat flour and were delicious. Then Rhee pulled forth a leaf of real tobacco.

"I don't mean to pry," I said, "but how in hell . . . ?"

"Remember on the train? You didn't really think we had to go to the latrine that often, did you, Bao? One of the guys found a bag of bread and a pile of tobacco leaves in a cupboard near the latrine. Must have been the warders' rations. There were so many of us on the train, they'll never know who took the stuff."

One of the Koreans toasted a hunk of bread on the stove. When the delicious smell went wafting through the building, the warder came galloping back. "Where'd you get that?" he demanded angrily.

"From my former camp," the Korean answered. "I'm toasting it because the doctor said it was better for my digestion."

The warder glowered, but had no real response.

NEXT morning the prison director, a fat little man named Chia, gave us some details. Our new home was called Liangxiang— Virtuous Village—Prison. To the outside world it was known as the New Capitol Electrical Machinery Factory. Its products were cheap aluminum goods, mostly pots and pans. The irony was evident; they were replacing steel pots and pans that millions of families had tossed into the collection bins during the Great Leap Forward.

For several days there were no work assignments for us, and we passed the time lounging and talking. Any illusions we harbored about food were dispelled. Veterans told us that the only place prisoners still got decent food was in Prison Number One.

Naturally, there were solitary cells—just in case—and the story I heard about them warmed my heart. At first the men of the construction battalion had built solitary cells that were more like dog kennels. Each was four feet high, three feet wide, and long enough only for a man to sit with his legs folded. When Director Chia saw them he ordered the chief architect and five of his foremen to spend five days inside their creations. After they were released they built new cells that differed from the standard cells only in that they had no windows. They were the nicest solitary units I had ever seen. I was happy not to try them, though.

The walls surrounding Liangxiang were about thirty feet high and formed a six-hundred-yard square. Besides the big, double-doored main entrance, there was a little door at the back, called *Tai Ping Men*—Gate of Peace. The only prisoners who passed through that door were in coffins. Ten yards in from the wall and running parallel to it all around the compound was a strip of whitewash painted on the ground—the forbidden line. Anyone venturing beyond it was to be shot without warning.

Besides me, our cell contained seven Koreans and two Japanese, so we were called the foreigners' team. Over the next few weeks I frequently caught sight of two large, pale-skinned prisoners who were the only non-Orientals I had seen in jail since Bartek. They were descended from White Russian settlers, and had no place to go home to, even if they were released. They looked strikingly out of place among all the Asians, especially Butolin, who had a great, Rasputin-style beard.

The first break in our routine came on January 3, when a tall man in a military tunic and surgical mask came to our cell. He was Li Tien-you, one of the prison doctors, and he checked our medical histories. In Chinese his name meant Heavenly Friend, and so he turned out to be. When our cellmates were assigned regular work shifts, Li ordered a few days' extra rest for me and another prisoner who had TB.

A functionary in the Ministry of Health, Li had accompanied

Chinese delegations abroad, but during a conference in Karlovy Vary, Czechoslovakia, he had let himself be tempted by a female comrade from the Czech side. When he returned to Peking, he was accused of illicit sexual relations. Naïvely, he had assumed that making love with a sister-Party member was ideologically satisfactory; but his superiors' only consideration was that she could have been a secret agent. Li got three years, and had already worked them off. He was a free worker when we met.

CHINESE New Year fell on February 5. After our meager supper the Koreans gathered in the hall and sang their country's wailing folk songs. I grew fretful and depressed, thinking of my family. Their New Year, I knew, would be even hungrier than ours this time, since my wife had written me that she had lost her ration book. I had invited Hui-min to the first visiting day after the New Year, but had no idea if she would be able to make it.

Later that night my Korean cellmates decided to augment our New Year meal. After the warders had gone home we scuttled down to the kitchen, set up lookouts and went to work. One man rapidly assembled five lengths of bamboo pole which had been concealed under clothing, and fixed a stiff, wire hook to one end. As usual, the kitchen window had been left slightly open to let out steam. On a table inside was a big pile of freshly made bean curd. We had buckets ready. The new curd was so firm that when the hook bit in, it lifted up from the table like magic. For his second act the Korean hooked some cabbage leaves and a bundle of vermicelli. We were all set to call it a day when Yoshida, one of the Japanese, decided to try for the gourmet touch. He attached his drinking mug to the wire and lowered it into a big earthen pot of soy sauce. Back in our quarters we made a communal stew on the stove in the hall.

Next day in the yard I ran into a man named Fourcampre. He was a Franco-Chinese *métis* like me, and I had known him in my childhood. He had become a free worker and so had the occasional chance for a visit to town. My spirits rose when he told me he had seen my family. They would be coming to visit me for sure.

As he had predicted, my wife and children showed up on visitors' day, February 11. It was obvious that they were in a bad way. Yung, the little one, solemnly handed over a package of biscuits. Selfishly I took it, without thinking that he probably needed it as much as I. As they were leaving I asked the warder if they could have three dollars from the pocket money I had earned, but my wife refused. In her next letter she told me that the warder had slipped her the three dollars from his own pocket.

THE recurrent TB had weakened me, and the dizzy spells still hadn't left me. At the infirmary I was pleasantly surprised to see that the head doctor was a man I knew—Yen, the bearded northeasterner who had been my second cell leader in the transit center.

"Well, so it's Bao," he said affably. "How did you get here?"

"With the other foreigners," I said, and told him about my symptoms. Doc Yen found a cavity in my right lung, but there was little he could do except assign me to light labor. Two days later I left my cellmates and moved in with the sick men.

We of the light-labor brigade lived in tents and did such chores as scraping bark from tree branches with pieces of broken glass, to be used by other prisoners for making baskets. Naturally, our decreased work loads were mirrored by lowered rations. I was down to less than thirty pounds a month—not much above starvation level. The consolation was that as a foreigner I benefitted from a new rule proclaimed that very year that accorded me a double portion of vegetables, the reason being that foreigners stood less of a chance of receiving food from their families. I was still permanently hungry, though, and after a month I asked to be put back on a regular work detail.

"Your duty is to do as the government tells you," the warder said. "When the time comes for you to leave the light-labor unit, you will go, no matter what your wishes are."

LATE in May we moved into a newly completed building. The cells were luxurious: whitewashed walls, high ceilings, plenty of light from twin windows, central heating, and straw mats on the floor. The warders were overweeningly proud of this building and made us maintain the cells with the same attention to petty detail as the boot-camp barracks my Marine friends used to describe. I was in charge of the windows and had to clean out the corners with a sharp stick after polishing the panes with damp newspaper. The warder also demanded that we polish the wooden floor so that he could see his own reflection in it.

Another innovation was the weekly lice inspection. The idea was intelligent, but it was a ludicrous routine: every one of us stark naked, teamed off two by two, picking over each other's bodies like so many curious monkeys.

In mid-June a security hysteria seized Liangxiang. The Taiwan Nationalists, hoping to capitalize on popular discontent bred by the famine, had attempted several landings along the coast. As usual, though, they miscalculated. As it turned out, the uprising they hoped for was directed against them as invaders. They never got anywhere, but they were taken very seriously.

Our mail and visiting privileges were cut off, and we were ordered to devote every study session to the Taiwan threat. The worst part of the new measures, though, was that every window in the prison had to be shut and curtained from dusk to sunrise. Sleeping in the stuffy rooms was a terrible trial, and a prisoner in another cell got himself into trouble over it. About 4:00 a.m., when he saw a faint glowing in the east, he opened the window. "Thank goodness," he said, "the day's here at last."

At the weekly examination of conscience an ideological warder ordered the prisoner to make an account of himself. The man gaped and stammered as the warder strode out of the cell. "But I don't know what he's talking about," he protested.

"Make an effort," the cell leader said.

Finally a cellmate accused him of wishing for the return of the Nationalists—hadn't he exulted the other day that a new day was dawning? He furiously denied any such intent, but the authorities refused to accept his denials. We struggled him for three days until he finally threw up his hands and said, okay, he had been hoping for the Nationalists.

I WAS TRANSFERRED AGAIN, this time to a special sick cell, after an X ray confirmed my TB. My jaw dropped when I saw that my new cell leader was none other than Ever Handsome Rhee. I don't know how he had managed to get transferred off work, but he was full of tricks. He immediately slipped me a pack of cigarettes. He got them from other prisoners, he explained, by the old Ching Ho general-services technique, the most profitable of which was Rhee's tailoring business: he made pants, jackets and even caps from any old cloth a prisoner managed to scrounge up. Rhee could do anything with his hands.

Life was pretty good in the sick cell. As a foreigner I was allotted not only extra vegetables, but ten and a half ounces of tobacco a month. The tobacco helped me forget the lack of food.

One memorable character in the cell was an old fellow named Wong, who had worked as an army medic for the Nationalists. He was a doctor of traditional Chinese medicine— herbs and acupuncture. That folk science was not then held in the esteem it now enjoys, and most of the prisoners used to refer patronizingly to Wong as "the Mongolian doctor"—Chinese slang for a quack. He took the kidding with aplomb. His great day came when one of the warders was stricken with a terrible toothache. It was impossible for him to get into Peking that day, and Dr. Yen's aspirin tablets had no effect. Wracked with pain, he called for Wong and his needles. It was child's play for Wong— toothache is one of the easiest things for acupuncture to cure.

Wong became a hero. From that moment on, he treated inmates side by side with the prison doctors. I, too, had a toothache that Wong fixed in a matter of seconds. But the most extraordinary sight was the way he took care of one prisoner who had epileptic seizures. He stuck needles in his upper lip and toes, and calmed him every time.

One odious zealot in the cell enjoyed informing. I had a bit of fun with him. We were speaking of sentences, and I told him that I deserved to be in for one day.

"One year, you mean?" he corrected me.

"No," I insisted. "One day."

He reported me for mocking the system of reform. When the warder inevitably came, I was prepared. "He must have misunderstood," I told him, in all innocence. "I only meant that I was thinking in the spirit of the Great Leap Forward."

The warder had nothing more to say. The slogan of the Great Leap Forward was "One day equals twenty years."

From my friend Fourcampre I learned about life as a free worker. Free workers were little better off than prisoners. They were organized into brigades exactly like ours, were locked into their cells at night, arose at the same hours, performed the same work, took part in the same study sessions, examinations of conscience and ideological summaries, not to mention the mutual surveillance and denunciation expected of them. True, they were permitted home visits twice a month if they had the money, but they were also eligible for solitary if their ideologies slipped. Of their average salary of twenty yuan a month, about fifteen went for food, which was no longer provided by the government, and tobacco; the rest was spent on items like uniforms and electricity fees. But at movies the first ten rows were reserved for them. That was something.

I often discussed the free-worker situation with the chief warder, a man named Tien, whom I came to admire. Like all the good warders I had known, Tien adhered strictly to the Maoist principle that the man who speaks his mind commits no fault.

"What's the use of making big efforts to reform ourselves," I once asked him, "if we end up with just about the same thing when we're through?"

"You've got your political notions all mixed up, Bao," Tien said patiently. "Most of you come to these places with no training or skills, and it takes the government lots of time and money to bring you up to the technical levels for the jobs you do here. Do you seriously think all that time and money should go to waste?"

That was a hard one to answer. Tien went on. "The records of the free workers are such that we have to be wary of them. It's true that they have expiated their sins. But if you drop a plate, there will always be cracks no matter how carefully you glue it back together. So why not keep them in the jobs they know? The government is served, and in the long run they're happier."

Elegant old Wong became a free worker while I was in Liangxiang. But by then he was too old to work. "Young fella," he told me in English, "things couldn't be better. Or worse. I offered to teach law or translate, but the state didn't want that. So now I'm living on fifteen yuan a month and they give me a little over thirty pounds for a ration. When I save a little money, I go into town and have a meal or see a movie, or I buy a book. You can come and visit me when you like, and we can talk some English together, no matter what they say."

Wong didn't give a damn anymore. Several months later I saw him being pushed by a guard toward the solitary block.

"Wong's problem," one of the other doctors said, "is that he's too American. He can't get over his mission-school childhood."

As MY internment in Liangxiang drew into 1963, my ideological progress had become so striking that Warder Tien appointed me deputy cell leader. It was quite an honor for a foreigner. Although I was not at all healthy, I had taken to the rhythm of the place and was, in my own strange fashion, happy. The news from home was bad, and my wife was making oblique references to a possible divorce (her only real chance to regain a decent standard of living), but what could I do about that?

By the summer of 1963 our living conditions improved slightly. We had rice or wheat flour at least once a week. As a sick person I was given only nominal jobs—picking metal scraps from slag heaps and cleaning sand from aluminum castings. I devoted myself more and more to studies and self-criticism. When my zeal was rewarded with approval, I began giving long discourses about imperialism, Soviet revisionism, or whatever subject was in vogue. I had become, if you like, brainwashed. Or perhaps I had simply accepted the bargain that my life in Liangxiang tendered to me: follow the path marked out for you, don't make trouble, and you will be comfortable.

The single exception to my good behavior was the letter I tried to send to the French consular agent in Peking. It rankled me that in the six years I had been imprisoned I had received nothing more from the French than two cartons of cigarettes and a little cash, while my family had been given only laughably small handouts of money. Yet the consular agent had known me well. France and China had no diplomatic relations at the time, but he was unofficially recognized as representing France's interests.

I decided to act. I asked Fourcampre to carry a note to the agent next time he went to Peking. The note was in French:

> I am writing you in haste. As you know from my wife, I have been sentenced to twelve years of labor. I assure you that the Chinese are treating me correctly, but my family is in a bad way. My own needs are modest. I need only some clothes and two dollars a month to help me through this bad period. Thank you in advance.

Unfortunately, Fourcampre was searched at the gate and the note was found. I was called in to see Warder Tien. "Tell me," he began, "are you satisfied with your ideological status?"

It was the old game of cat and mouse. And I had to play the innocent, even though I was ninety percent certain of what it was all about. "The government always knows what offenses you have committed," he continued.

"I can't recall anything."

After five or six more minutes we arrived at the point. "Do you know, Bao, the penalty for passing notes to the outside? Especially in a foreign tongue?"

I admitted everything. Poor Fourcampre got four days in solitary, but I was luckier—Dr. Yen examined me and told Warder Tien I was not fit to undergo solitary. I could have sworn he winked at me behind the guard's back.

Warder Tien ordered me to write him a report on my crime. A few days afterward I was called to the office of one of the ideological warders, a tall, strong, bearded man in the uniform of an officer in the People's Liberation Army. "Your confession is acceptable," he said. "Luckily for you, you didn't slander the People's Government when you asked the Frenchman for help. Considering that your motives were not reprehensible, we have decided to be lenient. If you have hardships, come to us. If we can help you to solve them, we will; if we cannot, we will at least give you an explanation."

"The government is doing enough for me already," I insisted. "But the consular agent gets money from the French government to help French citizens. It's his duty to help me."

"There are channels for that. What is it you want now?"

"Permission to write him again."

"Write a request to the factory director."

I pondered the situation. It was important to remain within the correct ideology. This was the letter I finally wrote:

REPORT
To: The Factory Director

Convict Bao Ruo-wang of Team Four, Seventh Brigade, respectfully submits the following to the Factory Director:

Of late I have been assailed by serious ideological problems which, if left unsolved, could have an adverse influence upon my reformation. Because I place full reliance upon the government, I am now exposing my innermost thoughts. I hope that the government will help me solve my problems and give me the necessary education to set me right.

From newspaper articles concerning the treatment meted out to Chinese subjects illegally detained in camps by the Indian expansionists (*People's Daily*, August 12 and 28, 1963), I have learned that Chinese consular officials have been denied the right to correspond with their compatriots, to visit them and to provide articles they need. As a result these detainees are now living under precarious and straitened circumstances. Moreover, they are permitted only two letters per month to the Chinese consulate, and in the English language only.

My first reaction was indignation and shock. However, very soon I began to have bad thoughts. I asked myself: Why does the Chinese government accuse others of doing things that she does herself?

Months ago I requested permission to write the Frenchman X for some material assistance. This man X looks after the interests of France and French residents in China, although he is not officially recognized by the Chinese government as a diplomat. My dossier will show that in the past the government has permitted me to receive some assistance from him. But my request to write him has not been answered to this day. The Chinese detainees are allowed to write two letters a month, but I, apparently, not even one.

Is it surprising, then, that I am beset by serious ideological problems? How can I pursue my reformation as the government wishes when the government demands of others what she is not willing to do herself? I know that these thoughts slander the government. However, I would not be sincere if I kept them hidden. My purpose in exposing them is to obtain the education needed to correct them. I hereby request that the authorities accord me the help for which I have so much need.

IT was more than two weeks before there was any reaction. Obviously my case had gone to the public security offices in Peking. I was finally called in by a discipline-and-education warder named Hseuh. He was officious, but accommodating. "You have a nerve," he began, "to make disparaging remarks about the government. Do you realize what the consequences for actions like that could be?"

"Yes, Warder," I said humbly, "but I have been taught that prisoners who reveal their thoughts to the government commit no sin and will go unpunished."

"The consequences could be frightful if you persist in harboring evil thoughts," Hseuh said stiffly. "However, you know that the government is always ready to listen to you and to help you solve your problems. Now tell me—what exactly is it you want from this man X?"

"I would like some material assistance."

"The government is looking after your needs."

"I know, but I would like to be able to help my family, too."

"Have no worries about them," he said with the usual fatherly assurance. "The government is conscious of their hardships."

"I was only trying to lighten the burden of the government."

We both knew it was a lie, but it was the correct ideological response and Hseuh accepted it. "Your attitude is good, but let the government make its own decisions. Now, then, we never turned down your request to write this Frenchman. We were merely studying the matter. The government will solve all your problems in due course. You may write this man X if you like, but there is no guarantee that he will help you."

"Permit me to report that I have a new bad thought."

"What kind of bad thought?" he asked suspiciously.

"You tell me I may write X, but at the same time you predict that nothing will come of it. I am wondering if this means my letters will not be mailed."

"You are speaking honestly, Bao, but you are also insolent. You may be assured that your letters will be mailed. Do you realize now how wrong you were in making those baseless accusations against the government?"

"Yes," I agreed humbly. "I beg the government to forgive me."

"All right then," he said with satisfaction. "You may return to your team now."

As I was walking out, he volunteered one last thought. "The letter must be in Chinese. And it must bear no return address."

Chapter 12

I SENT out eight letters in all, and the French consular agent never troubled to answer one of them. I hid my bitterness and sank more deeply into the life of Liangxiang.

At the study sessions I now became one of the stars. My gift of eloquence earned me a nickname—the storyteller. The only one of my mates who could lead studies as impressively was Ai Min, the one they used to call the theoretician.

Ai Min was a one-armed, one-eared bear of a man, who had been a Party member, a colonel, a political commissar in the army and a veteran of the Long March.* The two of us were an un-beatable team; I would set the stage with drama and color and he would take it from there, with Marxist-Leninist-Maoist chapter and verse. I had always had the good luck in the camps to be befriended by men more knowledgeable than I, and Ai turned out to be the most valuable of them all.

Like most former Party members, Ai was honest, but his experiences with sources of power had given him a cavalier attitude toward sacred institutions. He defined dialectics for me.

Imagine, he told me, that a group of journalists from the West is invited to Peking and receives first-class treatment from the government, with trips and interviews, plus the best food and lodging and a sumptuous banquet upon their departure. When the first articles appear in the Western press a few days later, they heap odium upon Peking. The ruling circles erupt into a frenzy of indignation, but the Great Man himself remains calm. "Be happy they wrote such things," Mao advises. "We should start worrying when the bourgeois press writes nice things about us."

When, several days later, there are some more articles, filled with flattering accounts of the new life in China, consternation runs through the ranks of the Party. All but the Great Man. "Why are you worrying?" he asks. "This proves that even the rotten bourgeois press has to admit the progress we have made."

The point about dialectics, Ai said, is that it can answer anything satisfactorily.

BECAUSE of my ideological progress I was temporarily appointed to take over a special cell of fifty backward illiterates. Mostly ex-peasants, laborers or mental defectives, they had spent their past study sessions either asleep or in witless stupors. I was given

---

* In 1934, forced by Chiang Kai-shek to evacuate Hunan and Kiangsi provinces, the Chinese Communists embarked upon a harrowing five-thousand-mile Long March, which by the end of 1935 brought the remnants of their forces to Shensi Province on China's northwest frontier. En route, Mao Tse-tung achieved unquestioned control of the Chinese Communist Party. [Editor's note.]

three months to set them right about the infidel Russians. Warder Tien told me that the results would be viewed as a test of my reformation. So I approached the job as a supreme challenge.

When I first entered the classroom cell, my students greeted me with all the intellectual animation of lumps of coal. I foolishly began my presentation in the rarefied political terms that would have been appropriate to Ai. Disaster. I could see their eyes glazing over. Obviously I would have to be more direct.

"What do you know about Khrushchev?" I threw out.

"What's *that?*" one asked. I swear it. He didn't even know whether Khrushchev was animal, vegetable or mineral! I was obliged to explain that he was first secretary of the Soviet Communist Party and premier of the USSR.

"Ah," came the pleased recognition. "Elder Brother."

It was my moment for revelation. "No, he is not Elder Brother," I said slowly. "Khrushchev is a *huai-dan*—a rotten egg."

This time there was a reaction. Their complacent pudding faces began to register doubt, perplexity or outrage, depending on how much they could remember from past studies. "We're warning you, Bao," one said, "any more talk like that about our great ally and we're reporting you."

When I continued in the same vein, the room exploded into a clamor of shouts and protests. Half of them were calling for a warder by then, and it didn't take long for one to arrive.

"What's going on here?" he asked at the doorway. "Is this the way you people study?"

"Warder," a spokesman for the group said, "we're sorry, but Bao has been insulting Elder Brother Khrushchev."

The warder held up his hand and the room fell silent. "Listen," he said carefully, "Khrushchev is not only a *huai-dan*. He is the biggest bad egg on earth!"

He went back to his office. My fifty students looked at me dumbfounded. Now, finally, it was their turn to learn that black was white. With painful, step-by-step care I explained to them how the unthinkable had happened.

My only problem was that I never succeeded in persuading

them to take Albania seriously. When I told them that the population of our doughty little ally was only around a million, they sniffed with exquisite Chinese scorn. One student even permitted himself the speculation that if we six hundred million Chinese got together we could sink Albania merely by peeing on it.

By the end of 1963 there was hardly a prisoner who didn't hate the Soviets. Among my students, though, there was one man who remained perplexed and tormented. He had been sent to jail in 1956 for having spoken of the Soviets just as we were speaking now. Didn't that mean that he now deserved a pardon? I promised to take the matter up with the authorities.

Warder Tien straightened me out. "What he said wasn't as important as why he said it. What he said might be progressive now, but in 1956 it was antigovernment propaganda. Do you see?"

I did. I was such a model prisoner by then that I took to going barefoot in the warm weather, in order to save the government the expense of shoe leather.

MY REFORMATION was all the easier since it was in the hands of Warder Tien, whom I admired for his humanity and honesty. Like Chao in Prison Number One, he had the uncanny ability to see into a prisoner's mind. As our living conditions improved in 1963, he assigned ration increases according to each man's needs rather than his production figures. The pains he took to judge each case individually were rewarded by our loyalty.

Even when things were at their worst Tien was able to control his charges with his own brand of applied psychology. The best example I can recall happened in October 1962, when hunger and resentment were at a high tide. He called the brigade together, marched us out to the main gate and climbed onto a stool for a little talk. There had been rumors, he said, that certain bad elements among the prisoners had been talking about escaping. This could be a dangerous influence on the rest of us.

With a dramatic flourish he ordered the guards to open the gates! "I don't want you to have ideological burdens," he said. "Since some of you have been talking behind the government's back, here's your chance to carry out your thoughts in the open. You can go on out the gate now. No one will stop you."

He clambered down and began striding back to the main building. Then he turned and threw out one final line. "Before you leave you'd better think about where you're going to eat from now on."

Of course no one left. We filed obediently back to the cells.

On another occasion Tien tolerated scandalous talk from a prisoner who had suffered deep humiliation when he was visited by his wife and their son, a mean little brat of around ten or eleven. The boy was wearing the red scarf of the Communist Young Pioneers. "I didn't want to come here," he brayed, "but my mother made me. You are a counterrevolutionary and a disgrace to the family. You have caused grave losses to the government. It serves you right that you are in prison."

Even the guards were shocked by his tirade. The prisoner returned to the cell in tears—in themselves forbidden—muttering, "If I had known that this would happen, I would have strangled him the day he was born." Tien let the incident pass without a reproach.

SOME weeks before Christmas I was summoned to the office of Prison Director Chia. There were four warders with him. That was very strange. Apprehensively, I took my place on the stool in the corner. Chia told me I did not have to keep my head bowed.

"Today the government has something very important to discuss with you." There was a portentous silence. I kept my mouth shut. "You are a French citizen. Have you ever been to France?"

What was he getting at? He knew very well I had never left Chinese territory.

"Are you married?" Again, a question to which he knew the answer. Jailer rhetoric.

"I beg to report to the director that I am married to a Chinese wife and have two children."

Chia looked pleased. He had reached the point for his speech. "So, Bao. There is Chinese blood in your veins from your mother.

You were born and raised here, and you have been nourished on Chinese food. Your wife and children are Chinese. You even look Chinese. Where is the French in you, Bao?"

He had a point there, and he probed a little further. "I don't have the feeling the French have done much for you, either. *You* may consider yourself French, but do you think *they* do? To them you're just a half-breed. The consular agent still hasn't answered your letters, has he? Do you think he would treat a hundred percent Frenchman that way?" Chia had found my weak point.

"The People's Government is taking care of you," Chia went on. "At the same time your own people are neglecting you. Do you ever wonder if there is any reason for holding on to French nationality? What does it get you? We know you want to be with your family. There might be a way out for you."

I felt the thrill of excitement and fear that comes when big decisions are at hand. I listened very carefully.

"The only way the government can tell if you have reformed yourself is by actions. If you really regret your past mistakes, you have to prove it. You have to break with the past. You have to decide whether or not you still want to be associated with the imperialists. If you made that decision, it would be the best proof for the government that you have learned your lesson well. Then there would be no more reason to keep you here."

That was quite an offer Chia was hinting at. Still, I had doubts.

"People like you who know foreign languages can get good jobs, Bao," he suggested.

"I don't know if it would be right for me to give up my nationality," I said.

"We're not asking you to do that," Chia insisted. "We have only laid some facts on the table. Don't say no or yes now. Just go back to your cell and think about it."

I rose to go. Then one of the warders called me over to look at myself in a full-length mirror. I looked like a cadaverous tramp.

"What's your sentence?" he asked.

"Twelve years."

"And you've served how many now?"

"Six."

"Halfway," he said. "Do you ever wonder if you'll make it?"

I went back to the cell depressed and troubled. If what they told me was true, it seemed that I had a chance of bettering my lot by renouncing my French nationality. It was Ai Min who made up my mind for me.

"What are we, Bao? You and I and the rest of us?"

"We are convicted felons undergoing Reform Through Labor."

"Yes, that's true, but put it more concretely."

"We are enemies of the people."

"The Communists don't feel obliged to keep promises to their enemies. As a means to an end, they feel free to use any scheme that serves them—and that includes threats and promises. Even if they should let you out, your dossier will follow you wherever you go. The first mistake you make, you'll be back here again—and then you'll *never* get out. But with your French nationality you'll always have some hope, even if it's slight. You understand?"

"Yes, old Ai," I said. "Thanks."

"Don't thank me. Just use your head. And remember another thing. Communists don't have any respect for turncoats, either."

So I didn't bite on the lure. I owe more than gratitude to Ai for his advice. Without it, I wouldn't be here now.

On January 13 I was called in to see Chia again. This time there were eight warders with him! And seated behind the desk with Chia was my interrogator from Grass Mist Lane.

"Sit down," he said. His voice was positively friendly. I took my place on the stool. "I came on some other business," he went on with studied indifference. "I heard that you were here and I thought I'd check on your progress."

That sounded like an obvious invention.

"I haven't seen you since 1957." He threw over a pack of Chung Huas. "Tell me what's happened to you since then."

Coming from an interrogator, that was no light request. In careful detail, watching my ideological step, I produced the entire history of my life as a convict. I went through five cigarettes before I had finished.

He stubbed out his cigarette. "What I'd like you to do now is write me a full ideological report. Tell me about how you viewed your crimes then and how you see them now."

"That will take a lot of time."

"That's all right." He turned to Chia. "Give him all the time and material he needs."

Even without Ai's advice I could see that the report was of highest importance—like a final exam. I started writing. Unlike my work in Grass Mist Lane, my report was in Chinese this time, the fruit of my studies at Ching Ho and Liangxiang. I spent two months composing it.

I wasn't even halfway into it when, one day at the end of January, a radio bulletin came over the loudspeakers at suppertime: France and China had established diplomatic relations. That evening the warder told us to make that the subject of our study sessions. Being French, I was the obvious choice to lead the talk. When I had finished, Warder Tien asked me into his office to tell him my thoughts on the establishment of relations.

"It is of greatest international importance," I said. "And it is clear that the relations were established on China's terms."

"You have no more views? Nothing personal, as a Frenchman?"

"No."

"Were you thinking that you might be released from prison?"

I suppose I did have those thoughts in the back of my mind, but I did my best to erase them. "I don't think my efforts have been strong enough for that," I said. "I've hardly been doing enough work lately to repay the government for the food I eat."

"You've come a long way, Bao," he said.

The next day my ration was increased to forty-six pounds, even though my cellmates were eating only thirty-six. I had to work even harder to drive thoughts of release from my head. That same week I was asked to translate *Lettres de mon moulin,* by Alphonse Daudet, into Chinese. It would be a useful service to the government, the warders told me, but I knew very well that Chinese translations of it already existed. So now they were trying to help me brush up on my French. . . .

THAT winter was no trial for us. Living conditions were improving all over China. Curiously, studies were emphasized more than ever; I could not have known it at the time, but this was a prelude to the Cultural Revolution. As food and consumer goods became more abundant in 1964, certain segments of the Party, and Mao himself, grew wary of the effects of the relatively easy times that had come upon us. Things were building toward the mass hysteria the country was to know after I had left.

In February I discovered Hui-min had divorced me. I received the news in a curt meeting with one of the warders. "Your wife is more progressive than you," he drawled. "You should be proud your sons have a mother like that."

I could hardly blame her, but I did feel a twinge of resentment on learning that the legal proceedings had been carried out in November. I returned to the cell in a daze.

In May came a Medical Parole Movement. Huang Kuo-chiang, one of the men in my cell seriously afflicted with TB, was among the first to be named to the two-hundred-man parole group. He was looking forward to returning to his village, he told me, but he felt dreadful premonitions: since his arrest, he had not received a single letter from his family.

The poor man was back after ten days. We were sitting on the bed preparing for studies when he appeared at the door, sunburned, dusty, breathing heavily and looking absolutely stricken. "I couldn't take it," he said.

He had been released with a little cash and a one-way ticket in his pocket. When he arrived in the village, his own father cursed him as a criminal element and ordered him to remain seated on a stool in the sun until he checked with the police to see if the letter of medical release was valid. After a week of being coldly tolerated by his family, taunted and scorned by the rest of the village, he took what money he had left, bought a return ticket, and literally begged Warder Tien to allow him back inside the gates.

ON AUGUST 30 my interrogator was back in Chia's office. "I've read your report," he said. "You've got the Chinese language almost perfect now. What you have written is positive, though it could be better. I've decided to accept the report, but I want you to keep thinking about improving your ideological status."

I promised to do my best. I was thrilled and flattered. What was more, he had quite a piece of news for me.

"The French embassy has asked to visit you. This place isn't suitable and it's too far from their embassy. We are going to transfer you to some place nearer. You should be ideologically prepared for a visit from the French. I don't think I need to explain what I mean. Get ready to leave as soon as possible."

Early the next morning a trusty brought me a new blue suit, underwear, black sandals, a towel and soap. He also handed me eleven yuan (close to four U.S. dollars). At 4:00 p.m. Director Chia officially turned me over to two plainclothesmen from the Peking Bureau of Public Security, who led me to a black Pobeda hardly newer than the one in which I had ridden the night of my arrest in 1957. We rolled through Peking, finally turning into the gate of Prison Number Two, the new interrogation center. Kung Deh-Lin, it was called—Grove of Virtuous Deeds.

A guard showed me to a small private cell, deadly silent. There were a raised bed and a stool. The guard asked if I was hungry. I thought I was, but when he returned with a plate of sautéed potato shreds, wheat *wo'tou* and soup, I was far too unsettled to eat. "The government is being too good to me," I said. But the guard ordered me to eat every bit.

The next day I had three meals. This place was like a hotel! In the afternoon they took me for a walk in the exercise yard. At the far end I saw a Westerner who looked American. I presume it was one of the unfortunate CIA operatives from the Korean War, Fecteau or Downey, who were not released until the 1972-73 improvement in Sino-American relations.

That evening a doctor came to examine me. "You need to put on some weight," he said.

Chapter 13

I STAYED on in my private cell eating myself goggle-eyed, reading old newspapers and trying to fight off boredom as I waited for the French to visit me. After all the years of living in close quarters, I found the solitude oppressive, even if the living conditions were better than I had ever dreamed. After ten days I wrote the warder a note asking to be sent back to Liangxiang if the embassy people didn't show up soon.

That was probably why he let me in on the struggle session. "We might be able to use your experience," he said. "We've got a prisoner we've been struggling for a week without any luck."

He filled me in on the case. Then I went back to my cell and put on my dirty old patched clothes. The guard watched me, his VIP prisoner, with scarcely concealed bewilderment, but I told him not to worry. When he led me to the struggle cell, I told him to shove me in as if I were a new prisoner just arriving to be interrogated. I kept my head bowed and hurtled awkwardly into the noisy, crowded little room.

"We're having our meeting now," the cell leader said. "Sit over there and I'll speak to you later." He seemed sure of himself for a man who had been directing a fruitless struggle for seven days. Even if the warder had not prepared me, I could have judged from insults being thrown out that the man they were struggling was an intellectual. He was stubborn, though. He simply refused to talk. After a few hours the leader called a break and told me to give a report on myself. I went through the normal procedure: name, age, background and the crimes I was accused of.

"Start working on your confession," he said. "Don't be like him and hold out against the government."

I repaired to my corner of the bed and contemplated the familiar scene, the shaking of fists, the harsh words spat out. Stinking intellectual. Scum of society. I kept silent.

At around 4:00 p.m. the cell leader—irate and frustrated— pointedly gazed at me. "Why aren't you talking?" he demanded. "Do you sympathize with him, or what? Just because you're new here doesn't mean you have the right to do nothing."

"My, my, my," I said politely, "the way you people work this session. How disorganized!"

Faces turned in surprise. The cell leader waited, curious.

"It seems that the only counterrevolutionary in this cell is that guy over there," I said. "That means the rest of us are heroes. I think we're forgetting that we're counterrevolutionaries, too."

Grumbling of angry voices. One of them shouted indignantly that I was insulting my fellow schoolmates.

"Put his remarks on the record," I suggested to the cell leader. "I have insulted him. That means he's not a counterrevolutionary. He hasn't committed any sins." That shut the shouter up.

"You'd better think about reforming yourselves before you feel so sure about jumping on other prisoners," I said importantly. "And let me tell you another thing: you're going to need each other in the camps, because the only way to survive there is to count on each other. I have been appointed by the warder to take over this session. Now let's see what we can do."

The cell was magically pervaded with quiet respect. The leader moved back against the wall in obvious relief. The rest of the session was ideological child's play.

Later I called the struggle victim aside. "You're being dumb," I told him. "The only way to get them off your back is to make a clean confession. It's like medicine: if you take it in little sips, all you'll have is the bitterness. The best way is to gulp it all down at once."

For the first time since that morning he smiled. I walked back to my cell with another mark of merit on my dossier.

On the afternoon of September 18 I was given a haircut and shave, and I climbed into the blue suit. I was taken to the office of the director, who motioned me to an easy chair. Things had changed quite a bit from the days of the stool and the bowed head. He told me that in a few minutes I would be receiving a visit from the French. How I spoke to them would be considered as a direct reflection of the progress of my reform. A hidden tape recorder would register every word I said.

Two guards led me to a large, bare room with a table in the center. In less than a minute the door at the far wall opened and a short, pudgy Westerner advanced toward me. This, I learned, was Marc Menguy, a middle-echelon embassy functionary.

"We want you to know that we haven't forgotten you," Menguy said. "We have been trying for some time to see you, but the Chinese authorities have not permitted the visit until now. Are you all right? Do you need medicine? How about food?"

"The Chinese government is taking good care of me. My rations are better than what the guards get. I have three meals a day."

"How about meat? Does your diet contain enough meat?"

"I can't tell you exactly how much meat I get," I said. "I don't have a scale to weigh it, but it is enough by Chinese standards."

"And cigarettes—can you smoke?"

"I am allowed to smoke outside during exercise period."

"Well, then," Menguy said with satisfaction, "everything seems to be all right. Is there anything else you would like from us?"

"I would like a dictionary, and maybe some newspapers."

"I think we can arrange to send you *Le Monde* and *Le Figaro*."

"No thank you, Monsieur Menguy," I said firmly, "I don't want bourgeois papers. I would prefer to have *The Peking Review*. And some novels by Hugo or Balzac, if you could manage that."

He left me with promises that the embassy would do everything it could for me, and advised me not to become discouraged.

BACK in my cell I could feel excitement surging through me, but I wondered about my performance. Would the warders approve? Would Menguy think I had been brainwashed? I got a hint that evening when the guard brought my supper. With it were two cartons of good French cigarettes and ten yuan. The guard informed me that the government was looking over some books the French had sent. If they were approved, I could have them. After supper I was taken to the director's office.

"The government is satisfied with the visit," the director told me. "We especially liked the way you dealt with the tricky questions. That was very good, about the meat and the scales. But do you really think they have your best interests at heart? Do you have any illusions about their getting you out of prison?"

That was easy to answer. I didn't even blink. "Of course not," I said. "I know I can't rely on the French embassy. If I started having those sorts of ideas, it would mean I was relying on the imperialists. It would prove that I wasn't reformed."

The director looked probingly at me for a long moment. "Do you really mean that, Bao? Are you really being sincere?"

"Look through my dossier," I suggested. "I think you will find that my attitude has always been the same."

On October 1 they gave me over two pounds of apples and full helpings of beef, pork, ravioli, noodles, bean curd and vegetables. I was feeling like a maharaja with a guilt complex, for I knew my ex-wife and our children were not eating as well, but all my requests to see them had gone unanswered. Four days later the guard informed me that they were in the prison visiting room.

Hui-min was there with Yung. Mow, our elder son, was already old enough to have been sent away to work on a state farm. Yung was ten now, but I was distressed to see how shabby his clothing was. In spite of the cold he wore only sandals, without socks. I asked the witnessing warder if I could give him the ten yuan that the French had left me.

"Of course," he said. "Bao has made progress," he told Hui-min, "but apparently he has doubts as to how well the government is taking care of you."

"Warder, I didn't say that," I protested. "I just want the boy to have some socks."

Hui-min declared that the government was taking good care of them. The meeting was over. I returned to the cell feeling miserable. There was precious little I could do for them, but I wanted to make at least a gesture. I took apart the padded mattress I had brought with me from Liangxiang and sewed it into a jacket for Yung. My guards even provided me with scissors, needle and thread. I gave them the jacket to pass on to my family.

On the thirty-first the guard tossed two books on my bed, a Chinese-English dictionary and a dictionary of idioms. They had come from little Yung. There was no chance for him to see me, but at least the guards had been good enough to deliver the books. He had bought them with the ten yuan I had given him. I never saw Yung again.

On the morning of November 5 a warder brought in a Western-style gray woolen suit, Chinese-made leather shoes and a white shirt. Both the shoes and the shirt were too big, so he took them away and reappeared later with another set, which fitted, except for the shirt collar. The next morning my guard led me out to a jeep manned by two armed Sepos.

We drove through the familiar streets of Peking, dodging bicycles, to the Supreme People's Court, a big, theaterlike place with the usual oversize portrait of Mao on the back wall. Up on the dais were an assistant judge, a secretary and a prosecutor.

The judge asked me the routine questions concerning my personal history, then read a short statement. "In view of the fact that Pasqualini has shown sincere signs of regret for his sins, the Chinese People's Government has decided, as a measure of special leniency, to remit the remainder of his sentence and to order him deported. He will be taken to the border under police guard and will be handed over to the competent authorities."

That was all. Release had come as swiftly as the ceremony that had condemned me to prison. Back in the jeep one of the Sepos ordered me to hold my head higher. "You're not a prisoner anymore," he said. "Why are you bowing your head like that?"

"Habit," I said. "Sorry."

At the prison the director was all smiles as he shook my hand. "Your ex-wife is here to see you," he said.

Our last meeting would have been strained even without the presence of the guard. What could we say to each other? She wished me luck wherever I happened to land. I promised to provide for the kids. This time they had a jeep to drive her home.

The director called me to his office and told me to prepare for the trip to the border. I made the mistake of asking him if I could ever bring my children out of China after me.

His voice became harsh. "Bao," he said, "if you had asked that question yesterday, I don't think you'd be leaving now. They are citizens of the People's Republic of China. Even if they wished to, which they do not, the government would not permit them to give their lives over to a corrupt bourgeois society."

On the afternoon of the tenth I left Prison Number Two. The guards drove me to the Peking railroad station and put me aboard a "soft" compartment that had been reserved. Chinese trains are divided into soft (padded seats) and hard (benches) sections in order to avoid the anti-Marxist connotations of first class and second class.

In the compartment was a plainclothesman from the Peking Bureau of Public Security. He wanted to make a few ideological points. "We are a young country, Bao, and the young often make mistakes. The best proof that the government is good is that you are alive and well today, even though you may have gone through some hardships. What you say about us outside China is your business, but we all hope you will stress the positive side."

We shook hands and my journey out of China began.

Fittingly, one of my two escorts was the same Sepo who had handcuffed me in my house seven years earlier. We rolled along in silence, while I gazed intently out the window. When I caught sight of the red brick buildings of Liangxiang in the distance, it was with a curious mixture of emotions—joy to be leaving it for good, but also a kind of melancholy nostalgia for all the good friends I would never see again.

Not long afterward a fresh-faced girl with a long pigtail, a train attendant, poked her head into the compartment and handed the Sepo a menu. It was then that I had an inspiration.

"I'd like a bowl of soup and two bowls of rice, please," I said.

My escorts smiled at each other. "Don't worry," one said. "Everything's paid for. You can order anything you want."

I kept my face expressionless. "I haven't finished expiating my sins," I said. "How can I order luxurious food? I should try to lighten the burden of the government as much as possible."

They looked at me glumly. They couldn't tell if I was simply putting them on. But they had no choice when it came to their own suppers. Could a guardian of the New Order show himself to be more bourgeois than a scum of society? That evening I had my last victory over the police: all three of us ate a bowl of soup and two bowls of rice apiece.

During the rest of the two-day trip my escorts took their meals in the dining car, alternating so that one always stayed with me. As for me, I kept to my soup and rice. We went through Hankow, across the river to Wuhan, then on to Canton.

I spent the night of November 12 in the Canton provincial jail. My cellmate was another Franco-Chinese *métis*, an older man named Rousset, from Shanghai, who also had been released. We smoked two of my cigarettes as a token of our new friendship.

MY LAST day in China was Friday, the thirteenth of November. Rousset and I boarded a morning train for Shumchun, the Chinese railroad terminus at the Hong Kong border. This time there were no compartments; we sat in the middle of a crowd of

Asian and Western businessmen returning from the Canton trade fair. China has truly come a long way, several Englishmen agreed among themselves. Everyone seems well fed and happy. Plenty to buy in the stores. It might just be the model for the future. Rousset and I held our tongues. Our two guards sat discreetly in a far corner of the car.

At Shumchun the guards led us through our own border formalities. We were allowed to keep six Hong Kong dollars apiece (one U.S. dollar). The rest of my savings from jail, we were told, would be sent to our families. We were permitted to write them a last letter. The customs inspector wrapped a sturdy band of paper around my three books—the only possessions I had been allowed to keep—affixed a red wax seal, and let us through to the transit restaurant, where our escorts ordered lunch for us.

At 1:30 they took us out to the Chinese side of the Lo Wu Bridge. At the far end I could make out an English policeman in his colonial uniform. Over to the right, steam locomotives chuffed back and forth in the Shumchun freight yards. Their tenders bore red-flag emblems signifying how many times their teams had overfulfilled their work norms. The boxcars parked on the sidings were covered with billboard-sized slogans: Long Live the General Line and Long Live the People's Communes. It was a bright, warm, optimistic, sunny day.

The guard held us up for an identification photograph. Just as he was about to click the shutter, another guard shouted and ran toward us. He roughly removed Rousset's hat and threw it on the ground. It might obstruct the picture, he said. Was he joking when he explained that the picture would be circulated to all the Chinese border posts, in order to prevent us from sneaking back in some day?

I picked up Rousset's hat. We walked across the bridge without looking back.

The Pasqualinis with Rudolph Chelminski at dinner in their apartment near Paris

Ten years after he crossed the bridge to Hong Kong in 1964, Jean Pasqualini—the former Bao Ruo-wang—is a satisfied middle-class Frenchman living in a comfortable suburban apartment near Paris with his second wife, his books, and his fondness for traditional Chinese cuisine.

He stayed in Hong Kong exactly thirty hours after his release, then boarded a ship for Marseilles. During the long voyage he met Pauline, a young Chinese girl on her way to London to study music. Five years later they were married.

In the meantime, Jean Pasqualini worked as a translator for a French government agency, and for the Paris bureau of *Life* magazine. It was there that he met Rudolph Chelminski, who advised him to write a book about his experiences in China. "I told him I was not a writer," says Pasqualini, "so I spoke into a tape recorder, my wife transcribed it, and from that material Chelminski wrote the book."

Pasqualini is now a librarian in the Paris bureau of *Newsweek*, and teaches Chinese at the Institut National des Langues et Civilisations Orientales. Despite a recurrence of the tuberculosis he contracted while in prison, he harbors no bitterness toward the Mao regime. In fact, life in the outside world often seems to him harder than life in the camps. "Apart from real friends, nobody cares what happens to you," he says. "If you can't work, you die. Not so in the camps; it was a curious world of interdependence."

His two sons, now twenty-six and twenty, are still in China, working in a factory—as does his first wife. "I send the boys money regularly," Pasqualini says, "and hope one day to bring them over here. Am I happy? How could I not be after what I have been through?"

Rousset, with whom he crossed the Hong Kong bridge, works at Orly International Airport. He and Pasqualini meet every November 13, to celebrate the anniversary of their liberation.

ACKNOWLEDGMENTS

Grateful acknowledgment is made to the following for permission
to quote from the sources listed after their names.

WILL ROGERS: HIS LIFE AND TIMES
THE BOBBS-MERRILL CO., INC.: *Will Rogers: His Wife's
Story* by Betty Rogers, copyright 1941 by Betty Rogers.
HOUGHTON MIFFLIN COMPANY: *Sanity Is Where You Find It*
by Will Rogers, selected and edited by Donald Day,
© 1955 by Rogers Company; *The Autobiography of Will Rogers*,
selected and edited by Donald Day, copyright 1949 by
Rogers Company.

ILLUSTRATION CREDITS

TIMES TO REMEMBER
Page 6: Mort Kaye Studios, Inc.
Pages 10, 19, 49 (top left), 71 (top left), 79 (top left, bottom): Kennedy
Family Collection.
Pages 35 (top), 49 (bottom), 70 (top), 71 (top right): Wide World Photos.
Page 35 (bottom): Keystone.
Page 49 (top right): Peter Hunter, Press Features.
Pages 70 (right, bottom), 71 (bottom right): Harcourt-Harris, Inc.
Page 71 (bottom left): Lisa Larsen, Time-Life Picture Agency.
Page 79 (top right): Jacques Lowe.

WILL ROGERS: HIS LIFE AND TIMES
Pages 234-235: Carl Fischer.
Pages 236 (bronze statue by Jo Davidson), 243, 249, 255, 259, 263, 267, 271,
276, 281, 284 (left), 309, 361, 373 (bottom), 386: Will Rogers Memorial
Commission, Claremore, Oklahoma.
Page 253: Oklahoma Historical Society.
Pages 284 (right), 299: Brown Brothers.
Pages 285, 330, 331: Culver Pictures, Inc.
Page 295: Museum of Modern Art, Film Stills Archive and
Samuel Goldwyn Productions.
Page 311: Smithers Collection, Humanities Research Center,
University of Texas at Austin.
Page 319: Underwood and Underwood.
Page 335: Cornelius Photography.
Page 347: Curtis Studios.
Page 373 (top): UPI.
Pages 380-381: Wide World Photos.